D. M. SHAPIRO

21 November 2012

HARVARD HISTORICAL STUDIES · 178

Published under the auspices
of the Department of History
from the income of the
Paul Revere Frothingham Bequest
Robert Louis Stroock Fund
Henry Warren Torrey Fund

Fighting for the Soul of Germany

THE CATHOLIC STRUGGLE FOR

INCLUSION AFTER UNIFICATION

Rebecca Ayako Bennette

HARVARD UNIVERSITY PRESS

Cambridge, Massachusetts

London, England

2012

Library of Congress Cataloging-in-Publication Data

Bennette, Rebecca Ayako, 1973–

Fighting for the soul of Germany : the Catholic struggle for inclusion after unification / Rebecca Ayako Bennette.

p. cm.—(Harvard historical studies ; 178)

Includes bibliographical references and index.

ISBN 978-0-674-06563-5

1. Kulturkampf. 2. Catholics—Germany—History—19th century. 3. Catholic Church—Germany—History—19th century. 4. Nationalism—Religious aspects—Catholic Church—History—20th century. 5. Nationalism—Germany—History—19th century. 6. Christianity and politics—Germany—History—19th century. 7. Germany—History—William I, 1871–1888. I. Title.

DD118.B46 2012

282'.4309034—dc23

2011045410

For James and Clara

Contents

Acknowledgments

It gives me great pleasure to acknowledge all of the support I have received that made this book possible. First, several organizations provided generous funding. I am grateful for grants received during my years at Harvard University from the Minda de Gunzburg Center for European Studies, the Krupp Foundation, and the German Academic Exchange Service (DAAD). I am also indebted to both the Andrew W. Mellon Foundation and Middlebury College for supplying continued funding to make the ideal combination of teaching and active scholarly production possible.

The research for this book comes from time spent in a number of archives and libraries. I would like to thank the archivists at the Archiwum Archidiecezjalne we Wrocławiu, the Bistumsarchiv Trier, the Bochum Stadtarchiv, the Bundesarchiv Koblenz, the Dom- und Diözesanarchiv Mainz, the Dortmund Stadtarchiv, the Landeshauptarchiv Koblenz, the Landeskirchliches Archiv der Evangelischen Kirche von Westfalen, the Staatsarchiv Münster, and the Stadtarchiv Münster. I am especially grateful to the Institut für Zeitungsforschung in Dortmund and its very patient staff members. I also owe my gratitude to the librarians at Harvard University's Widener Library and Middlebury College's Davis Family Library. Finally, I would also like to thank Kathrin Dupré and the Universitätsbibliothek at the Johannes Gutenberg Universität in Mainz.

Many people helped guide me at various stages of this project. First and foremost I want to thank David Blackbourn. I am ever grateful for his mentorship and support that has continued up to this day. I was very fortunate to have benefitted from the advice and support of Charles Maier and Susan Pedersen as well. Several individuals provided constructive comments after reading drafts of chapters or hearing conference papers. For their help, I would like to thank Margaret Anderson, Geoff Eley, Marjorie Lamberti, Till van Rahden, and Anthony Steinhoff. I would especially like to thank Michael Gross, Helmut Walser Smith, and Jonathan Sperber not only for their helpful comments but also for their kind words of encouragement at crucial moments. Of course, I am likewise indebted to the two anonymous readers who carefully read the manuscript and provided thoughtful suggestions. I am also grateful for the encouragement and help offered by all of my colleagues in the Department of History at Middlebury College, but special mention should be made of Febe Armanios, Ian Barrow, Cathy Bilodeau, Louisa Burnham, Paul Monod, Amy Morseman, Ann Nottingham, and Don Wyatt. A bit farther away, Heike Fahrenberg from the Middlebury School Abroad in Germany deserves a ton of appreciation too.

Finally, I would like to express my gratitude to those closest to me. To my friends for continuously cheering me on, even when this book meant not hanging out for long periods of time, I am indebted. I want to thank my parents James and Sachiko Bennette for their support, even though I am sure they were puzzled by my choice to spend so much time writing about Germans and Catholics, especially given that I do not belong to either group. I also want to acknowledge Clara, Lena, and Momo. Even after the longest and hardest days of writing, they lifted my spirits when I came home. Most importantly, I want to thank my best friend and husband, James Fitzsimmons. He made writing this book both possible and worthwhile. I truly could not have done it without him.

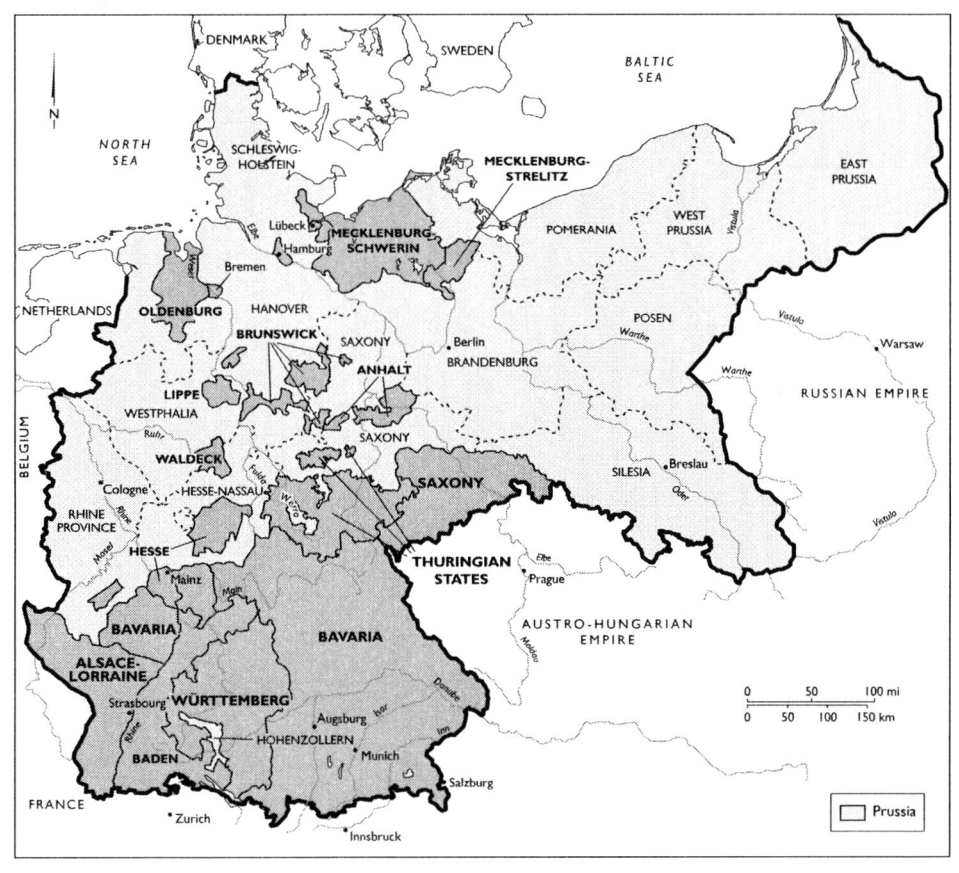

The German Empire, 1871–1918.

Introduction

"IF THE *REICH* is to have a future," the Catholic politician and newspaper editor Julius Bachem wrote in 1872, the people would need to decide carefully what the new nation should become. The right choice would lead to greatness. Yet Bachem bemoaned that liberals formed the "leading parties" at the moment and even the government was, in the end, at "their bidding." He asserted it was liberal influence that was responsible for the current "un-German" direction the nation was headed in. Only the "true friends of the Fatherland" could stop this. There was no time to lose, Bachem stressed, as even the new *Reich*—the culmination of so much work—was still fragile and easy to "demolish." He ended his plea by pointing to the central question in the *Reich*: "Which idea does it represent?" Which idea would "win existence" in the struggle taking place in the nation? The wrong choice would mean a *Reich* that was merely a "meaningless fact," nothing more than an "insubstantial phenomenon." It would mean a Germany with a "body" but no "soul." In his mind, this "soul" now needed to be fought for, and people could best do that by voting for the Center Party and supporting the Catholic press.[1]

What idea of Germany was Bachem referring to? How did the larger community of Catholics that he was addressing envision themselves as part of the nation after 1871? Though current scholarship clearly shows that Catholics generally rejected the idea of Germany proposed by liberals or the Bismarckian government, little is known about exactly how they tried to define the nation. If not anti-national, as many earlier accounts portrayed them, much of even the more recent scholarly literature still presents Catholics as largely unconcerned with national identity or simply not very involved in the construction of the new Germany after 1871. Most accounts prefer, instead, to concentrate on Catholics' separateness as a confession. This book, however, uncovers how Catholics' strong religious identity did not prevent them from constructing their own vision of the new nation and espousing loyalty to it after 1871, but instead fundamentally informed these developments. Furthermore, it argues that this alternative construction of national identity during the *Kulturkampf* played an important role in fostering Catholics' long-term integration, despite the decade itself being one of intense conflict.

Catholics have long come out of the "ghetto" as subjects of historical research for the modern period.[2] The innovative research of scholars like Wolfgang Schieder, Margaret Lavinia Anderson, Werner Blessing, and Jonathan Sperber laid the groundwork of Catholicism's larger presence in mainstream historical scholarship on Germany.[3] Subsequently, a lot of attention has been given to the high degree of cohesion within Catholicism as well as the resulting increase in scholarly efforts to differentiate among elements within it, both ideologically and regionally.[4] Historians have increasingly considered the complex interactions Catholics had with members of other religions, often noting conflict but sometimes pointing to cooperation as well.[5] Not surprisingly, a lot of attention has focused on the period of the *Kulturkampf* in a variety of contexts beyond merely a church-state dispute.[6]

Yet much of the scholarship focusing specifically on Catholic integration into the nation predates this more recent and broader attention to the social, political, cultural, and religious life of Catholics. Even after the end of the *Kaiserreich*, Catholic integration remained a topic of concern for political Catholicism itself, as the informative yet at times quite partisan history of the Center Party by Karl Bachem suggests.[7] Likewise, the differences concerning unification—either along the lines of a greater or a lesser German area—that divided many Catholic and Protestant proponents of the nation during the early and middle of the nineteenth century are quite well substantiated in the older literature.[8] Rudolf Lill, for example, researched these earlier differences between the confessions' views of the nation, particularly stressing that even after 1866 Catholics did not turn away from the nation. Highlighting the now generally accepted point that Catholics did not reject the nation in 1871, Lill asserted that only the *Kulturkampf* stopped this potential for greater integration.[9] Similarly, Ernst Deuerlein noted this initial acceptance but focused more on detailing the "return" of political Catholicism to the nation beginning after the *Kulturkampf*.[10] The focus on Catholic support for colonial politics in the later *Kaiserreich* as an indication of their ultimate national integration also found support in the subsequent research of both Horst Gründer and Wilfried Loth.[11] Most emphatic about the progress of Catholic integration in the nation before 1914 was the work of Rudolf Morsey. While he did not underestimate the degree to which the conflict of the 1870s slowed this process and certainly asserted that it proceeded much more quickly under Wilhelm II, Morsey also carefully pointed out elements from the *Kulturkampf* itself that made later cooperation possible, providing a more nuanced view of this period.[12] Not surprisingly, most of these works largely focused on the Center Party and political decisions rather than the masses of Catholics more generally.

Despite the greater attention paid to Catholics in the mainstream historical scholarship now, still relatively little is known about how they viewed the nation and their efforts to integrate into it. Some works continue to add to the picture, of course, while still remaining rather traditional accounts focused largely on politics.[13] Research has moved beyond considering only political events to include constructions of national identity and narratives of the nation, though this has also led to conclusions suggesting Catholics were largely separate from this process, abstaining from contributing any vision of the nation, especially during the *Kulturkampf* but also in later decades.[14] More assertive that Catholics actively strove to belong in the nation are the conclusions from the research of Jeffrey T. Zalar—again on the Wilhelmine period—and Pontus Hiort on Baden.[15] For the fullest account to date of Catholics and national identity in the *Kaiserreich*, one must still turn to Helmut Walser Smith's groundbreaking book *German Nationalism and Religious Conflict*. In it, Smith not only asserts that Catholics shared an interest in constructing the new Germany from the beginning but also provides the closest account in the literature of what this national identity entailed. He shows the constructive role of religion in national identity by highlighting the divisions created, however, which leaves the integrative potential of many aspects of the Catholic national vision unexplored.[16]

That so little is known about Catholic national identity stands in marked contrast to the wealth of studies on German nationalism more generally. Of course, the history of Germany has always had a close relationship to the nation created in 1871, one forged from the beginning with the works of so many nationalist historians writing scholarly accounts in support of unification led by Prussia.[17] Yet the focus on identity issues in many recent studies as well as the now far more flexible and complex understandings of the relationship between the populace and the nation have opened up how the topic is studied and have allowed for the inclusion of groups often excluded from traditional accounts. The issues of rhetoric, symbolism, and memory have been central to this approach, focusing on the constructed nature of nations and national identities.[18] Furthermore, scholars now understand identities to be multiple and overlapping, rather than singular and exclusive.[19] The innovative research on the binding national power of *Heimat* (a flexible notion of one's "homeland" tied closely to the local setting) later in the *Kaiserreich* in turn led to viewing even the earlier maintenance of regional identities as also having had integrative potential on the *Reich* level in the long term.[20] Some scholars have also emphasized the contribution made by traditions from the era of the Holy Roman Empire to how the nation was conceptualized both before and after 1871, providing further complexity and nuance to ideas of nationalism and national identity. A pivotal link here, of course, is again this idea of regional identities and federalism, which dominated the structure of the Holy Roman Empire.[21] Such recent approaches have also allowed historians to further study how conflict itself can lead to long-term consensus.[22]

Hence, this book sets out to provide a fuller account of the alternative national identity that Catholics cultivated to claim their place in the unified German nation that became the reality in 1871. Other scholarship that does consider the advance of Catholic integration into the nation mainly focuses on the 1890s, by which point not only had Catholics become far more supportive of government initiatives, but also the dominant vision of the nation had become far more accommodating through the emphasis on values like *Heimat*. The present account, however, focuses on the pivotal period of the *Kulturkampf* itself.[23] Existing literature has demonstrated that the decade of the 1870s proved formative for the long-term trajectory of the Catholic community.[24] This was also the period of the *Kaiserreich* in which the Catholic vision was the most distinct from the far more well-known official-liberal construction.[25] Yet little is known about Catholics' national identity during this decade because too often their opposition to the government and liberal nationalists' actions is conflated with their attitude toward the nation itself.[26] Moreover, what is known about their views of the nation—like the picture of Catholics during the 1870s more generally—presents division and difference.

Of course, the divisions and differences between Catholics and Protestants were certainly unmistakable and undeniable. Indeed, one objective of this book is to explore exactly how different this alternative Catholic vision of the nation was from that of their more studied opponents. At the same time, however, the present work argues that Catholic integration—slow and incomplete to be sure—also began in this formative decade, despite political opposition to the government and to the more dominant (Protestant) vision of German national identity. Even as Catholics rejected the actions of the government, they also claimed their place in the nation, emerging far more invested in it than they had been a decade earlier. Catholic arguments and attempts to define what the new Germany should be during the *Kulturkampf* ultimately proved indispensable in fostering their long-term integration, even if that only became obvious in subsequent decades. Therefore, this work attempts not to replace the well-researched portrayal of Catholics in the *Kaiserreich* as one marked by difference, but to present another part of the picture, one that focuses on the long-term integrative potential even during the height of conflict.

Of course, not all Catholics thought or acted alike regarding the nation (or anything else, for that matter), just as liberals or certainly Protestants did not. Though still more research needs to be done, scholars have provided accounts of several cases in which certain groups of Catholics did not act in accordance with the majority of their co-religionists.[27] Even the voting statistics from the 1870s, not to mention the *Kaiserreich* period more generally, clearly indicate not all Catholics supported the same policies or politics. Depending on which analysis of voting behavior one relies upon, approximately one-fifth to one-fourth of voting Catholics cast their ballots for parties other than the Center even at the height of election unity during the *Kulturkampf* in 1874.[28] These people, obviously, are not the subject of this book. Yet even among those who continued to identify themselves squarely with the Catholic community, the issues of region and class as well as a rural or urban setting, to name only a few of the more obvious issues, could cause differences.[29] Moreover, these particular subgroups certainly should receive plenty of focus in the upcoming research on Catholicism in Germany, as the general picture of the cohesion among Catholics has already been well demonstrated. Yet the "impressive homogeneity" of Catholics as a whole, especially during the 1870s, is impossible to deny, a point made even in scholarly attempts to provide more detailed views.[30] Indeed, unity of purpose and presentation was something contemporary Catholics not only confirmed as a characterization of the decade but also a development they actively promoted.[31] Furthermore, unity was not merely superficial, a hollow attempt to present a unified front versus opponents. Similar sentiments regarding the assessment of the situation and of the nation can be found tellingly repeated not only in public pronouncements but also in private correspondence. Especially given how little has been undertaken on Catholics and the nation for this period—indeed some of the existing literature has chosen to focus exactly on those individuals who broke with the majority of their co-religionists—an emphasis on the outlook shared by most of them, and not the undoubtedly extant differences and exceptions, is not only warranted but necessary.[32] Moreover, as the emphasis on visions of the nation and their constructed nature suggests, this study is centrally concerned with how Catholics articulated their understanding of—and place in—the nation, language that was commonly quite consistent.[33] Granted, this means, in part, rhetoric. But words mattered, and rhetoric not only stemmed from the reality of the conditions but had a way of shaping it as well.[34]

Though attempting to offer a definition of key terms used in the study of nations is beyond the scope of this book, terminological clarification is certainly in order.[35] This is a study of national identity, not nationalism. As many historians conceive of the latter term, nationalism in the 1870s was a phenomena that had limited weight among large groups of both Catholics and Protestants. National identity, however, is too broad without qualification since it could, on the most basic level, be equated with a general sense of Germanness, the development of which was neither specific to the period after the unification of Germany in 1871, nor particularly contested in scholarly accounts of Catholics in earlier decades. Moreover, discussing this more general sense of Germanness does not address the problem central to so much of the literature on national identity for the latter nineteenth century: how Germans were "made" from such a diverse group of peoples.[36] Hence, what this book explores is Catholic national identity that—while not the same as more dominant versions being proposed by liberals or the government—developed after 1871 in specific reference to the conditions that existed after unification. Of course the Catholic sense of Germanness after 1871 continued to draw upon earlier ideas and traditions that existed before 1866. Yet it also incorporated key elements specific to the post-1871 circumstances that not only accepted the reality of the *kleindeutsch* unification but also positioned allegiance and identification in reference to the *Kaiserreich*. Indeed, the elements that other historians have singled out to indicate Catholic integration later in the *Kaiserreich* as well as the ideas that allowed Germans more generally to share an "imagined community" were already present in embryonic form during the *Kulturkampf*.

Given the centrality of integration to this study, the various aspects of what this process could refer to should also be clarified. The beginnings of Catholic integration into the nation proceeded during the *Kulturkampf* on a number of related yet different levels, some of which advanced more quickly than others. Most basically, Catholics began to conceptualize many aspects of life along national lines as set in 1871. This involved everything from defending various actions as undertaken for the good of the nation or according to the wishes of the *Kaiser*, for example, to increasingly distancing the *Reich* from Austria-Hungary. On another level, integration also meant Catholics—like their Protestant counterparts— continued increasingly, though not exclusively, to identify themselves in relation to the national community beyond their locale or state, in other words as Germans. An example of this can be found in the harmonization of Catholic rhetoric on a national level, despite part of the message itself paradoxically emphasizing regional diversity as quintessentially German in nature. Finally, though the ideological conflict of the *Kulturkampf* clearly meant a high degree of separation existed between Catholics and their opponents in terms of how they defined the nation and German identity, the roots of long-term integration can be found even here. In the midst of the bitter ideological conflict that often led to Catholics claiming the exact opposite of their opponents, there also existed elements that could bridge the divide in defining Germanness and the nation, such as the emphasis on a common Christian heritage or the acceptance of *Wissenschaft* as an undisputed value. The alternative Catholic vision of the nation, in other words, was different on the whole but not always in the parts.[37]

A word on sources is also in order. While this study combines many different types of sources, ranging from formal complaints to the authorities made by private citizens that have remained stashed away in government and ecclesiastical archives to widely popular novels of the 1870s that went through many editions, newspapers occupy a central place in the analysis.[38] The study of Catholic national identity—so integrally connected to the conflict of the decade and the rhetoric it produced—cannot be undertaken without a heavy focus on the daily press of the period. The *Kulturkampf* consisted not mainly of physical battles but linguistic ones, and the language of newspapers is indispensable to the story of the 1870s.[39] Newspapers were a widespread medium in which Catholic notables could articulate their view of the German nation, reaching far more individuals than, for example, any address in parliament or speech at an associational meeting.[40] That is, of course, unless such addresses and speeches were subsequently printed verbatim in the newspapers themselves, which they often were for exactly the reason of greater accessibility. The connection between public opinion and the daily press is complicated to be sure. Newspapers have power, but they cannot simply construct any reality.[41] Yet the issue can only be one of debating the extent to which newspapers influenced the views of readers, not that they did so.[42] Nor was the relationship one way; newspapers provided a dialogic format that readers could influence, not least with their subscription money.[43] Catholics both encountered and constructed "their" vision of Germany on a daily basis in the newspapers. Especially given the limited examples for the Catholic community of other types of sources historians have often used in analyzing the construction of national identity, such as scholarly historical texts or national monuments, the importance of newspapers and other contemporary periodicals is undeniable.[44]

The case for the close relationship between Catholics and their press during the *Kulturkampf* is particularly convincing. Not only have scholars noted the high degree of cohesion in the Catholic community—including the press—during the *Kulturkampf,* but contemporaries also emphasized this. Prominent Catholic historian Johannes Janssen, for example, claimed the *Kulturkampf* had brought a "unity" surpassing anything before.[45] Likewise, contemporaries also saw the reportage in the press as not only a reflection of this unity but also as actively constituting it. Promoting unity was just one of the reasons Catholic organizations as well as individual notables within the community advocated so vociferously for the further development of the press, work that led to concrete results seen in the massive increase of established papers from 126 to 221 in the first decade of the *Reich*. It also fostered the great spike in overall circulation numbers, which doubled during this time.[46] Putting out a Catholic alternative to the "bad press" of the liberals was certainly another reason for the support of increasing newspaper numbers.[47] By the end of the decade, the circulation numbers for Catholic newspapers alone was 626,000. Including some of the other periodicals that appeared less frequently, the circulation reached approximately one million.[48] Of course this does not mean the "thorny issue of reception" is not a concern.[49] As Nancy Reagin rightly points out in her review of recent literature on the topic, reception is an issue in all studies of national identity and its construction, regardless of the source material.[50] It is never possible to tell exactly how a large group of people received and internalized such ideas and sentiments with a certainty. Yet one of the few points on which government and Catholic leaders agreed was the importance of the press and its influence on the larger community. A local Catholic club, for example, petitioned for the creation of a district press association to support Catholic newspapers, reasoning that "the press makes public opinion."[51] Likewise, seeing the press as the key issue, one public prosecutor tasked with keeping resistance to a minimum lamented the legal limitations on censoring the media, complaining to his boss that the Catholic "common man" put far too much stock in what the newspapers said.[52] Moreover, though Catholic leaders participated closely in overseeing the reportage of the press—

despite the latter's formal independence from both the Church and the party—newspapers did not merely act as vehicles for elite expression and manipulation of the broader public.[53] Influence went both ways. Beyond their purchasing power, readers could also register their objections, for example, in the form of letters scolding the editor, some of which were even published.[54] Furthermore, though the papers certainly contained elements included for "tactical" reasons, the bigger picture is not one of artifice or outright mendacity in place of true sentiment.[55]

The larger array of sources presents not only the same construction of national identity but also confirms the acceptance it found among Catholics more generally. The many sessions held at the yearly *Katholikentage,* meetings which Morsey highlighted as integral to Catholic cohesion from the 1870s onwards, presented the same ideas about Germanness and the nation.[56] These sessions were also not a one-way flow of ideas; the meetings presented an arena in which members of the community had a chance to react to and interact with Catholic leaders and their ideas in a much more direct and spontaneous way than reading newspapers and even writing letters to the editor offered. Pieces of private correspondence— from both notables and non-notables—expressed support for the ideas presented publicly, at times using the very same language. Indeed, the similarity of both sentiment and language across several different contexts means the Catholic construction of national identity cannot be dismissed as mere talk. Combined with what is known of Catholic actions more generally during the decade, including everything from the work done by individuals and organizations to voting patterns, the evidence suggests a period in which a close relationship existed between the rhetoric and the reality of reception. The ultimate indication that the rhetoric of the 1870s had real impact might, however, come from events decades later, given that the developments scholars have pointed to as indicators of more successful inclusion later in the *Kaiserreich* could already be found expressed as important ideas in the rhetoric of the *Kulturkampf.* In this sense, the present book argues that the 1870s were significant not only for the separateness of Catholics but also for their long-term integration.

This book consists of two parts. The first is a shorter section that reconsiders the narrative of the *Kulturkampf,* highlighting issues pertinent to the construction of national identity and especially to integration.[57] It proposes that Catholic efforts and ideas about how to effectively integrate themselves in the nation actually went through four different phases during the period. It begins in the initial chapter, however, with a very brief look at several developments earlier in the nineteenth century that not only influenced the outlook of Catholics on the eve of unification but also became important points of reference and memories called upon in Catholic national identity after 1871.

Chapter 2 starts the close examination of the 1870s, dealing specifically with the first two years of the new nation's existence. Upon unification in January 1871, and even after what historians now date as the beginning of the *Kulturkampf* by the middle of that year, Catholics maintained—and many rather enthusiastically—that 1871 meant not only a new era for the *Reich* but also for the world, a supposed German epoch in history. They attempted to reconcile their disappointments at the exclusion of Austria from the nation with the reality of a Prussian-dominated *Reich* by emphasizing the ability of Germany to spread German values beyond its borders. The year 1871 also saw the start of rhetoric that emphasized the beginning of revitalization domestically. In determining what positive changes could now be undertaken, Catholics drew heavily upon ideals valued within their own community. Yet the new nation promptly took on a cross-confessional definition in the Catholic construction. This period was not without its dissent, of course, but Catholics unified relatively quickly. Importantly, this drew diverging elements within Catholicism—some of which had been opposed to 1871 as, notably, many Bavarians were—together under a pro-*Reich* banner.

Chapter 3 continues the account through the period of 1873 to mid-1875. It argues that this period served as the low point of Catholic confidence during the decade. Catholics' efforts at conceptualizing Germanness reflected a real recognition of their dire situation. Though a main element of Catholic identity in Germany had always been based on support for state stability, this period saw the emergence of many formulations of allegiance that nonetheless included subversive undertones. Still, even at the nadir of their confidence in having a real future in the *Reich*, Catholics never stopped trying to claim their place in the nation.

Chapter 4 continues the chronology from mid-1875 into 1877, at which point Catholic efforts at creating a national identity switched from being primarily positive and inclusive constructions to heavily negative ones as well. The anti-Semitic content of Catholic rhetoric dramatically increased at this point. Considering Catholics' own difficulties as a religious minority, however, the anti-Semitism turned to non-religious issues with Jews. Hence, despite the repeated emphasis on the virtues of intense religiousness among Catholics, the efforts produced an anti-Semitism that largely disregarded theology and instead focused on the type of people Jews were, a version of hate that was informed by the increased attention to science during the nineteenth century and would be taken to a completely different level in the twentieth century. This chapter argues, however, that the attempt to rally around anti-Semitism at this point foundered relatively quickly. Instead, in the wake of this failure, Catholic rhetoric switched to portraying the main fight as one against socialism.

Chapter 5 completes the first section, focusing on the tail end of 1877 through 1878 and after, when the efforts to end the *Kulturkampf* began, ushering in a much more congenial relationship between Catholics and the government. With the main reason for Catholics rallying together in the new nation coming to an end, the Center Party and publications that owed their success in large part to the divisiveness of the *Kulturkampf* attempted to preserve the close bond that had existed between them and the Catholic populace. Amid fears of waning support among Catholics, Center notables focused on rhetoric that emphasized the broadness of the party and what it could offer beyond a focus on religious issues and opposition to the government. Importantly, this meant that even before the end of the active phase of the *Kulturkampf,* the Center Party began casting itself in terms that were much closer to those of the other political parties.

The second part of the book consists of four thematic chapters that examine significant, sustained elements in the construction of Catholic national identity. This part also links the specific developments of the 1870s to larger trends before and after the *Kulturkampf.* Chapter 6 considers how the location of the new *Reich* capital in Prussian-Protestant Berlin, combined with the concentration of the majority of the Catholic populace on the borders of Germany, inspired efforts to bring this periphery to the center and re-imagine the geography of the nation. To this end, the presentation of local events in Catholic regions as nationally important became prominent in news reporting. Yet even in touting diversity as the essential characteristic of Germanness, Catholic accounts disproportionately chose to emphasize the area that appeared most easy to integrate into what their opponents envisioned as appropriately German: the Rhineland and Westphalia. Furthermore, this emphasis on localities and regions as bridges to a shared national identity fit favorably with the concept of *Heimat* that would become so central to unity later in the *Kaiserreich*.

Chapter 7 focuses on gender. While much research has been done on the feminization of Catholic religion, this chapter goes further to show how this had implications for national identity during the 1870s. It argues that Catholics strikingly deviated from the German (and European) association of citizenship with masculinity, instead presenting constructions of national identity with a feminine gendering of the nation. This turned what had often been disparagingly alleged about Catholic effeminacy, about the women as well as the men, from a weakness into a strength upon which the nation should be based. Yet this tactic stemmed not only from a reaction to liberal criticism but also from a far larger reserve of positive connections with femininity. From the rise in Virgin Mary sightings to the manner in which average Catholics presented themselves in letters of complaint to local officials over daily confessional conflicts with Protestants beginning early in the century, a number of elements came together to inform the creation of a national identity that emphasized a feminine gendering of Germany. Importantly, it was a feminine Germany as subject, not merely the object of masculine actions.

Chapter 8 examines the educational conflict that raged between liberals and Catholics during the *Kulturkampf*, which must be viewed as encompassing far more than the often highlighted policies governing basic schooling or the training of priests. These issues formed only part of an interconnected and much more extensive debate over how knowledge should be constituted. The chapter argues that the central issue of *deutsche Wissenschaft* (German scholarship) was a value not championed by the liberal side alone. In this case, Catholic efforts at creating a national identity responded to allegations—indeed correct according to many statistical figures—of not meeting German educational standards, by this point lauded throughout the world for their excellence. Involving everything from encyclopedias to academic debates to popular books on science, these efforts re-examined what true *deutsche Wissenschaft* was.

Like many other Catholic activities of the period, the approach integrated both traditional and modern elements. Linking everything from faulty Latin to poor research methods, Catholic arguments did not dispute the value of German *Wissenschaft* but merely the liberal claim to it and to Germanness more generally. Importantly, such ideas promoting the value of scholarship did not remain the preserve of middle-class Catholics, who had often been more inclined to this position, but became the standard argument repeated even in more popular outlets. These arguments concerning higher education and scholarship recognized a shared value held by Germans above confession, a commonality that would later be drawn upon in the early twentieth century by individuals attempting to further integration.

Chapter 9 examines how Catholic attempts to define Germanness produced a very specific conception of the new nation's place on the world stage. Coming full circle and drawing upon the vision set out in the second chapter of a German epoch based on the spread of Christian values, this chapter shows how Catholic constructions of national identity created a larger moral map of Europe and, indeed, the world. The corresponding emphasis on ethical considerations, as opposed to *Realpolitik*, in the conduct of foreign policy led to a non-aggressive approach to international relations. At the same time, however, these constructions of Germanness fostered estimations of and attitudes toward other countries that spurred imperialism and contributed to the horrors of the world wars.

Given that the more dominant construction of national identity fostered throughout the 1870s by liberals and the government ultimately faltered at the end of the decade, in part due to the opposition of Catholics, it is important to understand how they fought for inclusion and how they understood their Germanness.[58] Of course, not all aspects of how Catholics defined the nation continued to inform their national identity after the *Kulturkampf*. Yet just as elements of liberal and official nationalism during the 1870s were reconfigured and recombined in the ongoing process of national construction, so were some of those from the Catholic version. Therefore this book argues that the significance and legacy of the *Kulturkampf* was not simply conflict but also the management of confessional differences in the service of national integration.

ONE

The German Question and Religion

JOSEPH GÖRRES WAS only eighteen when French Revolutionary troops entered Koblenz in 1794. Like many other educated Rhinelanders, he initially greeted the spread of republican ideals beyond the borders of France with enthusiasm. Indeed, the young writer who would become known for his support of German nationalism and contributions to a nascent political Catholicism got his start as a pamphleteer by writing pro-French pieces. A member of the first republican club in the city, the Patriotic Society, Görres used his pen repeatedly to prevent the return of Archbishop Clemens Wenzeslaus—and the *ancien régime* with him—to Koblenz, which the Elector of Trier had made his residential base just two decades earlier. Instead, Görres argued for French annexation of the left bank of the Rhine, a position promoted heavily in *Das Rothe Blatt,* a newspaper he founded in 1798. Hope quickly turned to disillusionment, however, and a deflated Görres retreated from politics at the start of the new century. Yet it was at this time that he moved towards Romanticism and nationalism. Once the Wars of Liberation that ultimately beat back Napoleon into France got underway, Görres returned to public life as head of the nationalist newspaper *Rheinischer Merkur.*[1]

While Görres hardly led a typical life, anti-French reaction and the Wars of Liberation played a similar role in precipitating nationalist sentiment for him as it did among other Germans at the time. Of course, France figured in the rise of nationalism in Germany beyond just the revolutionary and Napoleonic period.[2] Educated members of the middle classes had already begun asserting the primacy of German culture and language over French, often used by the royalty at courts throughout the Holy Roman Empire, in the decades before the Revolution.[3] Moreover, the rise of German nationalism did not draw solely on antagonism to France. Around the same time, the diffusion of the terms "nation" and "national" began picking up in German-speaking Europe with the translation of originally French works.[4] There were also cases of nationalist sentiment even after 1815 in which opposition to France played little role.[5] Yet the trope of France as archenemy would appear again and again to spur on nationalism, not least in moments like the Rhine crisis of 1840 or the Franco-Prussian War of 1870/71 that ultimately ushered in a unified Germany.[6]

Though the conservative settlement at the Congress of Vienna in 1815 dampened hopes for a unified Germany, various groups still kept nationalist sentiments alive. Choral societies and gymnastic clubs continued to have a nationalist bent to them, as did the *Burschenschaften*.[7] The involvement of these student associations in nationalist activities such as the festival at Wartburg Castle in 1817 prompted an alarmed Clemens von Metternich, chief minister of Austria, to outlaw them under the Carlsbad Decrees of 1819. That he also placed universities under close watch indicates the extent to which nationalism was still first and foremost championed by the educated middle class at this time.[8] The next big crackdown came in response to another nationalist festival in which students took part, though this one at Hambach Castle in 1832 had a broader social base of participants.[9] Not only the nationalism of such events worried authorities; liberalism went hand in hand with nationalism at the time. Both were ideologies of the opposition in the first half of the century.[10] Yet repression could stem the tide of nationalism for only so long, especially as many practical developments of the century spurred it along. Technological advances like the telegraph made communication over distances easier and speedier. Combined with the rise in publication of various printed materials, especially newspapers, this innovation helped provide the basis for a "national public."[11] Not just news but also people began travelling beyond their limited locales more easily with the advent of the railways. Of course, even more basic methods of travel improved with the expansion of the paved road system. Moreover, developments like the *Zollverein* meant not only people but also goods could travel more easily on this expanded transportation network.[12] Indeed, the greater development of such elements in Prussia as opposed to Austria contributed to the ultimate unification of the German nation in 1871 to the exclusion of the latter.[13]

Just as the Prussian-led, *kleindeutsch* unification of Germany was not a foregone conclusion earlier in the century, however, neither was the creation of clearly distinct understandings of the nation that so marked confessional relations during the *Kulturkampf*. Especially at the turn of the century, when nationalist sentiments were on the upswing, a pronounced irenicism between Catholics and Protestants ruled.[14] Such potentially divisive flashpoints like missionary events did not necessarily incite confessional conflict earlier in the century.[15] Again, the conflict could often be more easily understood as not between confessions but between Germans and French, an especially easy viewpoint to take for inhabitants of the heavily Catholic Rhineland who had experienced occupation firsthand and would be on the front lines of any aggression from the western neighbor.[16] Even the Hermann statue, the national monument that would later come to embody the idea of Catholic exclusion from Germany, found cross-confessional support when construction on the project began in the 1830s.[17] Prussian king Friedrich Wilhelm IV went especially far in promoting a sense of national unity that went beyond any religious differences between Catholics and Protestants. Married to Elisabeth of Bavaria, who only converted to Protestantism quite some time after the wedding, Friedrich Wilhelm also had faithful Catholics in his inner circle of advisors, including Joseph von Radowitz, who would later spearhead the ultimately thwarted efforts for unification in 1850 led by Prussia in the Erfurt Union.[18] The king's support for the building of the Cologne Cathedral and the festival associated with it in 1842 was an even clearer example of his vision of Germanness as equally inclusive of both confessions. He began the celebrations by attending both Protestant and Catholic services and again emphasized confessional inclusiveness and German unity in a speech he gave later in the day.[19]

Yet there were many developments pointing in the other direction and fostering diverging sentiments along confessional lines.[20] The ecumenism at the beginning of the century gave way to a more discordant relationship between Catholics and Protestants.[21] The vastly reduced number of territories after 1815 in the German Confederation that left the remaining states to deal with populations including both confessions had a part in increasing conflicts.[22] The religious revival experienced within Catholicism and Protestantism, however, likely played a larger role in underscoring confessional differences.[23] Both territorial reorganization and religious revival contributed to the major church-state conflict that erupted in 1837. Often called the Cologne Troubles, the dispute involved the confessional upbringing of children raised in Catholic-Protestant marriages. Previously, priests had performed marriages for mixed couples without requiring a promise that all offspring be raised Catholic. Nonetheless, Clemens August von Droste-Vischering, the new Archbishop of Cologne appointed in 1835, insisted on a strict handling of such unions, which meant mixed couples could only be married if the Protestant partner promised to raise any children as Catholics. Yet this directly conflicted with Prussian law, which indicated children should be raised in the father's confession. As all attempts to find a compromise on this issue failed, the government jailed Droste-Vischering. The conflict had grown beyond just him, however, as not only other Prussian bishops began to insist on a strict handling but also the Catholic populace came out in many instances to support their clergy, leading at times to fights with government troops.[24] Indeed, the conflict became one of the major events that reached the emerging "national public" through extensive reporting in the press.[25] At the same time, of course, it often elicited quite different responses depending upon confession. Not surprisingly, Görres's famous piece *Athanasius*, written in reaction to the Cologne Troubles, would also become one of the foundational works of political Catholicism.[26] Indeed, it is only in light of this confessionally divisive event that the full significance of Friedrich Wilhelm IV's insistence on religious inclusivity at the Cologne Cathedral celebration can be appreciated.[27]

Even aside from the direct conflicts and religious revival, however, indications existed very early on that at least some proponents of the nation viewed it in rather confession-specific terms. Beyond just the general opposition to France that many developed during the Revolutionary and Napoleonic Wars, the hostility could take on a particularly anti-Catholic bent among Protestants. Fearing especially harsh repression under Bonaparte's rule, especially after he signed a concordat with the pope, some Protestants already conceived of the French-German division as a confessional one too.[28] The Wartburg national festival likewise had a confession-specific message to it. It celebrated the 300th anniversary of Martin Luther's break with Rome and took place at the same castle where the reformer hid away from punishment for his actions.[29] Moreover, it was not only in the association of the German nation with Luther that such sentiments could exclude Catholics, as the regard for the Swedish king Gustavus Adolphus as a German national hero shows. Here, of course, the admiration was for his championing of the Protestant cause during the Thirty Years' War and his military feats against Catholic forces.[30]

Confessionally informed views of the nation were not only the preserve of Protestants either. The romantic nationalism of the period, with its emphasis on the splendor and unity of the Middle Ages—before the division of the Reformation—had a notably Catholic character to it. While there were some Protestant adherents of Romanticism, it did precipitate notable conversions to Catholicism among followers.[31] Moreover, it was not only the Prussian Friedrich Wilhelm IV who supported "national" projects. Bavaria's King Ludwig I did so as well, which could serve as a focal point for the nationalist sentiments of fellow Catholics.[32] His Valhalla project, conceived of during the Napoleonic period and constructed from 1830 to 1842, was built as a memorial to "the greats of the nation."[33] The persons originally included among the greats ranged from Hermann of the Cherusci to Saint Boniface, the eighth-century missionary, as well as Archbishop of Mainz, who was credited especially among Catholics with the original unification of Germany via Christianization. Reflecting Ludwig's qualms, however, Martin Luther did not make the cut in 1842, despite a bust for the reformer having already been sculpted for installation in the memorial shortly after construction began. The day after celebrating the completion of the Valhalla project, Ludwig I ordered work to begin on the *Befreiungshalle,* a monument to the deliverance of Germany from France during the Wars of Liberation.[34]

The events of 1848 and 1849 also showed both the possibility for cross-confessional cooperation on the national issue as well as its limits. Though the Catholic members of the Frankfurt Parliament voted together on issues specifically affecting the Church, they did not form a separate faction.[35] Moreover, many of the religious freedoms that would have been guaranteed by the "Basic Rights" resulted from Catholic cooperation with liberals on these points.[36] Even the *grossdeutsch-kleindeutsch* division cannot be simply ascribed to differences of religion. Initially, the vast majority of deputies at Frankfurt voted for the *grossdeutsch* solution, regardless of confession. Only after this possibility faltered on the response from Vienna did the Parliament more clearly break down into two separate camps of *grossdeutsch* and *kleindeutsch* supporters. While Catholics largely supported the *grossdeutsch* solution, it appealed to conservatives, South Germans, and those on the left end of the political spectrum as well. Moreover, a number of issues divided the deputies in Frankfurt, not merely the question of Austria or Prussia.[37]

These events also indicate the importance of divisions within the two confessions on the national issue, and not only for 1848/49. Especially early in the century, conflict within Protestantism remained a notable issue between the Lutheran and the Reformed versions.[38] When he ascended the throne, Friedrich Wilhelm IV smoothed over religious conflicts not only between the confessions but also within Protestantism too.[39] When divided into conservative and liberal wings, Protestants could differ significantly on their approach to and even support for nationalism. Sometimes liberals found the differences with their conservative co-religionists so great that they disparagingly called the latter "'Catholicizing' Protestants."[40] Not surprisingly in this light, the conciliatory approach of individuals like Friedrich Wilhelm IV or Ernst Ludwig von Gerlach, the conservative Protestant who would later cooperate extensively with Catholics during the *Kulturkampf,* often engendered liberal claims that the men were crypto-Catholics.[41] The reaction after the revolutions of midcentury only served to strengthen ties between conservative Protestants and Catholics. Furthermore, while by the 1860s conservative Protestants may not have been as close to Catholics as in the previous decade, they had also not yet moved closer to liberals as they would for a time after 1871.[42] The differences within Catholicism could also be significant, especially in the first half of the century. As the lack of a specifically Catholic faction in 1848 suggests, members of this confession could also be found across the political spectrum, at times following class more than religion.[43]

On the other hand, that the confessional division ultimately played a major role in the Frankfurt Parliament, where for the first time the national question was addressed more concretely, was impossible to miss. Moreover, while the Church found itself in a considerably better position after the revolutions, often cooperating—as it certainly did in Prussia itself—with the state in a partnership of "throne and altar," this did nothing to offset the increasingly conflicting paths along which political Catholicism and liberalism were developing. Liberalism remained closely intertwined with nationalism, but it also began to increasingly come into conflict with religion.[44] This came to a head most visibly in Baden, where liberals were already spearheading measures in the 1860s that were similar to those later passed in Prussia during the *Kulturkampf*.[45] The change was not only on the liberal side either, of course. Ultramontanism, which made inroads into German Catholicism before 1850, dominated the outlook of the community beginning in the second half of the century.[46] The opportunity for cooperation between liberals and committed Catholics as well as the possibility for individuals to fully identify as both at the same time became increasingly slight.[47]

Yet even if the developments of these decades tended to point in the direction of the liberal-Catholic conflict that would dominate the 1870s, the Austro-Prussian War really provided the turning point. More specifically, Prussian victory did. Leading up to the hostilities, of course, most people were united in opposition to the war, especially in Prussia itself. The conservative *Neue Preußische Zeitung*, commonly called the *Kreuzzeitung*, feared the disastrous consequences of the war, regardless of who won. Liberals—still engaged in the "constitutional conflict" with Bismarck over military financing and organization—did not support the war either. What little backing Bismarck did find for this war came from rather odd places at times. Some socialists supported it, for example, believing that victory and the vast changes that would accompany it would likely benefit them, especially in light of Bismarck's support for universal manhood suffrage. Among the other German states, opposition also reigned. Moreover, because most other states not only expected an Austrian victory but also feared the domination that might come with a Prussian triumph, they ultimately chose to support the former. That included not only the states of Baden and Bavaria but also those of Hanover and Saxony, making the division of support between the two great powers hardly reducible to any simple split based on confessional differences or even on north and south for that matter. Many of the Protestant churches of the various Austrian allies joined in backing the Vienna-based power as well. Yet in the wake of Königgrätz—the decisive battlefield victory of Prussian over Austrian forces—everything had changed.[48]

TWO

The Beginning of the German Epoch

CATHOLIC SUPPORTERS OF a *grossdeutsch* unification saw an end to all such hopes with the Prussian defeat of Austria in 1866, a loss that likely shocked them all the more because of the speed with which the Hapsburg forces capitulated. Yet realistic expectations of an Austrian-led Germany had already begun to wane before that.[1] However painful the final blow of 1866 must have been to some—and there are notable examples of this grief—it did not provoke an "apocalyptic mood" among Catholics, as Thomas Nipperdey rightly asserted.[2] Certainly some withdrew further from national affairs into particularism, especially in the South. Still others remained opposed to a Prussian-led Germany, despite taking active roles in the North German Confederation that prefigured it. Yet many of them both recognized the writing on the wall and accepted that a German nation unified by Prussia could still represent a positive achievement, a position that particularly applied to those leading Catholics pivotal in the founding of the Center Party and ultimately among its leading strata during the *Kulturkampf*. Among such men could be counted both Reichensperger brothers (though Peter came to this stance sooner) and Karl Friedrich Savigny.[3] Wilhelm Emmanuel Freiherr von Ketteler, bishop of Mainz, became the most notable advocate for accepting the leadership of Prussia in Germany, no doubt because of *Deutschland nach dem Kriege von 1866,* his quick response to the changed circumstances brought by Austrian defeat.[4] In it, Ketteler gave expression to both the

concern of many Catholics about Prussian leadership as well as the condemnation felt over the northern state's actions in a civil war many
believed never should have occurred. At the same time, however, Ketteler
argued for cautious optimism. Prussia was not beyond the pale; Catholics
could still believe in a *Reich* led by it. After all, good things often came
from wrong deeds, or as he put it, "a great misfortune often becomes the
source of the greatest blessings."[5]

Nonetheless, support for a Prussian-led Germany required time, and
the stance likely became the default position among the general Catholic
populace only with the advent of the Franco-Prussian War, though even
this did not win over groups like the Bavarian Patriots.[6] With the war's
end in sight, Ketteler penned another tract at the start of 1871, again
addressing the future of the German nation and Catholics' role in it. The
bishop reiterated many of the same points in *Die Katholiken im Deutschen
Reiche* that he had made in his earlier work. Yet the second text also suggests that Ketteler's already positively inclined standpoint on a Germany
led by Prussia had been further bolstered by the general populace's overwhelming support for the war and the rising enthusiasm over the
impending victory. Still cautious, Ketteler nonetheless reveled in what
had been achieved by the now unified nation: "We definitely stand before
a decisive moment. God has permitted that the German *Reich* has gained
power and a position such as are rarely entrusted to human hands."[7]

Though the text was not published until 1873, by which time conditions had changed, Ketteler held up the tract as evidence not only of his
own attitude but also as an indication of the welcoming attitude most
Catholics had for the *Reich*.[8] Indeed, most scholars who have addressed
the issue agree that a considerable "willingness to integrate" existed
among Catholics as they entered the new nation, a position shared by
historians who are nonetheless skeptical that this period of openness
lasted much beyond the first months of 1871.[9] This cautious optimism did
not rule out awareness of the potential problems that could arise in the
new *Reich*. Yet Catholics shared these concerns with many others across
both the religious and political spectrum. Even the nationalist historian
Heinrich von Treitschke worried about the potentially negative fallout
from 1871 on German culture.[10] Ketteler may have even underestimated
the extent of the "trusting attitude" many Catholics had regarding the

new nation, or more specifically its government.[11] After all, the Center
Party only gained slightly over half the Catholic votes cast in the first
elections to the *Reichstag* in 1871. Significantly lower than any returns
Catholic voters gave the party throughout the rest of the decade, the
results can perhaps be attributed in part to the faction's recent inception.[12] Yet that a sizable number did not even feel the need to vote for the
Center Party suggests a more general optimism among Catholics that
they too would be welcomed and at home in the new *Reich*.[13]

This chapter expands this point on the general openness Catholics felt
toward the new nation. Indications of it could be heard far beyond the
writings of a man like Ketteler. Certainly his words carried weight; yet
major Catholic newspapers, the speeches given at *Katholikentage,* and
private letters also tell a great deal about Catholics in the first years of the
Reich. Many of these sources reveal instances of not just openness and
cautious optimism but outright enthusiasm for the new nation. Certain
difficulties and objections from elements within the Catholic community
that presented potential stumbling blocks to acceptance of the new nation
were, at times, downplayed by co-religionists to help further general
acceptance. Even after moving into a more oppositional stance to the
government, Catholics remained committed to the *Reich* and continued
their efforts to construct a national identity and define Germanness. Ultimately, this chapter argues not only that the willingness to integrate in
the new nation existed among Catholics but also that the process of integration itself had already begun in the first couple of years.

With the advent of the Franco-Prussian War and a unified Germany within
grasp, alleged past wrongs were overlooked by many, if not forgotten.[14]
Johannes Janssen, for example, considered the sins of 1866 "atoned for"
just a month into the war by the common cause of "all German tribes"
against France. To his joy, one could now "again write a German history in
completely other [i.e., good] spirits" than had been the case after the defeat
of Austria, a sincere statement given his engagement over the next two
decades with his *Geschichte des deutschen Volkes seit dem Ausgang des
Mittelalters*.[15] Many Catholics, like Janssen, now focused on the future
before them, one they also believed would bring good things. The leading
Catholic newspaper *Germania* described approvingly the celebrations of

the "masses"—not differentiated by reference to confession—to fete victory over France. The article attributed such rejoicing not only to the elation over the return of peace and the euphoria of victory but also to the "sense" that Germany stood at the beginning of "a new era." With "the sense of German identity so powerfully strengthened," the nation would now not only undertake political reorganization but also improve society more generally. Recent events only constituted the "glorious dawn" of a future that promised an even greater "highlight."[16] This was no isolated example. Another *Germania* article described prospects for life in the new *Reich* as "full of hope."[17] Yet another wrote of the "confidence" it had that "Germany in its new arrangement [unification] heads toward a flourishing future."[18] The *Kölnische Volkszeitung* exhibited its characteristic restraint by stating "we too are pleased with the re-establishment of the German *Reich*. . . . We too pay tribute to the new empire *(Kaiserthum)*."[19] Yet just a few days earlier, while reveling in both the opening of the *Reichstag* and the success of the military that had "put itself to the test" against France, even this paper had gushed excitedly, speaking of a "spring day for the new German *Reich*."[20] Not only France found itself in a new position after defeat by Germany, however. Unification had changed everything internally and externally. With it "now the German [*Volk*] has the primarily leading job in political relations" above all "other peoples."[21] These others would now move to the background, and the *Reich* would determine things in nothing short of a "resurgence of the German way and the German character."[22] Similarly, the *Schlesische Volkszeitung* spoke of the German "mission," an idea that would become common in Catholic arguments for the importance of the *Reich*.[23] In short, such enthusiasm greeted unification as the beginning of a German epoch in Europe and the world.[24]

Indeed, given the later ferocity of the *Kulturkampf,* the allure that the advantageous situation enshrined in the Prussian Constitution held out for many Catholics, especially from states with more restrictive laws, is sometimes underappreciated.[25] The desirability Bishop Ketteler himself saw in the constitutional guarantees given to the Church in Prussia is well known and provided much of the impetus for the Center Party's attempt to have similar rights enshrined on the national level.[26] Yet Ketteler hardly stood alone in his quick recognition that Prussia's fortune in 1866 might well have a silver lining for Catholics more generally. The Bishop of

Limburg dismissed the attempts of members of the local Progressive Party to paint the Catholics of his diocese as possessed by "fanatic hatred of Prussia." While he admitted people still understandably had affection for the former ducal house of Nassau, the extension of favorable Prussian laws governing interaction with the Church to the newly acquired area would surely move Catholics to "quickly become fully content with the new order of things and devote themselves from the heart to his majesty, the king, and the royal house [of Hohenzollern]."[27] Eugen Thissen, parish priest in Frankfurt and later one of the co-founders of the Center Party, wrote even more enthusiastically of the advantage Prussian rule would bring to his city. The Church would now gain "the free position and dignified treatment of which it enjoys in the Prussian state above all other states, and the barriers that *Kleinstaaterei* produced [would] fall."[28] The Catholics of Mecklenburg had hoped for the extension of such advantages to them as well in 1866. Because the territory joined the North German Confederation at the time but was not directly annexed by Prussia, such expectations remained unfulfilled. It did not stop the surfacing of the same hopes again in 1871, however, as a letter to the editor from a Catholic in the city of Rostock made clear.[29] This idea found expression throughout the papers, with Catholics from southern states joining in as well.[30] In late January 1871, for example, the *Augsburger Postzeitung* acknowledged the "fear" among some in the region that Bismarck might ally with liberals in an attempt to wage war against Christianity. Yet, the paper contended that it found the "hope" felt by others that the chancellor would be a true friend to religion far more convincing, concluding "Catholic Germany need not fear him."[31] Even after hopes waned in 1871, calls for the state to follow the Prussian custom of increasingly better treatment of the Church over the past century continued to be voiced during the *Kulturkampf*, combining both an appeal to tradition that played a significant role in Center Party rhetoric as well as a jab at liberals in suggesting they were not following their own ideal of progress.[32] Friedrich Wilhelm IV so often received praise in historical accounts, for example, in part because his reign brought with it the advancement of the Church's position in Prussia.[33]

At the same time, however, early reportage also gave clear indication that the Catholic masses did not all share in this hopefulness. Of course stories on issues like the opposition to Bavarian entrance into the *Reich* by the Patriots provided explicit evidence of significant disunity.[34] Yet the variety of opinion also found expression in other more general articles, indicating that for some Catholics acceptance of the new nation stemmed largely from simple recognition of the facts. The articles of *Germania* are particularly telling in this respect, not surprising given its close connections with the event of German unification itself as well as its efforts to be a unifying force among all Catholics in the new nation.[35] Alongside the plethora of articles that praised the new Germany and portrayed such attitudes as reflected among the Catholic populace, there also appeared a more limited number that clearly stood out as attempts to inspire enthusiasm in readers still far more cautious than optimistic. At the beginning of January 1871, with debate in the Bavarian Parliament still raging and unification still unachieved, *Germania* ran an article entitled "Doubt about the New German *Reich*." In the face of rising concerns about unification in many corners, not just among Catholics, the article attempted to assuage any reservations readers might have. The article touched upon many different concerns, not denying their importance. Yet it concluded "to all these doubts and concerns there is one thing to say": this was only the beginning, not the end. The only decisive issue was whether the "seed and kernel" were those of the true *Reich* or not, a question the article alleged could only be answered in the affirmative.[36] Yet, even after the Versailles ceremony proclaiming the *Reich* on January 18, the editor of *Germania* still clearly felt some people needed to be convinced. Again the paper reminded readers that "nothing can enter into the world as finished." In the natural "process of becoming" that everything must go through, once more *Germania* asserted that the importance lay in the "seeds" of something bigger and better being present.[37] A similar defense of the new nation appeared again in late March.[38] By June 1871, however, the newspaper no longer felt the need to make such appeals. The disparity of attitudes among Catholics—as well as other Germans—was still present, and the article noted that unification did not occur according to the "expectations of all." Yet, it continued, "the conviction is universal that Germany won beyond measure through it and can win still more by it." Though "universal" was certainly an overstatement, *Germania*'s editors felt sure enough about the general acceptance of this position to conclude "we need not add anything further to our standpoint."[39] More importantly, even though the situation began to turn increasingly sour for Catholics as the

Kulturkampf began, the issue of division over unification ceased to be an issue, and support for the new *Reich* was taken for granted.

Nowhere is this clearer than in the articles of the leading Bavarian paper, the *Augsburger Postzeitung.* By this point, Bavaria had entered into the *Reich* despite the staunch opposition of the Patriot Party. Indeed, the opportunity for greater unity among Catholics throughout Germany came from within the Patriot Party itself, as thirty-two members ultimately supported entry, giving the measure enough votes to pass in the Bavarian Parliament. The *Augsburger Postzeitung* itself supported this position and also claimed the "Patriotic *Volk*" overwhelmingly did too.[40] While these moderate Patriots certainly acted more out of necessity than anything else, this pragmatism nonetheless paved the way for the larger Patriot Party's relationship to the Center to grow closer throughout the *Kulturkampf.*[41] Moreover, even while the *Augsburger Postzeitung* initially made no secret of its total disappointment in the unification of the *Reich,* it soon adopted the rhetoric of counterparts elsewhere in Germany. Within the first month, the paper went from decrying how much had been "destroyed," focusing on the "end of the history of our closer Fatherland [Bavaria]," to instead pointing out "there is truly still much salvageable" both in Bavaria and nationally.[42] While this change in tone might be attributed to seeing the glass half full versus half empty, by March 1871 there was no mistaking the attempt to leave this earlier opposition to the *Reich* behind. Even when alerting its readers to what it saw as alarming statements being circulated in opponents' papers, the *Augsburger Postzeitung* now referred to how it had "greeted the new German *Reich* with joy as an accomplished fact" in January 1871.[43] By the beginning of 1872, in its review of the last year's events, the *Augsburger Postzeitung* sounded far more like counterparts in Prussia did in January 1871 than its own articles from that time. The review spoke of the "splendid peace settlement" and how it "promised to secure Germany's power for a long time." While the article did note deep concerns about where the new *Reich* was headed, the tone hardly smacked of having believed this to be coming all along. Instead, it contended that such concerns "threaten[ed]" to disappoint all who had greeted the *Reich* "perhaps too sanguinely."[44] Continuing this trend, by September 1872 the *Augsburger Postzeitung* actually printed a more enthusiastic commentary on Sedan Day than the

Prussian papers, refraining from any negative statements.[45] Whatever opposition the paper now expressed was against the policies of Bismarck and the liberals, not against the *Reich* itself.[46]

The efforts to bridge divisions did not remain one-sided either. Though the two leading Catholic papers made clear their support for Bavarian entry into the *Reich* from the start—the *Kölnische Volkszeitung* by attempting to downplay any concerns of a confessional nature that the Patriots could have while *Germania* went further by aggressively chiding its southern brothers for what articles portrayed as misguided efforts— both publications largely dropped the issue after the deciding vote on January 21 and focused on the fact of unity.[47] Leading Center politicians did the same. Within days, Ludwig Windthorst, Hermann von Mallinckrodt, and August Reichensperger all wrote to Edmund Jörg, who as leader of the Patriots had voted against Bavarian entry into the *Reich*, impressing upon him the importance of ensuring that all members of his party now put past differences aside and present a united front on a national level with the Center.[48] Those Patriots who took up seats after the elections of 1871 did just that, forging the early bonds of a nationally integrated political Catholicism born of conflict.[49] Indeed, the *Augsburger Postzeitung* downplayed Patriot candidate losses in the *Reichstag* elections by noting that this was made up by gains in Prussia so that the Catholics would be as strong as they "ever dared to hope" overall.[50] The paper's prediction that "Catholics will gather together all the more closely from one election to another the more one threatens their sacred rights" proved to be true.[51] Even Jörg himself, though he stayed away from the *Reichstag* for the next few years, took up a seat there by 1874 and could admit that he felt "relatively happy" in Berlin.[52]

Bavarian autonomy, of course, constituted just one of several issues about which Center Party members were divided, not to mention the diversity of opinion within the populace itself. One need look no further than the already mentioned variety of candidates—Center and otherwise—Catholic voters supported in the first elections.[53] Even with the Bavarian Patriots on board, concerns over party unity within the Center itself always remained. August Reichensperger, for example, related to his wife Clementine late in March 1871 that the Center's organizing activities designed to present a united front were going well.[54] Yet the wording of a letter sent a week later in early April betrayed the real situation. Again reporting positively on Center developments, Reichensperger relayed the news by stating, "No trace of a split in our fraction," suggesting his very real concern that such a breakdown might occur.[55] Indeed, concerns over potential division only grew, largely a response to the recognition of how vital unity was in the unfolding *Kulturkampf.* The opening appeal of the Verein der deutschen Katholiken, made on July 8, 1872, cited the "division" that opponents were attempting to sow among them and stated the purpose of the newly founded society was to "create unification of all German Catholics."[56] The constant attention to divisions within Protestantism reflected not only the reality in that confession but also an anxiety about the same fate befalling Catholicism.[57] Even at the highpoint of the *Kulturkampf,* for example, leading Center parliamentarian Georg Hertling wrote about party cohesion in much the same way Reichensperger did to his wife. He addressed the fear of division only to conclude that such concerns were "completely unfounded."[58] Moreover, though votes throughout the *Kulturkampf* remained astoundingly united—both from the populace for the Center and among the party deputies for various stances taken as a fraction in the *Reichstag*—variations always remained.[59] In this sense, Wilfried Loth is right to caution against seeing Catholics as a monolithic milieu.[60] Yet it is hard to overlook the high degree of unanimity among Catholics and their representatives during the seminal decade of the 1870s itself. Hence, by the second year of the new *Reich,* Janssen proclaimed that he knew of no other time when the "unity" among Catholics was so great.[61] Significant for beginning the integration of Catholics into the new nation was, of course, the coalescing of the party and popular rhetoric around the ideas of openness and even enthusiasm for the new *Reich* represented by men like Ketteler and the Reichenspergers instead of the rejection, or at least reticence, of others like Jörg and even Windthorst.[62]

Even in the initial months of the new *Reich* when unity was at its lowest point during the decade, engagement with the new nation went beyond the enthusiastic words of some to include omnipresent statements from political and spiritual leaders reminding Catholics of the need to vote in the *Reichstag* elections. This first *Reichstag,* appeals asserted, would be the most important assembly in hundreds of years, since its job would be none other than to begin defining the new nation. Far from being just a concern for the government, this "colossal task" required the participation of the people, and certainly among them must be the Catholics as well. Their "involvement" was also needed to ensure "that the new Germany establishes itself in a [certain] way."[63] While such appeals made reference to the importance of securing the Church's position in Germany, this commonly did not appear as a singular goal but instead as part of the more general path to promising future greatness for the *Reich* as a whole. Less than two weeks before the elections, for example, Bishop of Breslau Heinrich Förster released his "Exhortation to Our Well Beloved Clergy," a statement reprinted in multiple newspapers to reach the laity as well. The article reminded readers that voting was a "religious duty, because religion commands [one] to work for the benefit of the fatherland in [one's] assigned sphere according to [one's] best abilities," to which Förster added afterwards that the results of the elections would likewise be of great importance for the Church itself.[64] The choice as such was not either the Church or the nation, but both of them for the good of each other.

Engagement with the new *Reich* did not remain only the talk of leading Catholics and publications; the masses followed in their actions. According to the statistics from 1871, Catholics were overrepresented among those voting in the first election in relation to their numbers among individuals entitled to participate.[65] As other historians have noted, such participation was neither a foregone conclusion nor an insignificant fact. Given that believing Catholics in Italy often abstained from voting, the fact that their German counterparts participated meant both a vote for a particular party and also one for the acceptance and the legitimacy of the new nation.[66] Of course, recognition of legitimacy aside, higher participation among Catholics likely also stemmed from concern over their position as a minority. Yet the votes that went to the Center Party—as only slightly more than half did—cannot simply be taken as opposition votes or signs of displeasure.[67] Some votes did register discontent, of course. Yet, given the importance of men like Ketteler and the Reichenspergers in founding the Center Party, for example, or the optimistic tenor of election appeals and of coverage of unification in the major Catholic newspapers, many votes were not mainly motivated by concern.[68] More importantly—regardless of whether it came from caution or optimism—Catholic participation in elections constituted an attempt on the most practical level to be included in the construction of the nation.[69] Even as the Center Party moved into a more clearly oppositional stance, this effort to construct—as opposed to merely obstruct—remained the case.[70]

Catholic efforts to join in the construction of the new *Reich* went far beyond basic participation in elections, however. Just a few days after the proclamation ceremony of January 18, *Germania* began a series entitled "Das Deutsche Kaiserthum" with the express intention of providing a Catholic interpretation of unification.[71] Far from representing the victory of Protestantism led by Prussia over Catholicism, as the accounts of many opponents suggested, the very significance of unification lay in the fact that it drew on a much more ancient heritage.[72] The article stressed the legitimacy of Wilhelm's title and the new *Reich*, noting that it was based on the heritage of the old one, the Holy Roman Empire of the German Nation, unlike other titles of rulers who simply proclaimed themselves emperors of something without drawing on any precedent—a telling reference to the century's recent examples from France and Austria. The article pointed out that January 18 marked not only the 170th anniversary of the Kingdom of Prussia but was also the date of the festival of St. Peter's Chair to commemorate the establishment of the papacy in Rome. It was from this much older tradition—represented by leaders like Karl, not Frederick, the Great—that the unified *Reich* ultimately drew significance.[73] Peter Reichensperger placed the same spin on unification in one of his initial speeches in the *Reichstag*. The parliamentarian asserted that on January 18 Wilhelm joined the lineage of men like Barbarossa, again setting aside the importance of Prussia's Frederick II (the Great) but likewise diplomatically distancing this interpretation from what might be construed as an Austria-centric position. He did so by also excluding from this distinguished lineage "Leopold II and Joseph II and all the other 'seconds'"—a reference to Francis II, both the last Holy Roman Emperor and the first for Austria alone.[74] How could Catholics be considered unpatriotic, another article in *Germania* asked, when they had been tending the very imperial heritage that gave the new *Reich* its significance centuries before Protestants even existed?[75]

The *Katholikentage* held after unification, none of which ever again met in Hapsburg lands until the Austrians began to convene their own separate meetings decades later, also served as another venue where Catholics staked their claim to the new *Reich*. Hardly surprising given Ketteler's early acceptance of Prussian leadership, the bishop also made a point of giving the *Kaiserhoch* at the 1871 meeting in Mainz and asserted, "We Catholics want to be second to none in terms of love of fatherland," a highly significant statement for Catholic integration as already noted by Rudolf Morsey.[76] While Ketteler was perhaps the most notable Catholic to take part in the meeting, the bishop's actions hardly stood out among many others undertaken to the same ends at the first *Katholikentag* after unification. Christoph Moufang, who did not transition after 1866 as easily as Ketteler did despite being a close associate, nonetheless opened the Mainz meeting with a speech that reminded the attendees of their duty to "represent the conviction of the 14 million Catholic Germans." In doing so, he clearly framed the meeting from the start as one concerned with Germany as unified in 1871 by leaving out those co-religionists in Austria. As for how integral Catholics were to this new nation, Moufang concluded, "It is true that [14 million] is only a third in the new German Reich, but it is truthfully not the worst third," to which there was general cheering.[77] Such an understanding also seems to have been held by those attendees from over the border too, as a speaker from Vienna introduced his talk by saying, "As I come from Austria, so may the question easily be directed at me: how is it with the struggle begun anew against the Church in your home *(Heimat)*?"[78] The meeting of 1872 was no less certain in these terms, despite all that had happened by then. Silesian Center politician Franz Graf von Ballestrem spoke at the opening ceremony in Breslau, asserting, "we are not only an assembly of Catholics, we are an assembly of German Catholics." There could be no doubt of the specific "Germany" in mind, as Moufang had just left the podium after reiterating his statement from the previous year with slight modification, this time exclaiming, "we are admittedly only a third, but one may nevertheless say a very respectable third of the German nation."[79] While sympathies with Austria still remained high, the *Katholikentage* framed the national community squarely as that of the *Kaiserreich*. As a *Westfälischer Merkur* article put it when discussing the new "shape" of things, "victor as well as vanquished must embrace it," and Catholics largely did just that.[80] Within the first couple of years after unification, for example, articles in the press already began chastising Austrian Catholics and defending Prussia from their rants.[81]

Catholics embraced the *Kaiser* especially, a figure who played an important integrative role for all Germans after 1871.[82] Newspapers on March 22, Wilhelm I's birthday, often featured not only celebratory congratulations to the emperor but also assertions of the utmost loyalty and love from his Catholic subjects. The *Schlesische Volkszeitung* spread a poem honoring the "hero emperor" across the top of its front page in 1872, waxing on about his deeds connected with Germany becoming "fully conscious of its power" in unification.[83] The *Kölnische Volkszeitung* made a particular point of underscoring their continued support that same year, stressing "Catholics are attached to this house of Hohenzollern with steadfast love, and—regardless of what has happened—this love has not wavered an inch."[84] *Germania* also made a point of this on the *Kaiser's* birthday in 1872, reprinting their well wishes from the previous year and concluding, "On the second imperial birthday today, we have about all of this not a word to take back and not a syllable to add."[85] Just as Catholics separated their opposition to the actions of the government from their love of the nation itself, they drew a clear line between Bismarck, "the highest civil servant of the state," whom they often targeted for a number of reasons, and the crown.[86] Not surprisingly, Catholic rhetoric often substantiated various arguments by claiming such was the will of the *Kaiser*, though it also chastised opponents for undermining the emperor's status as being above politics and "exploiting" him for their own ends when they tried to do the same.[87] Oft cited in support of the Catholic position was the *Thronrede* (speech from the throne) at the opening of the first parliament in 1871. The *Augsburger Postzeitung* wrote glowingly of what it interpreted as the peaceful intentions expressed in the speech and concluded it could only hope the *Kaiser's* "wish" would be followed.[88] Articles would return to the *Thronrede* and other statements by the *Kaiser* time and again to decry not only the direction Germany was taking in Europe but also the war being waged against Catholics with the *Kulturkampf*.[89] Even the *Historisch-Politische Blätter*, edited by the Bavarian Patriot Jörg, joined in this.[90]

In fact, the *Kaiser* also played an instrumental role in the cultivation of another theme that not only exemplified the Catholic attempt to define the new nation but also fostered integration: the rhetoric of a Christianity above confessions.[91] In response to attempts from Bismarck himself and others to present Germany as a "Protestant *Kaisertum*," the *Kölnische Volkszeitung* firmly asserted it only recognized a "German *Reich*," which had at its head "a devout, Christian, solemn prince, who wears the crown of the *Kaiser*, who belongs to the Protestant confession," a fact a Catholic could also view with "joy and great satisfaction."[92] Indeed, the Cologne-based paper had always emphasized this greater Christian unity not only by portraying the *Kaiser* as above the conflict but also by posing the battle from the beginning as between liberals and believing members of both confessions. Liberals had only a "slightly less hostile inclination" toward Protestantism than Catholicism itself, an article appearing shortly after unification warned.[93] Similarly, the *Westfälischer Merkur* asserted that only together could Protestants and Catholics ward off liberal attacks on religion, reminding readers that recognition of a shared Christianity had allowed victory over France.[94] The same division between "positive Christianity" and liberalism played out in the Catholic press all over Germany.[95]

While perhaps not so surprising when read in a moderate paper (for example, in the *Kölnische Volkszeitung*, which was particularly well-known for being moderate on all subjects, including the topic of Protestants), such conciliatory statements could also be found in a publication like *Germania*.[96] *Germania*, of course, was not only the most important Catholic newspaper in the *Reich*, it was also led, beginning in March 1871, by Paul Majunke, a man known for his strident tone that both led to his departure from the editorship of the *Kölnische Volkszeitung* earlier and quickly made his Berlin-based paper the target of many government crackdowns.[97] He had also been part of the ultimately unsuccessful push in 1870 for the establishment of an explicitly Catholic political party.[98] As one might expect, *Germania* included some anti-Protestant polemics. More significantly, however, these polemics are far more limited than assessments of Majunke or the paper he edited would suggest. Certainly, some articles claimed that the jig was finally up for the Reformation, having "used up" much of the "patrimony" taken in the split from the Church centuries ago; others expressed *Schadenfreude* at what was believed to be the end for Protestantism, not Catholicism, in Germany in light of the antireligious climate of the *Kulturkampf*.[99] Yet, like its more moderate counterpart in the Rhineland, and indeed major Catholic papers throughout the *Reich*, *Germania* also ran articles from the beginning stressing that the real division lie between liberals and believing Christians. Indeed, among the latter, differences existed concerning "less important things," but certainly not the "cardinal questions."[100] Another article again diminished the importance of confessional differences, finding them more "personal issues" than anything pertaining to national questions based on Christianity as a whole.[101] The *Kaiser*, of course, played a role in *Germania* in the toning down of confessional differences, with one article applauding Wilhelm I as an "orthodox Protestant" who gave Catholics no reason to worry and adding that "some Protestant kings in Berlin were more preferable to us . . . than some emperors in the Vienna imperial palace."[102] Perhaps most effective on this front was the ongoing article series simply entitled "Von einem Protestanten," often penned by conservative Ernst Ludwig von Gerlach, though published without attribution.[103] Prominently featured multiple times a month as the lead article, the series attempted to show the common ground shared by all believing Christians and at times encouraged goodwill more directly, as in one article's exhortations about "exercising moderation in confessional differences."[104] Not surprisingly, this particular article pointed to the shortcomings of opposing papers on this front. This was more than partisanship with a new-forged ally or simple wishful thinking, however. Over the course of 1872, the ratio between articles expressing anti-Protestant polemic and those stressing cross-confessional cooperation tipped even further in favor of the latter, a trend the paper would continue throughout the rest of the decade. Indeed, the continued appearance of the "Von einem Protestanten" series in part necessitated this, both logically and practically.[105] Though numerically insignificant as he was only one man, Gerlach and the series he contributed to served as concrete examples for Catholics and constant reminders that the conflict was not simply about confession, a position that became the default stance in the pages of even a vitriolic and aggressive paper like *Germania*. Even statements about political conservatism in particular remained more restrained than those concerning liberals. After initial hopes that the Center positions would gain support among conservatives based on shared ideas about religion and federalism faded, articles still spoke of them more as misguided than fundamentally wrong. Unlike the vitriolic attacks on liberals, descriptions of conservatives often focused on how muddled and weak they had become as a group, calling the leading conservative paper of the *Kreuzzeitung* "hardly still the shadow of its [former] self" and summing up the situation with headlines such as "The Disintegration of the Conservative Party."[106]

The events of the *Katholikentage* provide an even clearer indication that the default stance taken in Catholic rhetoric eschewed confessional polemics and underscored common Christianity. Speaker after speaker at the meetings that took place over the multi-day gathering expounded on the distinction between "Christian" and "the so-called modern ideas," seeing the attacks directed at "every positive faith."[107] Others lauded the *Kaiser* as a beloved "father of Christianity" from whom they only expected protection and help.[108] At times, the topic of confessional divisiveness received direct attention. A speaker at one of the sessions at the 1872 Breslau *Katholikentag* asserted, "At our meetings precisely every confessional polemic is strictly prohibited." He continued, adding that "already yesterday it happened that the president interrupted a speaker twice, because he permitted himself [to utter] confessional polemic." Such vitriol did not reflect the views of those in attendance at the meeting or the larger Catholic community they represented, the speaker concluded.[109] Yet his statements did reflect the emphasis placed on common Christian values over confessional division by many Catholic leaders during the decade, influential men such as the Reichensperger brothers, Savigny, Hertling, and Windthorst himself. Even Ketteler—likely more in his role as a pragmatic political thinker than as a religious leader—saw the value of this approach.[110] Most telling, however, was that the statement rejecting confessional polemic came not from one of these men, but from Paul Majunke himself. Regardless of what his personal inclinations might have been, Majunke had joined in the promotion of common ground between the confessions.

As noted in the Introduction, this book is about both the rhetoric of Catholic attempts to define the nation and the reality of their actions. Often the evidence points to a close relationship between the two. In this case, however, it is less clear. What we know of Majunke's own stridency, the acrid anti-Protestant quips that declined but never disappeared from the pages of *Germania* or other papers, as well as the silenced comments his speech referred to already suggests this. That more incongruity could possibly exist between how the main conflict of the day was crafted in papers and assemblies and how many individual Catholics may have viewed the *Kulturkampf* is even clearer when consulting archival records of communal disputes during the decade. Take, for example, the events of 1872 in Dortmund. In spring of that year, the procession associated with the feast of *Corpus Christi* caused such an uproar that officials were still dealing with the fallout months later. The priest and Catholic parishioners involved likely provoked the city's Protestants intentionally, attempting to show the latter "their own weakness" by ostentatiously parading past the entrance of one of their churches just as services were beginning. Many things contributed to the situation coming to a head at this moment, including population growth, but the role of the *Kulturkampf* is hard to overlook. After all, the procession had carried on without a hitch for the last two decades.[111] The Dortmund case formed just one of many problematic examples that government officials came to label as Catholic "street terrorism" during this period, though today's associations with the term belie the essentially symbolic nature of the disturbances.[112] The priest and his parishioners hardly had common ground on their minds that day, nor did events like it foster such an understanding.

On the other hand, this caution does not mean such ideas of Christian commonality had no anchoring in the masses, or, more importantly, fell on deaf ears. Tobias Dietrich's detailed study of several communities throughout the nineteenth century indicates that many places did not see a rise in confessional conflict during the 1870s.[113] Moreover, especially when considering the local politics in Dortmund, even this disturbance did not necessarily mean the Catholics involved rejected the manner in which publications and leaders formulated the situation. With liberalism on the rise in Dortmund during the 1860s, left-leaning Hermann Becker's election to *Oberbürgermeister* at the end of 1870 signaled what would be a long period of domination of local politics by the Progressive Party, which drew votes from a broad spectrum of the city's Protestants.[114] Indeed—as Becker was also elected to the *Reichstag*—if Dortmund exhibited similar Catholic voting patterns as prevailed in the election of 1871 more generally, an overwhelming majority of Protestant voters must have supported the left-leaning liberal Becker.[115] It is not hard, in this sense, to see the local conditions lining up with rhetoric portraying liberals as the ultimate enemy.

Of course, this also points to a certain flexibility of the Catholic rhetoric on shared Christianity itself. If the main point of such statements was to promote common cause, it still always left room for real differences between the confessions. Catholics, so the rhetoric claimed, remained united by their religion. Protestants, on the other hand, were divided by theirs. Even if its believing members were true Christians with whom the Catholics should cooperate, the ravages of liberalism were gutting Protestantism more generally. This was not tantamount to denouncing Protestantism as heresy like in the polemics of old, but it still betrayed a sense of Catholicism's superiority on the whole. If Catholics and believing Protestants were to work together, such rhetoric still suggested a partnership between the two in which the religion of the former was first among equals. It was a formulation that allowed for cooperation across confessions but also claimed a special role for Catholics in the *Reich*. Both elements promoted Catholic integration into the nation.

The Catholic populace at large clearly had mixed emotions regarding the confessional divide, just as various leaders of the community did, some more inclined to see the differences as secondary to a shared Christianity than others. More important for understanding Catholic attempts to define the nation during the *Kulturkampf*, however, is recognizing that this view emphasizing commonality between the confessions clearly—and quickly—came to dominate expressions in the community. This resulted from true conviction for some, tactical considerations for others, and probably a mixture of both in most cases. Regardless, this had important ramifications for integration. On a basic level, it provided a more inclusive definition of the new *Reich*. It only ever targeted liberals, not Protestants, as un-German, presenting the excluded group as even smaller by frequently playing up its elitism.[116] The same inclusive approach would even be applied to the masses increasingly attracted to socialism, if not to the ideology itself.[117] On another level, it left the door open to cooperation with the conservatives. The emphasis on common Christianity always allowed for a view of conservative Protestants—both in the religious and political sense—as more misguided and ultimately impotent than bad. While hopes for a constituency for the Center Party within the Protestant community never materialized, and attempts to form a united front with conservatives failed during the *Kulturkampf* itself, it was this black-blue coalition that ultimately heralded the end of Catholics' outsider status at the closing of the decade. The coalition and integral role of the Center in it may have been new for the *Reich* in 1879, but Catholic arguments for the necessity of this for the nation were by then already old. Catholic rhetoric had been building this bridge since the beginning. Indeed, such an idea drew upon the common experiences of religious revival that both confessions underwent earlier in the century. That devout contemporaries also feared society was becoming increasingly vulnerable to secularization provided another point of commonality, suggesting the initial hopes for a cross-confessional party were not unrealistic.[118] That the transition from the rhetoric of the 1870s to the real cooperation at the end of the decade was largely seamless should not be underestimated in importance either. Bismarck could and did change partners and rhetoric from one day to the next, a criticism expressed often by Catholics about both him and liberals. The Center Party, however, had from the beginning of the decade based its legitimacy and relevance on tradition and steadfastness to principle.[119]

Of course, this was all predicated on acceptance of and support for the nation. This was true of Catholics on the whole at the inception of the nation and remained so after any hopes of a smooth entry into the *Reich* disappeared. The *Kulturkampf* did not change this. One might even note that although the beginning of the *Kulturkampf* is often dated to mid-1871, more modest hopes still existed at that point that a major conflict could be avoided and likely did not entirely disappear until 1872. Until that point, the initial actions affecting the Catholic community still often received mention as reversible. This tendency appeared in multiple leading Catholic newspapers' recaps of 1871. The *Kölnische Volkszeitung* included a "warning" about what would happen if the new nation took the wrong steps at this crucial "turning point," suggesting nothing irrevocable had yet been done.[120] In the same tone, the *Westfälischer Merkur* contrasted the success 1871 had brought to Germany with the dangerous liberal elements "burrowing" in the foundation of the *Reich* at that very moment.[121] *Germania's* review stated things more positively, concluding, "We have confidence in the future of our beloved Germany," notwithstanding recent "alarming measures" that had been introduced.[122] Even the *Augsburger Postzeitung*, which was quicker to express concern over anti-Catholicism, also conveyed this sense of hopefulness at the worst being avoided by efforts "to prevent the malformation" of the *Reich*.[123] Only the *Schlesische Volkszeitung*, a newspaper that often tended to diverge from the leading Catholic publications more than others did, painted the conflict as unavoidable.[124] None of the papers rejected the nation itself. The *Kölnische Volkszeitung* went so far as to explicitly assert, "the German *Reich* is also our—the Catholics'—*Reich*."[125]

Even by the time the Catholic community clearly recognized the war was on and that its role in parliament would likely be an oppositional one for some time to come, its position on the new *Reich* itself did not change.[126] Professions of unwavering loyalty and love for both *Kaiser* and *Kaiserreich* resurfaced—down to the same wording intentionally—in 1872 as they did the previous year.[127] Catholic papers always distinguished between their "opposition against the domestic politics of Prince Bismarck" and the untrue claim that they bore any "enmity against the *Reich*."[128] Such a distinction also made it into the defense several men gave in May 1872 for their involvement with suspect Catholic organizations. Far from indicating any more "systematic opposition" or "hostile tendency," they clarified that involvement only meant to further their interests as Catholics in the current situation and in no way meant a decreased "loyalty" to Wilhelm I.[129] Indeed, in the Catholic position, opposition to *Kulturkampf* policies as well as other issues like centralization became inextricably woven together with love for the *Reich* and true Germanness. One newspaper article admitted, "We do not enter into the struggle imposed upon us lightheartedly." The article justified opposition, however, because "it is necessary now more than ever that it [the Catholic people] stand by *Kaiser* and *Reich* in customary loyalty."[130] Catholic actions not only stemmed from "German loyalty" but would be undertaken with "German seriousness."[131] This was yet another formulation of the central Catholic position that presented their opposition from the beginning as essential "for the sake of the Fatherland."[132] Though Catholics would remain true to this ideal throughout the *Kulturkampf*, the limits of this devotion would not go untested.

THREE

The Limits of Loyalty Tested

WHILE MANY CATHOLIC Germans greeted unification with acceptance as well as enthusiasm and remained hopeful about their prospects for inclusion longer than often acknowledged in the literature, this had its limits. Far from being the general attitude espoused throughout the 1870s or beyond, fundamental doubts about the very *Reich* itself arose at a particular point during the *Kulturkampf* and, more importantly, dissipated long before the end of it. Of course, other scholars have discerned the waxing and waning of events during the 1870s, often noting a certain highpoint of the *Kulturkampf* during the middle of the decade. The flurry of additional laws enacted at this time has certainly attracted scholarly attention to the expansion of the campaign, though historians like Jonathan Sperber and Ronald Ross have also taken into account the responses of the Catholic population itself to such oppression.[1] This chapter adds to the contours of the *Kulturkampf*'s timeline by looking at how Catholic constructions of national identity and particularly hopes for inclusion in the nation reflected the changed circumstances of the expanding legal onslaught by the government. Despite the continuation of larger arguments firmly asserting Catholics' place in the nation even during this time between 1873 and the middle of 1875, there existed underneath this a considerable sense of doubt, an unmistakable uncertainty about having a real future in the *Reich*.

* * *

The rapid passage of several laws beginning in 1873 certainly impacted how Catholics saw their position in the *Reich* for the worse.[2] Of course, the first two years after unification had brought with them oppressive laws. Both the "pulpit paragraph," which was intended to limit the ability of priests to urge parishioners to vote for Center candidates in their sermons, and a law prohibiting the Jesuit order originated during this time.[3] Within Prussia, the government also enacted the School Supervision Law that made inspectors representatives of the state and opened up those clergymen who staffed such positions to easy dismissal, a process mainly used against Catholic priests, not Protestant pastors.[4] Yet this did not even closely match the pace at which laws were passed beginning in 1873. This year saw the advent of the May Laws in Prussia, a series of four laws announced in the first half of the month that undercut the independence of the Church in disciplining its members as well as in training and appointing priests, the latter of which caused especially marked conflict between local government officials and Catholics in various communities.[5] The following year brought another round of laws further extending the Prussian state's control over affairs the Church had traditionally administered, including the introduction of civil marriage. The legislative volleys continued in 1875 with the passage of the Bread-Basket Law that allowed the government to withhold funds from uncooperative priests, the Congregations Law aimed at closing many additional religious orders in Prussia, as well as others that changed the structure of how parish possessions were overseen and gave Old Catholics common usage of such properties in some cases. So altered was the border between church and state by the middle of 1875 that the diet had to amend the Prussian Constitution by repealing articles 15, 16, and 18, which were designed to afford the two confessions wider scope over religious affairs.

Yet not just the passage of additional laws weighed on Catholics. The state increased efforts via monetary aid to support the development of Old Catholicism in Germany, which elected its first bishop in June 1873.[6] More problematic from the standpoint of internal unity was the statement issued that same month by approximately two hundred Catholics, many of them prominent nobles, that openly accepted the legislation enacted by the May Laws.[7] Another bombshell dropped when the correspondence between Pius IX and Wilhelm I from earlier that year became public knowledge in October. Composed with input from Bismarck, Wilhelm's response to the pope's initial letter attempting to show the *Kaiser* the error of Germany's current path had firmly rejected any sense of wrongdoing on the government's part. More important than this rejection, however, was the sensation the poorly worded letter by Pius caused among Protestants, angered by the claim that they also "in some way . . . belong to the Pope."[8] Indeed, the increased results for the Center at the polls in both the Prussian elections in November on the heels of these revelations and those for the *Reich* in January 1874 were a double-edged sword. The gains made political Catholicism stronger and even more united, but they also revealed an increased sense of being under attack in the new nation. At the same time, the parties most supportive of the *Kulturkampf* remained in control and showed no signs of losing steam, while conservatives in both houses dwindled even further.[9]

The next year brought setbacks of yet another nature. Hermann von Mallinckrodt, who had been so integral to the functioning of the Center that Bismarck credited him with giving the party the edge it needed to always be a "horse length ahead" in the struggle, died in May 1874.[10] Just a couple of months later, a young Catholic named Eduard Kullmann attempted to assassinate Bismarck in the spa town of Kissingen. Though the chancellor escaped the attack with only a minor wound, the incident both shocked the public and heightened suspicions of a "broad Catholic conspiracy."[11] Even though such rumors had no basis in reality, the Catholic community would bear the burden of the "wretched Kissingen assassination attempt" nonetheless, as August Reichensperger complained a couple of weeks after the incident.[12] Given the importance of the *Katholikentage* at the time, the absence of a meeting in either the previous year or 1874 also dampened spirits.[13] The outlook beginning in 1875 was hardly better, given the death in February of another Center leader, Karl Friedrich von Savigny, and the prison sentences meted out, ultimately, to five of the eleven bishops and archbishops with dioceses in Germany by that year.[14] Such cases only formed the most notorious of the many sentences and fines handed down by the government as the *Kulturkampf* began to focus heavily on punishing noncompliance.[15]

In light of this upsurge beginning in 1873, it hardly surprises that both sides of the struggle perceived a fundamental change around this time. In

January of that year, scholar and liberal parliamentarian Rudolf Virchow first spoke of "a great *Kulturkampf*."[16] Likewise, Catholic voices also changed in tenor around this time. Annual newspaper reviews of the previous year's events already struck a more ominous tone than those for 1871. The *Schlesische Volkszeitung* tried to cover both the good and the bad of 1872, summing up the balance of events with the rather uninspiring conclusion "we are admittedly behind but not defeated; we are outvoted, but not overcome."[17] *Germania* gave the top spot on the front page not to the yearly review as usual but instead ran an article on a recent confiscation of one of its issues as a "new year's greeting."[18] In the actual review of 1872, *Germania*, much in the style of Virchow, spoke of a "great struggle of principles" *(Principienkampf)* having broken out.[19] Gone was the sense that a battle could be avoided that had imprinted the annual reviews of the previous year. This recognition certainly reflected the laws of 1872, but the ongoing preparations for passage of the May Laws likely played a bigger role. Indeed, the initial drafts of these bills began surfacing around the turn of the year (1872 to 1873) and were widely discussed in the Catholic press.[20] Just weeks later, *Germania* again spoke of the "great struggle of principles" that had begun in an article appropriately titled "The Die Has Been Cast." Underneath this report, not surprisingly, stood an article on the draft of the bill regulating priests' training and appointment.[21] Internal correspondence among the German bishops also reveals this same recognition that the May Laws had taken the conflict to another level. Discussing how the episcopate should respond to these laws, Christoph Moufang pointed out that "the end of the forthcoming conflict is not foreseeable."[22] The change was even clearer in the reporting for the *Kaiser*'s birthday (March 22). *Germania* did not even mention the *Kaiser* on March 22, 1873, only approaching the issue a day later as part of its weekly review. Again, a sense that there was no going back from the struggle was unmistakable. Instead of well wishes, the paper chose to express "a scared feeling" given events taking place in the *Reich,* concluding, "At least at the moment, the crown can no longer turn back from the embarked upon path." Of course the article did add that it was because the ministers had too much sway over the *Kaiser.*[23] The *Schlesische Volkszeitung*, on the other hand, still printed a poem on the front page in Wilhelm's honor. Nonetheless, the format told as much if not more than its printing: unlike in the previous year when both Wilhelm and Pius received equal space in their birthday greetings, the emperor's 1873 poem turned out to be much smaller than the pope's.[24] Size mattered. By the end of 1873, the only bright spot in *Germania's* review of the past year was that the article concluded it would be better than the one coming up![25]

The weight of such events also impacted how the press presented the relationship between Catholics and the nation more generally. Despite the assiduous attempts to claim Catholics' place in the nation during the first two years of the *Reich*, beginning in 1873 the statements in the press— made for public consumption—reflect a real doubt about the situation. Part of this was a feeling of helplessness in the face of the rapid passage of so many oppressive laws. Indeed, an article in the *Schlesische Volkszeitung* zeroed in on this feeling around the *Reichstag* election time, pushing readers to vote and refuting those who would claim "But it doesn't do any good!"[26] Yet more common than shrinking back from the conflict was a quite notable rise in aggression, at least verbally. More importantly, statements began hinting that while the *Reich* had the loyalty of Catholics now, that might not be the case if things continued down the same path. The *Central-Volksblatt* published in the administrative town of Arnsberg compared the position of Catholics in the *Reich* to that of Jews in Babylonian— that is, foreign—captivity, of no small significance given it was published in response to Sedan Day.[27] Just a few days later, the *Kölnische Volkszeitung* also made suggestive comments about the celebration and what it meant to be German. With crafty use of the subjunctive tense, that paper concluded: "If we did not see and hear our surroundings, we would have to doubt that we still live on German soil; and if we did not love our *Vaterland* so ardently and deeply and did not have the confidence in a better future, we would have to be ashamed to be Germans."[28] Flipping allusions to their Irish co-religionists on their head—as they were so often lauded as a model of dogged yet peaceful means of resisting legal injustices that ultimately improved Catholic-Protestant relations for the better—*Germania* referenced a different image of Ireland. If the laws of the *Kulturkampf* continued to push the Catholics, the government might find itself "in the best case" with a "German Ireland" on its hands. Here the allusion was to the previous century, when Ireland had not only a spate of severely repressive laws directed at Catholics but also a rebellion at the end of the century, though the latter point was never directly mentioned.[29]

Perhaps the most consistent manner in which Catholics continued to affirm their present loyalty but also suggest its limits was by referencing Christian persecution in ancient times. Certainly the Catholic press never had a shortage of comments that called liberals "heathens" and liberalism the "new heathendom" before the *Kulturkampf* or during.[30] Yet allusions that had remained vague and limited then ballooned in both frequency and detail during the period between the turn of 1872 to 1873, when discussion of the May Laws first became public, and 1875. On the one hand, the reliance on narratives of persecution and the accompanying martyrdom fit with a much longer tradition that told and retold such continuously developing stories as part of Christian identity.[31] Yet not only those on the Catholic side saw the particular applicability of the ancient period to the events of the 1870s, especially given that early Christian persecution had also been linked to the idea that they were bad citizens. The famed politician and scholar of ancient Rome Theodor Mommsen made these connections and wrote them into his work as well.[32] The context of his own century and the *Kulturkampf* itself informed Mommsen's evaluations of the various emperors—persecutors of Christians and those more conciliatory—as well as of Rome's government system.[33]

On the Catholic side, Bishop Heinrich Förster of Breslau wrote to Archbishop of Cologne Paul Melchers in January 1873 of "martyrdom" and the "time of Julian" that had "returned," referring to the emperor commonly called the "apostate" in view of his effort to reject Christianity and return Rome to paganism.[34] In his letter sent from the Prussian bishops to the general clergy and Catholic populace a few months later, Melchers similarly asserted there was "hardly any time" since ancient Rome when the Church was so "threatened." Perhaps in an attempt to be slightly less pessimistic and look to the future, he nonetheless added a word about Emperor Constantine's ultimate conversion to Christianity early in the fourth century.[35] These references paralleled the noticeably increased accounts of Roman times in the daily press. The *Schlesische Volkszeitung* began a series entitled "The Lot of the Child in Heathendom," which included all the unsavory details of "Roman law" and the "thirst for the blood of Christians," right at the end of December

1872.[36] After that point, the references to the "pagan emperor[s]," like Julian and others, and the "three hundred years [of] pagan barbarity," referring to the early centuries of persecution in Rome, began to flow.[37] Similarly in *Germania,* the article "The Die Has Been Cast" did not fail to also invoke the idea of "martyrdom."[38] Now articles with headlines like "Since the Days of a Diocletian!" followed, claiming such "persecution" had not been seen since those times.[39] Ancient Roman references became common.[40] In 1874 alone, both the popular Catholic novelist known as Conrad von Bolanden and his co-religionist playwright Wilhelm Molitor penned works on Diocletian's persecution of the Christians.[41] Existing books in other languages had already been translated into German in the previous year. Titles such as *Die Märtyrer des Coliseums* (The Martyrs of the Coliseum) left little doubt of these books' focus.[42]

In their comparison of contemporary treatment to that of ancient Roman persecution, such references obviously expressed an increased level of anger over the new measures passed by the government. Yet it went beyond that basic level of discontent. Catholic notables of the time would have no doubt recognized that such references would only provide more "evidence," at least in opponents' minds, for the subversive nature of Ultramontanism because of the connection between persecution under the early emperors and the larger discussion of what subjects owed leaders considered to be tyrants. (That the early emperors so often featured as examples of tyrants in Catholic arguments was evident even in the first foray of the *Schlesische Volkszeitung* into calling up the imagery of Christian martyrdom of the early centuries, as below it appeared an article on "Modern Tyranny."[43]) Such a connection for both sides—liberal fears of Ultramontane subversion and Catholic efforts to discount them—was hardly specific to this particular phase of the *Kulturkampf* but had a history before 1873, not to mention a longer one even before the 1870s. The *Augsburger Postzeitung,* for example, already ran an article in July 1871 that summarized a larger publication refuting the idea that Jesuits, in particular, promoted the "murder of tyrants."[44] Yet, just as references to Roman persecution rose in the face of the May Laws, the efforts on both sides to prove or disprove the accusation that tyrants could be killed according to Jesuit teachings became more prominent. Not surprisingly, Roman emperors often came up again as examples in these arguments over the teachings concerning tyrants.[45] The topic of whether or not Jesuit teachings allowed the murder of tyrants became so discussed during these years of the heightened *Kulturkampf* that the issue was even mentioned in the *Reichstag* debates in May 1874.[46]

Hence, the increased willingness to make comments hinting at the limits of Catholic loyalty went hand in hand with the use of references to ancient Roman times, examples that also drew further attention to the threshold of allegiance by bringing up the issue of Jesuits and the permissible murder of tyrants, though Catholics refuted this. Catholics were walking a fine line between asserting loyalty and belonging while at the same time suggesting its limits. Indeed, even the choice of which emperor's persecutions to highlight played a role in this balancing act. Aside from the extremely rare mention of Nero, references were either to Julian or Diocletian. Yet even Julian came up relatively rarely compared to Diocletian, on whom the rhetoric settled almost exclusively, despite older references often noting both of them along with Nero all together. Evidence of how central Diocletian became to the Catholic statements about their treatment in the *Reich* can be seen in the way contemporaries of the events chose to recall them even years later. Figures as diverse as Julius Bachem, Bismarck, and Wilhelm II—just a teenager in the 1870s—used this allusion to Diocletian, though from quite different standpoints, to recall the period.[47] Of course, editors using Diocletian to headline newspapers at the height of the *Kulturkampf* did lend the stories a certain panache given the bloodier record of his persecutions, something that certainly played a role in creating the narratives of martyrdom. On the other hand, Christian narratives had been known to play up Julian's bloodlust as well, and regardless, it did not take much to constitute a martyr in Catholic discourses of the *Kulturkampf*.[48] There was even the occasional suggestion that such bloody executions associated with the earlier centuries were less of a problem for the Church than the more mundane, daily wearing down of Christians with law after law prohibiting various activities that worked all the more subtly but to the same end.[49]

Because the persecution under both Julian and Diocletian could—and, at least in some references did—fit when Catholics spoke of their predicament during the highpoint of the *Kulturkampf*, the big difference between invoking one over the other lay in the degree of subversiveness intended. Invoking Julian was a far more dangerous proposition than recalling the narrative surrounding Diocletian. Julian, after all, had long been associated in Christian tradition with the legend that either God had struck him down on the battlefield—by sending Saint Mercurius, who had been martyred by an earlier round of persecutions, down from heaven to do the job—or that one of his own soldiers, by some accounts a Christian, had killed the emperor.[50] Diocletian, on the other hand, died an old man. Just as important, the narrative surrounding Diocletian, especially in Christian tradition but more generally as well, saw not the emperor himself but his appointed second-in-command Galerius to be the real instigator of the persecutions.[51] Julian, on the other hand, allegedly needed no help in taking action against Christians. The popular accounts in novel and play form by Bolanden and Molitor—both of whom had their stories reviewed and retold in the daily and periodical press at the time—repeated these ideas closely. When Molitor had portrayed the life of Julian in an earlier play, notably published in 1866, his account left no doubt that the "apostate" himself was the driving force behind the persecutions.[52] Similarly, as Bolanden very briefly mentioned Julian in an 1875 novel, he referred to him simply as "the Christian hater."[53] Diocletian, on the other hand, received a much more gentle treatment. Bolanden invoked the authority of Lactantius, the source early Christian tradition also relied upon, to write his novel and constructed the same basic story, blaming the second-in-command; Molitor strayed somewhat from the traditional emphasis on Galerius as the enemy to instead focus on "the 'liberal' traitors to the *Reich* from the pagan world of the senators," clearly a reference to the majority in the Berlin parliament of the 1870s.[54] Yet Molitor's play did not ignore the culpability of Galerius entirely. Even though not a character, he receives criticism not only from the emperor but also from the main hero of the story, Sebastianus, who condemns Galerius for having "a hard and uncontrolled heart." On the other hand, Diocletian tries to convince his trusted body guard, Sebastianus, a Christian, not to choose martyrdom by pointing out, "you know I am no dark tyrant."[55] In short, references to the far more sympathetic Diocletian enabled Catholics to express their serious doubt without crossing over the line into disloyalty or even more subversive territory.[56]

Even though such narratives continued to focus on liberal instigators or Bismarck, in the character of Galerius, they also ultimately indicated doubt in the *Kaiser* as well, a feeling which found expression beyond merely the Roman references. The fallout from the publicized correspondence between Pius IX and Wilhelm I played a significant role in this change from the first years of the *Reich* in particular. Protestants were not the only ones upset by the correspondence. Catholics also expressed deep offense from statements made in the *Kaiser*'s letter, in particular at the allegation that they were involved in "machinations against the state." The Catholic reply to these allegations did still lay primary blame on those around Wilhelm I, noting they wanted to show the *Kaiser* that he was being misled.[57] Yet just as accounts of persecutions under Diocletian never completely absolved the emperor for going along with them, the subsequent treatment of Wilhelm in the press over the next couple of years also appeared less willing to fully distance the *Kaiser* from his ministers. Not only did *Germania* not include any birthday wish for the *Kaiser* in 1874, but the weekly review a few days later simply mentioned the difficulty of celebrating it with "undivided joy," making no mention of what any of his ministers may or may not have been advising him to do.[58] Doubt in what opinion the *Kaiser* himself may have had aside from his ministers was expressed even more clearly a couple of months later in May when a review open-endedly remarked, "It remains unknown how much truth there is in the widely held opinion that he only gives his approval with a heavy heart to the measures and laws that bring about so sad a fissure between the members of the *Reich*."[59] By 1875, the paper marked Wilhelm's birthday only by a side note, lamenting that the conflict between the Center and the liberals had gone so far "that the split that separates the parties is being deliberately extended out ever more to that place where the connection between the ruler and people occurs."[60] Regardless of who was driving the *Kulturkampf,* the article suggested the relationship of Catholics to their *Kaiser* was suffering.

In this context, it is not surprising that the expressions of the limits of Catholics' loyalty became even clearer. Nearing the bottom of confidence in the *Reich* and a Catholic future in it in early 1875, one article went so far as to blatantly remark that if the state continued on its current path, "with time it could lead to suggesting to the Catholics ideas of also seeking their moral point of reference somewhere else [than in the *Reich*]." Referring to Bismarck's recent attempts to intervene in other countries on the behalf of minority Protestants living there but at the same time continuing to impose oppressive laws at home, the article concluded by asking if those few foreign nationals "[were] to be more highly estimated than the 14,867,091 Catholics." Notably, it described the latter as those "who live [wohnen] inside the German borders," not as German Catholics.[61]

While this chapter has focused on the addition of rhetoric expressing doubt and distance to the *Reich* to emphasize what was particular to this phase of the *Kulturkampf*, it is important to note that largely the same arguments for inclusion and expressions of national identity leading toward long-term integration continued as well. The only element that really disappeared during this time is the emphasis on the *Kaiser*. While claiming Wilhelm as their *Kaiser* too played an integral role in Catholic constructions of national identity and belonging during the initial years of the *Reich*, between 1873 and the middle of 1875, the narratives of martyrdom replaced this focus.[62] While aggressive rhetoric never focused on the *Kaiser*, the sense of increasing distance from him and the *Reich* was clear. Yet, contrary to the narrative of alienation commonly seen in the historiography, Catholics never gave up on the *Reich* or their efforts to belong in the new nation. Even during this period of deepest doubt, Catholics' relationship with the new nation was strained, but not broken. In short, even viewing only this phase of the 1870s still hardly suggests a picture of Catholic opposition to the government as having crossed the line into opposition to the nation. This period does, however, suggest how close Germany might have been to a potentially quite different course of Catholic integration into the nation, one which may have more closely corresponded to the fears of liberals and Bismarck. Of course, several events came together in 1875 to both change the situation itself as well as Catholics' view of it, one in which this doubt faded and along with it the narratives focusing on persecution and martyrdom.

FOUR

The Real Threat Emerges

IF THE BEGINNING of 1875 saw the low point of Catholic confidence in the *Reich*, the end of the year brought with it a marked sense that fortunes were about to change. Continuously targeted as enemies of the *Reich* since its founding, Catholics now saw the chance to rid themselves of this outsider status by switching the focus to another group. Initially prominent Catholic voices identified Jews as this group. Scholars have written extensively on the outburst of Catholic anti-Semitic rhetoric during the *Kulturkampf*. While the literature also reflects the long-term opposition between political Catholicism and socialism, however, it has largely overlooked the significance of a similarly undeniable spiking of anti-socialist rhetoric on the heels of this anti-Semitic outburst in the 1870s. Yet it was the demonizing of socialism that ultimately proved more consequential during the *Kulturkampf*. This chapter argues that, although the efforts to find common ground with conservative Protestants initially focused on exposing the alleged crimes of Jews in the new *Reich*, the outburst of anti-Semitism was far more temporally specific than commonly suggested, though just as ugly nonetheless. Moreover, while this outburst undoubtedly drew on long-standing prejudices common among the Catholic populace, the timing of this ramped up anti-Semitism indicates its appearance had far more to do with tactics of integration in the *Reich* across the confessional divide than issues of internal cohesion or age-old hatred.[1] As a tactic, however, Catholic anti-Semitism quickly became too problematic.[2] Importantly, it was problematic in a way that anti-socialism turned out not to be. It was this socialist "threat" identified in the rhetoric that ultimately accompanied a renewed Catholic confidence in the *Reich* and became central to negotiating identity and belonging in the nation during the *Kulturkampf*.[3]

Scholars have largely addressed the anti-Semitic outburst during the 1870s as applicable to the entire decade more generally, making little or no distinction between any of the years or phases of the *Kulturkampf*.[4] In part, this understandably stems from looking at the 1870s as one segment of a much longer span of time, giving validity to the idea that the decade saw an explosion of particularly fierce Catholic anti-Semitic rhetoric.[5] Yet a closer look at the *Kulturkampf* itself reveals that the anti-Semitic outburst was particularly short lived. Indeed, the "Jewish Question" only burst onto the scene in 1875. Moreover, the anti-Semitic reportage surrounding it largely dried up by the end of the year, instead to be replaced by concern with the socialist "threat" from 1876 onwards.

  Certainly this is not to suggest that Catholics, their notables, and their publications did not exhibit the stains of anti-Semitism throughout the decade. They did. Even the *Kölnische Volkszeitung*, so often singled out among major Catholic papers for its distance to anti-Semitism during the *Kulturkampf*, carried more general comments referring to the negative trend of "Jewification" taking place in German society during the 1870s.[6] In this respect, Olaf Blaschke's argument about the prevalence of anti-Semitism that makes speaking more generally of any Catholic "ambivalence" toward Jews meaningless is right.[7] Yet the anti-Semitic commentary before and after the outburst in 1875 did not differ significantly in either intensity or content from such statements that could easily be found both before and after the *Kulturkampf* as a whole. Indeed, given the association in the literature of the decade more generally with Catholic anti-Semitism, what is far more striking is the absence of vitriol directed at Jews. Anti-Semitic comments in articles decrying liberals and alleging their role in the collapse of 1873, the use of the *Kulturkampf* as a cover for economic plunder, and the conspiracy behind these events linked to the Freemasons—all themes that would become central to the rhetoric of the outburst against Jews—are largely missing in this sense before 1875.[8] From the beginning in 1871, for example, an article denounced the "always very 'liberal' stock- and moneymen" and "fraudulent speculations."[9] Another article from two years later in early 1873 again hammered away at this theme, this time including the added specter of Freemasonry, by denouncing the nefarious connection between "the years of rapid industrial expansion [Gründerthum], the [Masonic] lodge, stock market swindle, and anti-Catholic rabble-rousing."[10] Yet another article from late 1873, after the economic collapse of that year had occurred, continued to make the same arguments about liberals' "stock swindle" and the deception of the "exploited populace" by the Kulturkampf.[11] Yet none of them, like so many other examples, even mentioned Jews as part of this corruption. When references to Jews appeared in these earlier years, they tended to be rather limited in scope, if negative nonetheless. Articles could refer to National Liberals like Eduard Lasker as "the Jew Lasker," as the review of the economically turbulent year of 1873 did.[12] Certainly this was meant as a jab, but the article went no further than that in its anti-Semitic rhetoric. Articles that expounded more on the Jews—again negatively— tended to focus on the religious differences between them and Christians. Not uncommonly the articles made reference to this long-standing division by drawing upon narratives of Jewish persecution of early Christians or going directly back to the crucifixion of Christ himself, for which they held Jews responsible.[13] Even more notable, all of these particular articles appeared in Germania, the paper commonly cited for being the most anti-Semitic of the major Catholic outlets and headed up during these years by Paul Majunke and Christoph Cremer, both anti-Semites.[14] If one would expect to find rampant anti-Semitism anywhere, it would be in these articles in this newspaper. But that is not the case. The early years of the Augsburger Postzeitung, another paper that would vociferously spew anti-Semitic rhetoric later on, present a similar picture.[15]

This relative reticence in terms of frequency and extent of haranguing Jews in the press, not to be confused with any ambivalence about their allegedly negative influence in society, did likely have much to do with the often cited Catholic concern about compromising their own position by attacking another religious minority when they themselves were such a minority.[16] Indeed, even the more overtly anti-Semitic rhetoric from the period often betrayed this Catholic concern. The Schlesische Volkszeitung cautioned readers from straying too far into intolerance, as "We are not in the position . . . to start shouting a true 'Hepp, Hepp' against our fellow

Jewish citizens."[17] An article in *Germania* similarly reminded readers of the need for Catholics to refrain from "hate of the Jews."[18] The concern would appear more generally throughout the reportage, often linked to assertions that it was more about guarding against the nefarious actions of Jews than negatively directed at the religious group as a whole.[19] A short booklet even chose to take this position as its title: *Not Incitement to Hatred of Jews—But Protection of Christians!*[20]

Incite hatred, however, is exactly what such publications did with a vengeance in the summer of 1875.[21] On August 17 of that year, *Germania* began its several-part series entitled "The Jewish Question."[22] In September it moved on to a second string of articles entitled "On the Jewish Question."[23] By mid-September the paper had begun yet another series, this time the three-part "Jewry and Stock Market."[24] October saw the rise of another series on the topic called "Joy for No Reason in Israel."[25] Not sufficient enough to convey all the points to be made against Jews, *Germania* added numerous standalone articles with titles such as "Freemasons and Jews" and "Jews and the Military."[26] Far from a unique outburst, other major papers exhibited the same spike. Among other anti-Semitic articles, the *Augsburger Postzeitung* also re-ran the series "The Jewish Question," ultimately dropping any attribution to *Germania* in later installments.[27] The *Schlesische Volkszeitung* produced its own multipart series on "Catholicism, Protestantism and—Jewry," the last of the three tellingly separated from the other two even in the title.[28] The relatively new periodical *Deutscher Hausschatz* that aimed to provide Catholic readers with a confessionally suitable counterpart to the liberal *Die Gartenlaube* also joined in the anti-Semitic rhetoric, providing an "entertaining" description of "The Jew City in Amsterdam," which spared no details in describing the "dirty mark" in otherwise "pure Holland."[29]

Why did any reticence in giving full vent to anti-Semitic ideas—ones clearly already well-formed in the minds of men like Majunke and Cremer long before this outburst—disappear in 1875? It had little to do with the alleged connections among liberals, stock market fraud, freemasonry, the *Kulturkampf,* and Jews, though the anti-Semitic Catholic rhetoric certainly zeroed in on these widely held beliefs that were all part and parcel of a supposedly larger effort to undermine German society. To suggest the reverse seems to mistake the content of this particular outburst of rhetoric with its specific cause in this case.[30] That cause, in short, was the appearance of a similarly anti-Semitic series in the conservative Protestant paper *Neue Preußische Zeitung*, often nicknamed the *Kreuzzeitung*. Several weeks before the rash of anti-Semitic rabble-rousing in the Catholic press, the *Kreuzzeitung* had run a set of articles beginning in late June that allegedly uncovered the liberal-Jewish plot of economic fraud plaguing the *Reich* from the outset.[31] Indeed, two weeks before *Germania*—widely acknowledged as the ringleader in this Catholic outburst as in so much of the rhetoric of the decade—began any of its series directed against Jews, it reported on the articles of the *Kreuzzeitung* with a mix of straight summary and clear approval of the content.[32] Portrayed in the historiography as having followed *Germania* in taking up anti-Semitism, the *Schlesische Volkszeitung* actually appears to have gotten the jump on this particular topic, already having similarly commented in its pages as the *Kreuzzeitung* series was still unfolding.[33] Regardless of which Catholic paper began the applauding of the conservative *Kreuzzeitung*, the sentiment spread to others. The *Augsburger Postzeitung* felt the series important enough that it reprinted the conservative paper's articles.[34] Even non-newspaper sources made reference to the significance of the *Kreuzzeitung* series.[35]

This is not to suggest that the responsibility for the anti-Semitic outburst actually lies with Protestants, not Catholics.[36] If ever the idiomatic expression "preaching to the choir" fit, it was in the connection between the *Kreuzzeitung* articles and the editors of *Germania*, Majunke and Cremer. Yet that these Catholic press outlets seized upon the appearance of this *Kreuzzeitung* series, which clearly posed an antagonistic line of thought to much of what the liberals had been doing since unification, as a means of trying to find common ground was reconfirmed time and again with references to the original articles in Catholic anti-Semitic rhetoric. Catholic anti-Semitic rhetoric did not fail to remember the "contribution" to the cause of saving Germany from Jewish machinations that the *Kreuzzeitung* articles had made.[37] This common front against the Jews (and liberals) would provide—or so at least some in the Catholic community thought—the basis for Catholic and conservative Protestant cooperation against liberalism that the Center Party had hoped for from the beginning.

Not only did the frequency and ferocity of Catholic anti-Semitism reach a completely new level in the middle of 1875, but it also tended to take on a rather different tone. Of course the distinction between a more anti-quated, religious anti-Judaism and a racially-based, modern anti-Semitism is often not clear, as much of the literature confirms.[38] Neither was it in this particular case. Unlike the earlier articles that focused on themes in early Christianity or the crucifixion itself, however, the pieces from this anti-Semitic outburst targeted Jews much more as a people, not a religious group. Largely passed over were reference to Jews as "killers of Christ," though no doubt some Catholics kept that age-old image in mind as well. Instead the articles pounded away at the idea of Jews as masters of the liberal "*Kulturkämpfer* press" and "kings of the stock market," though reference was also made to the long-standing idea of them as "usurers."[39] Indeed, religious and such theological differences were not the main issue at all, according to this Catholic rhetoric. *Germania* went so far as to tally up the numbers of Jews not only in Germany but throughout the rest of Europe, though it admitted the shortcoming of not being able to provide numbers for those "converted to other religions."[40] They, of course, still counted as Jews according to the article. They did not and could not, however, count as Germans.[41] At the same time the rhetoric continued to assert that "one [can] be a good Catholic and at the same time a good German," it denied that Jews could be anything other than Jews precisely because it was not a matter of religion in the latter case.[42] Differences in everything from morality to birthrate to ultimately national loyalty could be traced back, in part at least, to "characteristics of the [Jewish] race."[43] The supporting "evidence" came in the form not of statements stressing the religious differences based upon biblical testaments and the Talmud, but in quotes taken from members of the national canon such as Fichte and Goethe.[44]

As part and parcel of the attempt to find common cause with conservative Protestants came not only references to the *Kreuzzeitung* series but also repeated mentions of the distinction between Christian Germans of both faiths and Jews, including such assertions as, "We Christians and Germans cannot allow ourselves to be dominated by the Jews!"[45] As the Catholic anti-Semitic rhetoric posed it, the choice for true Germans of both confessions was simple: either stay the course of the *Kulturkampf* with its rampant infighting or smarten up and realize the true threat lay elsewhere. Accordingly, it was the machinations of the Jews that had so far been "the sorest spot of the development of Germany over the last years," something articles said even trumped the *Kulturkampf* itself.[46] Indeed, months of anti-Semitic rhetoric on both sides of the confessional divide allowed *Germania* to assert (hopefully) that the *Kulturkampf* was now "of secondary interest" as the real social and economic issues and their connection to the "Jewish Question" had become obvious to all.[47]

It was not only the potential for cooperation with conservative Protestants in this cross-confessional, anti-Semitic outburst that made Catholics hopeful. More subtle events had already begun prefiguring their rising fortunes. Already in the Prussian and *Reich* elections of late 1873 and 1874, the Center Party had gained increased support, although at the time the entrenchment of the liberals and *Kulturkampf* legislation dulled the impact of this achievement.[48] By 1874 Conservatives were becoming increasingly disgruntled with the liberal direction the government was taking on religious issues.[49] Already in February 1875 an article in the *Schlesische Volkszeitung* made renewed reference, even if only in passing, to the possibilities of a Christian conservative coalition, an appeal that had fallen on deaf ears in 1871 and seemed largely dead since then.[50] By 1875, Bismarck himself began to doubt the direction his reliance on the liberals was drawing the government in.[51] Perhaps even more important in the minds (and hearts) of contemporary Catholics, in early 1875 the *Kaiser* made the first of a series of comments that would be interpreted as taking a rather traditional, anti-liberal stance on matters of faith, both theologically and politically. Indeed, the *Schlesische Volkszeitung* saw this as a "great comfort," a clear sign dispelling any previous doubts about whether or not Wilhelm I agreed with those ministers around him, who at the moment had his "hands tied" by government procedure.[52] While there is certainly much truth to the idea of anti-Semitism as a reflection of fear and insecurity, the particular timing of the events of the *Kulturkampf* suggests that the outburst in summer 1875 also reflected a sense of possibility and increased hope that the situation could work to Catholics' advantage.[53]

With the advent of the anti-Semitic outburst, prominent Catholics clearly saw not only the potential for cooperation with conservative Protestants in the future but also believed they had finally taken the offensive against the liberals, a perception that certainly gained increased validity as the new legislation for the *Kulturkampf* slowed significantly in frequency and scope after this point.[54] The *Schlesische Volkszeitung* came to this conclusion rather quickly, asserting as the *Kreuzzeitung* series was finishing up, "the days of liberal power and splendor are numbered."[55] By fall of 1875 *Germania* was already boasting that the darkest part of the night had passed in an article appropriately entitled, "It is getting light."[56] Another article that headlined in the fall went so far as to appear under the title "The liberals are afraid."[57] The reportage around Sedan Day that covered a recent visit of the crown prince to the Rhine Province also emphasized that the fleetingness of current "ministerial experiments" and "chance parliamentary majorities" in no way lessened Catholics' loyalty to "inviolable institutions" like the ruling house, with the article reading much like a patriotic "love letter" to the Hohenzollerns.[58]

If such rhetoric rightly identified that Catholics had made it through the worst of the *Kulturkampf*, it wrongly saw anti-Semitism as the issue that would take them through the end of the conflict. Despite the daily articles on the topic during the second half of 1875, by 1876 the reportage largely dried up. Again, this is not to suggest that anti-Semitism disappeared from the pages of Catholic publications but that it did not play a prominent role. *Germania,* for example, claimed it would ratchet up its rhetoric again, as Jews were allegedly once more becoming "wanton," but nothing came of this idle threat.[59] Even *Tremonia*, the very local Dortmund paper for Catholics that got its start during the anti-Semitic outburst and would have a great deal to say on the topic in later decades, had largely discarded the theme just a year later.[60] The strident Catholic anti-Semitic rhetoric of the *Kulturkampf* disappeared as suddenly as it appeared.

If events external to Catholicism began the outburst in summer 1875, internal problems ended the tirade in its press.[61] If ever there was a time when the Catholic community stressed the importance of being unified and speaking with one voice, it was during the *Kulturkampf*.[62] But unlike in the case of most major topics of the decade, the community very definitely was not united on the issue of anti-Semitism.[63] Of course it was widespread. Beyond the outburst in the daily press, the issue of anti-Semitism made the rounds of more theologically-oriented publications like *Der Katholik* and the popular works of writers like Alban Stolz.[64] More importantly, however, the outburst did not appear in many particularly significant venues. The *Kölnische Volkszeitung*, most likely the second most important Catholic newspaper in the *Reich*, did not join in this anti-Semitic rhetoric in the summer of 1875. Windthorst is well known as having been opposed to such rabble rousing. Of course the caveat is always made that he was only one man. But he was not just any man. If he was an exception, he was an extremely important one as head of the Center Party.[65] From the letters written into *Germania* at the time, it is clear that there was both praise and criticism for the paper's anti-Semitic rhetoric.[66] Not surprisingly given this variability, anti-Semitism played little role at the *Katholikentag* of 1875, despite the meeting being held right as the rhetorical explosion was in full swing.[67]

Most striking, however, is the open fight over the spate of "Jewish articles" that broke out between two of the leading Catholic daily papers, *Germania* and the *Schlesische Volkszeitung,* in October 1875.[68] *Germania*—enraged over being contradicted by the Breslau-based paper but not wanting to damage Catholic solidarity any more than necessary—attempted to brush off the conflict as one not so much of viewpoint but of another editor getting too ambitious as well as being too fickle. It asserted the *Schlesische Volkszeitung* had said "entirely the same" thing in its series on the Jews as *Germania* had, only the former had done it several days later, a claim the Berlin paper backed up with rather selectively drawn quotes from the Breslau publication. Now, after the numbers for the last financial quarter had come in, *Germania* claimed the editor in Breslau decided to change direction.[69] In reality, the *Schlesische Volkzei-tung* had made anti-Semitic statements in its three-part series, but they had a far more religious and traditional quality to them. Indeed, the articles focused heavily on earlier centuries of conflict and also concluded with the idea that the Catholic Church had a particular knack for being tolerant.[70] Whatever other issues of rivalry and financial motivation became mixed up in the conflict, part of it, at least, stemmed from this rather different conception of anti-Semitism. Not satisfied with one headline article on the issue, *Germania* counter-attacked the *Schlesische Volkszeitung* once more a day later, though again not raising any of the rather different ideas that the two papers had expressed in their Jewish articles. At the end of the diatribe, *Germania* tellingly discussed the importance in the last years of the "truly exemplary unity of the Catholic press" and explained that it only felt the need to openly rebuke the Breslau paper because its disturbance was so rare and done in such "a reproachable manner."[71] In short, this was a huge and public blowup in a community obsessed with unity. Though several papers like *Germania* continued their anti-Semitic tirades over the next couple of months, others remained distant either to the entire issue or to the particular version the Berlin paper was asserting.[72] The only way this disunity was going away was if it disappeared as a major theme in general. Though the issue would rear its head again afterwards, disappear is exactly what it did for the rest of the *Kulturkampf* itself.

The topic that took anti-Semitism's place in Catholic efforts to find common ground across the confessional divide and reconfigure the struggle against another "enemy" was anti-socialism. The topic had already been discussed in the *Kölnische Volkszeitung* in 1875. No doubt the combination of separate smaller groups to form a unified party of Social Democrats in 1875 sparked part of this increased interest.[73] Not surprising given its reluctance to beat the drum of anti-Semitism too much, as the fight with Majunke's Berlin-based paper suggested, the *Schlesische Volkszeitung* had also already begun a several part series on anti-socialism in 1875.[74] *Germania* remained wedded to the focus on anti-Semitism longer, as did others like the *Augsburger Postzeitung* that reprinted the articles coming out of Berlin, but anti-socialism had clearly become the focus of the former's opposition rhetoric by 1876. Tellingly, given the recent debacle over differences concerning anti-Semitism, *Germania* specifically stated on the eve of this turn to highlighting anti-socialism that "in so far as concerns the rejection of social-democratic principles, the Catholic papers have always been, will be, and must be unanimous."[75] Then came the flurry of articles concerned with denouncing the various aspects of socialism, such as the article series "Catholicism and Socialism." Just as the anti-Semitic outburst had focused on Jews as un-national, this series lost no time in pointing to socialism as the un-German danger to the *Reich*, stressing that "the movement in itself is purely social and as such international."[76] The assertion not only moved the focus away from the supposed incompatibility of Catholicism and nationalism but also repeated allegations of internationalism made by other groups against the socialists. Of course, like anti-Semitism, Catholic anti-socialist rhetoric was certainly nothing new, present both earlier in the century and in the decade of the 1870s itself. The opposition between Catholicism and socialism, at least as contemporaries believing in the former posed it, was quite evident. At times the latter could even be presented "as the work of the devil."[77] Yet, again, it was the marked intensification of anti-socialism on the heels of the anti-Semitic outburst that really appeared at this time. Indeed, anti-socialism at this time paralleled the tropes used in anti-Semitic rhetoric just months earlier, suggesting how much the focus on one took the place of the other. Just as Jews in the military formed a notable issue in anti-Semitic formulations, so too did the issue of socialism and the military. The alleged problem with Jews was that they were far too underrepresented in the military, betraying a supposed unwillingness to shed blood and sacrifice for Germany.[78] The concern about socialism, on the other hand, was that it was far too alive in the military, seen as a particularly big problem in light of Catholic allegations of its purely international character.[79] Either way, however, the Catholic claim that the army, and hence the *Reich*, would be undermined by the particular threat being considered at that point remained constant. Indeed, anti-socialist rhetoric posed the entire issue quite the same as the anti-Semitic onslaught had: either stay the course of the *Kulturkampf* with its rampant infighting among true Germans or smarten up and realize the true threat lay elsewhere. As one article that described the attraction many workers had to socialist "radical agitators" concluded in exasperation, "in the face of such conditions as good as nothing has happened up to now; in comparison, one still always has time and attention for the '*Culturkampf*'!"[80] Yet, if the papers highlighted the potential cooperation of Catholics and conservative Protestants against liberals, there were attempts to even include some individuals among the last group, who had previously pushed the *Kulturkampf*, in the fight to beat back socialism. Again citing recent reportage from the conservative *Kreuzzeitung* that also decried the continued harmful effects of the conflict on religious life, an article added that help might be found among some "'liberals' who have not yet lost all sense for Christianity."[81]

While Catholic rhetoric made a clear transition from focusing on anti-Semitism to anti-socialism, the reality was never so cut and dry, of course. Just as supposedly intimate connections existed on all levels between Jews and liberalism, the same allegedly held true for socialism. Indeed, Catholic rhetoric also focused on the close relationship between liberalism and socialism, the latter being the logical outcome of the former in this line of thought.[82] Accordingly, most bad influences in society were linked to each other. Hence, likely some Catholics reading the papers or hearing other expressions of the anti-socialist rhetoric made the connection with anti-Semitism. Yet, importantly, it was not made explicitly in the reportage. Nonetheless, anti-socialism was not without its own potential drawbacks. Given the desire and need for political Catholicism to draw its support from all class levels, including workers, the "social question" and issues relating to what rhetoric portrayed as the rising impoverishment of the average German could not be ignored.[83] Indeed, the reportage shows a similar rise in concern about this issue, making what had always been a topic near to the hearts of certain Catholic notables like Ketteler a more central concern with rhetoric suggesting only the Center Party truly recognized the havoc the economy was wreaking on the populace at large.[84] Hence, Catholic treatments of those individuals tempted by socialism due to their own horrid living conditions included more sympathy than condemnation. The rhetoric reserved the latter for socialism itself, which allegedly based its platform on fundamentally wrong principles contrary to religion that could accordingly never be the solution to Germany's problems.[85] Of course, Windthorst personally appears not to have harbored the same fears about socialism as others in his own party did.[86] All in all, however, anti-socialism proved a far more unifying rallying point for Catholics—and potential allies across the confessional divide—than anti-Semitism did during the *Kulturkampf.* Indeed, by 1877 an article in *Germania* confidently concluded that there was now even little disagreement to be found among pro-government papers with the assertion that the "dangers" of the recent social problems needed to be concentrated on, among which socialism was counted.[87]

Beyond providing a threat against which Catholics hoped they could rally with other "true" Germans, anti-socialism also ultimately cemented the increased closeness between Catholics and the *Kaiser.* Further highlighting what were taken as anti-liberal statements by Wilhelm I in the arena of religion, Catholic reportage continued to reassert the claim to the *Kaiser.* In October 1876, the stance Wilhelm took regarding the inappropriateness of religious blessing for certain legally allowed civil marriages suggested increasing disapproval of the lengths to which liberals were taking the *Kulturkampf,* a development that Catholic articles were quick to point out conservative Protestants also objected to. Just as other missteps taken since 1871 came to light, so too did the particular "swindle of the *'Culturkampf.'*"[88] Reportage drew the same conclusion from the *Kaiser's* insistence on the traditional Apostle's Creed after a liberal clergyman named Hoßbach had been named pastor of a Berlin church despite rejecting central tenets of it. This was another example, according to one article, that Wilhelm was telling the *Kulturkämpfer* that they would go "no further!"[89] Not surprisingly, just a couple of days later, much was made of the *Kaiser's* recent "concerns because of the disintegrating efforts in the religious and social spheres," which also included the advance of socialism.[90] Just as Catholic rhetoric increasingly focused on only the combined efforts of believing Christians from both sides of the confessional divide being capable of stopping the dissolution of Germany into revolution—exactly the same position the *Kaiser* held according to the papers—liberalism became increasingly identified as on the outs. Indeed, by the middle of 1877, *Germania* concluded, "the moment has now arrived for 'liberals' to have to go against his majesty" if they wanted to continue with their destructive tendencies against religion, a development that would finally show their base "disloyalty."[91] Indeed, it would not only be Wilhelm that the liberals would have to battle against to continue. As a speaker at the 1876 *Katholikentag* in Munich had already surmised, "The time will come, and it is perhaps no longer far off, when one will not deny us the acknowledgement exactly from that high position from which we are most misjudged." Though Chancellor Bismarck remained unnamed, the reason for this approaching turnaround did not: "social democracy, the resulting child of liberalism."[92]

That not only Catholics remained underrepresented in their votes for socialist candidates but also that other political parties continued to exhibit a marked distance to the Social Democrats even as they became the largest block in the *Reichstag* on the eve of the Great War suggests this was not only an important issue during the 1870s.[93] Of course, anti-Semitism would viciously rear its ugly head again, both within Catholic circles as well as more generally as a political platform. Yet, given the difficulty it posed in 1875 for unity as well as the lack of emphasis placed upon it outside of that year in the rhetoric, it would be hard to portray anti-Semitism as central to Catholic attempts to define Germanness and assert their belonging in the nation.

FIVE

The Search for Continued Relevance

BY THE FALL of 1877, the long hoped for end of the *Kulturkampf* became something Catholics increasingly began to think of as a real possibility for the near future. Reflecting this, attention turned more and more to what role Catholics would play in the *Reich* after the end of the bitter struggle that had so deeply impacted them since 1871. Stressing openness to potential overtures of peace, one of the earliest newspaper articles to discuss how to move beyond the conflict noted that Catholics "have learned a great deal," including "to forget a lot." Indeed, highlighting the role of common memory in forging unity—much as Ernest Renan would a few years later in his seminal lecture "What is a nation?" and current-day scholars do in the literature on national identity—the article concluded that Catholics would be willing to forget this time again, placing the "religious and state well-being" ahead of any "bitterness" from the events of the *Kulturkampf*.[1]

Yet certainly a bitterness remained for many Catholics. In this sense, forgetting had its limits, as it usually does. One need look no further than the continued coldness of Catholics to the Bismarck cult. This distance was always there, despite the Center Party's cooperation in helping pass many of the Iron Chancellor's favored measures after 1878 to 1879, commonly noted as the end of the *Kulturkampf*, though the official settlement did not occur until 1887.[2] Of course, such reservations about Bismarck after the 1870s cannot be equated with distance to the nation itself any more than direct opposition to him during the *Kulturkampf* itself could be. After all, Catholics never made the integral connection between the chancellor and the nation in their constructions of German identity that many of their opponents at the time did. Indeed, they continued to describe their support of Bismarckian policies—at least many of them—after 1878 in the same language they had used for their opposition before: both were done out of loyalty to the *Reich* and in the name of true Germanness.

Although scholarly accounts of the 1870s and Catholics in the *Kaiserreich* more generally have emphasized the limits of this forgetting, it is also instructive to look at how contemporaries viewed this transitional phase at the end of the *Kulturkampf*. This chapter highlights what became a far greater concern among leading Catholics at the end of conflict than forgetting too little. Instead, they worried that many Catholics would forget too much and too easily lose the many lessons learned over the decade of struggle. It was this concern, one not unfounded given events within Catholicism at the time, that helps to explain why the rhetoric near the end of the 1870s recast the role of the Center Party itself on a platform that, ultimately, also helped long-term integration.

Much changed beginning in the fall of 1877 to suggest that the end of the *Kulturkampf* was on the horizon. Catholic newspapers had been keen on publishing any hints of grumblings regarding conservatives and even some liberals tiring of the conflict. Indeed, already during a February session in the Prussian *Landtag*, National Liberal deputy Eduard Lasker referenced the possibility of a revision to some of the *Kulturkampf* laws. Yet the statement by conservative deputy Meyer-Arnswalde in a November session made an even greater impact, as he called not only for a revision but declared himself and those Protestants like him to be "fed up with the *Kulturkampf*."[3] Change on the Catholic side also heightened the likelihood that the conflict would soon end, as Pius IX died in February 1878 to be replaced by the more diplomatically inclined Leo XIII. Indeed, the correspondence initiated between the papacy and the *Reich* by Leo XIII after his ascension proved important for the openness to ending the conflict expressed on both sides. On behalf of Germany, this was initially expressed by Wilhelm I; later the crown prince wrote to Leo after an assassination attempt left the *Kaiser* seriously wounded.[4] Cordial words were followed by a face to face meeting between Bismarck and the papal nuncio Gaetano Aloisi Masella at Bad Kissingen that summer.[5]

Certainly it is important to remember that the year 1878 itself did not bring an actual change in the alliance of parties voting for Bismarck's measures nor a repeal of any *Kulturkampf* legislation. Neither of these was a foregone conclusion, and the effects of the repressive laws continued to impact the daily life of Catholics in the *Reich*.[6] Yet Catholic contemporaries had the palpable sense that the situation was about to change drastically. Not only did the reportage repeatedly make reference to it, but even the articles which attempted to urge caution before getting hopes up too high also had to do so in the face of the widespread sense that a turning point had been reached, with people asking "if it will soon be better."[7] Windthorst himself, certainly savvy enough to know the process would not be quick or easy, believed that the moment was at hand when "the formulation of the conditions under which peace can be concluded must be seriously considered."[8] Moreover, if nothing else, Bismarck's efforts to blame the two attempts on the *Kaiser*'s life in 1878 on the pernicious effects of socialism, as opposed to Ultramontanism, did indicate that the Catholics were on their way in from the cold, regardless of the Center's own opposition to the chancellor's anti-socialist law. Of course 1879 brought more confirmation that a corner had, indeed, been turned. Not only did Bismarck make overtures toward peace in a meeting with Windthorst in March 1879, but he also graced the Center leader himself with a special invitation to a party at the chancellor's house two months later in May, an occasion marked by chummy if awkward rapprochement that even others in attendance remarked upon.[9] In light of the buildup of the previous year and a half, the dismissal of Minister Falk, so often seen to epitomize the *Kulturkampf*, in July hardly surprised. Indeed, it has been suggested that Falk's dismissal would have occurred even earlier, in 1878, had Wilhelm not been indisposed while recuperating from the second assassination attempt.[10] Such favorable events only gave more power to the validity of the old saying "God forsakes no good German," an article contended, combining the same usual defense of Catholic opposition to many of the government's policies with the claim of truly representing Germanness in the *Reich*.[11]

Yet these developments, which were positive in so far as they heralded a fundamental change in the fortunes of Catholics in Germany, had a double-edged nature to them, especially so far as the Center Party was concerned. The less embattled position of Catholics by 1878 led to a weaker showing at the polls for *Reichstag* elections that year. Depending on which indicators one takes into consideration, the elections of 1877 can be seen as already showing this drop in Center Party results. Even if a large part of the drop off stemmed from lower voter turnout among Catholics and the Center remained strong overall nonetheless, the signs of losing steam were there.[12] While a less mobilized constituency may have accounted for most of the lost votes, the potential fragmentation of political Catholicism also raised alarm bells among Center leaders. Splits arose on both the right and the left. In Bavaria, a reactionary group stressing the explicitly confessional character of their party broke off from the Patriots in March 1877, forming the Katholische Volkspartei.[13] In places like Aachen and Essen, the danger of fragmentation came from workers distancing themselves from the more bourgeois elements of the Center. In both cities, candidates promoting Christian socialist ideals ran against men officially backed by the Center Party in 1877, unseating the Catholic incumbent in Essen.[14] On top of this, the Center had to contend with yet a further issue of crumbling unity, as the diplomatic discussions taken up between Berlin and Rome created friction between the Papacy and Windthorst on how the *Kulturkampf* should be ended.[15] Nor did Catholics inside of Germany remain undivided over the issue of how to end this conflict, as both the usually united press as well as the community in general expressed disagreement.[16] Division was not the only problem associated with the negotiations occurring between Berlin and Rome. A large part of the problem this presented to the Center Party was one of diminished authority, as it "ended the Zentrum's convenient monopoly on political Catholicism at a stroke."[17] Righting the wrongs of the *Kulturkampf,* the bread and butter of Center efforts for the last several years, had now been taken up directly by the papacy, which gave party leaders little information on the negotiations and even less of a say.[18]

On one level, the Center Party responded via the press—which given the huge increase it experienced during the 1870s had a lot riding on the continued engagement and allegiance of the Catholic populace as well—to portray certain points of fragmentation as largely non-issues.[19] Obviously the split between the Patriot Party and the Katholische Volkspartei did not present as much of a problem for the Center. The leading Catholic national paper *Germania* suggested that when one knew the differences between the two parties, supporting the Patriots was the only logical course of action, not a surprising conclusion given that party's cooperation with the Center.[20] The growing distance between the Center and the papacy proved harder to deal with. The articles repeatedly stressed that Leo enjoyed the full trust of Germany's Catholics as well as the Center Party. Yet enough of these assertions reveal themselves ultimately as assurances to those worried that the pope would not fight hard enough to protect what the populace had "championed and defended with untiring perseverance" to indicate that the articles attempted to create unity more than reflect it in this case.[21]

Hence, signs of increased fragmentation not surprisingly led to greater efforts to foster unity, akin to those most notable at the very beginning of the decade before Catholics had more clearly pulled together. Yet, despite how pivotal a sense of being religiously besieged was to this unity that reached its height as the conflict itself did, a connection not lost on contemporaries from either side of the battle, the Center—and press which continued to have a close relationship with it—opted to significantly alter the rhetoric to distance the Party from the *Kulturkampf*. This began even before the close of the *Kulturkampf*'s more active half, not to speak of the official settlement in 1887 or the ending of many of its damaging effects on local parishes throughout Germany.[22]

The approach taken in light of the rise of socialist impulses within the Catholic community that threatened to funnel off parts of the Center's working-class constituency reflects this transition clearly. Though opposition to the Social Democrats remained part of the rhetoric, as did the sympathy expressed for the plight of poor workers, the larger impetus behind much of the discussion changed. No longer was the focus on combating socialism for its destructive effects on the religious fabric of the nation, though that remained an issue, but on working towards meeting what Windthorst himself referred to in a May 1878 *Reichstag* speech as the "justified demands" of the Social Democrats.[23] The idea of fulfilling the "complaints of the under classes that are justified" became a common call in the Catholic press around this time, leading to greater efforts to explicitly show the engagement of the party on behalf of workers.[24] As one part in an article series describing the numerous initiatives undertaken on behalf of "the distressed and [the] workers," rhetorically asked, "Which party has achieved more in positive creations in the social arena than the [achievements] of the Center?"[25] Not surprisingly given both the concerns of the local populace and the worries of the Center Party about losing voters, *Tremonia,* the Catholic paper in industrial Dortmund that often included articles specifically addressed to the coal workers in the area, published even more extensively on this topic, focusing on the "just demands of the miners."[26] In a speech held at a Dortmund political meeting, Center parliamentarian Schorlemer-Alst spoke on multiple topics, but saved the position of honor in his speech for "the most important subject, the social question."[27]

The choice of Aachen as the site of the *Katholikentag* in 1879 likely reflected the concern among leading Catholics that the Social Democrats would siphon off votes, especially given the hotly contested election there in 1877.[28] Whatever the reason the city was chosen, the events themselves leave no room for doubt that keeping workers within the Center Party was a top priority. The initial speech Windthorst gave at the meeting made this clear by addressing his audience as "my revered comrades in arms," continuing on to highlight whom he meant by pointing out that "the workers of Aachen are undoubtedly the first legion of the Center Party."[29] This he followed with an address devoted solely to the "many material questions . . . which especially concern the workers."[30] Explaining the Center's recent support of Bismarck's protective tariffs, Windthorst stressed that "above all" the party was interested in defending "the labor of our nation," to which he added for extra effect on the audience, "in other words your labor."[31] Indeed, the party leader went so far as to describe himself as "also a worker in my profession," someone who had toiled since his youth, though conceding "not always exactly with the hand."[32]

The Center Party did not only move away from highlighting the religious conflict in reference to socialism but also more generally overall. While it had always maintained its identity as a political, not confessional, party, explicit references to this claim became seldom after the initial year of the *Kulturkampf*. Regardless, the intense focus on the conflict during its height made such claims ring hollow.[33] But beginning in 1878, rhetoric began emphasizing the Center as an "eminent political party" again.[34] It "was always a political party and could not have been anything else," an article contended, explaining that the confessional affiliation of members "hinders in no way that the truths of Christianity transpose themselves in public life to political truths," the last being real concerns of the Center.[35] Completely aside from the *Kulturkampf* and other religious issues, another article assured that the Center had proven itself a "viable, rising" party, as it concerned itself with "all burning questions of the present," both of which were assertions that would appear in the rhetoric time and again.[36] Not only would the Center Party continue beyond the end of the *Kulturkampf*, but its existence was "a necessity."[37]

Such assertions meant to firmly deny talk and hopes by opponents that the Center would disband, of course.[38] Yet they also formed part of the Center's effort to rebrand itself as more than a party of opposition to something that increasingly looked like it was coming to an end. Instead, the Center portrayed itself as a party with much more to offer than just opposition. Not only did it try to highlight its political involvement with all "burning questions," but also attempted to ratchet up its appeal to specific groups within Catholicism beyond just the workers. Indeed, Windthorst's own understanding of a second speech given at the 1879 *Katholikentag* suggests as much. He concluded that the "meeting in Aachen brought about new courage and unity," after which he directly noted the content of his own speech was "calculated for a meeting from all groups (*Stände*) and in order to keep interest up."[39] Even beyond his speech, other speakers also stressed early on at the meeting that the party could address everyone's needs, "whether city dweller, country dweller, worker, *Bürger*, or aristocrat."[40] Given the liberal leanings of the bourgeoisie, among both its Protestant and its Catholic members, the Center attempted to shore up its image specifically in this arena.[41] Of course, the rhetoric up to that point had pitched the entire conflict as one waged against liberals. Yet liberals were always understood as championing something quite the opposite from true liberalism, the reason why Catholic newspapers so often placed the term in quotes when referring to their opponents.[42] Now, the Center began to trumpet itself as "the real liberal party," as a headline in the

Schlesische Volkszeitung declared, continuing on to assert that the party was fighting this battle "almost entirely alone."[43] The dominance of the Progressive Party *(Fortschrittspartei)* in Dortmund's local politics even elicited the claim in a Center political speech that its party represented "true progress *(Fortschritt)*."[44] Yet the Party also continued to emphasize its conservatism. This very reference to progress was immediately followed up with the assertion that the party also represented "the German loyalty *(Deutsch Treu')* of old," bolstering both the image of the Center as conservative and as truly national given the culturally prized value of fidelity. An article announcing the new *Reichstag* season in *Germania* further explained, the Center "will be conservative in all religious questions; liberal in all purely political and constitutional questions." Trying to cover all bases and be all things without obvious contradiction, other explanations simply played on the Party's name and concluded, we "now form the core and center of the political layout of the present."[45] Given the considerably changed politics on the national level after the end of the *Kulturkampf,* the play on words also included reference to the now central role the party assumed in passing legislation beginning in 1879.[46]

Perhaps one of the clearest indicators that the rhetoric was undergoing a significant change at this point is the loud insistence at the same time of the Center Party's stability and the steadfastness of its ideals. Articles repeatedly noted that the party's position was "not subjugated to the changing daily opinion that is today one way and tomorrow another"; instead, it asserted, "We know what we want and our principles suffer from no change."[47] Whatever opponents might try to call an about-face, another article explained, could be understood as "nothing more than the logical development of its [the Center's] earlier politics and its old principles."[48] Of course, there was some truth in this. None of these ideas about the importance of the social question, the difference between true and false liberalism, or even the party insistence on its constancy when compared to the vacillation of opponents was new. The ratcheted up attention to them, however, was.

This corresponded to a matching decline in emphasis on the *Kulturkampf.* Of course the issue never became irrelevant, but remained a part of the rhetoric. What is more notable, however, is not only the decreased attention to the religious conflict but also the striking change in the tone of the reportage surrounding it at this time. While the past several years had seen the conflict promoted as a struggle between good and evil, a fight for the very soul of Germany, most of the articles in 1878 already had begun discussing the *Kulturkampf* in less emotional and less heated terms. Long periods could pass without real focus on the *Kulturkampf*. The leading paper *Germania*, for example, remained conspicuously quiet on the issue in March 1878, which was not surprisingly also a point at which Windthorst believed major progress might be made in both ending the conflict and increasing the role of the Center in government.[49] Even when articles did appear that tried to rally Catholics around the banner of continuing the struggle, they still often suggested a more political than religious approach to the conflict. One article—written to convince those Catholics who appeared content to move on from the conflict and leave the rest up to diplomatic negotiations—tried to walk a fine line between asserting complete support for Leo's decisions while at the same time asking, "Should we idly lay our hands in our laps while we entrust our business with full confidence to the Holy Father and think it would be in the best and very best hands there?" No, the article firmly answered. Instead, it called upon Catholics to "go on energetically fighting until we have achieved full freedom and realized the entire program of the Center."[50] By now, of course, the focus of such a program had been considerably expanded in the rhetoric to include many diverse political goals.[51]

While the stance of the Center leadership throughout the *Kulturkampf* often reflected a mixture of both sincere beliefs and tactical considerations, the closing phase beginning in late 1877 betrayed a significant emphasis on the latter. Part of this is evident in the role a hoped for political realignment that included a rapprochement between the Center and Bismarck played in influencing Windthorst and the Party's actions. Measures designed to prevent the papacy from overshadowing the Center in representing German Catholics in the process of ending the conflict, which had grown far beyond simply one between Church and state, also indicate this.[52] Yet tactical considerations also played a major role in the relationship between the Catholic leadership and the masses of their constituency at this moment, particularly in the manner in which the rhetoric of the time was constructed. The Center Party's overall mission broadened far beyond one primarily interested in religious issues and the waging of the *Kulturkampf.* Attempts were made not only to address all Catholics but also to stress what the party could offer particular subgroups, a tactic that paradoxically attempted to bolster unity by tacitly recognizing the disparate elements that made up the constituency.[53] This deemphasizing of religious issues was all undertaken in the party rhetoric and appeals to voters despite Windthorst's own belief that "our first and main task, the resolution of which all other questions depends upon, is the getting rid of the *Kulturkampf,* and we may only commit ourselves with caution to the other questions, which are long-standing [ones]."[54]

This tactical rebranding of the Center to its constituency suggests that party leaders did not have confidence that continued emphasis on religious issues and appealing to voters only as a confessional cohort would retain its supporters. In other words, already in 1878 this response to the fears of party fragmentation and voter apathy in the face of a potential resolution to the *Kulturkampf* indicated a concern not that Catholics were too different from Protestant Germans, but that they were perhaps too alike and not so far removed from integration in the nation. That many Catholics would abandon the Center Party—not just by no longer voting but also by actively supporting other parties alongside their Protestant counterparts—seemed a real possibility at the time.[55] Again, the fear was that Catholics would forget too much of the last decade, not too little, and in doing so destroy the advantage of unity. That these fears of a major loss of support did not come to pass, with the Center Party remaining strong throughout the *Kaiserreich,* does not make this concern any less true.[56] Nor is it possible to know how the party would have fared had such a shift in its presentation not been undertaken. In any case, such efforts to broaden its focus beyond religious issues meant already by 1878 that the Center had recast its goals in terms sounding closer to—if still different from—those of other parties and would also continue to not only respond to but also influence the manner in which the party constituency viewed *Kaiserreich* politics.

SIX

Mapping Germany from the Borders to Berlin

IN NOVEMBER 1872, a lead article in *Germania* claimed with exasperation that never before had it read such inflammatory "confessional agitation" as that recently printed in the *Norddeutsche Allgemeine Zeitung* (NAZ), Berlin's semi-official government newspaper. Allegedly part of a recent, larger trend stemming from semi-official, liberal, and even Protestant church publications, these efforts to turn every issue into a conflict between the confessions only further damaged the process of true (internal) unification in Germany. Accompanying mottos such as "the State against Catholicism" were misguided enough, but the calls for "Protestantism against Catholicism" that had been appearing more often lately took the issue to another level, the article asserted. The NAZ supposedly subscribed to this divisive ploy to such an extent that it could not even stomach the presence of a Catholic newspaper in Berlin, or as *Germania* cited from the original article in its opponent's paper, "in the midst of the Protestant capital."[1]

While the agitation included everything from an incendiary account of the "bloody wedding of Paris" on the 300th anniversary of the St. Bartholomew's Day Massacre to allegations that Catholics committed cemetery "cannibalism," as only Protestant plots had suffered desecration in one Silesian town's graveyard, the NAZ's objection to Catholics being allowed a "voice" in the capital stung most. Of course, that stemmed in part from the objection being directed specifically at *Germania* itself. Yet the article protested this point the most because it also tied into a more general perception of Berlin as the Protestant capital of a Protestant nation, a view that found reinforcement in many ways, not least of which was the waging of the *Kulturkampf.* By definition, Catholics could never hope to be anything more than second-class citizens if this conception of the new *Reich* stood, nor could such a nation ever truly feel like home to them. Hence, the article went on to first refute the *NAZ*'s description of Berlin, pointing out that "Berlin, in the sense in which it [the *NAZ*] means it, is today not a Protestant city at all anymore," in part alluding to the high numbers of resident liberals, who accordingly did not truly count. More importantly, the counterclaim also pointed to the role of Berlin as the capital of the new *Reich* to assert that it could not, by definition, be a Protestant city. The article sarcastically argued that either the capital had to make a place for Catholics, or the *Reich* had to sever regions where they were a majority of the population: Posen, Upper Silesia, the Rhineland, Westphalia, and southern Germany. Then, the article ironically agreed, *Germania* would close up shop and the *NAZ* could have back its "Protestant capital." Otherwise, people would have to recognize that "the times have simply changed," as had the nature and role of Berlin in the unified Germany.[2]

Yet numbers were hard to argue with, and the population statistics pointed indisputably to a city that was inhabited overwhelmingly by Protestants.[3] Moreover, Berlin was not what most Catholics thought of when they envisioned their Germany. Even the Center parliamentarians who stayed in the city for long *Reichstag* sessions would have found the speech, customs, and landscape of the capital unlike that of their homes. Hence, while *Germania* began emphasizing the new role of Berlin from the beginning of the *Reich,* stressing that no German, regardless of who he was or what other region he came from, could any longer be considered "a foreigner" in the capital, the newspaper also asserted the reverse. No matter where in the *Reich* one went, the local inhabitants of even "the smallest village" would have "German life pulsating in themselves" and know their "small patch of earth belongs to the great Germany."[4] In short, unification in 1871 meant that not only could any German find himself at home in Berlin, but Germany could also be found in any town imaginable, no matter how small. Berlin may have been the capital, but it was no more German than any other place in the *Reich,* according to *Germania.*

As these efforts to recast both the character of the metropolis and its relationship to what many considered the periphery of Germany suggest, Catholic arguments concerning national belonging recognized early on the importance of geographical perceptions in defining the new *Reich*.[5] *Germania*, the central newspaper for Catholicism and uniquely based in the capital, stood at the forefront of this effort and consequently undertook a two-fold approach to create a mental map of Germany fitting its views of the nation. The first part meant challenging the role of Berlin, both as a Protestant city and as the center of Germany. The second entailed placing emphasis on events in Catholic areas, all on the physical periphery of the *Reich*, by bringing them back to the center, both literally by reporting on them from the capital and figuratively by presenting them as matters of national importance. Certainly the focus on these regions constituted not only an effort to portray a Germany relevant and recognizable to the Catholic readership but also an assertion of their integral role in the new *Reich*, an argument made for the benefit of their opponents as well.[6] Yet the manner in which *Germania* cast the new *Reich* as existing beyond Berlin also revealed a highly tactical approach to redrawing the mental map of the new nation, choosing to emphasize unproblematic areas like the Rhineland and Westphalia while exercising more caution concerning areas such as the eastern provinces.

Though scholars have always recognized the importance of regional variation in Germany, these differences have received increasing attention in recent literature.[7] While the emphasis in the literature on Catholicism during the 1870s continues to be on its homogeneity, and rightfully so in many cases, the greater attention to variation throughout the *Reich* has nonetheless also influenced research on this front. As Thomas Mergel asserts, despite Catholicism's "impressive homogeneity" on the national level, it "was essentially regional in character," indicating its concentration in the "four core regions" of Silesia, Bavaria, the Rhineland, and Westphalia, each with differing levels of wealth, urbanization, and religious practice, among other things.[8] Other scholars examining Catholicism have extended this regional approach even further, stressing not only the particular geographic distribution of the confessions in Germany but also exceptions in which local Catholics broke with the actions of most of their co-religionists throughout Germany.[9] The interest in regional variation has also had obvious importance for the study of nation-building and national identity formation. Indeed, beginning with Celia Applegate's pioneering study on the importance of the idea of *Heimat* (a flexible notion of one's "homeland" tied closely to the local setting) in creating Germans, examining the manner in which these more specific identities were fostered has been central to understanding national integration after 1871.[10] Yet, while issues of confessional difference have certainly been included in the literature addressing the connections between region and integration, the south German particularists being the prime example, the tendency has been to underscore Catholic distance to the nation in this arena as well.[11] On the other hand, the role of *Heimat* as a way of squaring the circle in national integration has largely been examined without reference to confession. Moreover, Alon Confino, whose book has provided the most in depth investigation of the *Heimat* idea during the *Kaiserreich,* specifically locates the development of this pattern of integration in the 1880s at earliest, after the major religious strife of the *Kulturkampf* had passed.[12]

Certainly part of *Heimat's* appeal for forging a nationally inclusive vision of Germany was its ability to stress the greater unity created from universal diversity, a process that meant downplaying potential tensions like those stemming from regional and religious identities.[13] Likewise, both its growth as a movement and its success as a dominant way of conceptualizing the nation occurred later in the *Kaiserreich,* as the literature suggests. Yet the roots of this integrative process took hold long before the 1880s and 1890s, as Abigail Green has convincingly demonstrated in her research on regional identities.[14] This chapter examines another aspect of these roots, focusing on confession and how Catholic efforts to conceptualize their place in the new Germany during the *Kulturkampf* relied upon a similar emphasis on particular locales as their connection to the nation. Of course, during the period of the 1870s, these efforts created clear lines of conflict with the Germany being envisioned by liberals and the national government. Yet, as both Green's and Siegfried Weichlein's works indicate, seemingly entrenched conflicts early on in the *Kaiserreich* could play roles as integral to ultimately creating a unified national identity as the greater openness to and acceptance of diversity that accompanied the *Heimat* idea later on did.[15] Similarly, these Catholic efforts to understand the nation from a local perspective, while not formally linked to the later activities of the *Heimat* movement, certainly paved the way for an easy transition to them, especially when compared to the efforts of liberals to impose a "univocal identity" in celebrations like Sedan Day.[16] Moreover, the particular localities that Catholic arguments chose to emphasize, those on the western versus the eastern or southern borders of the nation, also served to foster long-term integration.

Recasting Berlin

Given the importance of the daily press during the 1870s, Catholics needed a newspaper in Berlin, at least if they were going to have a voice in the new nation.[17] As the *Reich* capital, Berlin was center stage for all political activity, and newspapers there had an advantage in getting the inside story as well as the jump on presenting it to the public.[18] Numerous daily papers already made the city their home base. None of them, however, represented the viewpoint of the majority of the nation's Catholics. Even long before the proclamation of the new nation, notable German Catholics had realized the need for a centrally located newspaper to counteract the polemics of the liberal press.[19] Hence, in 1870 several Berlin Catholics, including the parliamentarian Friedrich von Kehler, formed a committee to establish the daily paper that ultimately became *Germania*.[20] Liberal and conservative Protestant papers had long existed in the main Catholic cities of the *Reich* and beyond.[21] Finally, the reverse was true: a Catholic paper had made Berlin its home. This was a victory in itself, a conquest of sorts. Certainly the language *Germania* used in reporting on the general reaction to its publication furthered this point, referring to other papers' accounts of Catholics "drunk with victory, making their entrance through the gates of the German metropole" to start a paper.[22] While *Germania* used such exaggerated language to summarize the position of its competitors as a way of poking fun at the alarmism and intolerance it saw in such articles, it nonetheless did not seek to undercut the achievement of founding a Catholic newspaper in Berlin.[23] That opponents still complained about the basing of *Germania* in the capital almost a full two years later, another article pointed out, only served as confirmation of this.[24]

Efforts to make a place for Catholics in the nation's capital also included challenging Berlin's reputation as a Protestant city. As with many other phrases representing positions opposed in the newspaper, such character-izations of the metropolis appeared in *Germania* with scare quotes, indi-cating disapproval. While not many Catholics lived in Berlin, neither did many Protestants, *Germania* argued. Instead, the city was inhabited by "heathens"—as Catholic publications commonly referred to liberals—and Jews.[25] The most vociferous objections to formulations about Protestant Berlin often appeared at the beginning of November, as articles responded to the events organized to commemorate Reformation Day on October 31.[26] In 1877, for example, *Germania* jumped on the results of Berlin's first city-wide synodal meeting, which was timed to coincide with Refor-mation Day commemorations, to show just what the local "Christians" were like. Representing the almost one million Protestants who lived in Berlin, Germania noted, the synod revealed a great deal about religion in the metropolis. Indeed, one needed to look no further than the person chosen as the clergyman to lead the meeting: Theodor Hoßbach.[27] Hoßbach, a preacher at St. Andreas in the Friedrichshain section of Berlin, had long been active in liberal Protestant circles, working alongside fellow clergyman like Gustav Lisco and Adolf Sydow to establish the *Deutscher Protestantenverein* in support of a more rational Christianity. When Sydow lost his clerical position as punishment for preaching that Jesus was the actual son of Joseph, Hoßbach along with several other Berlin pastors pro-tested to have the judgment overturned. By 1877, Hoßbach had himself become directly involved in preaching against the divinity of Jesus, holding a sermon on the topic in Berlin's St. Jakobi in May of that year.[28] Such people were "no longer Christians," *Germania* exclaimed, adding wryly, "So it is in the capital of Protestantism."[29]

The portrayal of Berlin as a city of heathens, not Protestants, fit well with the more general efforts in Catholic publications of the period to highlight the moral decay of the metropolis. It also furthered efforts to downplay confessional animosities and again cast the conflict as one of all believing Christians against corrupt liberals. From the beginning,

Germania spoke of the immorality gripping Berlin. Though liberal papers often decried the indecency of Catholic lands, *Germania* quoted extensively from recent editions of their competitors' own publications that pointed to growing problems in the capital. *Germania* wagered that Berlin surpassed all other capital cities in debauchery, despite the alleged benefits of liberal culture in the "city of intelligence." Extortionists, prostitutes, and cold-blooded killers filled the streets of Berlin, not to mention the overwhelming masses of brutes. Such people not only ran in the lower circles of the city, but could also be found in the higher echelons as well. The stock exchange swindle proved that unsavory characters also congregated among the well-heeled and powerful of Berlin, where, articles in *Germania* claimed, such fraud was even more prevalent than in other metropolises. Berlin allegedly even outdid Paris in its levels of debauchery, no mean feat.[30] *Germania* feigned worry that the Protestant churches in the capital would scarcely be able to survive monetarily, so reduced was their income from parishioners in the godless, corrupt metropolis.[31] The immorality would only increase without intervention.

Catholics hardly cornered the market on anti-Berlin sentiments in the founding decade of the nation. Inhabitants of other large German cities feared the loss of prestige they would suffer as all attention turned to Berlin. Members of many non-Prussian states felt bitter about the back seat they would have to take, a position made clear already in choosing the capital. The metropolis also evoked mistrust among many small-town Germans. These issues played a role in anti-Berlin sentiment, as did the quite real increase in problems facing the city after 1871: vagrancy, horrible living conditions, and masses of people willing to do almost anything to escape them. Even long-time residents and staunchly pro-Prussian patriots came to harbor doubts about Berlin during the 1870s, a city changing so rapidly it was no longer the same place they had loved.[32] Except for the last, these issues also played a role in the criticism of Berlin among Catholics, though the religious issue had the most impact overall, especially in forming the rhetoric.[33]

While *Germania* clearly denounced the corruption of Berlin, its ideas about how to remedy such problems in the capital nonetheless suggested a more complex relationship with the metropolis. The important role of religion in basic education had to be protected, *Germania* asserted, which could only be guaranteed in confessional schools in the city and throughout the *Reich*.[34] Berlin in particular needed more Catholic churches. Only then would greater numbers of the masses attain the needed religious guidance, *Germania* reasoned, as the multitude of empty Protestant churches indicated people were not receiving it there.[35] Berlin even needed religious processions to set it on the path to recovery, and an article complained of the recent banning of such events like the *Corpus Christi* march from Moabit and Charlottenburg to Spandau as yet another missed opportunity to turn the city around.[36] In other words, the articles argued that Berlin needed to become more Christian, and given the weakened and splintered state of Protestantism, especially in the metropolis, it was largely up to Catholics to do this. Hence, while rejecting the corruption of Berlin, such articles in *Germania* indicated that Catholics were far from giving up on recasting the capital, at least in part, in their own image. Each Catholic school, church, and procession in the capital would be another small victory, a conquest, just as the establishment of *Germania* itself had been. These efforts to claim public and social space in the capital undoubtedly stemmed from the realization that Berlin mattered, and now more than ever.[37] If Catholics were to play a role in defining the new nation, they would also have to make a place for themselves in Berlin. Despite the repeated denunciations of corruption in the metropolis, *Germania* articles also often noted how Berlin functioned as a linchpin for the nation. In short, this was a recognition of the centralizing elements of the empire, notwithstanding the preference for federalism among Center Party politicians. Even though it might take some people time to get used to it, no one could deny that the proclamation of the new nation turned Berlin into the "focal point" for everyone in the *Reich*.[38] Genuine pride was also involved, given sentiments that Berlin had also become important on the international stage and people would now look to it instead of Paris.[39] What had once been remarked on as a sandy nowhere by foreign travelers, if they bothered to visit Berlin at all, could no longer be denied its importance in a Europe with a unified Germany.[40] Hence, Catholic accounts of the poor state of the metropolis meant the decay and corruption of Berlin was a problem of national disgrace, one that they were integral to remedying.[41]

Despite all the rhetoric and the real actions taken to make a Catholic presence in the capital felt, including an influx of Catholics to the city after 1871, Berlin remained overwhelmingly Protestant.[42] Even if articles in *Germania* would always deny that the capital was a truly Protestant city, the paper certainly could not assert that Berlin was a Catholic one. Indeed, *Germania* largely ignored local Berlin news and affairs concerning the region in its editions. Focus on local events would have presented a picture of Catholics as largely marginalized, exactly what *Germania* attempted not to do. More practically, it would have held little interest for the readership of the paper, which was not only Catholic but also drawn mainly from outside of Berlin.[43]

In Search of the True Germany

While articles in *Germania* recognized that Berlin had become the linchpin of the new nation, the paper did not believe the capital represented the soul of Germany.[44] Instead, *Germania* positioned the capital as a nexus important for its ability to gather and combine the different parts of the new *Reich*, in all its regional and confessional diversity. *Germania's* role in the capital served to add the Catholic element into this mix. To do so meant not only promoting arguments about how Germany should be defined but also reporting on stories that highlighted Catholic events. Consequently, articles drew heavily on news from the borders of the new German nation, the areas with predominantly Catholic populations. The stories did not merely replace those that would otherwise have been covered in the local news section, however. Instead, *Germania* portrayed these events as nationally important, bringing Catholics from the periphery of Germany to center stage.

Of course, there were multiple areas on the borders of Germany that could be highlighted. Catholics predominated in Bavaria, to the east in Posen and Silesia, and to the west in Westphalia and the Rhineland. In addition to these "core regions," the same could be said of Baden.[45] The new *Reichsland* of Alsace-Lorraine also included a large number of Catholics. All of these areas received attention in *Germania's* pages. Not all of them were created equal, however, at least not for the purposes of Catholic inclusion in the nation.

Bavarian Catholics, for example, undoubtedly proved highly engaged in the national issue from the beginning, but strong allegiance to the their home state meant they were at times on the wrong side of the equation, at least as far as *Germania* and the majority of the Center Party were concerned. Indeed, the highest concentration of *Germania* articles on Bavaria throughout the *Kulturkampf* came at the very beginning of the period, when the newspaper dismissed the Patriot Party's efforts to scuttle a union with Germany as misguided and ultimately futile.[46] Even after overcoming this initial split and accepting the reality of a unified Germany, Bavarian Patriots always remained separate from the larger Center, adding a notable element of diversity.[47] Furthermore, despite Windthorst's own close interactions with south German Catholics, most leading members of the Center Party—men like Ketteler, Mallinckrodt, and P. Reichensperger—espoused far less hostility toward Prussia than their Bavarian allies.[48] For a publication attempting to highlight Catholic activity in the *Reich* as well as portray the utmost unity within the Catholic camp, Bavaria did not pose a good example.

Co-religionists in the East posed an even more difficult problem for arguments about Catholic inclusion in the nation. Catholics in the South may have thought of themselves as Bavarians first, but at least they were Germans too. The Catholics in the eastern provinces often included large numbers of Poles. While they accounted only for approximately 10 percent of the Prussian population and even less than that in the *Reich* as a whole, Poles made up more than half the inhabitants in Posen and Upper Silesia and almost exclusively espoused Catholicism. Despite many German Catholics also making their home in the East, especially in Silesia, the equation of Catholic with Pole in that area was often assumed.[49] Moreover, the cooperation between the Polish minority and the Center Party often proved a sticky issue. While the Center supported many of the Polish Party's goals, there were limits to how far the former could back the latter's cause, especially as their nationalist aims increased. Time only intensified difficulties in what was already a problematic relationship at the beginning of the 1870s.[50] Furthermore, cooperation between the Center and the Polish Party raised many suspicions, Bismarck's not least among them, making Catholics in the East an undesirable choice to focus on.[51]

The inhabitants of Alsace-Lorraine evoked the same suspicions, despite widespread support among the *Reich*'s populace for the annexation.[52]

Like among the Poles in the East, nationalist sentiment—in this case for France—compounded the resentment of and opposition to the government among the inhabitants of the new *Reichsland*. Most would have preferred to remain French. The *Kulturkampf* laws applied in the new *Reichsland* did little to win additional support for the government in Berlin, especially given that Alsace-Lorraine was the most Catholic of all areas in the *Reich*, with more than three-fourths of the populace belonging to the Church.[53] Practical reasons also made Alsace-Lorraine a poor choice to highlight as a way of bringing Catholics center stage. In addition to the always difficult cooperation between representatives of Alsace-Lorraine and the Center Party, for the first four years, Berlin did not allow the *Reichsland* to send any delegates to parliament. Moreover, the central government forbade the dissemination of newspapers considered potentially disruptive, *Germania* included, in the new *Reichsland*.[54] Given the thorny issues of allegiance that the inhabitants of Alsace-Lorraine raised as well as the lack of an accessible audience in the *Reichsland*, the territory did not represent the Catholic Germany that *Germania* wanted to show either its readers or its detractors. When articles portrayed Alsace-Lorraine, it was always as a missed opportunity.

Baden's majority populace, on the other hand, at times barely passed muster as belonging to the larger community of Catholics throughout the *Reich* in contemporaries' own estimations. Indeed, this explains its absence from the list of the "core regions" of German Catholicism.[55] Significant support for liberalism distinguished Badenese Catholics from their co-religionists more generally.[56] Indeed, Old Catholic numbers reached higher levels in Baden than anywhere else.[57] Given the slower development of political Catholicism in the region, it hardly surprises that the spotlight commonly passed over Baden.[58]

This left the neighboring regions of the Rhineland and Westphalia, two areas often grouped together, especially after becoming the westernmost possessions of Prussia early in the nineteenth century.[59] With the *Pfaffengasse* of German Catholicism running through these regions in the West, political participation in support of the Center always reached high levels.[60] Resistance to the *Kulturkampf* remained strong despite—or because of—the severity of its application in the West.[61] Given the events of the Cologne Troubles, the area could draw upon a reputation for holding fast against government pressure. Indeed, the very beginnings of political Catholicism itself could be traced here.[62] Not only was the area, the Rhineland especially, internally highly homogenous, but individuals from this Catholic hotspot also played extremely influential roles in the Center Party on a national level, while retaining a high degree of influence locally as well.[63] Men like Mallinckrodt, Ketteler, and the Reichensperger brothers were formative to political Catholicism in the 1870s.[64] Moreover, unlike in Bavaria, Catholics in the West had accepted unification much more readily.[65] Finally, the distance of the Rhineland and Westphalia to Austria should not be underestimated in making the region an attractive place to highlight. Given the sensitivity in Catholic circles to accusations of disloyalty, including that stemming from support for Austria, the shared border between the Hapsburg Empire and other Catholic parts of Germany could raise tricky issues.[66] When Bishop Förster of Breslau escaped imprisonment by the Prussian authorities, for example, by crossing the border into the Austrian part of his see, as did members of many local cloisters' mother houses, the case hardly yielded the same unambiguous tale of sacrifice as did that of the five bishops actually jailed in 1874 and 1875, four of whom came from the western dioceses.[67]

In addition to having none of the overt, political drawbacks of other regions, the Rhineland and Westphalia had many other positive attributes that recommended them for a portrayal of a vigorous Catholic Germany. The western regions experienced greater industrialization, urbanization, and prosperity, not a small consideration given liberal claims of Catholic backwardness.[68] They also had higher rates of literacy as compared to the East.[69] Unlike other areas of Germany that were losing inhabitants, the mushroom towns of the West quickly attracted immigrants, making it a region on the rise.[70] Indeed, some contemporaries liked to think that Cologne could rival Berlin in influence—a claim made all the more appealing to publications like *Germania* by the reputation of the former city as the "German Rome" for its thoroughly Catholic character.[71] The area also had adequate numbers of clergy and a well-developed press network, both conditions linked to strong political participation and cohesion.[72]

Articles in *Germania* reported on the events of the western provinces quite often. The specific subjects differed little from those dealt with by

Germania more generally. Schooling, for example, formed the basis for many articles. At various times, *Germania* ran articles on the efforts to establish interdenominational schools *(Simultanschulen)* in the Rhineland and Westphalia, obstructionist authorities preventing teachers from providing religious education, and the unfair extra burden placed on poorer local communities in insuring that their children did not have to be taught by members of another denomination, in particular Old Catholic instructors. Even when these issues also involved cases from other regions of Germany, the articles would often spend more time detailing those from the Rhineland and Westphalia.[73] Sometimes this showed a clear bias for reporting on Catholic events in the West. At other times the relatively advantageous circumstances of Catholics in the West likely led to events that simply made for better stories than those in other areas. For example, an article on sick care, a topic often infused with confessional tensions, highlighted the massive aid provided by various Catholic orders, especially to soldiers from the Franco-Prussian War. In addition to focusing on the Rhineland and Westphalia because of the greater proximity of religious orders there to soldiers returning from battle, the emphasis on the region also likely stemmed from the extensive sick care offered by Catholic institutions in the West, a development in no small part linked to the underlying higher urbanization, industrialization, and prosperity of the communities in the area.[74]

Resistance featured prominently in *Germania*'s reporting on the western provinces. Sometimes articles highlighted particular contemporary instances from the region.[75] Even more prevalent were references to the events of the Cologne Troubles.[76] *Germania* portrayed the *Kulturkampf* as round two of that 1830s church-state conflict, the same basic situation that Catholics were "experiencing again." Indeed, the articles asserted that much could be learned—by both Catholics and the government—from looking back to the Cologne Troubles as well as its "spiritual titan[s]" like Joseph Görres or Archbishop Clemens August von Droste-Vischering. Catholics could take as a model the years of "dogged resistance" that led to a government climb down, and the government should learn the lesson from its defeat the first time around. Indeed, if the government foolishly believed Catholics would act any differently this time, then, an article declared, it had "underestimated" them. More than a mere miscalculation, *Germania* asserted that it was an outright "insult" to assume that the Catholics had no "resoluteness of character" and would betray their stance of earlier decades. In this line of thought, the 1830s were not a specific case of resistance, but an example of Catholic character more generally. Furthermore, the Cologne Troubles did not just reflect Catholics in the region or in Prussia, but in "the rest of Germany" as well. The response to government pressure during the Cologne Troubles exemplified a fundamental truth about the "strength of the Catholic spirit in Germany," *Germania* asserted.[77]

While the Cologne Troubles had a more obvious significance beyond the region, other events that *Germania* reported on more clearly indicated the concerted effort of the newspaper to highlight the area and give local events a national importance. The paper reported on visits to the Rhine Province in the summer of 1875 by both crown prince Frederick III and by Minister Falk, for example, to address how Catholics more generally felt about the current situation. *Germania* seized upon the wide-spread enthusiasm that inhabitants of "the metropole of the Rhine Province [i.e., Cologne]" and elsewhere in the region expressed for Frederick as proof that one could be "a good Catholic and a good German at the same time."[78] On the other hand, *Germania* countered the reports in opposing papers that suggested the lack of demonstrations against Falk's Rhineland visit indicated a waning Catholic opposition to the *Kulturkampf.* It argued that the readying of police and military units in the region had more to do with the absence of demonstrations against Falk than any change of heart did. Nonetheless, *Germania* did agree with the implicit assumption of other papers that the region acted as a barometer for the rest of Catholic Germany.[79]

In addition to presenting the western provinces as *pars pro toto* for Catholic Germany, the newspaper also stressed their proximity to the capital. Another article countering claims that opposition to the *Kulturkampf* was waning asserted that liberals might be able to lull themselves into this false hope by looking no further than their own doorstep, but any glimpse of true "Catholic life and bustle" would dispel such illusions. For a good look, one merely needed to go west, with *Germania* suggesting that "some excursions to the Rhineland and Westphalia" would be "very advisable" for liberals. More importantly, these provinces did not exist at the ends of the *Reich* in out of the way places but could easily be reached from the capital. "[I]n each Berlin train station there is the largest selection of tickets, of which a person only needed to acquire one," *Germania* explained with a tongue-in-cheek earnestness, "to gain the indisputable right . . . to be dispatched into the province with the greatest willingness and courtesy." The article implied that nothing other than sheer desire to be clueless could explain the liberal claims, so effortless was the trip from Berlin to the western provinces.[80] Similarly, *Germania* included an article penned by a Protestant concerning the consequences of *Kulturkampf* legislation that exemplified the importance of looking beyond the capital, again to the West. From Berlin, "or in an area where mainly a Protestant populace lived," one could not see the attachment of people to their religion. In "areas with purely Catholic populaces," however, the picture looked different. The author did not have difficulty seeing this other side, the article reported, after traveling through various towns in the West. This did not result from some arduous fact-finding trip taken to the outer limits of civilization, but from a recent business trip that happened to take him to the Rhineland, which by the end of the decade *Germania* had no difficulty calling part of the "heartlands" alongside Westphalia.[81] Neither Catholics nor the regions they lived in, so such articles argued, were on the margins of Germany. Indeed, the new role of Berlin as capital of the *Reich*, now a nexus for all of Germany, made it impossible to discount them.

This came full circle to the idea that Berlin was not where Germany would be found, at least not the only place. Those who looked only in the capital or in areas like it sadly deluded themselves, *Germania* suggested. Finding the soul of true Germanness would no sooner happen by looking only in those areas than the *Reich* would be complete if it severed regions like Posen, Upper Silesia, the Rhineland, Westphalia, and South Germany, as the 1872 article had sarcastically dared it to.[82] While *Germania's* main emphasis was on highlighting Catholics, especially those in the West, it also couched these points in a larger argument supporting difference versus homogeneity. "Particularism," an early article quoting conservative parliamentarian Ernst Ludwig von Gerlach in an effort to describe life in the new Germany asserted, "is originally and essentially German." The multiplicity rooted in small places everywhere made up what was "characteristically German." While liberals wished to see a

Reich devoid of diversity, those who appreciated difference could lay far more claim to being "advocates of Germanness," be they labeled Ultramontane, conservative, or particularist. Even Bismarck had previously referred to particularism as the "height of Germanness," though *Germania* also agreed with the chancellor that it could be a weakness too. The new nation, therefore, now had the "truly German, good but difficult task of sustaining particularism as much as possible." Importantly, it was not just about regions, the article added, but also about religion. The differences from the "schism within the German *Volk*" also helped sustain diversity, part and parcel of how true Germanness was defined.[83] Not surprisingly, the article showed, regional and religious differences were often linked.[84]

Hence, what liberals and the government portrayed as drawbacks stemming from dangerous regional and religious differences, *Germania* spun as positives vital to the strengthening of the new *Reich*.[85] While *Germania*, like political Catholicism more generally, opposed the separatism of the Bavarian Patriot Party, the paper did not condone the liberal leanings of the current government in Bavaria either. Even if the Patriot Party had been misguided in its early efforts to prevent Bavarian inclusion in the *Reich*, the newspaper argued, its general opposition to the state government was correct. Only when the populace freed itself from the "mostly foreign" parasites in the state government would it again have a future. "Bavaria must again be the Bavaria [of old]," the article concluded, adding "if also in another way" in light of its new position in the *Reich*. Only then could the new Germany be strengthened by the inclusion of the southern state.[86] Similarly, the resistance offered by the inhabitants of Alsace-Lorraine only underscored the "Germanic tenacity and stubbornness" that had been preserved more so among them than among some other tribes. Once the government included those in the newly gained territory as the true brothers they were, not prisoners, the *Reich* would benefit from the injection of resolve into the population.[87] Indeed, doggedness was alleged to have been preserved more strongly in the Catholic populace of the *Reich* generally, given tribulations like the *Kulturkampf* that it had repeatedly endured. It fought so resolutely now, because Catholics had "preserved the tenacious character of its ancestors." Where would Germany be without people who stood by their beliefs "with German faithfulness" and "German earnestness," the newspaper asked.[88] In this way of defining the new Germany, difference did not necessarily mean dissolution. It could also mean greater strength.

Given its own home base in the capital, *Germania* played a special role in constructing a mental map of the new nation and Catholics' place within it. Yet the larger argument that stressed the advantages of multiplicity and located true Germanness in the cities, towns, and small villages of the borderlands as well echoed throughout Catholic publications. The other leading Catholic paper, the *Kölnische Volkszeitung*, for example, also emphasized the importance of regional differences in its discussions of what the new *Reich* should look like. While some "distinctive features" might have to be "sacrificed" for the "unity" of the entity, this did not equal a *Reich* that would "overwhelm all particular life of the provinces and local communities." Instead, it could "allow a Frank, Swabian, and Bavarian" to be just that. Any effort for the government in Berlin "to eradicate" these differences would be a "grave sin against the most inherent Germanic nature."[89] Of course the *Kölnische Volkszeitung* highlighted the West, but so did a surprising number of articles in other regionally based papers outside of the Rhineland and Westphalia when they discussed the importance of difference. While the *Schlesische Volkszeitung* had no trouble describing all "particularism" as "ancient" and inseparable from "German history," for example, it also ran a series on the Cologne Troubles that highlighted the importance of that event as well as the people there. It described the inhabitants of the Rhineland and Westphalia as particularly prominent not only within the *Reich* but also without. Indeed, the paper claimed that their significance stemmed from having retained particular "memories from the old German time" and that "the German character" had particularly "deep roots" in the Rhineland and Westphalia.[90] The Munich-based *Historisch-Politische Blätter* also included articles on this topic. The entry entitled "Pro Rheno," for example, championed the battle of "particular nature" *(Eigenart)* against the homogenizing effects of "un-German centralization." Moreover, this particular article—written by a Rhinelander—also echoed placing the emphasis on the western provinces for both their quintessential Catholic quality and the inhabitants' preservation of characteristic tenacity. Correspondingly, Rhinelanders were a "core tribe" that the new Germany would be incomplete without.[91] Similarly, the *Augsburger Postzeitung* included copious allusions to the importance of regional diversity and freedom—hardly surprising given its base in Bavaria as well. It continued to maintain that "nationality [was] not in centralization."[92] Centralization was "un-German."[93] Yet, like the example from the *Historisch-Politische Blätter* that was penned by a Rhinelander also suggests, the *Augsburger Postzeitung* went to great lengths to support its insistence on the importance of regional diversity with quotes or evidence provided by non-Bavarians. Given previous opposition to unification by Patriots, these efforts were undoubtedly meant to give the paper distance from such earlier events while still arguing the same point as other Catholic publications throughout the *Reich*.[94]

Despite repetition of the same larger arguments throughout a multiplicity of Catholic outlets, a coordination that only increased over time as the *Kulturkampf* continued, differences remained, many linked to regional circumstances.[95] Even the two leading Catholic newspapers, *Germania* and the *Kölnische Volkszeitung*, often emphasized different elements in their reports. The latter always remained partly a regional newspaper, including numerous reports on events in the province of Cologne. While the paper increasingly reported on national and even international events over the decade, the emphasis on these local events continued.[96] More importantly, unlike *Germania*, the *Kölnische Volkszeitung* had no need to justify its focus on the region nor did it go to the same lengths to cast the events as nationally important. Its home in Cologne and the location of its primary audience was justification enough. Similarly, reporting in the *Kölnische Volkszeitung* stressed the importance of local identity and questioned the Germanness of Berlin itself, but it never expressed the same degree of interest in recasting the capital as a Catholic city. It already had the German Catholic metropolis of Cologne.[97]

The relative strength of Catholicism in the West also likely affected the extent to which the *Kölnische Volkszeitung* highlighted certain themes, though they were still present as in other publications. The proliferation of feminine imagery—especially portrayed on the receiving end of violence—that became linked with Catholic passivism in the face of government oppression, for example, never received as much attention in the articles of the *Kölnische Volkszeitung*.[98] Whereas the Berlin context might bring to mind traumatic cases like the storming of the Moabit monastery in 1869, the Cologne context could also remind readers of events in which the resistance of local Catholics had boiled over into physical aggression, despite what the rhetoric said about passive resistance.[99] More generally, the pages of the *Kölnische Volkszeitung* remained free of the vitriol expressed in the pages of *Germania*. No doubt this was linked in part to the personal style of the lead editor for the latter during almost all of the 1870s, Paul Majunke.[100] Yet it also likely had to do with the greater confidence Catholics enjoyed in the West as compared to other areas of Germany, especially Berlin. Even though many of the same Catholic notables contributed articles to both papers and, indeed, hailed from the West themselves, location made a big difference, as articles in *Germania* had acknowledged from the start. What appeared as understood in Cologne did not necessarily seem so in Berlin, where Catholics felt a need to scrape for any advantage.[101] Even so, these differences were largely in tone, not substance, particularly during the *Kulturkampf*. This was all part of what a leading Catholic on the national level like Ketteler could nonetheless assert was "legitimate" in "particularism." His assertion was only another variant of the same sentiment expressed throughout Catholic publications: "This love toward the *Heimath* and toward the *Heimathslande* is also the natural foundation for the love toward the common German *Vaterlande*. Where the first is missing, German patriotism also has no solid ground and no deep roots."[102]

Geographic perceptions of the new nation played a key role in Catholic efforts to define Germany and gain inclusion. Given its unique base in the capital along with its *Reich*-wide scope, the daily newspaper *Germania* had a pivotal function in these efforts, though other Catholic outlets asserted the same basic argument. While none of the Catholic regions were ignored, the Rhineland and Westphalia received most attention in the reporting, an emphasis that worked on multiple levels. Practically speaking, most of *Germania*'s readership lived outside of Berlin; a large segment of the readership lived, instead, in the West itself. More importantly, the emphasis on the Rhineland and Westphalia made tactical sense given the strength, vibrancy, and political reliability of Catholicism there as well as the "modern" features of the area linked to industrialization and urbanization. This was the view of Catholic Germany that could best withstand the aspersions of opponents. A symbolic level also existed, of course. *Germania's* articles attempted to both bring Catholics from the periphery to Berlin as well as to cast national attention on these border areas in efforts to pinpoint the heart of Germany. By arguing for the indispensability of places like the Rhineland and Westphalia—thoroughly Ultramontane regions—the articles clearly countered constructions of the nation that marginalized or actively excluded Catholics. From the beginning, this alternative construction placed Catholics firmly in the heartland of the nation, even when that sometimes required a stretch of the (geographic) imagination. Given the newness of the *Reich* to all citizens in 1871, however, highlighting local Catholic events as nationally important held significance beyond just opposing the ideas of *Kulturkämpfer.* It also served to make the new Germany less abstract and more recognizable to Catholic readers themselves.[103]

The connection of these efforts to the integration of Catholics in the new *Reich* was not limited to their more immediate and direct countering of exclusive constructions of the nation and providing Catholics with a recognizable version of the new Germany. Though quite oppositional to the emphasis on homogeneity preferred by liberals and the Berlin-centric focus of the government itself during the 1870s, the Catholic argument emphasizing regional—and the accompanying religious—variation as the soul of Germanness itself ultimately had much in common with the *Heimat* idea that became central to imagining one's self a part of a national community later in the *Kaiserreich.* By the 1880s and 1890s, the adoration of local *Eigenart,* the assertion that 1871 meant German life now "pulsat[ed]" in every small village, and the notion that to have a Germany one needed "Frank[s], Swabian[s], and Bavarian[s]" were all points well known and rehearsed by Catholics who had lived through the *Kulturkampf* as the cultural argument linked to the Center Party's federalist stance in the face of Bismarck's centralization.[104]

SEVEN

Femininity and the Debate over the
Guiding Principle of the Nation

IN AN APRIL 1874 letter to Gerhard Schneemann, a Jesuit living in the
Netherlands at the time, fellow priest and historian Johannes Janssen wrote
of his mixed feelings about the situation in Germany. On the one hand, he
felt optimistic about how the Church would weather the attacks of the
Kulturkampf. Yet, apprehension pervaded his mood when thinking about
the fate of the *Reich*: "It is just that as a patriot I am so very sorry the
German *Volk* is being so ruined in its noble qualities that it has still preserved from the past, above all that the youth is being so de-Christianized
and corrupted *(entsittlicht)*." Janssen mentioned a specific example of this
moral ruin from recent events in his own Frankfurt: a drunken eleven-
year-old boy had stabbed his sister. This was also to be counted among the
"marvelous 'fruits' of this struggle," Janssen sarcastically reminded his
friend.[1] Indeed, Janssen saw the example as indicative of a larger moral
blight affecting even the highest circles of government and politics. One
needed only look at how the leading *Kulturkämpfer* acted to know that
"behind these blokes is nothing other than brutal force." Driven by the
basest of urges, they could no sooner do the right thing than a dog could.
Only force mattered to such people.[2]

Janssen provided his most extended critique of the new Germany's
direction in his monumental *Geschichte des deutschen Volkes seit dem
Ausgang des Mittelalters*.[3] Though initially conceived in the 1850s and
occupying the scholar up until his death in 1891, Janssen's massive study

received the greatest impetus from the events of the 1870s, when the first two volumes were completed.[4] Though the immediate topic was the late Middle Ages, as the title suggests, Janssen clearly used the tumultuous events of that era as a proxy for those of his own time in which massive changes were occurring in Germany. After detailing all of the strengths of cultural, economic, and political life under the Holy Roman Empire during the Middle Ages, Janssen explained how this all led to the disasters of the Thirty Years' War. Writing in part to defend the Middle Ages against the critical treatment it received in non-Catholic accounts, Janssen not surprisingly made connections between the decline and Luther's Reformation.[5] The actions of Protestants came off as largely destructive. At the same time, Janssen did not spare Catholics of all blame either. More importantly, Janssen located the primary reason for the undermining of medieval society not in the religious but in the legal sphere:

> Above all else the disastrous effects, already glaringly apparent by the end of the fifteenth century, of the newly introduced, foreign pagan-Roman law imposed themselves here, which stood, in principle, in opposition to the entirely Christian-Germanic legal and economic system, . . . This opposition must be clarified and in particular the influence foreign law wielded on the development of princely absolutism [and] on the cancerous damage of all later molding of German life, already long before the outbreak of the revolutionary movements of the sixteenth century, must also be discussed.[6]

In this formulation, Janssen cast the conflict as one between German and foreign, Christian and pagan, tradition and deviation.[7] Though *Geschichte des deutschen* could not escape being labeled as "Catholic scholarship," its inclusion of the religious aspect of this conflict as only one among many allowed it to gain acknowledgement from certain Protestant critics, including mention of Janssen's evenhandedness on confessional topics.[8]

According to Janssen, Roman law began rapidly replacing the indigenous Germanic version from the middle of the fifteenth century. This stemmed in part from the attraction it held for rulers, emperors and princes alike, as Roman law gave the state ultimate authority. Contrary to "the Christian-Germanic legal view" that recognized law as ultimately coming from God, the transplanted system recognized only the role of the state, as had been the case under the pagan emperors of Rome. Hence, far from being guided by any morality, law became merely another tool at the disposal of the state. Janssen particularly noted how the princes of the empire began to usurp more and more power for themselves. Yet they could not have done it alone. Ultimately, Janssen laid blame with the "plundering lawyers."[9] These men's "idolatrous worship of the foreign law" made them argue that princes were above even the Church itself "long before the outbreak of the Church schism."[10] Once the jurists shunted God and morality aside, law no longer acted as a protection against injustice and a check on depravity. Power-hungry princes, willing to do anything to advance, became traitors and destroyers of an era of greater moral consensus, bringing to an end a period of peace during which the empire had been a protective shield for all of Europe. The only thing that mattered was force, nowhere more apparent than in the violent battles of the seventeenth century. Ultimately, for Janssen the conflict boiled down to one between morality and might, with the latter ethos unfortunately prevailing at the end of the Middle Ages. Having the ravages of war still fresh in their memory, readers were to take Janssen's account as both a work of scholarship and a cautionary tale, an example of a mistake not to be repeated by the new *Reich*.[11]

Janssen was hardly alone in his concerns or in drawing upon a "lesson from history" to make his point.[12] Articles in *Germania*, for example, went further and recounted history from antiquity to the present in much the same terms. Back in pagan antiquity, the Roman Empire led the world by force, recognizing nothing other than its own power to dominate. In such times, "war [was] not an emergency, but a normal state."[13] Only with the rise of the Church and the Holy Roman Empire did peace become the norm, with Christian morals protecting weaker entities from being completely overrun as they had been in earlier times. The Empire remained on top as long as it held to these "noblest political ideas" that cultivated "Christian teaching, Christian morals, [and] Christian thinking." But with the growth of the "pagan Renaissance culture and the unhappy [religious] schism in the sixteenth century," Europe also saw the end of "German splendor and German leadership."[14] The Protestant princes, determined to gain the upper hand against the emperor no matter what the cost, went so far as to ally with Germany's "traditional arch enemies," including the French. Just as in the *Geschichte des deutschen Volkes*, this complete abandonment of Christian morality in favor of unlimited power led the people to the horrors of the Thirty Years' War.[15]

Not surprising given the more general readership of the newspaper, *Germania* made the connections between the calamities at the end of the Middle Ages and the present situation even more explicit. Articles continued to recount the history of Europe after the Thirty Years' War as one only freed from the catastrophe of the seventeenth century by a delicate balance of powers *(Gleichgewicht)*. Still this amounted to only a fleeting respite since this system was nothing more than another regulated completely by power, which had to remain carefully parceled out among multiple countries. The first failure of the balance of powers came with Napoleon's conquests at the beginning of the century. The second began with Prussia's victories in the 1860s. Now Europe would be at the mercy of whoever happened to be strongest, especially distressing considering that could change: "Russia and Germany alone have control over war and peace in Europe, and our part of the world is protected from the arbitrary use of power of one empire only by the jealousy of the other. Should in any given moment this rivalry cease to exist, so all of Europe would be left to the will of one man, an [entire] part of the world would be given laws from the study of a single statesman."[16] Hardly a comforting thought to any of the peoples of Europe, *Germania* asserted.[17] Hence, though some might envy Germany for being at the forefront (even more than Russia) of this new era and ushering in the German epoch, articles cautioned against such a view. What was the point of being on top if the opportunity was being wasted by not leading according to "the highest ethical ideas"?[18] Instead, guided by the ideas of liberals, the "modern" age—with its "preference of power over right" that left power "no longer bound to the eternal laws of morality and religion"—had actually brought Europe right back to where it started, always in fear of the next war. It had merely replaced the pagan times of the Roman Empire with those of *Neuheidenthum*.[19] In the articles of *Germania* as much as in the larger point of Janssen's history, the beginning of the new *Reich* was turning out to be as much a series of wrong turns and missed opportunities as the end of the old one.[20] If the country remained on this course, which was becoming more and more set by the day, the future could not hold anything much better than the fate that befell Germany during the Thirty Years' War. True patriots, Catholic arguments stressed, could not stand by and let that happen. Just as one statesman could set down the law for all of Europe if no one stood in his way, the same individual—Bismarck, though not named specifically— would also do it for Germany unless someone stopped him. Completely devoid of principles, the liberals had allied with Bismarck and could not be expected to do it. Conservatives better understood what was needed, including the important role of religion, but had largely become irrelevant, both politically and within Protestantism itself.[21] Catholics, at least as their arguments portrayed it, were Germany's last hope.

It was in this context that Catholics asserted a different definition of what the new Germany should stand for. While Catholics stressed that they too had died for the nation in the war against France, they took issue with the militarism they saw pervading all aspects of society. Morality, not might, should be the first principle in Germany. In their view, this represented a continuation of the traditions of the old *Reich*; this charac- terized true Germanness. Such arguments did not always remain free of anti-Protestant sentiment, to be sure, but this element usually remained in the background, like it did in the earlier volumes of Janssen's *Geschichte*. More commonly, Catholics tended to identify liberalism, the enemy of all Christianity, and the Bismarckian state as the real culprits in promoting the corrupt idea of might makes right.

In addition to detailing the Catholic arguments in this debate over what the guiding principle of the new nation should be, this chapter high- lights the inseparable coalescing of elements of this argument against an alleged excessive reliance on raw force into a concerted effort to produce an alternate construction of identity that ultimately gendered the nation as feminine. One might see this potential gendering already suggested by Janssen's chosen example to represent the moral decline of the *Reich*: a boy who stabbed his sister. Of course one can never know exactly why the historian specifically chose to cite that case. Maybe that the assailant and the victim were siblings caught his attention. Possibly their youth shocked him. Perhaps no other violent crimes occurred that week in Frankfurt. Nonetheless, this pairing of the aggressive male and the wronged female appeared so often in Catholic arguments over the direction of the new *Reich* during the 1870s that the implications for the gendering of the nation cannot be overlooked. While a sizable body of literature on the role of gender in national constructions already exists, much of it focuses on masculine conceptions of the nation. Several scholars have shown the connection between femininity and Catholicism, both as a reproach made by opponents and as a statistical and cultural shift occurring from the feminization of religion.[22] Yet the positive feminine imagery associated with Catholic conceptions of the nation and Germanness has largely been untouched.[23] In part, this feminine depiction stemmed from a desire to counter the dominant national identity—imbued with masculine imagery—being proffered after unification. The approach also reflected real constraints facing Catholicism during the *Kulturkampf*, however. At the same time, the use of feminine imagery had long-term roots in the more general situation of Catholics throughout the nineteenth century in Germany.

Protestantism, Militarism, and Masculinity in German National Identity

Obviously, Protestantism played a significant role in many aspects of the construction of national identity undertaken during the 1870s, including the emphasis on militarism and masculinity. In part this stemmed from the population statistics. In the Holy Roman Empire, Catholics formed a majority. In the German Confederation, the confessions balanced each other out. With unification in 1871, however, Catholics sunk to a mere one-third of the population.[24] The exclusion of Austria in 1871 precipitated this significant reversal, giving Protestants greater strength in numbers. Moreover, Prussia not only had a large Protestant majority, it was also identified with Protestantism both by outsiders and internally by the most influential groups in society.[25] Of course, it was Prussia that dominated the newly created Germany, unified through war under the auspices of Bismarck, a Protestant, and "ruled by self-consciously Protestant emperors."[26] While varying constructions of national identity could adapt different aspects of the image of Wilhelm I to suit their needs, the importance of the emperor as head of the Protestant Church as well as commander of the army should not be underestimated in visions of the nation attempting to exclude Catholics.[27]

The connection between the Protestant imprint on the construction of identity and the role of militarism appears prominently in the creation of Sedan Day, the closest thing Germany had to a national holiday.[28] Occasioned by the efforts of various Protestants, most notably Pastor Friedrich Bodelschwingh, it never received official sanction as a national holiday.[29] Nonetheless, the connections between the volunteers who organized Sedan Day festivities every September 2 and those in government, as well as Wilhelm I's scheduling of ceremonial events on the same day, lent the holiday a "quasi-official" approval.[30] While Sedan Day fit with the way Protestants chose to construct national memory, it did not for Catholics.[31] Catholics commonly remained distant to Sedan Day festivities, contemptuously referring to it by other names like "Satan's Celebration," and instead chose to celebrate specifically Catholic events.[32] The inclusion of obvious anti-Catholic rhetoric in the festivities gave them little reason to celebrate, nor did the conception among many Protestants of the military triumphs over Austria and France—Sedan Day commemorating the later event specifically—as "Victories of the Reformation and Protestantism" against Catholic countries.[33]

Certainly many of the earlier advocates of Sedan Day never conceived of the holiday as a celebration of the military, and often liberals continued to commemorate the day largely devoid of heavy militaristic overtones.[34] Yet Wilhelm's undertakings, such as the ceremonial beginning of construction on the Lichterfeld cadets' school or the yearly parading of the Berlin troops on Sedan Day, clearly linked the holiday to a celebration of the military.[35] After all, the day itself commemorated an important military victory.[36] This emphasis on the military in the foundation of the German Empire was prevalent beyond Sedan Day as well. The *Kaiserparaden* centered on a display of martial strength, and monuments drawing on the imagery of the military sprang up to embody national memory in stone.[37] Unification—seen as the result of a series of victorious wars waged by Prussia—earned the military greater prestige, and even among bourgeois liberals who had earlier been more critical, the esteem attached to soldiering and becoming a reserve officer increased.[38] Prussia led, of course, because of its might: it was "the strongest of the strong."[39] This connection between nationalism and the military via war was hardly new (nor a distinctly German phenomenon). The long nineteenth century began with such a connection in the fight against Napoleon, an association that would have long-lasting effects throughout the century.[40] While the importance of militarism in German national identity should not be considered all encompassing, it was undoubtedly significant.[41] More importantly for the consideration of how Catholics attempted to posit different constructions of national identity, this became a major issue that they latched onto in their opposition.[42] As the historian Janssen complained, "in the new German *Reich* almost nothing counts more than the Jew and the *Pickelhaube*," the spiked helmet worn by military men.[43]

The creation of the dominant German national identity also revolved around men and drew mainly upon male imagery. Obviously the importance ascribed to the military in unification meant a preference for those who could soldier: men.[44] The "nation was seen as a fellowship of men," and women's inability to serve militarily provided yet another rationale for their less than full inclusion.[45] Along the same lines, contemporary notions of gender proclaimed that men, not women, acted and acquired. Men had reason and rationality. The public sphere belonged to them to shape as they would.[46] Men embodied what the nation stood for, a connection made in other countries too.[47] Contemporaries expressed this common gendering of Germany and Germanness in everything from the manner in which they built monuments to the way they wrote literature.[48]

In this highly Manichaean system of representation, those allegedly not part of the nation became feminized in the imagery of identity.[49] Both the French enemy and the Jewish outsider could be labeled feminine.[50] Likewise, the coding for Catholics became feminine. Not only did priests lack manliness, but Catholicism in general bred femininity. The religion based itself on feeling, not reason, and at the behest of priests, women could play far too disruptive a role in the public sphere by goading their husbands to vote for the Center Party. In contemporary terms, such alleged femininity barred Catholics from full inclusion in the national community.[51]

Protestantism, militarism, and masculinity combined prominently in the construction of the Hermann Monument in Detmold. Situated in the Teutoburg Forest at the site where the battle was thought to have occurred in AD 9, the monument commemorated the total defeat of Roman soldiers by the rebellious Gaius Julius Arminius, better known as Hermann of the Cherusci.[52] Viewing the battle as a reclamation of Germany for Germans, nationalists viewed Hermann's victory as the foundational act in their construction of memory.[53] While architect and sculptor Ernst von

Bandel made his initial sketch of the Hermann statue in 1819 and the construction of the actual monument began in the 1830s, the project was only completed in the new *Reich* in 1875.[54] The funding of the monument indicates the multiplicity of actors involved in creating national identity in the nineteenth century: not only citizens' organizations, the *Reich,* and the Kaiser, but also German patriots living in foreign lands.[55] Furthermore, earlier on the monument had garnered support from members of both confessions, with a notable contingent of advocates during the *Vormärz* coming from the Catholic areas of Bavaria. By the midst of the *Kulturkampf* in 1875, however, the unveiling of the completed monument proceeded with the marked exclusion of Catholics.[56] While this was not the initial idea and some Catholics did try to fit Hermann into their own versions of national memory, precedent had long existed for this association of Hermann with Protestant Germany.[57] Even before the Reformation itself, German humanists invoked the figure of Hermann in their efforts to assert themselves *vis-à-vis* their Italian counterparts as well as to challenge the abuses they associated with the Roman papacy.[58] Especially in the context of the *Kulturkampf,* the connection between Hermann and Protestantism was unmistakable.[59]

While an earlier design of the Hermann Monument posed the figure with his sword downward, Bandel's final creation stood with weapon raised.[60] Given the general importance placed on the military for unification, the choice of a more aggressive posture hardly surprises.[61] Hermann fit with the general trend of monument building in the *Reich* that glorified the military.[62] Connected with this militarism was the wish to "embody the nation in a human figure,"[63] a task that could in this context only be accomplished by a male symbol: Hermann, "*man* of the army,"[64] with his "phallic" sword.[65] The weaving into national memory of the values of Protestantism, militarism, and masculinity resonated not only with those responsible for creating the monument but also with significant numbers of the populace. Compared to others, the monument to Hermann received a sizable number of visitors.[66] More importantly, the image of the monument was spread further through its inclusion on goods packaging and in use as a logo.[67]

Of course, this is not meant to suggest that the imagery in German national memory, even when focused on this dominant form, was only about Protestantism, militarism, and masculinity. Germany also needed femininity. Alon Confino has emphasized this in the emergence of *Heimat*, gendered feminine, during the 1890s.[68] Indeed, femininity had long played a role in the creation of Germanness. The mythical figure Germania was a favorite symbol in nationalist literary and visual arts.[69] Karen Hagemann has pointed to the importance in the formative imagery during the Napoleonic Wars of both genders: warrior men were valorous because they could protect their honorable womenfolk.[70] Women were the wives and mothers, the embodiment of hearth and home, for which German men worked and fought.[71]

The masculinization of Germany and Germanness was not about a complete irrelevance of femininity in the national memory. It was about how each gender was included. When national imagery concerned men, it was about Germany as an active subject. When national imagery concerned women, it was about Germany as a passive object. This conformed completely to the dominant gender polarities of the period: men acted, women were.[72] Even when women attempted to create a larger role for themselves in the nation, they often continued to contribute to this division that limited their representation in imagery and reality.[73] As Confino writes in his discussion of gender, "Fatherland and nation, therefore, could go to war, while *Heimat* could never do that."[74] The pairing of Fatherland and nation together under the gendering of male concurs with Hagemann's research for the Napoleonic period: "The familialization of the concept of the nation did not contradict the simultaneous tendency towards militarization and masculinization, but was rather a necessary part of it."[75] Just as women were second to men in contemporary society, they were subsidiary to them in the dominant national imagery of the 1870s.

Catholicism, Morality, and the Revalorization of the Feminine

Catholics posed their own idea of what Germany should be to fight more exclusive conceptions of national identity promoted by opponents and also to articulate their role in the new *Reich* for themselves. Obviously, they rejected the Protestant identification of the nation. They also countered the other elements that had been so prominently linked in the creation of the dominant national imagery of the 1870s. Catholics continued their criticism of Prussian, and now German, militarism. Instead, they emphasized the importance of morality, commonly demonstrating this in their conflict with the government by advocating passivism. Ultimately, this formed part of a more general rejection of the masculinity permeating the mainstream national identity, with Catholics turning to feminine imagery instead. In this case, however, it was not femininity as object, but as subject.

That Catholicism, as opposed to Protestantism, should reach for the feminine as subject was probably more likely even outside of the particular circumstances of unification and the *Kulturkampf*. As George Mosse notes, masculine representations of the nation appear less commonly in Catholic countries than in Protestant ones (among which he tellingly includes Germany). Even though these female icons in Catholic countries likely consisted of representations as objects, not subjects, it is an important insight. Mosse suggests a connection between female national icons in general and the Virgin Mary, emphasizing her maternal, soft qualities that served to further underpin the dichotomy between men and women in imagery.[76]

Undoubtedly, it was this idea of the Virgin Mary that brought succor to many Catholics during the nineteenth century. Yet they knew another side of the Virgin too. She appeared strong, at times angry, and could mete out severe punishment when necessary.[77] In punishing or rewarding, Mary was powerful. Protestant critics of the Catholic Church did not completely miss the mark when they identified the inordinate power ascribed to the Virgin Mary. The official distinction made between Mary answering a prayer herself—which she did not according to the Church—and acting as an intermediate and passing it along to Jesus to respond to was not very clear.[78] To the individuals praying it probably made little difference. This was a Virgin Mary who not only deserved love but also commanded respect. Veneration of her became increasingly prominent in nineteenth-century Catholicism. Pilgrims who had once travelled to local sites began to favor more distant ones dedicated to the Virgin Mary, and religious organizations devoted to her worship increased.[79] The tough times of the *Kulturkampf* brought multiple claims of Virgin Mary apparitions.[80] From this ubiquitous Mary, Catholics could draw on the imagery not only of the traditional mother figure, but also of the strong woman, an actor in her own right.

Catholic experiences of communal conflict, in a setting of more general disadvantage in Prussia and other German states in the period leading up to and after unification, also lent themselves to a particular understanding of the role played by gender.[81] In interactions with Protestants, the Catholic community could identify with the injured, female party, though the frequency with which this occurred must have varied as the confessional composition of the region varied. Mixed marriage disputes, not a private matter given the social divisions between the confessions that they transgressed, could bring out the gendering of sides. One priest involved in a confessional dispute about an illegitimate child, for example, concluded, "Catholic priests, parents, and families in the area around Siegen really have a [valid] complaint that, as it appears in the often arising cases, the Protestant boys set out to seduce Catholic girls into an illicit life, to impregnate and disgrace [them]."[82] Even when relations between the genders and confessions were legitimized, Catholics considered themselves disadvantaged by the manner in which the legal code was structured. In Prussia, for example, a notable issue was the law regulating the confession of children from mixed marriages: as a rule they should be raised in the religion of the father, not the mother.[83] The results of this could be damaging, as a priest from Krefeld concluded:

> Protestant officials from the old provinces buzz over like swarms of bees into the new . . . [and] work their way into the most respected and affluent Catholic families [via marriage]. By the power of the Cabinet order, through their offspring [they] devour the religion and with this also the properties of the Catholics and thereby gradually set themselves up as the rulers of the country.[84]

Based on his impression that mixed marriages usually meant the grooms came from the opposing religion more often than not, the priest feared that Catholic mothers would increasingly bear Protestant children.[85] Eventually the entire footing of Catholicism would be undermined. While concerns about the unequal gender distribution between men and women in such confessional interactions could be discussed in terms of a more typical idea of men trying to protect their womenfolk, in the particular case of Siegen Catholic fathers trying to protect their daughters it also carried the implication of Catholicism in its entirety being imagined as a female in the designs of an aggressive Protestant male.

Moreover, Catholics could also draw upon the image of the woman as a significant actor in the face of Protestant advantage in mixed marriage conflicts. Midwives appeared in accounts as an ally of Catholic mothers in issues concerning how offspring were to be baptized. The mother would have been weak and often did not attend the baptismal ceremony anyway.[86] The midwife's physical proximity to both mother and child made her a likely source of help. Complaints tell of fathers who learned only after the fact that the attending midwife had already taken the baby to the local priest for baptism. The *Wochenblatt für Kreis Bochum*, for example, reported the case of a Catholic baptism being surreptitiously performed on a Protestant man's child from a mixed marriage. The article merely labeled the culprit as "a certain female individual."[87] Given the repeated mention of midwives undertaking such actions in records of baptismal disputes from the period, however, it is likely that this general reference was one the article's author felt most readers would understand.[88] In the case of a man named Thiemann, he only discovered the initial Catholic ceremony after taking his daughter and having her baptized Antonie Dorothea by the pastor. He then found out that the Catholic register already listed her as Anna Dorthea, the name given to the child when the midwife had earlier snuck out with the baby and took it to the priest for baptism.[89] Of course neither the imagery of the Virgin Mary nor the associations of Catholicism as the female in confessional conflicts was exclusive of more traditional gendering ideas among Catholics. Yet they did provide more complex strains of gender imagery that could inform Catholic national memory when the promotion of the feminine became more explicitly understood in terms of Germany as subject.

Beyond issues of communal conflict, women were playing an increasingly prominent role in the Catholic religion. Part of a more general pattern across the confessions and affecting countries beyond Germany during the nineteenth century, this feminization of religion meant that women began outnumbering men in religious orders and comprising a larger percentage of the lay practitioners.[90] Catholic women involved in philanthropic endeavors increasingly permeated society in roles such as teachers and welfare workers.[91] The feminization of religion even influenced the issue of who claimed to have seen apparitions of the Virgin Mary, as female visionaries finally became more common than their male counterparts in the nineteenth century.[92] While these women, like most others during the nineteenth century, often found expression in undertakings that conformed to the gender differences held in society, they nonetheless afforded themselves more active roles.[93] Moreover, they were roles that did not go unnoticed. As Catholicism had experienced a far lesser degree of secularization over the century and the Center Party was intimately concerned with religion, German Catholics were more inclined to draw inspiration from events in the Church and to draw upon strengths coming from the religious sphere. This stood in marked contrast to Protestantism, which had been more affected by secularization and many of whose members did not necessarily look upon this as a negative occurrence.[94]

As the situation moved closer to unification in the 1860s, Catholic discourse reacting to the rise in Prussian power focused on the state's heavy reliance on force and on the military. Alongside a number of other groups skeptical of Prussian expansionism that included particularists, democrats, and workers, Catholics spread the term *"Militarismus"* to decry what they saw as a heavy-handed use of inappropriate force via troops, but they also extended the critique to the general organization of society, including economics.[95] The critique expressed the sense of generalized violence and lack of respect for rights that they believed was overtaking Prussia, though some pointed to this militarism as a wider European phenomenon as well. Furthermore, Catholics argued that it was not merely a problem limited to the traditional proponents of the military found in the *Junker* elite, but had become part and parcel of the modern, capitalist society run by the bourgeoisie. Yet the criticism of Prussian militarism cannot be separated from its anchoring in the horror felt towards very real military conflict, with the war between Prussia and Austria in 1866 being formative.[96] In the eyes of contemporary Catholics, the ultimate reliance on force by the (after 1866) unquestionably dominant Prussia, however, was also considered a danger in domestic politics.[97] Catholics expressed their opposition in the pages of the *Historisch-Politische Blätter für das katholische Deutschland*, for example, and demanded an end to this militarism.[98]

Hence, by the founding of the *Reich,* there were already ideas and experiences that could inform the creation of a definition of Germany and Germanness among Catholics that preferenced feminine imagery in connection with the emphasis on morality over might. Even before the *Kulturkampf* drove Catholics to pointedly emphasize this oppositional understanding of Germany, an intimation of this alternate gendering appeared in the title chosen for their new national paper established in December 1870. With the name *Germania,* Catholics also chose to emphasize their ancient lineage in the nation by drawing upon antiquity as Protestants so often had with Hermann. Yet they linked themselves to the oldest name known for Germany, a name embodied by the mythical Germania, a female icon of the nation, instead.[99] Germania was a multifaceted female icon. She could be a seated lady or a motherly figure of the nation, yet she could also be seen valiantly defending all that was German. Importantly, however, she did not represent the military figure that Hermann did.[100] Of course the Catholics realized the importance the title they chose would have, as opponents would thoroughly scrutinize it in all of its connotations. The name *Germania* proved no exception, as a discussion in one edition indicated, and the newspaper even had to defend against accusations that it chose a Latin version of *Deutschland* to emphasize the power of Rome in the new nation.[101]

While many notables had already developed critiques of what they saw as destructive militarism, the *Kulturkampf* brought more general attention to the topic, as Catholic publications portrayed it as another example of the reliance on violence, now turned inward. Papers like the Bavarian *Augsburger Postzeitung* highlighted the issue from the very start.[102] Militarism, the paper claimed, posed a fundamental threat to "the German national character."[103] Even *Germania,* which had initially downplayed concerns over militarism in the unification process, targeted the excessive reliance on force in all sectors in the *Reich,* including the treatment of Catholics.[104] Earlier articles sounded almost like pleas to stop the impending catastrophe: "We could only lament it in the interests of the state itself, if the German government were to provoke a fight with the Catholics, as the power of the bayonet [alone] cannot offer a state security for any length of time."[105] Indeed, *Germania* stressed the desire for peace on all fronts: "Externally the German *Reich* enjoys peace . . . may the same also be able to be said of the domestic circumstances!"[106] By 1872, however, there could be no mistaking the situation for anything but a war turned inward. Instead of the army, liberals and the government now primarily employed the domestic arm of militarism, using mainly "police measures" in the campaign against "dissenters."[107] Articles noted that the "battle" primarily targeted Catholicism but also "affected devout Protestants."

As the above reference to the "bayonet" of the state suggests, the words used to describe the government's campaign against the Catholics emphasized the militaristic, violent nature of the acts: "There is no longer any doubt. One wants the battle, the oppression, and the persecution of the Catholic Church in Germany. It is condemned without being heard. One declares war against it, the battle to the bitter end [bis auf's Messer]!"[108] While Catholics were merely trying to protect themselves by any "means" (Mitteln) possible in this attack, other parties were using the "most impermissible, dishonorable weapons."[109] Catholics returned to the Blood and Iron so important in unification, but now asserted they would be on the receiving end of the "brutal violence" in the next battle.[110] Of course such references also highlighted the role of Bismarck in both campaigns. It was with the same use of war imagery that Catholics defended their unwillingness to participate in celebrations once Sedan Day emerged as a holiday: "And when the happy time of inner peace and holy unity . . . returns with God's help, then and only then do we, too, want to take part in a holiday. . . . Then we, too, want to take part in a national celebration. Until then it is not the time for a celebratory fuss because of an *external* victory that was followed by a great *inner defeat*. Until then it is not the time to rejoice and jest—but probably to *mourn* and *pray!*"[111] As Bishop Ketteler suggested, Sedan Day did not so much commemorate the victory over France, but a hoped for triumph in the current war against the Church.[112] In light of this contemporary language used to describe the 1870s, it is more apt to translate *Kulturkampf* as "Battle for Culture" with the more militarized connotation, as Margaret Lavinia Anderson has done.[113]

The charge of militarism applied not only to the actions of the government against Catholics but to the ordering of society in all aspects. Critics like Georg Pachtler continued to rail against "the [state's] claim on all human and material strengths and resources of the people for the sole purpose of war."[114] State budgets ballooned to support the needs of the military, financed by draining taxes on the populace.[115] While capitalists benefitted, the German people continued to sink into misery under the burdens.[116] Above all, Pachtler pointed to the moral consequences of militarism. During the course of their military service, some individuals would undeniably be bettered by military training, he admitted. Young men with particularly bad characters would at least learn order and punctuality. Yet any who had a good character would doubtlessly be ruined, carousing with buddies and (tellingly) seducing innocent young ladies. More generally, Pachtler criticized the disregard for people that militarism brought with it.[117] Only this could result from a system that viewed the world as a series of "power issues" that assumed "the strongest is in the right."[118] Like Janssen, he described this moral decline on an individual and *Reich* level as stemming from the abandonment of Germanic-Christian values of the Middle Ages, resulting in the rise of the state as the only source of all law.[119]

Certainly differences existed among the specific ideas of men like Janssen, Pachtler, and Majunke, chief editor responsible for all staff writers at *Germania*.[120] While Janssen had always been more open to Prussian leadership in Germany, one cannot miss the disdain for the northern power by Pachtler, a Jesuit born in Württemberg and exiled to the Netherlands in 1872.[121] The differences did not end there, nor were they absent among the various segments of the Catholic populace.[122] Yet the emphasis on unity during the *Kulturkampf* and the efforts of leading Catholics to make the various political and social organs of Catholicism inclusive meant such differences became muted during this period.[123] More notable than the variations during the 1870s is the consistent rejection of force as the guiding principle of the nation and the concerted effort to define the true Germany as one based on morality above all else. Indeed, objections to *"Faustrecht"* appeared in the works of men like Janssen and Pachtler as well as throughout the daily press and leading periodicals for Catholics.[124] Adherence to the statutes of the legal system, at least as they were being treated in the new *Reich*, did not solve the problem either. Laws only functioned if their genesis came from morality.[125] Bismarck, with his decision to "undertake *Realpolitik* and not *Idealpolitik*," did not understand this, nor did the liberals, who "want[ed] to preserve nothing beyond their own power" with their decidedly amoral

"*Interessenpolitik*."[126] Without morality, laws became nothing more than another extension of the state's uninhibited power, another weapon in its arsenal of persecution.[127] They could be changed to suit the state's latest needs without regard to any other principles.[128] Catholic arguments positioned themselves as the brake on this arbitrary rule of force. Ultramontanes, they argued, believed in more than *Real-* and *Interessenpolitik*; the state had "a moral function to fulfill."[129] This opposition between proponents of morality as a guiding principle and those who relied on force, as Catholics suggested the government and liberals did, formed the heart of the key question in the new nation: "What should count in Germany in the future?"[130]

While one might be inclined to see the government as the stronger contender of the two, Catholic arguments cautioned against relying on physical power in the face of moral force. Articles throughout the Catholic press repeatedly described how fragile and fleeting a system based on armies and police was in reality, a point driven home in critiques of militarism.[131] Catholics knew "that it is more difficult to defeat moral resistance than to triumph over physical obstacles, and that police measures are powerless against the former."[132] Moreover, without morality—and the religion necessary to instill it—even the most inculcated of the state's arms of power, the army, would quickly become unreliable and as corrupt as society in general was becoming.[133] Still, it was not only this alleged practical superiority that Catholics pointed to when they explained their own reliance on moral force. They relied on such methods because only those were worthy of their cause, which "represented the greatest moral interests of humanity."[134] Unlike their opponents, they were not willing to use any means to achieve their goal.[135] Hence, continuing the militaristic language of the *Kulturkampf* but rejecting the reliance on force at the same time, Catholic arguments promised that only "spiritual weapons" (*geistige Waffen*) would be used.[136] An article in *Germania* posed the contrast in both principles and methods even more clearly when it quoted Saint Ambrosius as saying, "Against weapons and soldiers, tears are my weapons."[137] These weapons could also be more tangible, of course, including the "press, associations, and public meetings," which would be "far more effective means" than "the fist."[138] Accordingly, Catholics asserted they would not merely win, but "morally destroy" their opponents.[139]

In efforts to exclude Catholics from the new nation, liberals drew upon the general association between women and religion set up in the dichotomy of traits between the sexes and labeled their opponents as feminine.[140] Yet even as they countered this exclusion, Catholics obviously argued from a position that embraced religion as necessary for proper national development. Hence, by setting up Church versus troops and morality versus force, Catholics were doubly identifying themselves with feminine qualities, as nineteenth-century society likewise tended to code morality as feminine. Already in the Napoleonic Era, the contrast between men and women in national imagery meant that " '[v]alorousness' became the masculine, and 'morality' *(Sittlichkeit)* the feminine 'character trait' *par excellence.*"[141] More generally in national symbolism throughout the century, "feminine virtues held society to its moral goals, while man was the soldier, the heroic figure who translated theory into practice."[142] Indeed, Windthorst himself explicitly made this connection, referring to woman as "called upon to be the guardian of religiosity and good morals."[143] Yet if the pairing between military men and moral women had often complemented each other in national imagery, the use by Catholics of the claim to represent the moral high ground took this coupling and produced a very different message: now soldiers destroyed morality.[144]

This identification with the feminine, portraying Catholics as the quintessential bearers of morality in the new German nation, did not remain on the level of discourse composed for public consumption. Catholics gendered themselves feminine not only by their identification with morality but also by how they chose to counter government attempts to oppress them in actuality. Catholic leaders, both religious and secular, gave the utmost importance to the use of non-violent, passive means of resistance.[145] Indeed, passivity appears to have been decided upon as a formal position in face of government suppression.[146] Beyond formal decisions and public pronouncements, private correspondence also indicates the commitment to this position. Regarding the centenary celebration for Daniel O'Connell, for example, the priest and Center parliamentarian Christoph Moufang praised the fellow Catholic most for helping coreligionists in Ireland by opposing the government "in peaceful ways and with spiritual weapons."[147] Though occasions did arise in which crowds grew restless and boiled over into acts of aggression, the overwhelming character of the resistance eschewed such acts.[148] Of course, nineteenth-century gender assumptions categorized passivism as a trait more generally and also in specifically military contexts that denoted an aversion to war as feminine as well.[149] While passive resistance as a tactic was neither an exclusively Catholic approach nor did it always conjure up such strong associations with femininity, it did in this context.[150] Indeed, Catholics sharpened this general association with more tangible links to a feminine gendering. Flowers, so commonly associated in the nineteenth century with femininity that literature written by women was condescendingly referred to as "flower verse" *(Blumistik)*, became ever-present in public displays of support for the Church and resistance to the government.[151] They were placed in Catholics' windows and presented to clergy as they were celebrated on their release from jail.[152] Women took center stage in the resistance to the government in general, resulting in far-ranging implications: "Their [women's] loyalty to the Roman Church with acts of religious faith and state resistance and more fundamentally Catholicism itself gendered as a woman defied the strictures of society organized according to public or private."[153] This real activity by Catholic women was further highlighted by reportage giving it particular coverage. Indeed, *Germania* boasted that they had nothing to fear from women being in the fight.[154] It reasoned the government could not win against a group "whose women even did not shrink in the face of the superior strength of an enemy power and happily hurried over in sympathy with their men to sacrifice themselves for the common cause."[155]

The tactics of the Center Party to represent Catholics gendered as female could go beyond supporting the symbolism of masses of women protesting peacefully in the face of Prussian troops. It not only encouraged women to become involved in promoting the party's cause, but members could also invoke the ideal of "the Catholic woman" when trying to give authority to their message. Far from referring necessarily to real women's opinions, however, this was "a useful political fiction into whose mouths commentary was put whenever a Centrum author or speaker wished to interject the voice of healthy common sense, or indeed, the voice of the community as a whole."[156]

This "feminine" passivism was set in sharp contrast to the heavy-handedness of the state. *Germania* rhetorically questioned the actions of the "statesman," most certainly Bismarck: "It is asked, is it chivalrous to set oneself, with the enormous material aid of the state that he has at his disposal, in battle against people, who only can and wish to counter him with passive resistance?"[157] Not surprisingly, dishonorable behavior towards women specifically became a particular issue. During the First Spanish Republic, one article detailed the attacks of "'liberal' German knaves" on the Spanish *Infanta* Maria. Pointing out that Maria herself was German, as her mother was Princess Adelheid von Löwenstein, the article chastised the way many liberal papers wrote negatively about the *Infanta*. Alluding to the question of inclusion in the nation, it asked "should there really still be a knave in the German Fatherland who is not ashamed of the affront committed?" It urged such men to "honor women!"[158] While the case involving the *Infanta* tended to revolve more around words, more commonly examples focused on the repeated actions against the "defenseless women" living in convents who were being thrown out in the streets.[159] While Catholic women were not afraid to go up against a stronger opponent, *Germania* nonetheless asserted that the state should be ashamed to "declare war even against the world of women."[160] In doing so, such arguments both went against and with the grain of gendering in the nineteenth century.

This imagery of passive, Catholic femininity versus militaristic, (Protestant) state masculinity corresponded to the reality of the situation as well. Actions by troops and the police to break up Catholic gatherings during the *Kulturkampf* were certainly oppressive and at times became frighteningly violent.[161] For example, Julius Bachem reported the violent use of force against pilgrims at Marpingen, leaving some injured, in an article written for the *Historisch-Politische Blätter für das katholische Deutschland,* the same journal that Catholics had used beginning in the 1830s and 1840s to counter Protestant versions of history and in the 1860s to develop their critique of Prussian militarism.[162] At times even liberals could be shocked by the severity of the *Kulturkampf*.[163] Complaints abound in the archival files from the period of cases in which the police swept in to end meetings, if not worse.[164] Even just the shock from the rapidity with which the authorities pressed for dissolution of religious houses struck those involved as incomprehensibly heavy-handed and added fuel to the already heightened tensions in the Catholic community at large. The mother superior of a branch of nuns in Marienthal bei Mün-ster, for example, repeatedly protested the "force" used to drive her com-munity of "defenseless women" from their "dear Fatherland," pointing out that even "non-civilized peoples and governments" would have given more consideration to the "weakness and defenselessness of [their] sex."[165] Imagery, bolstered by harsh reality, posed the choice between the position of the state and that of Catholics plainly: guns versus flowers, a form of opposition that has often resonated among people in favor of the latter.

Finally, Catholic imagery also gendered Catholics as feminine by using the trope of the raped woman in wartime. Unfortunately, war has com-monly involved sexual assault, but unlike under other circumstances, war-time rapes are not primarily about the women affected but about the entire enemy community.[166] As Ulinka Rublack indicates for the early modern period, the description of wartime rapes often centered on the responses of the men who could not prevent the violation of their wives and daugh-ters.[167] Hagemann discusses the impact of male fears that French soldiers would rape German women in the creation of a masculine nationalist dis-course around the role of men as warriors capable of defending their wom-enfolk.[168] In Catholic discourse concerning confessional conflict there had also been recourse to the imagery of "violated Maria," referring to the Virgin Mary and the need to defend the Church.[169]

Already in the middle of 1871, *Germania* predicted what would be in store for Catholics during the impending conflict: "the Catholics of Germany" would be "in constant danger of violation *(Vergewaltigung)*."[170] This use of the word *"Vergewaltigung"* (violation or rape), commonly employed in descriptions of the government's actions against Catholics, not only played into the militarized language of the conflict with its inclu-sion of the root *"Gewalt"* (force or violence) but also highlighted the gen-dered nature of the battle. The word would similarly be used numerous times over the decade, even paired in cases with other suggestive terms. An article in the *Schlesische Volkszeitung*, for example, suggested that only true respect for the law—something Catholic arguments always claimed liberals had no hint of—drew the line between similar ideas, tellingly including the example of the difference between *"Leidenschaft"* (passion) and *"Vergewaltigung."*[171] Indeed, the allusion to the sexual aspect of the gendered battle was heightened by additional references to offences against women's honor. A review of a play about Hermann of the Cherusci noted not only the dubious historical accuracy of the work but also that it degraded German values, including "chaste female sense."[172] *Germania* described the Sisters of Charity as a "blossom" to be destroyed by the "rough hand" of the state.[173] Set among such articles asserting only Christianity raised up women from a position as mere objects of "sensuality" (versus their place in antiquity and in the *Neuheidentum* of the liberals) and that religion was necessary to curb excessive desires, the sexual imagery of defloration was impossible to miss.[174] Beyond the daily press, folksy works such as those by Alban Stolz continued to add to this context in pieces like *Schreibende Hand auf Wand und Sand* (1874), where he detailed multiple cases in which saints' images were attacked. All five cases that he chose to describe involved the Virgin Mary, including one in which a soldier suggestively yelled up at her picture, "You've stood up there for a long time, wouldn't hurt a thing if you laid down in the grass once."[175] Given the multiple ways in which the arguments of Catholics portrayed themselves as feminine, however, this Catholic use of the trope of rape during the *Kulturkampf* did not focus on male actors attempting to defend female victims. It did not speak primarily of the need to protect others, though that could be an element, but of Catholics themselves being the victims.[176] This, again, produced imagery that gendered Catholics as a group as feminine.

This chapter has examined the efforts by Catholics to define Germany in a manner opposed to the construction relying on Protestantism, militarism, and masculinity permeating the culture of the newly unified Germany, especially from liberal and official activities. There were many possible sources that suggested an identification with the feminine for Catholics and from which Catholics could garner imagery of women that both confirmed but also transgressed the boundaries of traditional gender divisions. In particular, the relationship with the Virgin Mary, the experiences of communal conflict, the feminization of religion and Catholics' continued referencing of this sphere, and the development of a critique of militarism contributed to this pool of memories from which this opposition could be constructed. Yet while these may have provided material for the creation of a Catholic definition of Germany based on morality and on the feminine, the importance of the *Kulturkampf* has to be acknowledged for its role in rousing Catholics into a concerted effort to champion this particular understanding of the nation.

The attempt to assert an identity that emphasized religion hardly surprises given the lesser degree of secularization within Catholicism and the long-term proclivities of Catholic nationalism.[177] That morality would become a linchpin issue and that passive resistance would be used by Catholics was also relatively foreseeable. The invocation of morality by victims of oppression is hardly revolutionary. The use of passive resistance underscored this moral high ground, though the fact that the state's physical and political power over Catholics left them little other choice should not be overlooked.[178] What is perhaps most striking about the construction of national identity analyzed here is how it used feminine imagery. Considering the labeling of Catholics as feminine that was used to exclude them from the nation and the general acceptance of the larger context of the division of society into separate spheres (undoubtedly by Catholics too), this assumption of the feminine gender was a rather striking departure. Yet Catholic efforts did so not only by association with the female coding of morality and passivity but also by consciously representing the community as feminine in acts of opposition to the government that presented both the symbolic and the real participation of women. When they wanted to legitimize their speech for the community as a whole, they portrayed it as the opinion of a Catholic woman. Using the trope of wartime rape, as they truly did see the *Kulturkampf* as militarism turned inward, rhetoric took up this feminine gendering for Catholics to underline that might did not make right, regardless of what the state did. This revalorization of the feminine exemplifies Foucault's point that the very same words and categories in a discourse that are used by one group to control another can be turned around in resistance.[179]

Contrary to nineteenth-century sensibilities, this feminine gendering did not exclude Catholics from Germany—at least in their definition of it—or from representing the nation as subject. Catholics were not only part of the nation because of their claim to a German lineage more ancient than that of Protestants but also because they were necessary for the proper development of the nation, as the history of the *Reich* had shown. Without Catholics and their link to the true German past, Germany's future would continue down the path of militarism and social debauchery. Accordingly, it needed the Catholics because they were the bearers of morality. Only by including them in the nation could Germany gain this moral impulse. Only with this moral impulse could Germany use its greatness for a true German epoch and become what it was meant to be. This morality, however, was integrally linked to and based on the representation of Catholics as feminine, a gendering even bolstered by the choice of Germania as an icon in the national memory. Catholics did not deserve inclusion in the nation in spite of this femininity, but because of it. It was this construction of national identity that allowed Catholics, gendered feminine, to represent what the nation should be, to represent Germany as subject.

Of course, imagery is not reality.[180] This departure from a masculine gendering of Germany as subject cannot be taken as evidence of an equally enlightened change in practice. Though women gained greater room for activity in their charitable work and participation in acts of resistance to the government, the fact remained that the authors of articles in newspapers like *Germania,* the priests organizing events, the politicians of the Center setting the program for political Catholicism, and the people voting for them were all men. Moreover, just as other strains of national memory were being constructed and accepted by the same groups that promoted Protestantism, militarism, and masculinity, others existed within Catholic imaginings of the nation too, though only in the background during the 1870s.

It appears that this national identity centered on a feminine Germany as subject faded after the stress of the *Kulturkampf* passed.[181] According to the research of Norbert Busch on imagery in Catholic piety, for example, representations of Jesus during the *Kulturkampf* became highly feminized, but after the conflict and its effects subsided, there were attempts to transform the image of Jesus into one conveying more masculine qualities.[182] This coincides with Confino's situating of the decline of Sedan Day—as well as its militaristic masculinity that Catholics were trying to combat—and the transition to emphasizing a more inclusive identity via references to *Heimat.*[183] The evolution of the use of *"Vergewaltigung"* as a word in *Germania* articles also indicates that the promotion of a feminine Germany was closely linked to the pressure of the *Kulturkampf.*

Articles employed the term numerous times throughout the decade to describe the situation of Catholics in Germany and elsewhere. Yet "*Verge-waltigung*" appeared less and less as articles expressed more confidence after the middle of the decade, even though many of the issues initially described as "violations" still remained. Tellingly, by the end of the decade, *Germania* applied the word not to Catholics, though hardly out of the woods yet, but to the liberals.[184] This connection between the stress of the *Kulturkampf* and the feminine gendering of Germany as subject indicates that just as times of crisis can produce circumstances in which established oppositions among people within a community are diminished, they also have the same potential to mute traditional divisions in the realm of symbolic representation.[185]

The Catholic approach to the debate over the fundamental guiding principle of the nation during the 1870s represents a defining of Germany and Germanness that, although ultimately short lived, nonetheless adds an important element to understanding the heavily conflict-ridden process of nation building and the alternative gendered images that could accompany it. Furthermore, its legacy for the long-term integration of Catholics did extend beyond the *Kulturkampf* itself. Although Catholic rhetoric could certainly be exclusionary, such as that against Jews, it usually did not equate the corrupting influences on the *Reich* with Protestantism. Specifically in the debate over the guiding principle of the nation, the main emphasis remained on the conflict between Christian morality and un-Christian disregard for it. This as well as the complete abjuration of violence undoubtedly made later efforts to forge national unity less difficult.

EIGHT

The Battle over Schools and Scholarship

IN 1872, A new edition of Center parliamentarian August Reichensperger's book *Phrasen und Schlagwörter: Ein Noth- und Hülfsbüchlein für Zeitungsleser* appeared.[1] Though Reichensperger had written the original in 1862 and had put out only one more edition since that time, the drastic change in the social and political climate produced by the *Kulturkampf* prompted him to offer readers a significantly enlarged version.[2] Despite the changed circumstances, Reichensperger's intentions remained the same: he wanted to expose what he saw as the shaky foundation of German liberals' ideas. A prolific writer, Reichensperger believed that words mattered. He even included a saying by Pius IX on the title page of his book: "One must give words back their meaning." He saw no better way to lay bare the problem of German liberalism than by providing a detailed account of the many terms that had become perverted by liberal usage, especially in the press, resulting in a system of thought and practice in which no distinction was made between "right and wrong, good and bad, truth and lies."[3]

Formatted as a small dictionary providing entries for over 120 terms, *Phrasen und Schlagwörter* posed as a scholarly cataloging of words whose meanings could no longer be taken for granted. Indeed, "to the degree that concepts have changed and turned themselves inside out," Reichensperger claimed that the average person needed assistance deciphering what terms like "tolerance" or "civilization" signified anymore.[4]

Phrasen und Schlagwörter could provide much needed aid to the new nation's newspaper readers. Through explanations that included references to philosophical ideas, examples from history, and quotes from contemporary thinkers, the book systematically detailed how liberals used key terms. For any shortcomings that might arise throughout the work, Reichensperger begged pardon, as "the keen insight and methodology of one like Linnaeus would hardly suffice to bring order to the muddle."[5]

At the same time, Reichensperger used a tongue-in-cheek tone throughout the work. As he explained the words as used by liberals, Reichensperger attempted to make clear to his readers the absurdity of it all. The twists and turns in the definitions and the need for countless qualifications served to highlight what he saw as the illogical liberal viewpoint. By employing the form of a dictionary, he lampooned the scientific manner in which liberals often presented their viewpoints. As Reichensperger's main audience was Catholics, not liberal newspaper readers as his introduction facetiously suggested, the humor resulting from this tactic served to further underscore the charge of liberal absurdity. *Phrasen und Schlagwörter* allowed Catholics not only to laugh at Reichensperger's jokes but also at liberals themselves. The combination proved successful, as demand for the book prompted the Catholic publisher Schöningh to release two more editions within six weeks.[6]

Just as Reichensperger chose a two-pronged approach to making his case, using both humor and facts, he identified the basis for his insight on quite disparate sources: common sense and *Wissenschaft* (which depending on the context can be translated as "science," "scholarship," or "knowledge").[7] The latter itself needed explanation, however, as Reichensperger believed *Wissenschaft* had changed and deserved an entry in the book as well. "Not often achieved and difficult to attain," the *Wissenschaft* Reichensperger based his work on had little to do with what he argued liberals commonly meant by the word.[8] His much rarer *Wissenschaft* was the "traditional" kind that had developed over centuries and "blossomed in the universities and monasteries, institutions established by the Church."[9] Employing this type of *Wissenschaft*, Reichensperger hoped to show readers clearly that the current usage of the term bore no relationship to the old one. Instead, *Wissenschaft* was now "modern" and "free." It based itself "absolutely on its own feet," not bothering with the traditional sources of knowledge.[10] Not so much the university as an institution but the "liberal professoriate" formed the base for this new *Wissenschaft*. This group's "infallibility had taken the place of the infallibility of the Church" in all matters, allowing it to make authoritative pronouncements on all possible subjects.[11]

Reichensperger's *Phrasen und Schlagwörter* exemplifies the Catholic approach to battles over education and, more generally, knowledge during the *Kulturkampf*. The arguments had a basic, common-sense element backing them. They could champion the common man (or woman, as the previous chapter has shown) as a source of deep wisdom, while parodying those considered educated (*gebildet*). Yet there also existed a more complex argument, one that not only invoked the ideals of *Wissenschaft* and higher education, including the much vaunted idea of *Bildung*, but also tried to demonstrate a mastery of the techniques that led to good scholarship, self-cultivation, and ultimately the ability to know the world.

Many works of scholarship on how the larger issue of education formed a central battlefield during the *Kulturkampf* and how it also linked up with debates about national identity exist. Accounts, from general works like Thomas Nipperdey's *Deutsche Geschichte* to more detailed treatments like Marjorie Lamberti's *State, Society, and the Elementary School in Imperial Germany*, have largely focused on the importance of primary schooling.[12] When discussing secondary schools and universities, or the related ideas of *Bildung* and *Wissenschaft*, scholars often emphasize Catholics' distance to, or even outright rejection of, these. They cite factors like the connection made by contemporary Catholics between *Bildung* and heavy-handed Protestant Prussianness.[13] Scholarship mainly suggests that the attention of leading Catholics turned towards realms associated with higher education in the 1890s, also a time by which modes of national integration had indeed become far more inclusive of them by focusing on flexible points of identity like *Heimat*.[14] Accordingly, only by this later decade did any notable impetus within the Catholic populace develop that urged greater attention to the dominant (Protestant) notions of culture concerning education, promoting involvement with "modern" issues like *Wissenschaft* and a change in the types of books borrowed for reading.[15] Scholars associate this change with the increased attention to the parity question from the Center Party during the 1890s.[16] This decade saw the use of "scholarly objectivity" by Catholics who had long been largely absent from the fields of *Wissenschaft* linked with the modern production of knowledge.[17] For the earlier decades of the *Kaiserreich*, however, the emphasis remains on points such as the conversion of many Catholic professors after 1870 to Old Catholicism, the resistance to the education of priests—unlike Protestant clergymen—in universities, and the efforts of the Church to discount many of the results of research that were seen as cutting edge in the scholarly community.[18] Even well after these early years, Catholics, it has been suggested, preferred to define themselves by values other than those like achievement in higher education.[19]

Certainly, as this existing scholarship shows, Catholics did not have the same relationship to education and viewed the fundamental basis of knowledge and its production differently than Protestants. Hence, the Center Party always fought most vociferously over legislation affecting basic education. Moreover, real disparities in levels of schooling between the two groups, to the advantage of the Protestants, undoubtedly existed.[20] Though there were individual exceptions, there was no Catholic counterpart to the vibrant Protestant *Bildungsbürgertum* that defined German education and research during the nineteenth century.[21] Greater efforts by Catholics to integrate themselves into a Protestant-dominated academic world did see advances in the 1890s, but even this did not meet huge success during the imperial period. Yet this chapter offers greater complexity to the more general picture of Catholic distance to education, especially at higher levels, during the early years of the *Reich*. While the attention of political Catholicism in the legislature focused on *Volksschule* policies, the larger argumentation put forth to represent the Catholic viewpoint on education saw the problem as embedded in a far more extensive complex of issues. Indeed, the Catholic position expressed greater acknowledgement and appreciation of the importance of education, including more specialized endeavors linked with the active production of knowledge, than existing scholarship suggests. Considerable reluctance to accept liberal Protestant ideals more generally did not preclude at times championing values like *Wissenschaft*, as Reichensperger did in *Phrasen und Schlagwörter*. On the one hand, this involved establishing differences from how liberals had come to view such concepts. On the other, however, it meant invoking many of the same ideals of scholarship as liberal Protestants did. Catholic defenders nonetheless insisted that it was their scholars, not the "liberal professoriate," who truly understood how to implement these ideals. In doing so, especially given the association of Germany with academic excellence in the nineteenth century by both those within the new nation and without, Catholics were claiming to embody true Germanness.

German Education and Scholarship

"In the nineteenth century," so Thomas Nipperdey wrote, "Germany became a land of schools."[22] Here he referred to the rise of compulsory schooling and its impact on the development of modern Germany. Yet his statement applies just as much to the perception that contemporaries had of Germany, or of Prussia especially.[23] Other countries saw Germany's prominence bolstered as much by schools as by factories and troops. Educators elsewhere attempted to emulate the German educational system.[24] Though the internationally applauded ideal of, for example, the Prussian elementary school system may not always have corresponded to an equally efficient reality, the achievements of German educational institutions cannot be denied either: by the beginning of the *Kaiserreich* a "reading revolution" had occurred, increasing literacy rates from around 25 percent in 1800 to encompass approximately 87 percent of the populace.[25] The dramatic accomplishment in just seventy years cannot be overstated. Real successes and continued renown meant that the education system featured prominently in Germany's exhibits during both the 1893 and the 1904 World's Fair.[26]

Higher education, especially, received international acclaim, producing a flow in and out of Germany. The German university model and the ideas being developed within the academic community there traveled to other countries to be adopted; students from elsewhere came to study in Germany.[27] Part of the strength of German universities stemmed from numbers: nineteen existed in the newly united *Reich*.[28] More fundamentally, the extensive reforms undertaken early in the century to reinvigorate education led to both the perception and the reality of excellence.[29] Led by men like Wilhelm von Humboldt, it was these early nineteenth-century reforms—undertaken during a time of nascent nationalist sentiment and in part as a measure against French domination—that revolutionized the university.[30] The University of Berlin, founded by Humboldt and ultimately taking his name, came to be recognized as the leading institution during the century.[31] Having studied at multiple institutions, theologian Philip Schaff concluded that "the University of Berlin occupies the first rank of all similar institutions in Germany not only, but in the world."[32]

In particular, the German educational system came to be noted for the quality of scholarship it produced.[33] The prominence of German *Wissenschaft* spanned the gamut from achievements in the humanities and law to advances in the sciences and medicine.[34] So much cutting-edge research came out of Germany that considerable discussion in the international scholarly community took place in German.[35] No doubt the reputation of German universities meant they attracted prominent scholars to undertake first-rate research. Practical conditions, such as generous funding, might also be noted as contributing factors.[36] What contemporaries—at least Germans—often saw as the reason for scholarly success, however, lay more in a particularly German way of thinking, or as philosopher Friedrich von Schelling called it, "the German mind."[37] Hardly surprising given the context in which university reforms occurred, this idea of a quintessentially German way of thinking that defined the nation's scholarship and, indeed, led to its high quality did not pass with the Napoleonic threat but continued to be repeated by subsequent generations. Rudolf Virchow, for example, believed that his countrymen produced better research than the French because of a particularly German way of thinking.[38] Hence, long before unification, education played a significant role in defining Germanness.

The founding of the nation only increased the salience of educational issues. As the repute of German education and scholarship grew over the century, so did the importance of these defining characteristics.[39] The nation had more basic links to education and scholarship as well. The common rudimentary education that increasing numbers of people received as the nineteenth century continued, such as in the Prussian *Volksschule*, fostered similar experiences that, on a basic level, could bind ever larger groups together.[40] Likewise, the *Gymnasium* also fostered commonalities among students in different states. This resulted not only from sharing similar experiences but also from the curriculum of the schools, with its emphasis on the universal and attention to general knowledge. While the numbers affected by this remained limited by the exclusive nature of the

Gymnasium, those marked by it often belonged to the groups most supportive of and active in nationalist efforts.[41] *Gymnasium* graduates also
could go on to attend university, the place where education perhaps most
tangibly helped form a national community. Students moving from one
university to another fostered a certain harmonization of general standards
throughout the network of German institutions, something most notably
required in fields like law, where the individual might go on to practice in
yet another place entirely.[42] Moreover these mobile students forged real
connections among individuals from disparate places, relationships that
could revolve around organizations such as the *Burschenschaften* and
could be quite strong.[43] Hence, it hardly surprises that students and professors commonly supported nationalist causes.[44] The relative weakness of
Hapsburg universities can be considered a factor in the ultimate success of
the *kleindeutsch* version of Germany.[45]

The greater importance of education and scholarship also came from
attempts to use them as tools for the inculcation of the German identity
that needed to be created after 1871. This more targeted utilization of the
system to engender national identity had already been happening since
the beginning of the century.[46] Though speaking more abstractly, Goethe
and Schiller had also exclaimed, "Germans—you hope in vain to become
a nation. Therefore, you can do it, educate yourselves to become a freer
people!"[47] After 1871, efforts to imbue students with a sense of Germanness only increased. Though still controlled by individual states, schools
nonetheless concerned themselves with fostering national identity as
well.[48] Attempts to Germanize other ethnic minorities in the *Reich* also
often centered on primary schools and language education.[49] Universities
could be used similarly. Hoping to reverse efforts to Gallicize Alsace that
had just been undertaken by the French earlier in the century, before the
Reich gained the territory in the Franco-Prussian War, the German government tried to staff the university in Strasbourg with ardently nationalist professors who would not fail to inculcate a corresponding sense of
national identity in both students and the local populace.[50] While real
limits to the effectiveness of such tactics existed, they were tried nonetheless.[51] Beyond language policies and the examples of specific institutions,
scholarship more generally was used to engender national identity. Not
only more obvious fields like *Germanistik* but also those such as biology

played a role in the efforts to define Germanness.[52] Commonly noted in the scholarship on national identity, the field of history had an especially large role, from the debates between scholars like Ficker and Sybel to the more general influence of popular accounts and historical fiction.[53] As the situation had drastically changed after 1871, education, in its many forms, enabled people to come to know the new nation, shaping how they understood Germanness both factually and ideologically.

The confessional divide produced distinct educational patterns for Catholics and Protestants. Catholics largely attended the *Volksschule* and went no further. While this remained the case for Protestants more generally during the century, a significant number completed higher levels of education at the *Gymnasium* and university. Contemporary sources reported widely on this educational deficit *(Bildungsdefizit)*, a point that often found its way into religious and political polemics. Though these polemics often included unsubstantiated causes (and effects) for the disparity, they also pinpointed a number of relevant factors.[54] Practical reasons often played a large role. Cost, for example, was one. Education at higher levels involved not only school fees but also other expenses, such as money for activities in university social groups. Consequently, students came mainly from wealthier families.[55] Catholics, of course, tended to be poorer than Protestants. Location also made a difference. Catholics tended to be rural dwellers in comparison with Protestants and lived mainly in areas that did not have easy access to a *Gymnasium*, the first step to university entrance. Higher education remained largely a preserve of urban Protestants.[56] Catholics also found it hard to break into higher education, as it tended to be a self-perpetuating system. Educated fathers had educated sons. The most obvious way this disadvantaged Catholics came in the form of absence: priests, unlike Protestant pastors, did not pass on their proclivity for learning to children.[57] The impact becomes even greater when considering that enrolled Catholics disproportionately tended toward the faculty of theology, which was also one of the less expensive study programs.[58] Beyond these practical reasons, discrimination played a role in keeping Catholics out.[59] Hence, though education allegedly favored merit over birth and wealth, it hardly surprises that the affluent, urban bourgeoisie formed the bulk of those considered educated *(gebildet)* during the century or that, among Christians, this group consisted almost exclusively of Protestants.[60] The rarity of educated, middle-class Catholics makes it difficult to talk of a Catholic *Bildungsbürgertum* at all.[61]

Values also factored in the educational deficit. *Bildung*, that which in part came from a *Gymnasium* and university education, mattered to Protestants in a way that it simply did not to Catholics.[62] A difficult word to translate, *Bildung* could be rendered as "education" or "culture," though "self-cultivation" might be best as it also captures the active role of the individual in the process that the *Bildungsbürgertum* so often stressed.[63] Though *Bildung* involved active development on an individual level, it also emphasized general knowledge and universalism.[64] While not the same as *Wissenschaft*, it was closely linked to scholarship as a form of self-cultivation, though tensions would later become obvious as research grew ever more specialized by the end of the century, producing conflicts with the emphasis on general knowledge.[65] *Bildung* was connected with many other elements as well, influencing reading habits, interest in the arts, and even fostering certain architectural styles.[66] The ambiguous role of religion, however, formed the biggest hindrance to Catholic identification with the value of *Bildung* in this sense. For many of the educated, *Bildung* served as a replacement for traditional religion.[67] "Modern" scholarship often posed contradictions with the Bible, repelling some believing Christians and instead attracting those with weakened faith.[68] The greater degree of secularization among Protestants meant they formed the majority of those in the latter group.[69] At the same time, *Bildung* also contained religious elements even in the nineteenth century.[70] Alongside Humboldt, theologian Friedrich Schleiermacher had played a fundamental role in educational reforms earlier in the century.[71] Indeed, many saw educational reform as initially beginning with a religious event: the Reformation.[72] Of course, this religious element also dulled Catholic interest, as the traditions prominent in the institutions associated with *Bildung* were Protestant.[73] The rising neohumanist emphasis in *Gymnasien* and universities on Greek language and culture in the nineteenth century, for example, served as an alternative to Latin-centered studies that were associated with Catholicism.[74] This is not to even detail the many social values associated with these institutions that gave them a Protestant flavor, such as the integral role dueling—an act Catholics refrained from due to the pope's pronouncement against it—played in student life.[75]

For most Catholics, the Church and its traditions occupied the place that *Bildung* did for the Protestant bourgeoisie.[76] Especially as the nineteenth century progressed, Ultramontanism dominated Catholicism in Germany and stronger regimentation by the Church structures conflicted with many aspects of *Bildung* lauded by the Protestant bourgeoisie. While Catholic theology retained its place in the university during the century, it tended to restrict scholarly inquiry more than its Protestant counterpart, for example, and the influence of the even more regimented seminaries increased.[77] Well-known actions against theologians like Georg Hermes and Ignaz von Döllinger restrained dissent.[78] Even beyond theology, the Catholic Church attempted to exercise greater control over the intellectual pursuits of the entire flock by methods such as forbidding the reading of certain books. One should not overestimate the actual effectiveness of such methods.[79] Yet, the different approach within Catholicism to education in all its aspects cannot be denied.

Despite the reality of the *Bildungsdefizit* and the different value system promoted by Catholicism, Catholic attempts to create a national identity could not simply ignore the larger subject of education, even if they had wanted to. People identified Germans with educational excellence at all levels. Liberals, dominant in politics and in nationalist activities, held *Bildung* sacred. Not just something difficult to translate linguistically, *Bildung* expressed something particularly German, as the French and British middle classes did not have any true correlate value.[80] In the polemics of the *Kulturkampf*, liberals hammered home their claim to this German value. Their rhetoric portrayed Catholics as incapable of true membership in the nation because they were not cultivated enough to have attained political maturity.[81] Hence, the importance of education, extending far beyond primary school policies, for German identity was too great for Catholics to ignore it in their efforts to provide their own definition of Germanness.

Separate but Equal: Catholic Arguments for Confessional Schools

Catholic arguments on education often focused on the bread and butter issue of primary schooling.[82] This formed a major concern for both confessions in the 1870s and more generally throughout the century.

Complaints of contemporaries to local officials regarding confessional conflicts commonly revolved around primary schooling issues. A parent could initiate the complaint, often reflecting disagreement between spouses of different confessions as to which school their child should attend. The disputes easily grew into larger affairs, as clergyman, often also serving as school inspectors, became involved in protecting what they saw as the child's best interests.[83] Of course, they understood the fight related to the larger task of preventing attrition from their own confession. A concern that plagued clergymen throughout the century, souls gone astray could be lost to the other confession or to secular life, both allegedly dreadful outcomes, and at least from the Catholic viewpoint, increasingly linked developments by the latter part of the century.[84] Not just the impact of religious instruction would be lost by a child switching schools. Everything from who staffed teaching positions to which books a pupil learned grammar from combined to educate the student as a member of a particular confession. Hence, non-confessional schools (*Simultanschulen*) likewise elicited opposition from parents and clergy, who feared these allegedly non-religious elements would in reality be controlled by the other side.[85] Instead of choosing a nearby questionable school, parents often had their children walk to another community to attend one they felt could be trusted in every respect. The Catholics in Niederkostenz, for example, fought to keep sending their children two miles away to the school in Kirchberg, despite the difficult path between the two communities causing frequent absences during the winter and leaving many children sick from daily exposure to the elements.[86] Especially after 1871, new legislation affecting education and the increased attention to creating Germans only heightened the importance of primary schools, where the majority of the nation's new members would be educated.[87] The stakes were high, and everyone knew it.

Under these circumstances it hardly surprises that Center politicians spent considerable time on the issue of primary schooling. Already in earlier decades education repeatedly formed a central rallying point of Catholic political efforts in the states, such as Prussia in the 1850s under the leadership of the Reichensperger brothers or Baden in the 1860s by Catholics reacting to the struggle with liberals already underway there.[88] Windthorst himself devoted energy to educational issues in his early political career in Hanover.[89] Even at the end of the 1860s as political Catholicism was reorganizing and realigning itself in Prussia, it still high-lighted school policy, a focus also evident in the formation of the national Center Party.[90] An election manifesto from 1870 (*Soester Programm*) needed no more than two words to convey its position on basic education: "confessional schools."[91] With the advent of the *Kulturkampf*, the atten-tion only increased, as the government (in Prussia more so than the *Reich* generally) targeted Church influence on education. From the opening salvoes on the education front with the School Supervision Law of March 1872 to the piecemeal banning of thousands of priests from offering religious instruction that only received greater codification by decree in February 1876, legislation increasingly removed the Church from the classroom.[92] Of course, these policies often represented reform attempts that were not necessarily confessionally motivated, and they affected Protestants too. Yet the lesser extent to which officials applied them to Protestants and the bias of some laws designed specifically to address perceived Catholic problems—such as the insufficiency of priestly train-ing—also indicates their role in the struggle between state and Church.[93] Moreover, while the legislation angered many conservative Protestants, it never provoked the same degree of outrage from them or played the same defining role in their politics as it did among Catholics and the Center Party during the *Kulturkampf*.[94]

Mirroring the importance of the issue among the populace and Center Party leaders, newspapers devoted plentiful space to school policy ques-tions. *Germania* prioritized articles about primary education from the beginning, even before the onslaught of the *Kulturkampf*. Some articles remained straightforward, providing only basic factual reports. Others, however, went far beyond this. For example, when the district govern-ment instructed school inspectors in Wiesbaden to check that all local schools were using one of the two approved non-confessional textbooks, *Germania* reprinted the order in its entirety then proceeded to make the standard arguments for confessional education. While religious instruc-tion continued to be offered separately by confession, the article stressed that ignoring religion in other subjects taught from the non-confessional textbooks gave students an incomplete education. The issue of compre-hensiveness and the integral role of the Church in all education only scratched the surface. Underneath lay the freedom for communities to regulate their own local affairs and, more fundamentally, for parents to choose how their children would be instructed, in this case a choice clearly expressed in favor of confessional schooling.[95] While the particular books in question did not appear dangerous, the article warned against letting such issues slide. After all, the article argued, who knew where this could all lead? Non-confessional religious instruction could be introduced just as quickly as these seemingly innocuous textbooks. If it existed in Wiesbaden, could it not spread to the rest of the newly unified *Reich*?[96] Moreover, even if these particular texts were not so bad, *Germania* left no doubt in readers' minds that most non-confessional school books filled children's heads with lies. In Berlin itself, the newspaper reported, the city had distributed books considered appropriate for both confessions that spoke of issues like "the papal entity's profound loss of morality."[97] Omnipresent in *Germania*, this type of story was commonplace throughout the Catholic press.

Germania also reported on schooling in the newly acquired *Reichsland*, matching the central government's own recognition of Alsace and Lorraine as an educational hotspot.[98] Like in eastern areas with large Polish populations, students in Alsace and Lorraine supposedly needed extra attention if they were going to become good Germans. They were handicapped in Bismarck's eyes by not only their questionable state allegiance but also by their Catholicism. Hence, on both edges of the *Reich*, the government stepped up school supervision.[99] The new administrators in Alsace and Lorraine instituted curricular changes that promoted German language and culture as efforts to reawaken an alleged German essence of the inhabitants.[100] Many of these changes came under heavy fire from *Germania*. It detailed the prohibition of orders such as the Dames du Sacre Coeur from teaching, the training of instructors regardless of confession in the same institution, and the naming of school authorities who all, not coincidentally, were Protestants. Fully non-confessional schools, the article warned, loomed just around the corner. Again, the article noted that all this occurred against the express wishes of the parents and the individual communities. Though done under the banner of "national progress" and supposedly bringing German excellence in education with it, the schools had actually been better under the French. It hardly surprised, the article continued, that the local populace bore no great love for their new country, asking rhetorically, "What does Alsace Lorraine have to thank Germany for after three years?" If this is what being German was going to mean there, it was hardly worth it.[101] Given the role that educational excellence played in issues of national identity, of course, the article implied that the changes were not German at all.[102] Certainly the bigger point was that the *Reichsland,* controlled directly from Berlin as it was, showed everyone what the rest of the *Reich*'s future would be if nothing stopped the government.

The Same, but Better: Higher Education and Catholic *Wissenschaft*

Secondary schools also made the papers, though infrequently. Most notably, *Germania* included many articles on the conflict that surrounded Braunsberg's Catholic *Gymnasium* and its religion instructor, Dr. Wollmann. The Bishop of Ermland had excommunicated Wollmann after a disagreement over papal infallibility. From the Church's standpoint, Wollmann could no longer serve as religion instructor and should be removed. Concerned Catholic parents circulated petitions rejecting Wollmann, publishing them in *Germania* to rally support to their side.[103] As far as the state was concerned, however, Wollmann still held his post, which meant that Catholic students would have to receive their religious instruction from him. Initial attempts to resolve the issue met with little success, and ultimately the government cited problems over how the *Kultusministerium*'s Catholic section handled the affair as the reason for its dissolution in July 1871. Resolution came in 1872 under Minister Falk, when he exempted students from taking religious instruction with Wollmann and subsequently had the teacher reassigned elsewhere.[104]

While dealing with a higher level of the system, commentary such as that in the Braunsberg case could reflect the same basic arguments that commonly applied to primary schools. Yet Catholic efforts during the *Kulturkampf* to protect their rights and assert their German identity—intertwined but not identical goals—did not stop here. Moving beyond the often noted practical policy issues associated with the *Volksschule,* standalone publications, daily press articles, debates, speeches at public meetings, and the work of organizations all combined to address the higher ideals of self-cultivation, culture, and scholarship. In short, this marked a battle over the concepts of *Bildung* and *Wissenschaft*—what they meant and who represented them—that required a more complex argument concerning education.

Attempts to remedy the Catholic lag in educational achievements had begun long before the notable activities of the 1890s. Calls for a free Catholic university first appeared formally at the General Meeting of Catholic Associations in 1862.[105] Yet they had been long in the making even by that point. The devastation wrought to Catholic institutions during secularization also elicited calls for the reinvigoration of higher education to prevent Protestants from completely dominating the field.[106] The Reichenspergers spoke of creating a Catholic university in Prussia already in their early years as parliamentarians.[107] In 1854, Bishop Ketteler wrote of his concern over higher education, concluding that only by having Catholic institutions could the "scholarship [which is] almost a monopoly of unbelief" coming from the existing universities be combated.[108] Indeed, Archbishop Melchers believed the establishment of a Catholic university to be "a question of life and death for Catholic Germany."[109] Georg von Hertling, the man who would become central to fostering scholarship later in the century, also involved himself in many endeavors during the 1860s, such as organizing Catholic student associations at universities.[110] More generally, journals like *Der Katholik: Zeitschrift für katholische Wissenschaft und kirchliches Leben* attempted to showcase leading scholarship.

Certainly some of the Catholic support behind institutions like their own university reflected an attitude similar to the rationale used in arguments concerning primary schooling. On the most basic level, the demand desired separation, one believed necessary for an education reflecting the particular needs and outlook of Catholics, whether they be schoolchildren or university students. Badenese parliamentarian and higher education advocate Franz Joseph Buß insisted that existing institutions emphasized the wrong-headed value of "self-direction of the students," an approach that any future Catholic university would have to reject.[111] Indeed, a large impetus for a Catholic university came not from students but from parents seeking a trustworthy institution, another similarity to arguments concerning primary schooling.[112] For many supporters, their own university entailed not only Catholic students and professors but an expression of a fundamentally different concept of education.[113] This meant one that would undoubtedly lead to a different scholarship, one "in the Catholic sense."[114] Such scholarship would not add to the "inner restlessness and confusion, dissatisfaction with the existing and a desire for the new," which came from Protestant-style thought that overly glorified "understanding."[115] Such support for a Catholic university highlighted the relationship between religion and scholarship in all other areas, and in that order.[116] In this vein of thought, Catholic arguments posed knowing the world through study at all levels as something controlled by confession. Confession heavily imprinted scholarship every step of the way, leading to different results and processes for learning and scholarship for each group. Scientific scholarship, an ideal so vaunted by liberals, this clearly was not.

Just as calls for a Catholic university continued during the *Kulturkampf* so did reference to these underlying ideas. An article in *Germania*, for example, asserted that:

Religion rules all fields of knowledge, and there are hardly scholarly doctrines that do not stand under the influence of religious views. . . . Since there has existed a Christian thinking, all human thought is Christian or un-Christian, in sharp opposition of one to the other. Nothing in scholarship and art, that deserves such a name, remains untouched by Christianity, neither subject to it nor scandalously against it, and even a craft, when it raises itself above unimaginative mechanical activity, does not remain free of its beneficial influence. . . . Furthermore, it is not dogma alone that separates the Catholics from non-Catholics. How different the judgment, under the influence of the teachings of their Churches . . . , of the former from the latter proves over most historical events.[117]

Not surprisingly, this point came in conjunction with commentary about confessional schools as well. Likewise, it showed the same association—here only implicitly made—between Protestantism and the dangers of secularism.

Yet while such ideas about a religion-centered scholarship were not absent from the pages of *Germania*, they formed only one aspect of the

Catholic rhetoric on education. When dealing specifically with higher education and *Wissenschaft,* the argument that religion should dominate scholarship received scarce attention. Indeed, striking given the historiography is the paucity of such statements. While the sentiment also exhibited itself in general comments about society and religion—ones which when applied to scholarly life could suggest a controlling imprint coming from the Church—in the argument specifically on education and scholarship circulated in numerous different venues during the *Kulturkampf* beyond just the leading paper *Germania,* this attitude did not form a dominant discourse. Instead, the main line of thought expressed in Catholic arguments promoted a *Wissenschaft* undertaken by Catholics that was no less, and usually more guided by the universally lauded values and methods of rigorous scholarship than that produced by their opponents. The very future of the new nation, *Germania* argued, depended on this.

These ideas of a more complementary, not controlling, relationship between religion and *Wissenschaft* had many antecedents in the period before the *Kulturkampf* and Catholic attempts to form a national identity during it. Alongside the support for a Catholic university that stressed the need for total separation to enact a particular vision of education incompatible with that of non-Catholics even at the university level, for example, also stood backing for the institution that stemmed more from a recognition of the limited opportunities for advancement in the existing system.[118] One reason did not exclude the other, but neither did the two mean the same thing. Those who advocated for a different sense of scholarship almost certainly agreed with the need for a free university to allow Catholics to advance. Yet those who realized the limited opportunities the existing universities offered did not necessarily perceive the same stark gulf between Protestant and Catholic *Wissenschaft,* nor see the latter as controlled by religion. As the above quote from Ketteler in his 1854 treatise would suggest, he cited the lack of opportunities for Catholics as a reason to create their own university.[119] While emphasizing the issue of inequality may have in part been guided by the text's topic of legal protection for the Church, Ketteler limited himself to the same reasoning again in 1867, when he wrote from both a political and a religious standpoint: "We do not have any bearers of Catholic scholarship, no Catholic faculty, and therefore the efforts for the establishment of a

Catholic university are inherently so justified and for the life of the Church so necessary that they deserve general support and finally must lead to success."[120] Priest and theologian Martin Deutinger, considering the connection between the Church and various fields of study more generally, posed the relationship as one of give-and-take on both sides: "[Religion] may not exclude scholarship anymore than scholarship may renounce religion."[121] Georg Hertling, who despite his own difficulties advancing in the university system due to his religion, found the idea of a chasm between the two confessions' scholarly activities so wrongheaded that he referred to the "entire Humbug of the Catholic university." Instead, he believed that "one should above all else inspire love in our students for the existing universities and only create a remedy for the existing evils." Of course, even for a man like Hertling, whose views fell at the other end of the spectrum from those of men like Buß, religion still played an important role. Yet it was not one that needed to divide the confessions. Indeed, Hertling even thought that "the right way of philosophical research is suitable for leading to a bridge between Catholic and Protestant scholarship."[122]

The efforts of both liberals and Catholics to create a national identity and the importance of education to ideas of Germanness made the distinction particularly important during the *Kulturkampf*. Catholics themselves were aware of this fact, living as they did in a country "so generally praised" for its academics.[123] Espousing a scholarship incompatible with the existing system of higher education so integrally connected to the new nation would have been disastrous to Catholic efforts at dispelling the *Reichsfeind* (enemy of the *Reich*) accusation, not to mention being contrary to how men like Hertling actually felt. Of course, this did not mean a total silencing of variations within the Catholic camp. As the above quote from the leading newspaper *Germania* also indicates, arguments for one did not always preclude those for the other even from the same source. Generally, however, scholars note the uniformity that characterized Catholic efforts during the *Kulturkampf*.[124] In intellectual fields particularly, the literature stresses the stifling effect of the Syllabus of Errors, the dogma of papal infallibility, and triumphant Ultramontanism that in part contributed to this uniformity among believing members of the faith, as opposed to those considered merely Catholics in name.[125]

Certainly, these did pose serious difficulties for learned Catholic individuals, highlighting tensions that had always been there but became even starker during this period. One need only look at the massive conversions among the professoriate to Old Catholicism, which were more visible examples of a dissatisfaction that also spread among some educated Catholics who never converted but nonetheless felt ill at ease with the rising Ultramontanism.[126] Paradoxically considering the rising potential to stifle independent thought, however, and in part linked to this greater uniformity, the Catholic argument overwhelmingly encountered in public discourse concerning higher education during the *Kulturkampf* became the one de-emphasizing the excessively confessional nature of Catholic *Wissenschaft*. The underlying tension that had existed about how Catholic *Wissenschaft* should be understood, with the adjective distinguishing more so the product and especially the process leading to the scholarship or instead to the identity of those who created it, was increasingly decided in favor of the latter.[127]

In 1873, Ketteler wrote *Die moderne Tendenz-Wissenschaft (The Modern Ideological-Scholarship)*.[128] The treatise exemplified the direct connection the topic of scholarship had to the larger struggle raging during the *Kulturkampf*, as the book specifically sought to undermine the work of prominent liberal professor of law Emil Friedberg. Because Friedberg was involved with *Kulturkampf* legislation, with his scholarship promoting an interpretation that buttressed the government's position, criticizing his work meant attacking the state's policies too.[129] *Die moderne Tendenz-Wissenschaft* formed part of a larger exchange between the two men, since the treatise was written to counter a public response from the liberal professor to yet another text by Ketteler.[130] The bishop's book took the form first and foremost, however, of a treatise on scholarship. Already in the second paragraph, Ketteler wrote of Friedberg's response: "It offers us quite a perfect example of that more and more proliferating ideological-writing that acts like scholarship, but is just as far removed from true scholarship as Greek sophistry was from true wisdom."[131] Throughout the book, Ketteler repeatedly called Friedberg's work "alleged scholarship."[132] While the text certainly expressed complete disagreement with Friedberg's points, Ketteler emphasized the scholar's faulty methods, sources, and reasoning.[133] The logic of the professor's public response struck the bishop as so contorted that he characterized it as "Dr. E. Friedberg contra Dr. E. Friedberg."[134] Not only did Friedberg's argumentation defy logic, the professor wrote in a "coarse" manner that lacked all standards of professionalism.[135] Ketteler contrasted this all to the airs put on by Friedberg and other "alleged men of scholarship," concluding that they were hypocrites when it came to claiming that they, not Catholics, represented learning and culture in Germany.[136] Ketteler sarcastically asserted "that the 'intellect' that stands in danger of being exterminated [by the Church, according to liberal arguments] here is only the intellect of Dr. Friedberg himself."[137] While the bishop did not forgo a reference to the role of religion in scholarship, he waited until almost the end of the treatise to add: "One needs to have only a superficial knowledge of the Church and its scholarship in order to be convinced of how deeply it is filled with the awareness that belief is genuinely rational and true *Bildung* is the best friend of Christian truth."[138] Hence, the treatise posed the conflict as not between a Catholic and Protestant *Wissenschaft* but between a true and a false one. Ketteler concluded that it was Friedberg and (Protestant) liberals like him who did not follow the methods of scholarship so lauded by them.[139] The importance of the argument for issues of German identity could not have been lost on Ketteler either given that previously he had been attacked specifically for undercutting national ideals with even his relatively measured reasoning backing a Catholic university.[140]

Arguments taking a scientific approach and claiming greater validity than those of liberal scholarship did not remain limited to more specialized publications.[141] Indeed, articles expressing the same ideas filled the pages of Catholic newspapers. *Germania*, for example, recognized the central role of scholarship from the beginning. When discussing what the new German nation would mean for Europe and the world, the newspaper stressed that beyond politics "religion and scholarship are indisputably very much higher spheres of intellectual life."[142] The German epoch meant not only the rise of a new political power in Europe but also "the spread of its [Germany's] character over the other peoples," the realm of scholarship receiving specific mention in connection with this development. Far from being a negative for others, the "German way and German character" in "scholarship too, in art as well, [in] generally all

aspects of the mind" would bring better solutions to the current problems
in society that other peoples, like the French (who were singled out in the
article), could not solve.[143] Expressing confidence gained from recent
military success and hope for the new nation, *Germania* posed the
dichotomy as one between German and French scholarship, not Catholic
and Protestant. Religion remained important, but with—not instead of—
scholarship. Nor did the coming of the *Kulturkampf* sour *Germania*'s
outlook on the importance of scholarship. Repeatedly, articles invoked
"deutsche *Wissenschaft*" and other formulations of the special relationship between Germans and education, calling them the "most cultivated
people in the world" and a "nation of thinkers."[144] Sometimes the individual articles did use these phrases sarcastically. This did not represent
a disavowal of the ideal itself, however, but expressed disgust at how liberals were misusing it: "The much extolled 'German thoroughness' and
'German scholarship,' in which Catholic scholars have no part at all, is
becoming a downright mockery in the present religious struggles."[145]
Here the sarcasm also applied to repetition of the claim that backwards
Catholics had contributed nothing to the realm of scholarship, one often
employed by liberals.[146] Peter Reichensperger, for example, felt the need
to counter this widespread idea in a *Reichstag* speech by asserting "that
modern nations owe their entire *Bildung* and culture to Catholicism."[147]
Newspaper editors also took the allegation seriously and often countered
it by reporting on Catholic activity in various intellectual fields.[148] Given
the importance of staking a claim to Catholics' scholarly proficiency,
Germania even argued that the belief in miracles—something that
provided many Protestants with what seemed incontrovertible proof of
intellectual incompetence—had support from their "most detailed, scientific study of all fields of knowledge."[149] Throughout the *Kulturkampf,*
Germania insisted the conflict was not between scholarship and faith. It
was between true and false scholarship. Depending on the particular
article, the newspaper linked the latter with the French, socialists, Free
masons, and, most commonly, liberals.

Like Ketteler's treatise, *Germania* stressed that the scholarship of their
opponents was false not because it conflicted with the Bible—though
that was a byproduct of being wrong—but because of faulty methods.
The problems stemmed from employing "fishy" as opposed to "uncorrupted

sources" in research.[150] Playing fast and loose with the "demands of logic" also lessened quality: "Hypotheses are put forward, accepted as proven, and then arguing continues as if a sentence is therefore already right because it finds representation in a 'liberal' paper."[151] Such incompetence at basic research methods could only be called "scholarly carelessness."[152] Factual inaccuracies allegedly plagued liberal arguments. *Germania* reasoned that such sloppy work was unacceptable for someone who was "a representative of 'German *Wissenschaft*' in good standing" that addressed an "educated" audience.[153] To counter these inaccuracies the paper frequently offered—as one of its most valuable public services it believed—detailed, line by line corrections of these errors in scholarship and the pronouncements of the government based on them.[154] Because so much of the salient scholarship on the *Kulturkampf* involved statements about the Catholic Church and its doctrines, a particular focus in the pages of *Germania* became factual errors resulting from "the lack of knowledge in religious and Church matters shown by our 'liberals.'"[155] Many articles targeted Rudolf Virchow as a chief offender given his role in both scholarly and political life. *Germania* argued that even a man of his "talent and education" had no real knowledge about things affected by his support of *Kulturkampf* legislation. The paper found such ignorance hardly surprising given the sources consulted by men like Virchow: "The main and really richest library of our parity state does not possess at all, or only incompletely so, many of the most important written aids for information about Catholic matters." Still, things like this did not excuse the faulty methods employed in approaching the subject, *Germania* contended. When men like Virchow did not follow the "fundamental rule[s]" of scholarship, it resulted in a "disgrace of the 'thoroughness' and the moral solemnity of 'German *Wissenschaft*!'"[156] As opposed to supporting Catholic over Protestant beliefs, articles like these focused on issues in the "realm of facts," though the implications for the confessional struggle were clear.[157] *Germania* attempted to argue on scholarly grounds, not religious ones, that liberals' work (and corresponding legislation) had to be disqualified. An article responding to an account of saint veneration in an opposing paper began by clarifying what was to be achieved: "'Germania' is no Church paper and should not be one. . . . We mention right from the beginning that we do not intend [by this instruction] to appear as a proselytizer. . . . We simply want to explain to it [the other news-paper] that for the assessment of Catholic matters Protestant bias is not sufficient, but that, above all, a knowledge of Catholic doctrine is necessary. . . . We are far from demanding that a Protestant accept the inner correctness and truth of this [belief]—it takes more than mere study for that—but one could at least demand that Catholic doctrine would be reported by the opposing side objectively, in accordance with these discussions [by Catholic thinkers on the meaning of saint veneration]."[158] *Germania* concluded that all of this scholarly incompetence shown in attacks against Catholics "proves the talk about German *Wissenschaft* and its influence on life to be a lie."[159] Even beyond the realm of doctrine, learned liberal professors showed "examples of ignorance, [so bad they are] probably not possible by any Prussian Catholic clergyman."[160] Ultimately, *Germania's* point was that liberals, not Catholics, were being un-German in this case, harming chances that the German epoch would change things for the better.

Beyond issues regarding specific scholarship, *Germania* questioned the extent to which its opponents could claim to be *gebildet*. The newspaper pointed to problems even at the level of language. For example, some of the factual inaccuracies allegedly stemmed from false translations, particularly from Latin. An article on Virchow suggested as much when its author felt the need to include both the Latin original and a German translation of an important papal statement that the scholar had commented on. Despite the "humiliation for the learned gentleman" that this might produce, *Germania* asserted Virchow's linguistic confusion had led him to mistakenly interpret the document.[161] Targeting the liberal *Kölnische Zeitung*, *Germania* reprinted a long passage of translation from its opponent's columns and concluded, "If our readers should find the reading of this document difficult and in some places only come to understand the meaning with difficulty, we can say to you in consolation that the blame is not yours." Just like in previous cases, the liberal paper had provided a translation in "incomprehensible and senseless German."[162] A series of articles on Luther went so far as to bring the biblical translations of the reformer himself into question.[163] References to faulty Latin translations had a larger symbolic significance as well in the face of widespread philhellenism among the bourgeoisie of the nineteenth century, an enthusiasm that came with both a dose of anti-Romanism extending to the modern Catholic Church and also often a particularly Protestant understanding of national identity.[164] Moreover, despite this bourgeois philhellenism, the language of Latin itself remained more central to advanced studies with the average *gymnasial* student, for example, devoting more time to learning it than Greek.[165] Hence, the attention to Latin, including reproductions of full texts in the original, and appropriate translations served the dual purpose of countering philhellenism and of undermining the *Kulturkämpfers'* claim on *Bildung*, suggesting they had not paid much attention to their school lessons.[166] Referencing the multifaceted meaning of *gebildet* that included being both educated and cultured, the style in which opponents wrote also came under scrutiny. Bismarck drafted a statement about papal succession including so many clichés that one article quoted the beginning of it and asked, "Can one stylize any worse than has been done in these two sentences?"[167] It was not just a question of aesthetic appeal, though, as *Germania* took another paper to task for the "offensive, coarse manner" it employed in its writing. Like Ketteler's complaint about Friedberg's "coarse" manner, *Germania* argued that such issues mattered. If "le style est l'homme," as the article dared to assert, then such words did not belong to "men of intellectual cultivation and aesthetic taste" but were mere "weapons of ignorance."[168] Returning to Pius's exhortation that "one must give words their meaning back" just as Reichensperger did in his book, *Germania* asked, "These days is not frequently the one who is described as an 'educated person' the one who is in truth most uneducated?" *Bildung* was important, but "a thoughtless speaking and writing of words" cheapened it. Instead of true *Bildung*, such men had nothing more than "*Scheinbildung*."[169] Far from raising any specifically Catholic or even religiously-based claim, however, *Germania* drew upon what had long been a concern primarily of the educated themselves: the dangers of pseudo-education.[170]

Nothing better exemplified the alleged spuriousness of much that liberals presented as learned and scholarly rigorous than its inconsistency. Given the approval liberal papers showed for his rejection of papal infallibility, Döllinger often received attention in the Catholic press for his about face on the topic.[171] Similar to Ketteler's claims about Friedberg's self contradiction, *Germania* ran a series of articles titled "Döllinger then and now." The articles recounted the theologian's earlier conclusions on infallibility and asserted his current ideas were "considerably different."[172] Since the liberal press cited Döllinger as an authoritative source for many of its points on Catholicism, *Germania* attempted to turn this back on opponents by quoting from the theologian's earlier publications, especially lines in which he wrote of the Church's positive attributes and decried as false the efforts to portray papal authority negatively.[173] Using evidence from these writings of Döllinger and other Old Catholic professors like Johann Friedrich von Schulte, *Germania* asserted that Bismarck himself had been proven wrong by this *"deutsche Wissenschaft."*[174] Through all of this, articles focused on Döllinger as a scholar, not as a reformer in the tradition of Martin Luther. *Germania* stressed that when Luther defended his views at the Diet of Worms, he asked for God's help; Döllinger, on the other hand, "called upon *Wissenschaft* to assist him."[175] The paper bemoaned not the spiritual but the scholarly consequences of the professor's fickleness: "Mistrust! With regard to his students, definitely the worst for a teacher."[176] After all, *Germania* asked, if Döllinger's previous understanding had been flawed, had he not also "dragged his students into [this same mistake] with his earlier teaching?" Luckily, *Germania* assured, other Catholic scholars supported the earlier conclusions, finding only Döllinger's recent ideas to be false. Hence, *Germania* made the issue not one of Döllinger's religious beliefs but of his scholarly competence. Given how much liberals depended upon opinions like his, the paper sarcastically warned its opponents that they should look to more reliable sources, "otherwise the scholarly basis of the '*Kulturkampf*' will receive an all too shoddy appearance."[177]

While the work of Döllinger himself allegedly showed the inconsistency that plagued false scholarship according to Catholic arguments, the changeability of the natural sciences in their entirety provided a more general target. *Germania* carefully clarified that its analysis did not indicate a denigration of the natural sciences: "We really do not despise them; on the contrary, we highly esteem them, like every scholarly field in which the searching human mind strives for the truth." But the paper cautioned that the natural sciences experienced rapid changes, using the specific example of chemistry, the "modern science *par excellence.*" *Germania* pointed out that the history of chemistry "teaches us that the entire point of view that it takes today is already an absolutely different one from that which was regarded as authoritative twenty years ago." The article noted that even the ideas of early pioneers in modern chemistry simply no longer held weight. To suggest that the natural sciences had provided any definitive answer to the rhyme and reason of religion did not heed the precepts of logic itself, *Germania* concluded. Had not Socrates, the paper reminded, suggested a similar caution with his statement, "I know that I know nothing." Likewise, the philosophy of Germany's own Kant declared the limits of man's knowledge, the article adding that "neither the newest scholarship, despite all of the indisputable advances, can change this fundamental theorem, nor will the scholarship of the future be able to." That religion also supported similar caution was only added at the end of the article with a short reference to the biblical saying "For we know [only] in part."[178]

Darwin's ideas received special attention in Catholic publications. This stemmed in part from the conflict between the ideas of Darwin and Ultramontane Catholic teaching but also from the use of Darwinism in anticlerical attacks by liberals.[179] The issue had symbolic meaning as well, given the importance of the increasingly influential natural sciences for middle-class, liberal identity.[180] Popularized versions of Darwin made easy targets for being parodied in passing by *Germania*'s writers. Poking fun at other liberal publications' (such as *Die Gartenlaube*) fascination with the natural sciences, *Germania* included a tongue-in-cheek article entitled "The Frog" on its front page.[181] It waxed on about the life of a tadpole, noting that its development into a frog just happened as opposed to an ape's, which occurs "if he happens upon the idea" to turn into a human![182]

Aside from such satire, however, *Germania* also dealt with Darwinism and its popularized versions from a scholarly standpoint.[183] Again, articles pointed to issues such as inconsistency. Accordingly, they argued that many of Darwin's conclusions stemmed not from logical, step-by-step thinking but were "based on pure arbitrariness" that could just as easily support other findings, a weakness that Darwin's own work supposedly acknowledged by using "words like: 'probably,' 'it is to be assumed,' 'it appears,' 'might,' 'could,' etc. that turn up on almost every page of the text."[184] Furthermore, *Germania* asserted that, just like Döllinger, Darwin had changed his ideas about how the process worked.[185] The paper also reported on research from other fields of scholarship that appeared to contradict many of Darwin's assumptions.[186] *Germania* even used the work of Alfred Russel Wallace, another British scholar working on natural section whose methods the newspaper suggested were superior, to undercut Darwin by showing inconsistencies in how these two men believed the process occurred.[187] Ludwig Büchner, the noted popularizer of Darwinism in Germany, did not fare any better in the pages of *Germania*. Far from being a true scholar, his work could "claim originality in barely one of his sentences." Hence, "'German scholarship' celebrated no great triumph abroad," despite the wide availability of Büchner's work in other languages as well. It also did not help that Büchner, despite being a "compatriot," had really only copied the work of Darwin, "the Englishman," who did not say that much fundamentally different—so far as *Germania* was concerned at least—than "the Frenchman Lamarck."[188] Darwinism was German neither in quality nor in origin.

Though many of these articles refuting Darwinism had a more religious tone than most others concerning scholarship and higher education, they still mainly countered the ideas on a scholarly basis. Indeed, the objections raised by articles in *Germania* concerning the limits of knowledge had also been a point of discussion among natural scientists themselves since midcentury. Committed liberals such as Emil Du Bois-Reymond and even Virchow questioned the boundless capacity for knowledge that often characterized scientific research.[189] Certainly one cannot miss the greater skepticism of scientific progress inherent in the Catholic arguments. Yet the position was, in these cases, articulated from a scholarly standpoint, in a tone more akin to the caution of a thinker like Edmund Burke than the outright rejection of anything that disagreed with the Church doctrine so often associated with Ultramontane Catholicism.

Catholic arguments considered faulty scholarship and spurious education as connected to an array of corrupt, non-German ideas. Turning Protestant associations of Catholics with the French enemy around, *Germania* posed that the source of such corruption in liberals' scholarship came above all from France. Not only were more recent scientific ideas like Darwinism ultimately French, but the entire century had been a

process of Germans copying their western neighbors. Instead of looking
to native sources, "at the end of the previous and at the beginning of this
century the German nation had, so to say, forgotten itself. Back then the
educated of our nation were mad about the modern France of Louis XV
and the Encyclopedists and for the classical paganism of Greece and
Rome. The great traditions of German history were essentially unknown
and incomprehensible even to a Lessing, Herder, Göthe, Schiller. Hence,
true enthusiastic patriotism was an entirely unfamiliar feeling to all those
men of the 'Enlightenment'-Era. One felt ashamed of his Fatherland and
its glorious past, which already since the 'Reformation'-Era, but especially since the 30 Years War, had sunken more and more into darkness
and oblivion."[190] Here, of course, *Germania* also referenced the conten-
tious historiography of the early modern period in Germany.[191] The "educated" of Germany continued to draw inspiration from the French in
other areas of culture as well, the paper claimed, using "French models"
for other endeavors such as literary creations, leading to nothing short of
an "intellectual dependency."[192] *Germania* sarcastically noted that such
copying seemed all the more "peculiar," given how much liberals touted
their "much extolled . . . Germanness (*Deutschheit*)."[193] In this line of
thought, much of what those allegedly educated individuals valued as
German culture and *Wissenschaft* really came from France. This claim
also furthered the allegation of inconsistency in liberal scholarship since
such work merely followed the latest trends of "Parisian fashions."[194]

This alleged corruption of German educational and scholarly excellence
had consequences beyond academia as well. Darwinism, for example, not
only came from France (via Lamarckism) but also led back there by
inspiring materialism and socialism, nowhere more evident than in the
Revolution and the Commune.[195] Attempts by liberals such as Virchow to
increase the teaching of the natural sciences in the German educational
system could supposedly only quicken this descent.[196] Indeed, the contemporary scholarly laxity and spurious *Bildung* was symptomatic of what
Catholic arguments saw as the more general lack of concern for basic principles pervading the new *Reich* on all levels. It came as no surprise to
Germania's writers that the people could easily be ruined by stock specu-
lation. After all, the newspaper concluded, "the situation is not an ounce
different with the *Scheinbildung* than with the *Scheinpapieren* on the

stock market."[197] The liberals were responsible for both, and neither was backed up by anything of value![198] One supposedly needed to look no further than the relationship history between liberals and Bismarck to realize that the former exhibited as much inconsistency in their political positions as they did in their scholarly work.[199] Just as the ethos of the natural sciences often led to a "pragmatist" outlook, *Germania* argued that middle-class liberals stove for practical gains.[200] Finding a connection between a particular scholarly style and Bismarck's political approach was not exclusive to Center politicians. Academics themselves saw a similarity between the process of producing German scholarship and Bismarck's *Realpolitik*: both eschewed ideological bias.[201] Of course, the Catholic arguments assessed this connection negatively, concluding that all this activity was devoid of principles.

Indeed, Catholic arguments about false scholarship frequently included reference to both problems with methodology, such as source selection, and a more general failure to follow ethical standards of the field, though the latter was often expressed through insinuation. Professors, particularly those who worked in the parliament too, served as frequent examples of this two-pronged accusation.[202] Concerning a statement by Rudolf von Gneist that *Germania* took issue with, an article supposed that viewing the problem as one of sloppiness beat the alternative explanation: "We cannot and do not want to accept that Herr Gneist . . . intentionally said the falsehood."[203] Responding to a description of Heinrich von Sybel as "first among the currently living German historians," *Germania* preferred calling him "first among the currently living German master concocters of history," emphasizing the constructedness of his retelling of the national story.[204] *Germania* could also be more direct in its accusations, as it was in the title of an article questioning Virchow's ideas about church-state relations: "Ignorance—or Lie?"[205] Another article sniped, "A liberal German professor must always be right, even if history should say otherwise," making fun of the "infallibility" of liberal professors that Reichensperger and other Catholics had parodied in a variety of outlets.[206] Here the vaunted element of self-direction in *Bildung* had allegedly gone completely awry, with the liberal professor the perfect example of being unhinged and conforming to no standards or principles beyond his own. Instead of exercising the caution that true scholarship necessitated, Catholic arguments asserted that such individuals showed unwavering acceptance of all their own conclusions. This meant nothing short of an "idolization of *Wissenschaft*," supposedly far more dangerous than the idolization of saints that Catholics were often accused of. Whether from incompetence or from political bias—also a breach of scholarly ideals—these professors were portrayed as not upholding their duty as bearers of German *Wissenschaft*.[207]

These claims that liberal scholarship lacked principles and often resulted from intentional deception did link the discussion to one of morality, or more specifically, its decline in society, a stock issue for Ultramontane Catholicism. While Catholics saw a solution to this decline in the assurance of practices like confessional schooling and a greater religiosity in general, this hardly meant their arguments could simply be reduced to mantras of faith over reason. After all, that they ultimately worried about the impact the wrong policies would have on morality hardly expressed an unshared concern. The fixation on convent atrocity stories, for example, expressed a similar worry among liberals, not to mention the larger moral implications of *Bildung*.[208] Consider how Catholics backed up many of their arguments on moral decline: statistics. In a "time of unscrupulousness" and "weak character," *Germania* felt it necessary to examine not only population numbers but also more complex school statistics broken down by confession.[209] Looking back on what the *Kulturkämpfer* had wrought, *Germania* posed no better example of the decline existed than the "criminal statistics" indicating Germany would "soon become the most pitiable country in the world," a stark contrast to its reputation as the land of education.[210] *Germania* even produced the numbers to show this was a trend among countries with liberal leadership, pointing out that Rome now had a higher rate of murder than all other provinces in Italy except Sicily![211] Particularly prominent was the concern over what papers called "suicide mania," a problem allegedly caused by the loss of religion, especially among Protestants. According to the *Schlesische Volkszeitung*, the point was no mere supposition, however, and an article stated with professed impartiality, "The statistics lead to such conclusions."[212] Indeed, articles used "statistical comparisons" to make a wide array of arguments, engaging in debates over the validity of various results.[213] Though dating back to earlier advances, statistics experienced a particular rise in importance during the nineteenth century, with various efforts at setting up specific bureaus to collect data beginning with men like Humboldt and coming to successful fruition at the *Reich* level and in various states after 1871.[214] Connecting the legitimacy of the state as well as of scholarship, universities had offerings in statistics, including a special seminar established by the head of the Prussian statistical bureau, Ernst Engel, in 1870 to educate future officials in the methods.[215] Hence, when Catholic arguments provided a statistical basis for their positions, they not only laid claim to this legitimacy but also to the reputation statistics had achieved as a "guarantee of precision, rationality, and impartiality attributed to science."[216] Combined with the rebuffing of the scholarly underpinning of *Kulturkampf* policies, Catholic arguments used such data to provide a more "scientific" basis for their policies, even ones directly concerned with morality.

Hence, according to Catholic arguments, the famous German *Wissenschaft* had little in common with what liberals now pushed as scholarship and the government more than happily used as evidence to support its own ends. Such scholarship was inconsistent, biased, foreign, and too faulty to be aware of its own limits. Despite opponents' claims that Germanness was being safeguarded by the *Kulturkampf,* Catholic arguments proposed that liberals with their false ideas about education were creating not *Bildung* and the associated ideal of *Kultur,* but its exact opposite: *Verwilderung* (return to the wild).[217] If no one opposed these developments and ultimately the state became "the lone source of all right and all *Wissenschaft,*" as *Germania* argued the liberals were allowing to happen with their unwavering obedience to Bismarck's government, Germany would no longer be a "constitutional state" (*Rechtsstaat*) but a "prison state."[218] As in the wild, only force would matter.[219]

Hence, Catholic arguments posited that fostering scholarship was important not only for their own confession but for the future of Germany. More specifically, Germany needed the scholarship of Catholics as a counter to that produced by the state's liberal puppets in order to protect academic freedom, something that would inevitably vanish in the "prison state." *Germania* argued that the effects of the current idea of "national education" were already surfacing in the destruction of "creative mental ability." In part, the paper targeted basic education, as it noted the need for compliant soldiers. Yet the criticism encompassed the entire "much vaunted" education system, since the state needed to produce "blindly obedient" civil servants as well, an inclusion that certainly referred to university professors.[220] In the same vein, the *Augsburger Postzeitung* asserted that "Wissenschaft" had "abdicated in favor of the sabre."[221] For a time when "*Wissenschaft* could still express itself freely," the paper contended, one had to go back a few years.[222] Beyond the specific benefit to academic freedom, Catholic arguments posited the importance of fostering scholarship for the more general pursuit of truth, especially given the concerns raised about the ethical standards of certain liberal scholars.[223] In this line of argument, academic freedom and truth through scholarship, both ideals claimed by liberals, were actually the preserve of Catholics.[224]

In the dire times of the *Kulturkampf,* therefore, the need for Catholic scholarship existed more than ever according to leading Catholics, and the founding of the Görres-Gesellschaft in 1876 formed part of the efforts to fill this requisite. Growing out of ideas discussed at a small gathering of mostly young, educated Catholics in September 1875, the society would offer the kind of support to its members that had often remained elusive to them in the universities.[225] It was not just a matter of academics, however. As head of the section for philosophy, Paul Leopold Haffner, argued, only greater efforts from Catholic scholars could reverse the larger social trend that "in our beloved German fatherland *Wissenschaft* is not power at all, but conversely power [is] *Wissenschaft.*"[226] When announcing plans for the Görres-Gesellschaft, the *Kölnische Volkszeitung* went so far as to claim, "The decisive battle against liberalism must be fought out not in political debates and election campaigns, but on the level of ideas, of scholarship and literature." The article concluded that if this point would be understood anywhere, it should be in Germany.[227] Indeed, as he was laying the groundwork for the society, Hertling felt no lack of support for his work, relating to co-founder Hermann Cardauns his satisfaction with the progress of the arrangements for the society and specifically noting his happiness over the unified front that would be put forth despite how many people had truly had a hand in preparations.[228] The Görres-Gesellschaft received warm acceptance from the Church as well, evidenced by the response from among German bishops and Pius IX too, but this did not detract from the society's emphasis on scholarship.[229] In the announcement for the opening meeting printed in *Germania,* for example, the society repeatedly noted it was an organization for those who valued scholarship and wanted to support scholarly endeavors. It referenced issues of belief only twice by noting the hostile attitude to the Church of much (liberal) scholarship and the goal, among others, to support research on issues potentially relevant to "apologetic interests."[230] Reporting on the recent centenary celebrations for Joseph Görres's birth linked to the founding of the society, *Germania* chose to describe his spirit as one "striving for truth," again a formulation that allowed for the importance of belief but did not detract from the value of scholarship.[231] This distinction between theology and scholarship did not merely appear on paper either but was reflected in the organization's structure. While its founding statute included sections for natural sciences, philosophy, history, and a combined one for jurisprudence and social sciences, theology did not gain a place among the focus areas of the society.[232] The founders emphasized that though the society had interest in efforts to harmonize belief and science, the results needed to be "completely at the top of scholarly research."[233] As in so many other instances, Catholic arguments for support of the Görres-Gesellschaft emphasized "real *Wissenschaft*" against "false *Wissenschaft*."[234]

This hardly surprises, given the importance Hertling had for the founding and development of the Görres-Gesellschaft, undertaken on the heels of the scholar's dashed hopes of being promoted at the University of Bonn.[235] Indeed, Hertling's efforts to invigorate Catholic scholarship and push for greater integration into the dominant academic culture have been noted by multiple scholars. Yet the emphasis has mainly been on his later activity from the 1890s and onward.[236] But the attempt to emphasize the scientific, rigorous methods and values of mainstream German scholarship—here it is problematic to speak of "modern" scholarly methods since, in contemporary Catholic arguments, the word came to have a particular meaning associated with everything that was wrong with dubious, fashion-driven, liberal scholarship of the *Kulturkampf*—was already there from the foundation of the society. The idea of a "bridge" that could bring together the scholarship of both confessions did not remain merely a dream that Hertling wrote of to his friend.[237] Hertling urged the philosopher Franz Brentano, for example, to consider publishing a recently written article in a more neutral journal than the Catholic *Theologisches Literaturblatt*, a source that would limit its reception among Protestant scholars.[238] Hertling also made bridging scholarly divides among the confessions part of his own proposed "specific scholarly plan" that he would undertake in the future, an effort that came to fruition even as clouds began gathering in the new *Reich* with the ideas of his 1871 book, *Materie und Form und die Definition der Seele bei Aristoteles. Ein kritischer Beitrag zur Geschichte der Philosophie.*[239] In the same year that he helped found the Görres-Gesellschaft, Hertling also sought to create a bridge between the confessional reading cultures by "modernizing" the book offerings of the Borromäusverein with the addition of non-Catholic selections.[240] From the 1860s into the twentieth century, the words and actions of Hertling consistently represented this standpoint, including during the *Kulturkampf.*[241] That the efforts of the Görres-Gesellschaft to foster connections between Catholic and Protestant scholars started from the beginning is confirmed by Cardauns's account as well. Despite focusing on Catholic scholars specifically, Cardauns clarified that that never meant a "personal or intellectual barrier" to others in the academic community. Instead, the society "was always . . . conscious of the necessity to serve scholarship in intellectual contact with differently minded researchers under the implementation of the strictest scientific methods."[242] To Hertling, the value of fostering such scholarship during the *Kulturkampf* was obvious, as "the Church cannot and may not do without *Wissenschaft*." Indeed, by the society's general meeting in 1896, Hertling did not feel the need to remind others of the importance of the Görres-Gesellschaft's work during the *Kulturkampf* years, but to caution against thinking that the organization had become "superfluous."[243]

More complex than current scholarship would suggest, Catholic arguments on education took two quite different approaches. On the one hand, arguments could stress difference and confessional separation, as was the case for primary education. Yet, on the other hand, they also made attempts to emphasize and to embrace the same ideals that the academic establishment promoted. Of these two approaches, the latter was clearly the main stance toward higher education and *Wissenschaft*. Indeed, the rhetoric even went so far as to claim Catholic ownership of these scholarly ideals by providing evidence intended to show how little liberals themselves followed them. In doing so, the Catholic position on higher education did appeal to values that were "modern" in the sense that liberals then and historians of today use the word. Rigor regarding source use, consistency of argument, and intellectual freedom were all highlighted in Catholic arguments. That Catholics refused to label them as "modern"—because of the larger association of that term in the struggle—does not undercut this. Certainly there were limits, however, to how well such ideals were actually achieved by Catholic *Wissenschaft*.[244]

Given the importance of education for conceptions of Germanness, both to the Germans themselves and to others, such arguments by Catholics were at the same time efforts to define the new nation. In this case, they did not do so by proposing a different idea of Germanness as they did in the events described in the previous chapter. Instead, Catholic arguments also touted the value of academic achievement that the liberals so often lauded. Yet they went further to assert that it was Catholic scholars, not liberal scholars, who truly represented the real "*deutsche Wissenschaft*." Hence, instead of being the backward enemies of the *Reich* to be excluded, they were, by definition, indispensable to the new nation. Discourse cannot be mistaken for reality, of course. Yet the effect of such arguments on public opinion among Catholics cannot be overlooked either, especially since they found expression in a wide array of venues, both specialized and popular. While certainly efforts to integrate Catholics into the educational mainstream and their corresponding nationalization advanced significantly during the 1890s, as scholars note, these processes had notable roots extending back into the *Kulturkampf*-era itself. That Catholic approaches to defining the new nation during the 1870s also included points of agreement on the centrality of education and scholarship with even their most vociferous of opponents must be included among these roots.

NINE

The Moral Geography of Europe and Beyond

IN THE MIDST of the *Kulturkampf*, the priest Joseph Bischoff added another book to his literary arsenal in defense of Catholicism with the publication of *Urdeutsch* in 1875.[1] Bischoff, better known by his pen name Conrad von Bolanden, had already written books on Luther, Gustavus Adolphus, Franz von Sickingen, and many other confessionally charged topics. Indeed, on the eve of the *Kulturkampf*, Bischoff had become such a prolific and popular author among Catholics that he resigned his pastorate of ten years in Berghausen to become a full-time writer in 1869, living well off his literary income alone. Not only the approval of his reading public prompted this move, however, but also the disapproval of the Bishop of Speyer, who told the young priest it was time to retire his pen for good. In part, this decision by Speyer's Bishop Weis likely reflected both a view of Bischoff's limited literary talents as well as taking into account the books' "too extreme" tone, one that hardly encouraged "Christian peace." Not surprisingly, Bischoff continued to be a controversial figure during the *Kulturkampf* as well. In 1872, Pius IX honored him with the title of Privy Chamberlain; only a year later he made the papers by being the target of death threats at his home, though their delivery in the middle of the night by screaming, drunken *Gymnasium* students suggests they were largely more a nuisance than anything serious. In the end, Bischoff dropped all charges against the students to spare them from expulsion.[2]

Meant for a popular audience, the story of the historical novel *Urdeutsch* was simple. It told the tale of St. Martin as he attempted to spread the gospel among the pagan Germanic tribes living scattered throughout the dark forests. Facing many dangers as well as the skepticism of his own servant, Eustach, St. Martin steadily conquers both hearts and minds among the Germans by singing, preaching, and revealing via miracles the virtues and truth of Christianity. Within this larger framework came two subplots. One dealt with the feud between rival tribes, a vendetta so deadly that it had reduced the weaker of the two down to only the remaining sibling pair of Bissula and her younger brother, Hermanreich, who had still not yet come of age. The other focused on the love story between Bissula and Vithimer, a nobleman of yet another tribe. Already deeply in love at the beginning of the novel, the two suffer through most of the plot convinced that they will never be able to marry.

Bischoff intended his book to be far more than mere entertainment, however. In the forward, he specifically attacked the "swindle" being spread by *Kulturkämpfer* alleging the incompatibility of German ways with "Rome," in this case Christianity.[3] In particular, Bischoff wanted to expose the true nature of the early Germanic tribes, which, after 1871, were so often touted as quintessentially German by liberals in accounts like the Hermann myth. Hence, though a novel, *Urdeutsch* included numerous footnotes citing Tacitus—a source for the Hermann myth as well—and others as evidence of the general accuracy of the author's rendering of tribal life among the Germans.[4] Bischoff reminded readers of his purpose again at the end of the book, noting, "I have turned historical evidence, not products of the imagination, into the form of the novel."[5] The facts, as he presented them, added up to a picture of early Germanic tribes as lascivious, lazy, and bloodthirsty. He spared no detail in relating everything from the grisly battles to the ease with which mothers would abandon their babies. Models of culture on which to base the new nation, these early Germanic tribes were not.

Instead, Bischoff lauded the achievements of Christianity, the true source of culture as he saw it. St. Martin, the messenger of God in the novel, brings light to the darkness of the forest as well as to the primeval Germans. It is he who insures the children are clothed, the women not mishandled, and the blood feud ended. Before Christianity, the story relates, "[there was] no trace of actual culture." Even the forest ground remained fruitless, figuratively and literally: "in all of Germany not a single fruit tree."[6] Through such examples, Bischoff hoped his fellow Germans would recognize the importance of Christianity and the danger he believed *Kulturkämpfer* posed to it. Yet even in the forward Bischoff assured readers who were not German that the story applied to them too. Far from resorting to any "petty" examples of German bragging, he asserted that his novel attempted to showcase "Catholic" ideals. Hence, "readers of all Christian nations," not just Germans, could see how religion had helped them.[7] Throughout the body of the story as well, St. Martin repeatedly assures those he meets that Christianity is not Roman, nor Greek, nor belonging to any other nationality; it is simply divine. Bischoff returns to this point at the end of his novel, stating, "There is only one light, only one truth, only one way of salvation for all nations of the Earth."[8] Without it, even the early Germanic tribes were nothing more than "barbarians," a point that Bischoff asserts on almost every page.

Comments downplaying national differences in favor of Christian universalism appeared throughout Catholic publications. On the eve of Germany's proclamation, an article in *Germania* already spoke of the importance of keeping in mind the "unity of humanity," repeatedly stressing the Christian character of the new *Reich*.[9] Another article appearing only weeks later went so far was to criticize the idea of "nationalities" holding too much weight, which it referred to as a "swindle."[10] Reflecting on the lack of support for the pope, the *Kölnische Volkszeitung* lamented the wrong path Germany was heading down with its disregard for the "common bond of a civilization created and preserved by Christianity" and loss of any sense of the "solidarity of nations."[11] The word "swindle" also came to mind, like it had for Bischoff in *Urdeutsch* and in the pages of *Germania*, when a contributor to *Stimmen aus Maria-Laach* eschewed the "vanity" that led to "an overestimation of one's own tribe" versus other "peoples."[12] Such statements hardly surprise given the cooperation between the Center and the Polish Party, the deputies from Alsace-Lorraine, and the Danish Party as well.[13] Similarly, though initially seen as progressive, Pius IX had by the 1870s long shown himself opposed to the rising nationalism throughout Europe, not to mention his direct conflicts with its supporters in Italy on repeated occasions.[14] Given the continued sympathies of many Catholics for the now "foreign" Austria, the evidence of their international—and hence anti-national and anti-German—position seemed clear to many contemporaries, as the charges of *Reichsfeindlichkeit* indicated.

Certainly many of these factors have influenced how scholars have presented German Catholics in the process of national definition and identity formation during the early years of the *Reich,* more by their being overlooked as participants in this process than anything else.[15] Even in accounts that clearly reject the charge of anti-nationalism, the attention given to Catholics is relatively scarce and more focused on the role they played as "enemies," if only in the minds of *Kulturkämpfer.*[16] Other historians, of course, give more weight to the contention that Catholic integration into the nation faltered on their significant focus on international ties beyond the borders of Germany.[17] Even Thomas Nipperdey suggested that Catholics "emphasized against all national exuberance the supra- and international," though he added they did not do this to the extent the socialists did.[18]

Yet while German Catholicism's reluctance to look only at national differences and the clear importance they placed on remembering a common humanity across all borders undoubtedly separated them from nationalists during the *Kulturkampf,* a point the former not only conceded but insisted upon at the time, it did not prevent them from nonetheless developing an increasingly defined sense of Germanness.[19] Earlier in the nineteenth century, after all, German nationalists felt a close connection to similar movements elsewhere, including among the Poles.[20] Left-leaning liberal nationalists continued to emphasize this cosmopolitanism even after the foundation of the *Reich.*[21] Even for the late *Kaiserreich* one should be careful not to overemphasize the "dichotomy between cosmopolitanism and nationhood."[22] Certainly, Catholics during the *Kulturkampf* did not perceive their insistence on a common Christian civilization, especially throughout Europe, as preventing a sense of their particular place in the world as Germans. Indeed, unification only made this role all the more important.

Hence, *Germania* felt the need to distance itself from the "swindle" it believed nationalism represented largely because the article and several earlier in the same series had already spent pages considering how the foundation of the *Reich* represented the rise of "German character and German nature on top," which was nothing short of "the leadership of the world." The article wanted to clarify that this role Germany would assume complied completely with the idea of the commonality of a "Christian foundation." Indeed, "difference had a right" and the "assertion of such an entitlement" as the "realization and implementation of the German nature" did nothing to undercut the importance of the commonality of all humanity. After all, the German epoch had been "ordained by God."[23] A couple of years later, when the *Kölnische Volkszeitung* article appeared, it criticized the lack of "solidarity of nations" indicated by non-intervention, condemning this as "un-German." Ignoring what made the *Reich*'s people special, their "justice, maintenance of morality, and the respect for religious authority" would have catastrophic consequences not only for Germany but for the world.[24] Similarly, the "swindle" of "vanity" that the contributor to *Stimmen* warned readers against did not prevent him from finishing the same sentence with "nonetheless I cannot ward off the conviction that our German people—with its particular nature in talent and development—was, is, and will remain one of the decisive factors in the history of Europe." Perhaps feeling that this had not really captured the importance of Germans enough, he added in the next sentence that really the importance was not just for Europe, but for "the world."[25]

Even a polemical text written by a divisive priest with the express intention of rebuffing any notion that the original Germanic tribes—the initial founders of the nation at least as much of the nationalist rhetoric of the period portrayed them—could have stopped killing themselves off much less become anything greater without the benefit of Christianity did not forgo plentiful references to the specialness of Germans and their role in the world.[26] Before he begins his conversion efforts, St. Martin knows that "the future holds in store a German life of wonderful magnificence."[27] When the process of Christianization is finally underway by the end of the novel, "Even the non-sentient nature seemed to intuit to what the foundation here was being laid." Bischoff referred not only to the "seeds of Christian culture" but also "the first born of a great people."[28] Indeed, though barbarians, the early tribes of Bischoff's *Urdeutsch* have a particular proclivity for conversion. While learning the language and customs of the locals, St. Martin realizes many kernels of divine truth are held in their legends, concluding, "O certainly, there are enough links for Christianity [to easily take hold]."[29] These early Germans, according to *Urdeutsch,* have a sense of heaven and hell and know there is "only one all-powerful God," though even Bischoff had to add the qualifier "strictly speaking" to stand by the latter assertion.[30]

The time period in which Bischoff set his novel also aids in intensifying this connection between the Germanic tribes and Christianity. Though combating what he saw as the lies of nationalist rhetoric built up around the Hermann mythos, Bischoff set his novel not during the Cheruscan's time but hundreds of years later in the fourth century. Most tribes in *Urdeutsch* are still barbarian, of course, but some have already converted to Christianity, such as the one from which Vithimer comes. As much as Bischoff wanted to undercut any ideas suggesting true culture came from anywhere but Christianity, he also did not abandon the sense of a special German role in this process. The most striking example of this comes from multiple references to nineteenth-century Japan in a historical novel about ancient Germans. When describing the ease with which early Germanic tribesmen would take their own lives, Bischoff offered in an aside, "The educated Japanese have up to today remained at [the level of] stomach slitting and other barbarian customs."[31] To insure his criticism of early Germanic tribes would not be taken as denying contemporary German culture, Bischoff resorted to a comparison with the Japanese again in the conclusion, stating that the "educated Japanese" still amounted to nothing more than "wretched barbarians," a fate the Germans escaped in the fourth century.[32] While he of course noted this only came via the benefits of Christianity, it did not change the point from Bischoff's perspective that contemporary Japanese were barbarians and Germans were not.

Even the ambiguous meaning of the title could feed into this idea of a particularly German proclivity for true culture, regardless of the universal benefits offered by Christianity. The first sentence of the novel proclaims, "The present-day Germany bears hardly a resemblance to the old pagan Germany as the Christian missionaries found it."[33] Bischoff substantiated his claim by offering up descriptions of pagan norms that allowed children to be thrown away, women to be taken against their will, and other generally brutish occurrences. He also, not surprisingly, spent time noting both the utter disarray and dirtiness in which ancient Germans lived as well as their distance to communal life. Given the growing relationship of cleanliness and orderliness with national identity during the nineteenth century that Nancy Reagin's work has articulated, in addition to the well-known vibrant associational life in nineteenth-century Germany, it is not hard to believe readers—at least those among the Catholic community who were receptive to Bischoff's larger point— would conclude that what was "primevally German" was not what was "quintessentially German" at all.[34] Instead, the latter only came with the addition of Christianity, making Germanness and Christianity by that point inseparable, which was exactly the Catholic standpoint.

Hence, contemporary Catholic arguments about what the new *Reich* should stand for did pose the conflict revolving in part around choosing Christian universalism over "nationalism." At the same time, however, Catholic arguments did not equate this with espousing an international or anti-national position versus a German or national one. Instead, the choice as Catholics saw it was between Christianity and paganism, culture and barbarism. Furthermore, even long before the Center Party became a reliable supporter of the government's military and colonial plans later in the *Reich* that would become part of the *Weltpolitik* aimed at achieving "a place in the sun," Catholic rhetoric had also defined a special role for Germany. In part this came from the integral connection contemporary arguments posited between Germany and Christianity, not least in what was portrayed as a heritage passed down from the Holy Roman Empire, seen as both a quintessentially German and Christian institution. Yet it also stemmed from the extensive picture Catholic rhetoric of the era painted of the rest of the world. While a few nations appeared as positive examples, most others fell beyond the pale of what Catholics saw as the cultured world of Christian civilization.[35] This chapter examines how contemporary Catholic arguments located Germany's place in the moral geography of the world its rhetoric created.[36] Only by placing the promotion of Christian universalism in this larger context can the extent of Catholic efforts to define Germany and Germanness and their effects on integration be understood.

European Christendom and the German *Reich*

Part of the conflict posited between culture and barbarism also turned on the idea of a common European civilization, one seen from the Catholic viewpoint as representing the heart of Christendom, though it played into more general associations made across the political spectrum between the continent and cultural superiority relative to the rest of the world.[37] The Catholic *Kölnische Volkszeitung* argued that denying the "common bond of a civilization created and preserved by Christianity" meant Germany "only still recognized a nominal Europe," the embodiment of that principle.[38] When countries allowed barbarous acts to be committed on their soil, *Germania* asserted that they "lost all respect in civilized Europe," concluding it showed how little "hordes" elsewhere were really like the Europeans.[39] Yet within the common European civilization emphasized by such Catholic publications, vast differences, both moral and practical, among the various nations meant only the new German *Reich* could and should lead Europe, and in turn the world.

No country better represented Catholic attempts to define the new Germany by applauding positive developments situated elsewhere in the moral geography of Europe and the world than Britain, or as contemporaries usually called it, England.[40] German Catholics had not always been keen on English laws and customs. Instead, in the first half of the century, pro-English sympathies often appeared strongest among liberals. Publications like the *Historisch-Politische Blätter* and Catholic sentiment more generally tended to sympathize with Irish co-religionists, seen as being oppressed by a heavy-handed English government.[41] Moreover, the position England had taken on the two previous wars of unification and ultimately its willingness to sell arms to France, despite remaining formally neutral during the Franco-Prussian war, meant the adoration for Britain also began to lose its appeal among many liberals, a shift both welcomed and fostered by Bismarck himself.[42] Given the ardent support all Germans, regardless of confession, gave to the Franco-Prussian War, the mercantile activities of the English also received negative attention in the Catholic press. *Germania,* for example, wrote a scathing article entitled the "Neutrality of England." Though the government professed neutrality, this did not stop English businessmen from selling arms to the French. Indeed, even though an individual businessman might want a German victory, the article contended, he would still sell to the French, since in the English mind "business is business."[43] Such faulty thinking character-ized not just English society, but also that of the French, *Germania* noted not surprisingly. Indeed, such ability to separate different spheres of life constituted a "symptom of sickness" appearing more and more.[44] Such articles, written during the last push before the French signed the armi-stice, joined in the general anger in Germany over the behavior of the "craven race of tradesmen" the English had become.[45]

Yet merely a year later by 1872 the situation had completely changed. The sale of arms no longer played an issue as the Franco-Prussian War ended successfully for the *Reich*, and the main battlefields were those of the *Kulturkampf*. Likewise, Catholic commentary, from newspaper arti-cles to parliamentary speeches, now praised English laws and customs as exemplary for the new *Reich*. Many of the references simply included excerpts from religious as well as mainstream sources like the *Times* to show the disapproval that *Kulturkampf* measures elicited from the Eng-lish, undercutting any "intensions" by the liberals or the government to suggest support from their British counterparts.[46] Other statements went further, however, and applauded the nobility of English character. The mistaken belief that the British would approve of the *Reich*'s current actions against the Church revealed how little the *Kulturkämpfer* really knew about "English *Bildung* and morality," the *Kölnische Volkszeitung* alleged.[47] Indeed, the "inherent feeling for freedom and justice" insured that the English could not approve of the *Reich*'s current treatment of the Church.[48] Catholics praised the British sense of right not just on religious matters, but more generally.[49] In a *Reichstag* address concerning the con-ditions of the recently gained territory of Alsace and Lorraine, Windthorst emphasized the importance of the "victorious nation" to treat conquered areas "chivalrously and liberally." To underscore how much that was not the case, he concluded that its English counterpart would hardly approve of how the *Reichstag* had handled such issues up to this point.[50] Given the long affinity between German and British liberals, often banking on a shared sense of Germanic and Protestant identity, as well as hopes by

Bismarck that *Kulturkampf* measures might find support from across the Channel, it hardly surprises that Catholics often returned to the English example to support their side.[51]

Of course, Britain had had its own religious conflicts with the Irish, a point the opposing parliamentary members quickly shouted to Windthorst during his speech. Yet this made the English case even more exemplary in Catholic arguments. The Center leader quickly retorted to his detractors that he was not speaking of "the barbarians in England that treated the Irish barbarically" but the "present-day England that is *gebildet* and free."[52] Newspapers carried news of ever more vestiges of Catholic oppression being swept away, highlighting that as the *Reichstag* was passing increasingly restrictive laws, the British parliament was repealing them.[53] Even the "Manchesterism" that Catholic publications had faulted the British for at the beginning of the decade became something largely of the past in this positive view of England.[54] The shortcoming Catholic publications now hinted at when referring to England no longer centered on morals but ability. After all, an article concluded, "England's military power has not kept up with the wartime capabilities of the continental armies." Its government would only engage in European affairs "to a modest degree," *Germania* stated, providing a practical explanation for British isolationist impulses.[55]

A look to the British Isles provided not only a good example for the new *Reich* government but also for the Catholics of Germany. The Irish, of course, were that example, regaining popularity from earlier in the century in the Catholic reportage of the *Kulturkampf*.[56] *Germania* called Ireland a "shining example" for German Catholics that oppression of the Church could not succeed if they "do not give up."[57] Tributes became so widespread during the *Kulturkampf* era that the *Kölnische Volkszeitung*—based in the Rhineland where admiration for Irish political leader Daniel O'Connell had grown to such an extent that houses often displayed his picture—felt it necessary to add that despite praise for their fellow Catholics they were not nor did they want to be Irishmen![58] Particular fascination with O'Connell did not remain limited to the West, as publications all over Germany, such as the *Schlesische Volkszeitung* out of Breslau and *Deutscher Hausschatz* based in Regensburg, ran detailed serials on the man.[59] German Catholics did not just find the tenacity of their Irish brethren laudable but extolled the manner in which the latter pursued the entire cause. O'Connell became a hero for Catholics not only for his defense of their religion but also because of his commitment to peaceful means.[60] The Pius-Verein, involved with initiating the midcentury *Katholikentage* that continued throughout the 1870s up until today, modeled itself on O'Connell's Catholic Association.[61] Far from being treasonous or insurrectionary, the Irish as continually loyal to the crown found repetition in articles again and again.[62] Like the evidence Catholic arguments cited for the English feeling of justice transcending any more limited religious sympathies the British may have shared with their Protestant German cousins, the cases highlighted in the Irish fight against oppression showed people also rising above such sectarian concerns. For example, *Germania* published a series of tributes to individual Irishmen involved in fighting oppressive legislation, noting repeatedly how the cause found avid supporters among both Catholics and Protestants.[63] Of course, as images of other places often are really about the home country, these articles were more concerned with Germany than Ireland, and the reality of the Irish case was often quite different.[64] Yet by tailoring the presentation of the case to highlight only elements compatible with their own situation, German Catholic publications could present the Irish not only as an inspiration to their readership but also as a vision of what they hoped their own role in the new nation would lead to. Hence, when the Irish at last received identical treatment to the English, they would allegedly become true "brothers" with the same everything: "country," "state," "prince," "duties," and finally "rights."[65] Increasingly closer to seeing a let up in the *Kulturkampf* at home, the estimation of the ultimate outcome in Ireland grew even rosier by 1878. After everything the "island people" had gone through, mistakes and hardships aplenty, one could finally see that with "freedom" and "justice" as the pillars of society, the "English, Scots and Irish have become 'a unified *Volk* of brothers.'" This "harvest" of the British Isles was one the German Catholics hoped soon to be enjoying at home as well.[66]

As much as Catholic publications focused on the British Isles for positive inspiration, they turned to France for a view of what should be avoided. While, according to the portrayal in Catholic publications, France never fell beyond the pale of European standards and at least the continued presence of men like the conservative Patrice de Mac-Mahon suggested it might not fall completely from Christendom, everything French was stressed to be clearly not German. It was a conclusion Catholics shared with other Germans more generally, their liberal opponents included, even if the specifics of what fell on which side of the divide differed. This antithesis rose to prominence with the Revolution in 1789, and despite continued attraction the western neighbor held for some Germans on the left end of the political spectrum early in the nineteenth century, the Franco-Prussian war and the foundation of the *Reich* cemented the view of France as the quintessential enemy.[67] Given the extent to which the more general antithesis has been addressed in existing scholarship, two particular elements of the Catholic argument concerning the nature of the French deserve attention here. First, Catholic rhetoric portrayed the *Kulturkampf* as fundamentally a French idea, a view that pointed to the defeated neighbor as a cautionary tale of what would happen if such a course was followed at home. Addressing attendees at the first *Katholikentag* held in the new *Reich*, Bishop Ketteler described the beginning attacks against the Church as following "those French principles and precepts of Godlessness." They had already been defeated in the Franco-Prussian War, bringing France to its knees, but now Christians had to be vigilant that these "French principles" did not find any root among the "German people."[68] Similarly, the *Augsburger Postzeitung* warned of the "un-German" ideas being "imported from France."[69] Indeed, several major daily Catholic newspapers included such portrayals, often focusing on the defining role of the French Revolution.[70] In particular, *Germania* published a several-part series retelling the events following 1789 as they impacted the Church and Christianity. The revolutionaries of 1789 such as Danton, Marat, and Robespierre became rebranded in Catholic publications as "the '*Culturkämpfer*' of the period," and everyone knew where that had led for France.[71] Such articles presented England's reaction, not surprisingly, as one of the few bright spots of the period. England's willingness to stand up to the French and help clerical refugees signaled the "magnificence" of its people, something they would always retain as a "badge of honor," especially given that confessional differences might have suggested otherwise.[72] With the *Kulturkampf* raging by the mid 1870s, England appeared in the Catholic press as "the only one in all of Europe" that was resisting these allegedly French ideas.[73] Catholics believed even beyond the Revolution, the history of France showed the country as trying to destroy the Church like no other.[74]

Second, France was old news, or as the Germans would have expressed it figuratively, yesterday's snow. Just as Ketteler emphasized that the French had been defeated by Germans in the war, so too did the newspapers. Even before war's end, *Germania* concluded the French, "according to their character as a people," would surrender and "have to avow what they do not want to, that they are inferior alone to the Germans, as Germans." This meant not only a change in the relationship between the two countries but also with the world now that Germany had assumed the top position in Europe.[75] The founding of the *Reich* began the German epoch. Other nations had had their chance, France most recently, but now it was Germany's turn to put things right.[76] Of course, given that the French were a "bellicose" people, Germany could not let its guard down against a possible "war of revenge."[77] At the same time, however, Germany's western neighbor was certainly not its biggest worry. Going even further than *Germania,* the *Kölnische Volkszeitung* felt so secure in this estimation by 1877 that it concluded, "The German *Reich* has at present nothing to fear from France," citing the former's 49 million people and an army "incontestably the best in the world."[78] While this feeling of superiority did not differ fundamentally from the general view of France during the time, its importance for the present chapter lies in not underestimating how much Catholics—even in opposition—continued to draw upon the common German victory over the archenemy France as a source of pride and national definition well into the *Kulturkampf.*

Of course, Catholic arguments attempting to define the nation gave attention to Austria as well, but not as much as might seem the case from their earlier *großdeutsch* inclinations. As Helmut Walser Smith has rightly asserted, the conflict over defining the new nation after 1871 revolved around fundamental differences of how the state should be organized that went far beyond Austria's inclusion. Nor did Catholics' continued interest in a closer union with Austria indicate a lesser allegiance to the German *Reich* itself.[79] Beginning with calls from Bishop Ketteler of Mainz, those within Catholic circles slowly but surely recognized the changed circumstances facing German unification after 1866 and accepted the legitimacy of Wilhelm I as emperor of Germany in 1871.[80] The start of the *Kulturkampf* did not change this. Despite allegations of *Reichsfeindlichkeit* from their opponents, German Catholics did not see the issue as Germany or Austria, but one of Germany and Austria.[81] Whether arguing for a close union with Austria as they did early on or accepting a looser connection to it later in the decade—almost always vague on the specifics regardless of what kind of association they were supporting—Catholics advocated the relationship as something for the good of Germany.[82] This certainly meant both the advantage of including all individuals of German ethnicity in the nation as well as the practical benefits to the *Reich*'s position in Europe. Over time, however, the calls for a closer union with Austria increasingly focused on the security needs of the *Reich* itself as the prime motivation. By the end of the decade, Catholic articles had long made clear distinctions between the needs of Austria in international relations as opposed to those of their own country, Germany. Indeed, Austria could even appear as a potential enemy, as Catholic rhetoric drew on the same fears of isolation that none other than Bismarck himself had about Germany being encircled by enemies.[83] The *Schlesische Volkszeitung* felt comfortable enough in 1877 to unleash the type of tirade normally reserved for liberal opponents but this time directed against the Vienna-based Catholic paper *Vaterland*.[84] Given the emphasis on unity among the Catholic press in the *Reich* during the 1870s, such an act was significant. Though a special relationship undoubtedly still existed between the two countries, and not only in the minds of Catholics, even a paper like *Germania* limited the relevance of closer connection to Austria by early 1878 to one stemming from "remembering old love."[85] Too much water had passed under the bridge by that point, including conflicts between Catholics in the two countries, for the Center and its supporters to call for more than the Dual Alliance that came in 1879, which appeared as the "realization of many ideal hopes after so much confusion and suffering."[86] Just as for most Germans, Catholics accepted the Dual Alliance as recognition enough of whatever common brotherhood they shared with their Austrian counterparts.[87]

Yet it would be wrong to think that German Catholic arguments defining the nation only presented the *Reich* as distinct from Austria due to a *fait accompli*, a missed opportunity that was too late to get back. As problematic and unfortunate as the war and defeat of Austria had been in 1866 according to Catholic accounts, this did nothing to change what they also recognized by the 1870s: the waning of the Hapsburg Empire. If England's primary shortcoming was its lack of continental power and France's was its corruptness, Austria in the 1870s exemplified both. While it could still serve a role as an ally to Germany to stave off isolation, it clearly had its limits. The *Kölnische Volkszeitung* referred to it as a "passive, sick [power]."[88] *Germania* jeered that its neighbor lacked the power to even "run an independent foreign policy," its attempts to act otherwise "capable of deceiving no one other than its own government."[89] An article in *Tremonia* concluded that Austria's "turn" was coming soon, as it would likely be "digested" by Russia in the future.[90] Such articles did not express much hope for Austria righting itself either, given that it was moving in the wrong direction, burdened with its own anti-clerical policies instituted by liberals internally and positions in international affairs that one could only "condemn."[91] In disarray politically, religiously, socially, and economically, Austria was just getting by. A review of 1877 admitted that one could understand if the Austrians had "almost lost the hope of better days."[92]

Beyond the British Isles, France, and Austria, the Catholic press did not highlight other European states as models, potential rivals, or much-needed friends. Rhetoric would reference countries like Belgium or Switzerland, but such places almost always gained their significance by being placed in a larger assemblage of events led by the major powers. The unified Sweden and Norway, for example, made a rare appearance in the back pages of *Germania* as yet another version—this time from the Swedish *Aftonbladet*—of the citations commonly included from English newspapers about how "truly liberal peoples" viewed the *Kulturkampf.*[93] Italy received mention more often. Yet much of the attention focused on just how undeserving the country was of any note whatsoever, asserting the idea that the Italian nation was destined to follow the wrong principles and fail miserably. As Catholic accounts retold it, the German nation had at least been greeted initially with "a jubilation [that] could be just as enthusiastic as common," but the Italian nation had from the beginning been a moment of "deepest pain" that inevitably divided the people in two. With its financial difficulties and an army that would not even be able to beat the French or Austrians, Italy had too many problems with its "foundations," making "a lasting, continued existence of the unified Italian state a chimera."[94] An article even suggested that a problem like Freemasonry seemed coded into the Italian "national character," which certainly did not bode well.[95] Unlike Germany, which became more German through its regional diversity, different groups in Italy remained a bunch of "separate" people who believed unity to be nothing more than "an [empty] phrase."[96] Both Germany and Italy shared in being young countries, but the latter was like a "sick corpse" to the former's "healthy" one.[97] Hence, unlike France, at least potentially, Italy posed no real threat in the German Catholic view of Europe, as the comment about its military weakness indicated. Reportage suggested Italy was nothing more than a joke. When the courts of Berlin and Vienna received Victor Emmanuel II, for example, *Germania* suggested not too much should be made of this. After all, it noted, these courts had also received leaders from the most far off country of no importance. Any effort by the Italians to construe their king's reception as a deserved honor was "laughable."[98] An article in the *Schlesische Volkszeitung* called Italy a "great power" just so it could immediately add that the title was "not remotely deserved."[99] While a large part of the vitriol stemmed from the direct conflict between the government of Victor Emmanuel II and the Vatican, such targeted rhetoric likely had in mind the views of German liberals too, who looked to Italy and saw another young country embodying the same nationalist principles as their own.[100] Catholic rhetoric rebuffed the idea that any real similarity existed between the two, however. Drawing a clear distinction between them, the Catholic argument asserted that one could rightfully reject Italy, while at the same time truly loving Germany.

Hence, among the moral but "modest" Britain, the corrupt and "inferior" France, the lost and "sick" Austria, and the crumbling and "laughable" Italy, the new Germany stood out as a leader in Europe. Not only the downplaying of the potentials of other nations but also the direct statements throughout the Catholic press touting the strength of Germany indicated this view of European affairs. An earlier article claimed the year 1871 belonged to Germany because it saw the *Reich* "gloriously restored," making it the "most powerful" country by which the rest of

Europe would orient itself.[101] Throughout the decade, others continued to speak about the "overwhelming strength" that had "completely changed the map of Europe" and "reshaped the balance of power," making Germany the "top, commanding power."[102] According to accounts, this dominance did not result from good luck but had its roots in the German character itself: from the beginning *"furor teutonicus"* meant that "such a people will not go though the world without making a mark."[103] This trait even Bolanden's *Urdeutsch* conceded had indeed come from the pagan Germanic tribes, though only with Christianity did it become a power for good, the "brilliance of the Christian knighthood" that protected the weak and fought infidels.[104] Hence, despite eschewing what Catholics saw as the government's militarism, these accounts of the new *Reich*'s role in the world did betray a feeling of pride in being the most powerful nation, especially when set against portrayals of the other states, so many of which were dismissed as "not even requir[ing] mention."[105]

This strength did not exist for its own sake alone, however. Like their opponents, Catholics also spoke of the "mission" Germany now had before it, though the two sides understood this proposed task quite differently.[106] With the new epoch after 1871 came not only the ability but the "vocation" to spread "German character and German nature."[107] Indeed, "Such a high position imposes great duties," reminded one article; "not just for one's own glorification but also for the benefit and salvation of the entire world," asserted another.[108] Even the more restrained *Kölnische Volkszeitung* went so far as to suggest it was the "knowledge that Germany alone" was capable of saving Europe that drove the German people to fight so hard against the French and achieve unification. As the "most powerful *Reich* in Europe's heart," it now had a "mission" to lead at this "turning point in world history."[109]

Of course, how Catholics pitched the mission reflected how they defined the new *Reich*. Just as Catholics stressed the primacy of morality in the internal politics of the new *Reich,* so they did in foreign relations.[110] Accordingly, the bullying and jockeying for practical advantage in every situation needed to stop since this only ratcheted up tensions that could easily lead to another war, one in which Germany would have everything to lose.[111] Instead, the new *Reich* should use its power for the common good, especially in Europe, by protecting the rights of all and standing up for weaker entities when necessary. Of course such arguments always led back to aid for the embattled papacy.[112] Indeed, this conflict came to a head at the start of the first *Reichstag* with passage of the liberal written response to the *Kaiser*'s opening speech in which non-intervention in papal affairs was underscored, but not without opposition from the Center Party and its production of an alternative draft.[113] The conflict turned on a question far more fundamental than whether or not the *Reich* would aid the pope, however. Such a position meant not only declining aid for the pope, but also abandoning fellow Christians in infidel lands and German minorities repressed by other states that Catholic reportage included as needing protection.[114] In visions of the nation put forth by Catholics, the policy of non-intervention equaled an abjuration of a responsibility to common humanity and Christian civilization by the *Reich*.[115] As shorthand for this view of what Germany should be, Catholics repeatedly returned to the old *Reich*, something which in and of itself made their loyalty to the new nation suspect in the eyes of many contemporaries.[116] It did not help that their account always stressed the old *Reich*'s overarching Christian character that drew on what they presented as harmonious cooperation between the Holy Roman Emperor and the pope himself. As one article noted, "the old German *Reich* meant—significantly—the '*respublica christiana*'."[117] Armed with this civilizing idea, the emperor of the old *Reich* acted as protector of legitimate rulers and oppressed peoples thoughout Europe, promoting a harmonious coexistence of states.[118] Janssen drew on this same vision of the old *Reich* as a model for the new one in his *Geschichte des deutschen Volkes*, speaking of the former's role as a "great peace-preserving Power."[119] Bolanden did as well, presenting the highpoint of history as coming during the Middle Ages with the Holy Roman Empire, a point alluded to in *Urdeutsch* and solidified in his follow-up novel *Altdeutsch*.[120] What made the old *Reich* worthy of emulation, accordingly, was its recognition of the "unity of humanity."[121]

Who made the old *Reich* great, however, was quite a different story. Catholic accounts never left any doubt that honor belonged to none other than the Germans. Again stressing the particular role Germany had to play, the *Kölnische Volkszeitung* added to its description of the old empire that "it was not coincidence that the German state system stepped up to the top of the *Reich*."[122] In a review of Bolanden's *Urdeutsch*, even the young Jesuit Joseph Spillmann, who later became a popular Catholic author himself, could not refrain from eagerly looking ahead to the next volume that would show the period of the Holy Roman *Reich* of the German Nation—including the latter part of the title as well, like Catholic accounts commonly did—a time when "our people [were] put on the top of all peoples."[123] Janssen's account of the Holy Roman Empire even linked a lessening of its German character to the beginning of its end.[124] One needed read no further than *Germania*'s series title, "Das deutsche Kaiserthum," referring to both the Holy Roman and the new empire, to know who was responsible for the splendor of the Middle Ages that such articles touted as the model for the young nation.[125] That Catholic characterizations of the old empire not only went as far back as to claim even Charlemagne himself as part of this particularly German development, but also employed an understanding of the nation, not surprisingly, far more appropriate to the nineteenth century than earlier ones did not prevent them from asserting an undeniable continuity between the old and the new *Reich*, despite being "separated by centuries."[126]

Of course, such highlighting of the brilliant role Germans played in both the old *Reich* and the new, now at the head of Europe, precipitated corresponding instances of humility in which Christian universalism arose and assurances were made that other peoples would not find themselves at a "disadvantage" because of this. *Germania* even went so far as to concede that Germany's leadership in terms of its overall power did not mean other peoples did not have a chance to make their mark on the epoch by fulfilling a "vocation" in the other arguably even more important realms of "religion and scholarship."[127] Yet it turns out these other peoples did not have much of a chance, as the developing rhetoric not only claimed *Wissenschaft* as quintessentially German but also continued to play up the inherent connections between Germanness and Christianity, the flip side of the equation of Frenchness and secularism.[128] Germany was on top all around, Catholics believed, and they thanked God for it.

At least, such arguments asserted this is how things after 1871 should have gone, could have gone, and hopefully still would turn out if the new nation acted as its nature and history dictated. Yet Germany was being

"I[ed] astray."[129] The general decline in "the reputation . . . of the German people" among other countries provided a clear example of this, articles contended, invoking the nation's standing in much the same way that Windthorst did when he appealed to "Germany's honor" as the reason why its current policies had to change.[130] Raw force alone, even that of the strongest state, only went so far, *Germania* argued: "To be the leading state in Europe is of dubious value if this position is not used for the protection and assertion of the highest ethical thoughts in international life," a point considered so important that another article a year later included the phrase verbatim, except for replacing "dubious value" with "no value."[131] Without such commitment, "a mere belligerent and conqueror" could not hope to achieve much "of permanence."[132] It would not leave much of a mark on history. That the new *Reich* was failing in its mission to lead equaled nothing other than a "disgrace" that "the weight of the German nation" was not being asserted.[133] In short, the German epoch was slipping away. Hence, even in statements chastising the current course of the government and the *Reich*'s failure, Catholic efforts to define the nation appealed to a strong sense of Germanness and pride in it. Indeed, given the alleged destructive and misleading machinations of Bismarck and the liberals, Catholics during the *Kulturkampf* more than ever conceived of themselves as having an "extremely glorious mission" in the nation to right its path.[134] The country needed "to rule entirely and completely in a German manner again, in the spirit of German freedom and German loyalty."[135] Only this, Catholics argued, could save "true culture" and "true nationality."[136] Only this "[was] national-patriotic in the best sense of the word."[137]

Even the emphasis on greater respect for other nationalities, something Catholic criticism of the new *Reich* always noted as a strength of the old, did not undercut this sense of German leadership in the world.[138] Here, of course, the main sticking point was the Poles, a nationality within the *Reich*. The earlier sympathy expressed by German nationalists for their Polish counterparts, already on the wane after midcentury, as well as the rather tolerant treatment of them by the Prussian government, changed with the founding of the *Reich*. After 1871, efforts to forcibly Germanize Poles went ahead full steam, accompanied by an increasingly negative view of Polish culture. The measures intended not only to

Germanize them but also, as part and parcel of that process, to "civilize" them.[139] While Catholic support, most notably in terms of Center Party votes in the *Reichstag*, commonly threw its weight behind efforts for milder treatment of the Polish minority, there were clear limits to this. Poles and the Center Party joined forces at the moment for mutual benefit. This did not mean no differences existed, however, but only that the "discord" could be "fought out" later.[140] Just how large these differences were only became apparent later, but they already existed from the beginning.[141] Interests of the *Reich* came first.[142] Even Catholic arguments for the better treatment of Poles came infused with what they asserted was true German sentiment. One article argued, "We make no secret of it that we have always valued German civil rights and German nationality too highly for us to be able to ever have gotten used to forcible nationalization [i.e., Germanization]."[143] Indeed, such sentiment was what Catholics presented as the difference between Germans—allowing for the inclusion of their Anglo-Saxon cousins in Britain—and other people, including the Poles. It was also what made them better, worthy of their world mission. Even a comment from as staunch a defender of the Poles as Windthorst could include such double-edged implications, as his reasoning regarding the imposition of language restrictions suggests: "The Poles are not given to us to be Germanized, but that we treat them (legally). Now, if one has the desire that they be Germanized, then you can be sure that they will be Germanized much sooner and much more through the most careful consideration for the rights which have been provided them through a measure like this (Official Language Law) which must make the blood boil in the veins of these people."[144] It was not so much the end but the means he attacked, tacitly accepting an idea—that Poles would be drawn to the greater German culture—not so unlike the views of his political opponents.[145]

The World Beyond

If a return to German ways was necessary to save the *Reich* and Europe, the rest of humanity needed this all the more, according to Catholic portrayals of the world's moral geography. For as much as Germany's neighbors left a lot to be desired in their actions, the rhetoric presented an even gloomier picture beyond the continent. Drawing on their idea of European civilization, Catholic accounts saw in much of the rest of the world its opposite. Sometimes they termed it the "uncivilized world," but most articles minced no words in calling it what they believed it to be: "barbarism."[146] While they shared in asserting this division in the world with their contemporaries across the political spectrum, Catholics emphasized the central role Christianity played in determining which camp a given place fit into, a formulation expressed in their touting of European Christendom.[147] Hence, many examples of the barbarism dominating the rest of the world appeared in cases of attacks on the Church.

Though not mentioned much overall, the New World did win attention in articles for various cases of barbarity. Brazil, hardly of pivotal interest for German affairs more generally, nonetheless garnered significant attention from the Catholic press for the waging of its own *Kulturkampf*. The *Kölnische Volkszeitung* ran a several-part series on the events there beginning early in 1874 and lasting well into 1876.[148] Compared to the detailed descriptions of its Rhenish counterpart, *Germania* expressed Catholic views more succinctly and more sharply, summing up the entire matter by blaming it on Pedro II, Brazil's emperor, who it suggested "had learned nothing better on his repeated, long-term travels through Europe." Only that could explain how a ruler with European heritage (Pedro II was grandson of the last Holy Roman Emperor Francis II) would allow his country to undertake such activities that "immersed the rest of South America in barbarism."[149] While reluctant to dismiss North America as quickly, Catholic portrayals of it also passed along hearty skepticism to readers of what civilization could be said to exist there. After all, an article cautioned, "everything that glitters is not gold."[150] Another article suggested that the Americans had enough sense to view the *Kulturkampf* negatively, like the British did. Of course, the compliment was backhanded, as it implied that even the Americans, questionable as their degree of culture was, had enough sense.[151] Windthorst used the Americans in a similarly ambiguous manner in a Prussian parliamentary speech, to which his opponents seized on the negative half and dismissed the value of the United States completely with an interjection of "barbarians!"[152]

Asia, also mentioned alongside America in Windthorst's speech, fared even worse than the New World. While backhandedly complimenting the Americans for having the sense to see the problems with the *Kulturkampf*, the same *Kölnische Volkszeitung* article continued on to show just how wrong liberals actions were by adding that they used China and Japan as "models."[153] Another article sarcastically took this idea of China as a model for liberals even further, noting additional similarities between the Asian country and Germany, such as the "lack of belief" of the higher classes in both places.[154] Of course, China also appeared in various articles for actions it allowed against local Christians, events like "persecution" and "massacre."[155] Japan might have received slightly more attention if only because of its own recent successes. One article noted that the island, though "seemingly powerful and coming into bloom," could only expect "ephemeral" gains given its continued reliance on "sham knowledge," a criticism that tied back into Catholic claims that the scholarship of liberals did not meet German *Wissenschaft* standards.[156] Just like Bolanden's *Urdeutsch* pointed to the Japanese as still being "wretched barbarians," other references spoke of the need for European states, also referred to as "all nations calling themselves civilized," to intervene in Japan's actions toward Christians.[157] Of course, it turned more on who Catholics, not inhabitants of the nations themselves, called civilized.

Asia could apply to a much closer East than that of places such as China and Japan, as usage of phrases like the "Oriental Question" to describe problems in the Ottoman Empire indicated.[158] It did not merely stem from the literal meaning of Orient as the East, however, but also from European perceptions of shared characteristics.[159] In this latter vein, articles spoke of the "Asiatic steppe peoples," bunches of "hordes" meting out "Turkish barbarism," and despotic government in the "style of Nebuchadnezzar," drawing on examples from the more general region.[160] Of course the Catholic press highlighted Christian victims of these acts, which also stressed the difference between Islam and Christianity. It was not only in the distant past that barbarians "under the banner of the crescent moon" pushed at the gates of Europe, as one reprinted letter from a reader reminded.[161] Drawing on the close connection they posed between religion and civilization in the idea of European Christendom, Catholic portrayals went one step further in claiming Muslims were "pagans" as well, drawing specifically on "pagan cruelty" against Christian minority groups.[162] Much like Bolanden's pagan tribes, Catholic reportage asserted the Turks could not be expected to act much differently without the light of what they believed to be true religion.[163] Such atrocities and the "cry of horror they in the civilized world call out" proved decisively, according to one report, that such "hordes . . . did not belong to Europe."[164]

While all of these other areas of the world continued to underline not only what Catholics touted as the superiority of German culture—at least in its authentic form—in the world but also the importance of Germany's mission after 1871, they even paled in comparison to the main reason the *Reich* needed to lead: Russia. Despite the efforts of the government to court Russian friendship, Catholic rhetoric from the start presented the Empire of the Czar as one of the main reasons German unification constituted an event important to the salvation of the world.[165] Now "stronger than ever," the *Reich* could be "a guarantor for the future and the peace of Europe and the cultured behavior (*Gesittung*) of the world," since a strong Germany could protect the continent from "the flooding of barbarism embodied in Pan-Slavism" led by Russia.[166] Such statements accompanied frequent reports in both of the major daily newspapers of "Russian barbarities" perpetrated against minority groups like Catholic Poles or Ruthenians.[167] Despite bordering the *Reich*, the northeastern neighbor belonged not to Europe but to the rest of the world, most commonly a force in itself but also thrown in with Asia in Catholic portrayals. Articles spoke of "Mongolian brutality" and the despotism of the "Russian-absolutist" kind that completely went against German standards.[168] More importantly, there could be no mistaking that Russia acted completely out of step with standards "among civilized peoples" in Europe, the Catholic position claimed.[169]

Such alleged clarity on the part of Catholics as to Russia's true barbarism only made the developments of the 1870s doubly alarming to them, for both domestic and foreign relations. As the decade progressed, estimations of 1871 changed. Even in the first year of the *Reich*, Catholic arguments on the direction the nation should move in warned of the potential danger posed by "the Russian national fanaticism growing day by day," though the article added assuredly that one on one, Germany had nothing to fear.[170] Yet just a few years later, Catholic arguments increasingly pondered if 1871 might have been the beginning not of the German epoch but of one of a different kind, suggesting that "less so Germany and more so Russia has drawn the greatest benefit from the most recent European changes."[171] Despite Germany being the power that had ended France's disastrous leadership of the continent, an article complained, the new nation's energies were being sapped, leaving Russia waiting in the wings to take the "position of honor" that should be Germany's.[172] By 1876, the Catholic press increasingly spoke of the balance of power having already tipped, with "not Germany, but Russia having command over the history of Europe" now.[173] Of course, Catholics believed it was the *Kulturkampf* that was "undermin[ing] the well-being of the German nation."[174] It was this specific loss of influence to the Russians that could allow alleged barbarians to "proceed in the name of Europe" that Catholic opinion presented as a "disgrace" to the nation.[175]

In particular the "Oriental Question" brought the presentation of the German-Russian conflict to a head in Catholic rhetoric. While initial reports, especially in *Germania*, expressed support for some type of intervention to prevent Ottoman actions against minority Christian groups there, the general position of the paper quickly changed.[176] Reportage switched from highlighting the "sufferings which our Christian brothers must endure under the Turkish yoke," certainly something European hearts could not remain unmoved by, it concluded, to presenting the situation as far more complex than "Cross and crescent moon," as one later article was entitled.[177] In this light, the suffering of Christians, while not dismissed, certainly became less an issue. Articles emphasized that while German Catholics had no love for Turkish Muslims, Russia by far posed the larger threat.[178] Part of it stemmed from Russia's mistreatment of Catholics, certainly. Yet the plight of Baltic Germans, mostly Lutheran, also gained attention.[179] Indeed, as always, the opposition was anchored in both "objection out of political grounds as Germans and out of religious grounds as Catholics."[180] The former, however, came to the forefront during the "Oriental Question," with more and more emphasis placed on Russia as the "Slavic great power" in contention with the *Reich* as a German nation.[181] If Russia was allowed to gain in strength and clinch its dominant position through gains in its war against the Ottoman Empire, so Catholic opinion worried, "what will culture, freedom, and *Bildung* have as fruits from a further pan-Slavic development?"[182] Whether emphasizing the religious or the ethnic dangers posed by the "northern Colossus," Catholic rhetoric made the choice simple: German civilization or Russian barbarism.[183]

This was the choice that made the new nation so important in the larger world, according to Catholics. The events of 1871 had brought about both a "Europe-threatening barbarism" in Russia and a Germany that "alone [was] in a position" to stop it.[184] Catholics argued that success in this contest required not only that the German nation remain true to its roots but also that all its members pull together to vanquish the threat. Working together against the "most dangerous enemy of the West" meant including not only Protestants but also Catholics, whom articles portrayed as on the front lines of the struggle against such barbarism.[185] Continuing the *Kulturkampf*, on the other hand, could only lead to an impotent Germany that, through its "squandering of the best powers in domestic feuds," would end up on the losing end of history.[186] In short, this was why German unity was so desperately needed, according to Catholic arguments about the new nation. Stopping the barbarians *inside* the gate, as Catholic rhetoric so often painted the *Kulturkämpfer*, was the only way to stop those outside of it.[187]

As has often been noted for Germany as well as other countries, national integration often received a fillip from animosity directed at enemies. In the case of the *Reich*, scholars have commonly focused on France's role as a foil for the development of German identity.[188] Certainly, Catholics shared in this national demonization of the French foe as much as any other group of the 1870s, despite efforts of opponents to link them to the western neighbor via a shared religion. Moreover, Catholic attempts to define the new nation and its course cultivated a particular sense of Germanness by placing the new *Reich* in a larger frame of geographical reference constructed from portrayals of other places in Europe and the world that went far beyond this Franco-German rivalry. Not only France but also the other major nations in Europe and beyond functioned as a foil for the special qualities of the *Reich*. While the basic ideas of Christian universalism did mute some of the most direct statements of national difference, the larger discussion left no doubt that Catholic definitions of the new *Reich* also conceived of Germany as possessing qualities that distinguished it from the rest of the world and, more importantly, entitled it to lead, including over other national minorities within its own borders. Certainly the emphasis Catholic rhetoric had on religion meant many of the proposed distinctions between Germanness and otherness stemmed from more narrowly defined moral differences, but given the unbreakable link they posed between Christianity and civilization, these divergences easily bled into general cultural ones as well. Likewise, Catholic rhetoric also took pride in the military strength of Germany, though always asserting that might alone was insufficient to fulfill the *Reich*'s mission. Appeals could also play on national economic interests. Even expressions of dismay at the direction liberals and the Bismarckian government were taking Germany in continued to call upon the idea of a special German mission, which needed commitment from Catholics for its success now more than ever, but would require the unity of Germans of both confessions. Barbarism could only be fought back by civilization, and Catholic rhetoric even during the height of the *Kulturkampf* made every effort to portray civilization as a common Christian value that all true Germans could unify around.

The Catholic emphasis on Germany's special place in the moral geography of the world after 1871 not only bolstered acceptance of and integration into the *Reich* during the decade itself by making commitment to the nation an issue of humanity's salvation—a position which made opposition to the government's course all the more necessary at the same time—but also contributed to long-term integration in a much more straightforward manner as well. While the view of other nations expressed in Catholic circles in the 1870s might have been out of sync with the trends in German foreign policy at the time, it did not remain so for long. The Dual Alliance with Austria came in 1878. A German break with the "Slavic great power" Russia was not a foregone conclusion by that point, despite the increased distance generated by the Berlin Conference and grain tariffs, yet ultimately this came to pass as well.[189] Indeed, the constellation of major allies on both sides of the conflict leading up to World War I did not look so different from that suggested by the Catholic moral

geography of the *Kulturkampf,* including the somewhat ambiguous relationship with Britain that oscillated between courtship and belligerence
by the *Reich* government almost up to the very end.[190] The similarities
should not be overstressed, of course, nor should the effect. More than
three decades had elapsed. Yet given the importance of World War I
and the rallying of Germans in 1914 against the nation's enemies as a
moment for national identity, the point deserves mention. Men like
Windthorst were long dead, and those like Matthias Erzberger—a leading
figure in the Center Party who rose to prominence after the turn of the
century—had been small children during the *Kulturkampf.* On the other
hand, individuals like Georg Hertling and Julius Bachem remained in
the thick of things during both periods. Certainly, continuity between the
prejudices of the *Kaiserreich* and later German epochs should not be
overemphasized. Moreover, the extent of racism as well as the consequences of it in the Catholic rhetoric of the nineteenth century were of a
different order than that of World War I and later. The *Kulturkampf* era
hardly prepared Catholics for the propaganda or the horrors of World
War I, not to even mention World War II, but such rhetoric did have a
familiar ring to it at least in 1914.[191]

Scholars who largely see Catholic integration as not occurring until
later in the *Kaiserreich* focus on the importance of the Center's support
for the *Reich's* military (especially the navy) and colonial efforts as indicative of this shift.[192] Though emphasizing this connection too much would
be overly simplistic and problematic in some of the conclusions that it
suggests—most notably equating opposition to such activities with opposition to the nation itself, which such a formulation implies—it nonetheless remains an important indicator given the significance of both the
military and colonies for the construction of national identity.[193] In particular, Catholic support for colonies offers another opportunity to trace
the roots of this group's integration back into the 1870s. Explaining why
the Center Party supported the government's colonial politics, for
example, Georg Hertling concluded that "Germany's position in the world
made such a [stance] indispensable."[194] This comment likely alluded to
the idea that Germany's status entitled it to hold colonies like other major
powers did. Yet the "indispensable" role the *Reich* had to play undoubt-

edly carried civilizing implications with it as well, as the emphasis on missionary work among indigenous people in the Center's support for colonialism suggests.[195] The campaign appeals of the Center Party, for example, commonly also included this reason for supporting colonies, such as asserting the importance of "spreading of the Christian belief and culture" in 1903 and again in 1912, though this time the text also noted the economic importance of the protectorates.[196] The 1884 election appeal, not surprisingly, was much closer to the language of the 1870s, stating colonialism would be supported "if and to the extent that the practical [tasks] and higher missions of the *Reich* . . . make a conscientious consideration seem advisable."[197] Even the dramatic protest spearheaded by Erzberger, which led to a renewed campaign by the government to undermine the national reliability of Catholics in the Hottentot elections of 1907, really revolved around ending specific abuses perpetrated against indigenous populations, not ending colonialism itself or the paternalism born of alleged German cultural superiority that came with it.[198] While certainly tactical considerations and the hope of practical advantages played a role in Center support for colonial and military buildup, so did a belief in a particularly German mission for the advancement of civilization.[199] After all, even Erzberger described work in the colonies as "a valuable Christian and national service." He also stressed the importance of "Catholics tak[ing] their proper share in this work," just as appeals of the 1870s emphasized the necessity of the same group's commitment to the new *Reich*'s mission against barbarism.[200] While such appeals had links to a much longer history of missionary impulses coming out of Catholicism and the tradition of the Church militant itself, on the one hand, and also to the general idea of a German *Kulturnation* that predated the *Reich* as well, on the other, the clear assertion that 1871 had fundamentally changed the international situation as well as the enthusiasm over the German epoch that arose with the country's new status binds them specifically to the national identity being created after unification. That even in the *Kulturkampf* era the rhetoric of Catholics highlighted and further promoted the sense of a German mission and enthusiasm for the *Reich*'s role in spreading culture throughout the world suggests their backing for colonies later in the *Kaiserreich* was as much a continuation of certain aspects of integration into the new nation as it was a "return" to support for the central government.[201] For belief in the new nation's special mission as a world leader, if not always in the decisions of Bismarck and the liberals, was something Catholics did not abandon even in the depths of the *Kulturkampf*.

✄

Conclusion

THIS BOOK HAS uncovered how German Catholics constructed their own vision of the nation, their own idea of what the true Germany was—and could be. Contrary to the idea that their confessional identity kept them from developing a national one after unification in 1871, Catholics' religion fundamentally informed how they understood themselves as belonging in the new Germany. Certainly they imagined a very different Germany than that proposed in the dominant, largely Protestant vision of the first decade. The acrimonious conflict of the *Kulturkampf* that raged throughout the 1870s was as much about religion as it was about what the new nation should stand for—for both confessions—and fundamentally influenced how Catholics envisioned their place in Germany. It did not, however, simply leave a legacy of division that separated Catholics from their fellow Germans as is so often suggested. The 1870s also laid the groundwork for Catholic integration into the nation. Catholic efforts to define what Germany should stand for, only intensified by the very fact that opponents tried to exclude them during the *Kulturkampf*, left the embattled group far more invested in the nation than they had been at the beginning of the decade. The fight for the soul of Germany was all the more proof to Catholics that they had a role to fill in the new nation, one that only became more necessary the more divisive the conflict grew. Furthermore, the particular vision of Germany fostered among Catholics during the 1870s also played a role in integration. Despite the undoubtedly

187

distinct aspects of this alternative Catholic vision of the nation, significant elements allowed for points of commonality to be found across confessional lines, either at the time or more obviously later on.

At the beginning of the *Reich,* divisions within the Catholic community were largely put aside, as was the opposition that some had initially harbored toward unification. Certainly this represented tactical expediency, but it also drew on the notable hope and enthusiasm many Catholics greeted the new nation with in 1871. In contrast to the exclusively Protestant vision of the nation promoted by the liberals in conjunction with the Bismarckian government, Catholics quickly harmonized their rhetoric concerning national belonging in terms of a shared Christianity. It was liberals who became the focus of Catholic attacks, not Protestants more generally. Of course, the hope initially arose among Catholic political leaders that cooperation with conservative Protestants could be achieved. That this effort to build a coalition among believing Christians faltered does not undercut the effort. Nor did the initial failure of this coalition to materialize alter the Catholic rhetoric emphasizing common Christianity. Similarly, Catholic arguments shied away from attacking political conservatism head on, preferring to see it as more muddled than wrong. Certainly the failed support from conservatives and the continued attacks by liberals and the government meant that Catholics had a turbulent transition into the *Reich.* Of this there is no doubt, even if the recognition that a major conflict was unavoidable came only in 1872, somewhat later than many scholars would place the start of the *Kulturkampf.* Regardless, this conflict did not lead Catholics to turn against or even away from the nation. Instead, in the Catholic view, fervent opposition to the *Kulturkämpfer* and the government allied with them was inherently linked with devotion to the *Reich* and a concept of true Germanness.

Despite the initial hopes that the *Reich* would bring about a German epoch that all could take part in, the zeal shared by Catholics had its limits. A flurry of laws enacted in 1873 that significantly worsened the position of Catholics resulted, not surprisingly, in greater expressions of reservation and doubt. While much of this continued to be directed at the government, it was hard to miss that Catholics also began to distance themselves from the *Kaiser,* a much more integral symbol of the *Reich* itself. Catholic newspapers, books, and plays highlighted the themes of age-old Christian persecution and martyrdom with metaphorical comparisons between life in the *Reich* and that under certain emperors during the ancient Roman period, a language that could also include subversive undertones. Yet even at its most aggressive this rhetoric never truly promoted an anti-national stance. Rather, it still focused on the *Reich* being led down the wrong path, one Catholics argued was fundamentally un-German. Given that this was the height of the *Kulturkampf,* it is important to note that even at this point Catholics were not alienated from the *Reich.* Moreover, this was a phase that passed by the middle of 1875.

Attention again turned to engendering cooperation across the confessional divide by attempting to rally Christian Germans together against Jews. Close investigation of the events starting with the outburst in the middle of 1875, however, reveals that the spike in anti-Semitism was more limited in duration, if not in breadth, than has often been suggested. Whatever potential this attempt may have held for precipitating a coalition between conservatives and the Center remained untested, as developments within Catholicism quickly squashed this anti-Semitic outburst that was moving in the direction of a more racially based hate. Indeed, the fallout between two of the leading Catholic newspapers of the time over this issue, as well as the continued distance of other papers to the outburst more generally, provided very public evidence of the lack of agreement among Catholics more generally over the issue of anti-Semitism. What took the place of this anti-Semitism was none other than anti-socialism, which experienced a similarly marked spike. Much of the same rhetoric used against Jews was now employed against socialism, which provided a less problematic common "threat" around which Catholics and non-Catholics could rally.

By the fall of 1877, Catholics began to have hope that the *Kulturkampf* was coming to an end, and, correspondingly, concern turned already in these last years of the conflict toward what role they and the Center Party would play in the *Reich.* Leading Catholic politicians especially worried that many would too easily forget the lessons of the *Kulturkampf,* not a completely unwarranted fear given signs at the polls and the appearance of cracks in unity. Catholic leaders combated these problems by trying to leave open the possibility for cooperation with Bismarck at this time and by taking measures to prevent the papacy from completely overshadowing the

Center Party. The Center also broadened how it cast its mission to try to appeal to the various factions becoming more prominent as the conflict began winding down. In doing so, the rhetoric de-emphasized religious issues and stressed what the Center could offer more generally. If this period shows the height of tactical considerations influencing rhetoric on the one hand, it also, on the other, shows how much papers—the major outlet for such language—as well as Center Party leaders themselves had to respond to what they saw as the sentiments of the larger Catholic community. The creation of rhetoric was always a two-way process. Importantly, this rebranding of the Center Party's role—as well as that of Catholics in the *Reich*—employed language that cast its purpose in terms that sounded far more like those of other parties than the highly religious focus of the middle of the decade. In many ways, however, this change was also a return to the broader-based focus from the beginning of the decade.

Thematically, Catholic rhetoric reacted to the centralization inherent in the new nation by drawing attention away from Berlin and focusing it on the borders. Yet that the areas of dense Catholic settlement were borderlands did not make them peripheries, nor did it make the people who lived there peripheral to the nation. With an emphasis on the idea of local and regional distinctiveness as the quintessentially German (national) trait, Catholic rhetoric argued that only by including Catholics and the areas they lived in could the new *Reich* truly be complete. In short, areas in danger of being portrayed as liminal both for their location and confessional composition were instead pitched as integral to the nation. Yet this was only one level of this effort. On another level, the clear attention given to Berlin—most notably in the establishment of the first Catholic newspaper there around the time of unification—did mean a tacit recognition of these very centralizing aspects of the new nation that Center leaders were uncomfortable with. Moreover, the place that came to stand in for regionality more generally in the rhetoric was the place that most easily fit with what opponents thought Germany should be and chided Catholics for failing to conform to: the industrialized, educated West of the Rhineland and Westphalia. By highlighting the national importance of local and regional events in the West, the rhetoric attempted to assert an imagined topography or a mental map in which Catholics occupied a central and integral position. Long-term, of course, this rhetoric focusing on the constitution of the national through the very diversity of the local and regional fed right into the ultimately more successful integrating idea of *Heimat*.

Cautioning that the militarism of the new Germany was leading it down a destructive path—the dominance of power over right—Catholics argued that they were the best hope to get the nation back on track. Catholic leaders stressed that morality, not might, should be the foundational principle of the nation. In doing so, the rhetoric—as well as even more private understandings of the conflict that could draw on many trends over the century pointing in such a direction—equated the struggle between power and right to one between an aggressive male and a wronged female. The former was, of course, supposed to be the liberal-backed government and its forces; the latter was the Catholic community. Such arguments coalesced into an alternative construction of national identity in which the *Reich* was strikingly gendered as feminine. Such femininity was not only attached to concerns over what should be the leading value in the *Reich* but also to the ways in which Catholics emphasized their passive resistance to oppression during the *Kulturkampf.* Yet the imagined feminized nation faded quickly after the end of the *Kulturkampf.* Not insignificantly, however, the rhetoric of the period was still a major service to the progress of integration. That the battles of the 1870s remained linguistic and symbolic, despite the exceptions to this, had much to do with this understanding of Germanness and the nation.

As is generally understood, Catholics did not view fundamental ideas about knowledge or education the same way that Protestants did. This did not mean, however, that Catholics gave up their claim to the German value of *Wissenschaft.* Indeed, it was not so much that Catholic rhetoric disputed the value of *Wissenschaft*; instead, the arguments debated who actually embodied it most. Catholic arguments hinged not on justification by faith but on the assertion that Catholics themselves actually followed the ideals of scholarly production far better than the liberals, who had turned to bending knowledge to fit their ideology. In this context, the common derision of the "liberal professoriate" was more about the first part of the phrase and less about the latter. Moreover, as general excellence in academia had become associated with Germany in both domestic and foreign perceptions, Catholic arguments claiming the value of *Wissenschaft* also asserted Germanness. As much as the common story of Catholic efforts to maintain confessional primary schooling meant division—and it did—the position on higher education and scholarship presented the possibility for bridging this divide. Not surprisingly, efforts of notable Catholics to further integration around the turn of the century drew on this same idea of scholarship as a bridge that rhetoric had presented in the 1870s. More importantly, such ideas were not only the preserve of middle-class Catholics during the *Kulturkampf* but found dissemination to the larger community in the newspapers too.

Catholicism had deep traditions of Christian universalism that did not disappear in the wake of 1871. Yet this opposition to the ideology of nationalism, which the rhetoric saw as a "swindle," in no way meant for Catholics a stance against the nation. Indeed, what the rhetoric so commonly said about Christian universalism was that it was also a fundamentally German affair. Liberals and the *Kulturkampf* were undercutting this in the favor of allegedly French ideas. In short, stressing Christian universalism did not preclude defining increasingly oppositional understandings of Germany's role and value in comparison with other nations. Indeed, Germany's special role in promoting Christian civilization throughout Europe and the world had very much to do with the idea of "mission" work to spread such values to less fortunate (and less civilized) places. Hence, far from underestimating the value of the *Reich* after 1871, Catholics saw the new nation at a pivotal point in history: it could either lead civilization or be led astray. Liberals were dangerous because they, according to this view, were ruining the chances for a German epoch and leading the world to barbarism, and into the hands of Russia no less.[1] The importance for integration was threefold. First, Catholics understood their national identity in part based on stark oppositions to other peoples just as liberals and Germans more generally did. Although universalism was important, all nations were clearly not created equal in the moral geography of the world painted by Catholic rhetoric. Second, this emphasis on a sense of "mission," in this case linked to the idea of spreading German culture more generally throughout Europe, was connected to the later missionary impulses that fed Catholic support for colonialism in the Wilhelmine period, a development that scholars have rightly recognized as important for integration. Third, while certain parts of the Catholic moral geography aligned with that created by Bismarck or the liberals—such as the omnipresent opposition to France—the real integrative power of the rhetoric of the 1870s appeared after the turn of the century. The reality of German relations on the eve of World War I was not much different than the understanding of the nation's place in the moral geography created by Catholics during the *Kulturkampf*.

Of course, beyond the specific links that can be drawn from the way Catholics envisioned the nation to the long-term "making" of Germans, the *Kulturkampf* also fostered integration on the most basic level because it did not lead to a complete breakdown of relations, something not to be taken for granted given the fervor of the conflict or notable counterexamples from national struggles in other places. Aside from the rhetoric and the specifics of the national identities being constructed on each side and whether or not points of commonality were being forged, Catholics and their opponents kept the conflict within the bounds of the *Rechtsstaat* system. In particular, even at the height of the struggle and the nadir of Catholic morale, they contributed to this continued process of negotiation to settle their differences and promote their respective visions of what Germany should stand for by largely constructive, not obstructive or destructive means.[2] It was a lesson other groups could likewise draw upon when they were on the political outs, where liberals would find themselves at the end of the decade and, perhaps more significantly, where socialists remained until the end of the *Kaiserreich* despite their growing popularity. To the extent that nations are "imagined communities" based on shared identities, they are also rooted in different groups learning to manage conflict and to live together. That Catholics and their opponents who proposed a Protestant definition of the nation did so despite the bitterness of the *Kulturkampf* was good "practice" for the long-term integration of all Germans into the nation.[3]

Notes

Introduction

1. *Die Sünden des Liberalismus im ersten Jahre des neuen Deutschen Reichs* (Leipzig: Leuckart, 1872), 3–4, 29, 38–39.
2. See Oded Heilbronner, "From Ghetto to Ghetto: The Place of German Catholic Society in Recent Historiography," *Journal of Modern History* 72 (2000): 453–495. On religion—both Catholicism and Protestantism—becoming mainstream even in post-1945 historiography, see Mark Edward Ruff, "Integrating Religion into the Historical Mainstream: Recent Literature on Religion in the Federal Republic of Germany," *Central European History* 42 (2009).
3. Wolfgang Schieder, "Kirche und Revolution. Sozialgeschichtliche Aspekte der Trierer Wallfahrt von 1844," *Archiv für Sozialgeschichte* 14 (1974): 419–454; Margaret Lavinia Anderson, *Windthorst: A Political Biography* (Oxford: Clarendon, 1981); Werner Blessing, *Staat und Kirche in der Gesellschaft: institutionelle Autorität und mentaler Wandel in Bayern während des 19. Jahrhunderts* (Göttingen: Vandenhoeck & Ruprecht, 1982); Jonathan Sperber, *Popular Catholicism in Nineteenth-Century Germany* (Princeton: Princeton University Press, 1984).
4. For an emphasis on differentiation, see Wilfried Loth, "Soziale Bewegungen im Katholizismus des Kaiserreichs," *Geschichte und Gesellschaft* 17 (1991): 279–310; Thomas Mergel, especially *Zwischen Klasse und Konfession: katholisches Bürgertum im Rheinland, 1794–1914* (Göttingen: Vandenhoeck & Ruprecht, 1994); Oded Heilbronner, "Regionale Aspekte zum katholischen Bürgertum. Oder Die Besonderheit des katholischen Bürgertums im

ländlichen Süddeutschland," *Blätter für Deutsche Landesgeschichte* 131
(1995): 223–259; Thomas Mergel, "Mapping Milieus Regionally: On the
Spatial Rootedness of Collective Identities in the Nineteenth Century," in
Saxony in German History: Culture, Society, and Politics, 1830–1933, ed.
James Retallack (Ann Arbor: University of Michigan Press, 2000), 77–95;
Eric Yonke, "The Problems of the Middle Class in German Catholic
History: The Nineteenth-Century Rhineland Revisited," *Catholic Historical
Review* 88 (2002): 263–280; Rebecca Ayako Bennette, "Threatened
Protestants: Confessional Conflict in the Rhine Province and Westphalia
during the Nineteenth Century," *German History* 26 (2008): 168–194.

5. See Helmut Walser Smith, ed., *Protestants, Catholics, and Jews in
   Germany, 1800–1914* (Oxford: Berg, 2001); Olaf Blaschke, *Konfessionen
   im Konflikt: Deutschland zwischen 1800 und 1970: ein zweites konfessionelles Zeitalter* (Göttingen: Vandenhoeck & Ruprecht, 2002). See also
   Dagmar Herzog, *Intimacy and Exclusion: Religious Politics in Pre-
   Revolutionary Baden* (Princeton: Princeton University Press, 1996); Till
   van Rahden, *Juden und andere Breslauer: die Beziehungen zwischen
   Juden, Protestanten und Katholiken in einer Deutschen Grossstadt von
   1860 bis 1925* (Göttingen: Vandenhoeck & Ruprecht, 2000). For a close
   look at Catholic-Protestant daily interactions, see Tobias Dietrich,
   Konfession im Dorf: Westeuropäische Erfahrungen im 19. Jahrhundert
   (Cologne: Böhlau, 2004); Rebecca Ayako Bennette, "Confessional Mixing
   and Religious Differentiation in Nineteenth-Century Germany," (Ph.D.
   diss., Harvard University, 2002).

6. For example, compare Ronald Ross's more recent book with the many
   older titles on the topic: *The Failure of Bismarck's Kulturkampf: Catholicism and State Power in Imperial Germany, 1871–1887* (Washington
   D.C.: Catholic University of America Press, 1998).

7. Karl Bachem, *Vorgeschichte, Geschichte und Politik der Deutschen
   Zentrumspartei, zugleich ein Beitrag zur Geschichte der katholischen
   Bewegung, sowie zur allgemeinen Geschichte des neueren und neuesten
   Deutschland, 1815–1914*, 9 vols. (Cologne: J.P. Bachem, 1927).

8. Nonetheless, more recent work on this difference has also shown greater
   contours of how Catholics envisioned possible unification during this
   earlier stage. See especially Wolfgang Altgeld, *Katholizismus, Protestantismus, Judentum: über religiös begründete Gegensätze und
   nationalreligiöse Ideen in der Geschichte des deutschen Nationalismus* (Mainz: Matthias-Grünewald, 1992); Nikolaus Buschmann,
   "Auferstehung der Nation? Konfession und Nationalismus vor der
   Reichsgründung in der Debatte jüdischer, protestantischer und
   katholischer Kreise," in *Nation und Religion in der deutschen*

Geschichte, ed. Heinz-Gerhard Haupt and Dieter Langewiesche (Frankfurt a.M.: Campus, 2001), 333–388.

9. Rudolf Lill, "Die deutschen Katholiken und Bismarcks Reichsgründung," in *Reichsgründung 1870/1871: Tatsachen, Kontroversen, Interpretationen*, ed. Theodor Schieder and Ernst Deuerlein (Stuttgart: Seewald, 1970), especially 358, 361, 365. See also his subsequent works including "Der Kulturkampf in Preußen und im Deutschen Reich (bis 1878)," in *Handbuch der Kirchengeschichte*, vol. 6, no. 2, ed. Hubert Jedin (Freiburg: Herder, 1973), 28–47; "Grossdeutsch und Kleindeutsch im Spannungsfeld der Konfessionen," in *Probleme des Konfessionalismus in Deutschland seit 1800*, ed. Anton Rauscher (Paderborn: Schöningh, 1984), 29–47; "Katholizismus und Nation bis zur Reichsgründung," in *Katholizismus, nationaler Gedanke und Europa seit 1800*, ed. Albrecht Langner (Paderborn: Schöningh, 1985), 51–64. For the years 1866 to 1871, see also George C. Windell, *The Catholics and German Unity 1866/1871* (Minneapolis: University of Minnesota Press, 1954).

10. Ernst Deuerlein, "Die Bekehrung des Zentrums zur nationalen Idee," *Hochland* 62 (1970): 432–449.

11. See Horst Gründer, "Rechtskatholizismus im Kaiserreich und in der Weimarer Republik," *Westfälische Zeitschrift* 134 (1984): 107–155; "Nation und Katholizismus im Kaiserreich," in *Katholizismus, nationaler Gedanke*, ed. Albrecht Langner (Paderborn: Schöningh, 1985), 65–87; Wilfried Loth, "Zwischen autoritärer und demokratischer Ordnung: Das Zentrum in der Krise des Wilhelminischen Reiches," in *Die Minderheit als Mitte: Die Deutsche Zentrumspartei in der Innenpolitik des Reiches, 1871–1933*, ed. Winfried Becker (Paderborn: Schöningh, 1986), 47–69; "Integration und Erosion: Wandlungen des katholischen Milieus in Deutschland," in *Deutscher Katholizismus im Umbruch zur Moderne*, ed. Wilfried Loth (Stuttgart: Kohlhammer, 1991). Though the focus in his work is different, Martin Baumeister's book also sets the integration of Catholics in these later decades: *Parität und katholische Inferiorität: Untersuchungen zur Stellung des Katholizismus im Deutschen Kaiserreich* (Paderborn: Schöningh, 1987). Likewise, Thomas Nipperdey largely portrayed the integration of Catholics as something of later decades, despite his oftquoted statement that "the history of Catholicism between 1871 and 1914 is also a history of its nationalization." See *Deutsche Geschichte, 1866–1918*, Band I: Arbeitswelt und Bürgergeist (Munich: Beck, 1990), 456. The quote is taken from a section that originally appeared separately under the title *Religion im Umbruch* (Munich: Beck, 1988).

12. See Rudolf Morsey, "Die deutschen Katholiken und der Nationalstaat zwichen Kulturkampf und Erstem Weltkrieg," *Historisches Jahrbuch* 90

(1970): 31–64, especially 35–37. Morsey also offered subsidiary points on integration in "Ludwig Windthorst. Größe und Grenzen von Bismarcks Gegenspieler" and "Streiflichter zur Geschichte der deutschen Katholikentage 1848–1931," both of which are in *Von Windthorst bis Adenauer: Ausgewählte Aufsätze zu Politik, Verwaltung und politischem Katholizismus im 19. und 20. Jahrhundert,* ed. Ulrich von Hehl et.al. (Paderborn: Schöningh, 1997): 145–157, 187–200.

13. See, for example, the argument against integration in Christoph Weber, *"Eine starke, enggeschlossene Phalanx": Der politische Katholizismus und die erste deutsche Reichstagswahl 1871* (Essen: Klartext, 1992).

14. Frank Becker, "Konfessionelle Nationsbilder im Deutschen Kaiserreich," in *Nation und Religion,* ed. Heinz-Gerhard Haupt and Dieter Langewiesche (Frankfurt and New York: Campus, 2001), 389–418. Barbara Stambolis also looks at these aspects of national identity formation for Catholics. The *Kulturkampf* era is addressed for only two pages, however, and her emphasis at least for the 1870s still suggests distance to the nation. See "Nationalisierung trotz Ultramontanisierung oder: 'Alles für Deutschland. Deutschland aber für Christus': Mentalitätsleitende Wertorientierung deutscher Katholiken im 19. und 20. Jahrhundert," *Historische Zeitschrift* 269 (1999): especially 70–71.

15. Zalar mainly connects reading with integration beginning in the 1890s. See Jeffrey T. Zalar, "'Knowledge is Power': The *Borromäusverein* and Catholic Reading Habits in Imperial Germany," *Catholic Historical Review* 86 (2000): 20–46; Jeffrey T. Zalar, "The Process of Confessional Inculturation: Catholic Reading in the 'Long Nineteenth Century'," in *Protestants, Catholics, Jews: 1800–1914,* ed. Helmut Walser Smith (Oxford: Berg, 2001), 121–152; Jeffrey T. Zalar, "Knowledge and Nationalism in Imperial Germany: A Cultural History of the Association of Saint Charles Borromeo, 1980–1914," (Ph.D. diss., Georgetown University, 2002); Pontus Hiort, "Constructing Another Kind of German: Catholic Commemorations of German Unification in Baden, 1870–1876," *Catholic Historical Review* 93 (2007): 17–46; Pontus Hiort, "Negotiating Identities: South German Catholics and the Formation of National Identity, 1871–1914," (Ph.D. diss., Northern Illinois University, 2007).

16. Helmut Walser Smith, *German Nationalism and Religious Conflict: Culture, Ideology, Politics, 1870–1914* (Princeton: Princeton University Press, 1995). Though largely showing division for the early decades, Stefan Laube hints at possibilities for long-term integration: "Konfessionelle Brüche in der nationalen Heldengalerie—Protestantische, katholische und jüdische Erinnerungsgemeinschaften im deutschen Kaiserreich

(1871–1918)," in *Nation und Religion in der deutschen Geschichte,* ed. Heinz-Gerhard Haupt and Dieter Langewiesche (Frankfurt and New York: Campus, 2001), 293–332.

17. On this relationship, see Stefan Berger, *The Search for Normality: National Identity and Historical Consciousness in Germany Since 1800* (Providence: Berghahn, 1997), especially Chapters 1 and 2.

18. This approach is often associated with the work of Benedict Anderson and his seminal book *Imagined Communities: Reflections on the Origins and Spread of Nationalism* (London: Verso, 1983). It is also linked to the more general work of modernists and the idea of a nation as constructed. See Ernest Gellner, *Nations and Nationalism* (Ithaca: Cornell University Press, 1983); Eric Hobsbawm and Terence Ranger, eds., *The Invention of Tradition* (Cambridge: Cambridge University Press, 1983). On memory, see Maurice Halbwachs, *On Collective Memory,* ed. Lewis A. Coser (Chicago: University of Chicago Press, 1992), especially 182–183; Paul Connerton, *How Societies Remember* (Cambridge: Cambridge University Press, 1989), especially 1–4, 14, 16; Aleida Assmann, *Arbeit am nationalen Gedächtnis: Eine kurze Geschichte der deutschen Bildungsidee* (Frankfurt a.M.: Campus, 1993), especially 46, 50–57; John R. Gillis, "Memory and Identity: The History of a Relationship," in *Commemorations: The Politics of National Identity,* ed. John R. Gillis (Princeton: Princeton University Press, 1994), especially 3; Alon Confino, "Collective Memory and Cultural History: Problems of Method," *American Historical Review* 102 (1997): 1386–1403. For Germany in particular, see Alon Confino and Peter Fritzsche, *The Work of Memory: New Directions in the Study of German Society and Culture* (Urbana: University of Illinois Press, 2002). Memory has also become important for the field of religion: Danièle Hervieu-Léger, *Religion as a Chain of Memory* (New Brunswick, NJ: Rutgers University Press, 2000), especially 123. For Germany, see Stefan Laube, *Fest, Religion und Erinnerung: konfessionelles Gedächtnis in Bayern von 1804–1917* (Münich: Beck, 1999).

19. David Blackbourn and James Retallack, "Introduction," in *Localism, Landscape, and the Ambiguities of Place: German-Speaking Central Europe, 1860–1930* (Toronto: University of Toronto Press, 2007), 7. On religion specifically, see Heinz-Gerhard Haupt and Dieter Langewiesche, eds., *Nation und Religion in der deutschen Geschichte* (Frankfurt and New York: Campus, 2001).

20. On the later period, see Celia Applegate, *A Nation of Provincials: The German Idea of Heimat* (Berkeley: University of California Press, 1990); Alon Confino, *The Nation as a Local Metaphor: Württemberg, Imperial*

Germany, and National Memory, 1871–1918 (Chapel Hill: University of North Carolina Press, 1997). On the earlier case, see Abigail Green, *Fatherlands: State-Building and Nationhood in Nineteenth-Century Germany* (Cambridge: Cambridge University Press, 2001).

21. See Dieter Langewiesche and Georg Schmidt, eds., *Föderative Nation: Deutschlandkonzepte von der Reformation bis zum Ersten Weltkrieg* (Münich: Oldenbourg, 2000). See also, Otto Dann, *Nation und Nationalismus in Deutschland, 1770–1990* (Munich: Beck, 1993); Otto Dann und Miroslav Hroch, "Einleitung," in *Patriotismus und Nationsbildung am Ende des Heiligen Römischen Reiches*, ed. Otto Dann, Miroslav Hroch, and Johannes Koll (Cologne: SH-Verlag, 2003), 9–18. On federalism, especially in this context, see Maiken Umbach, ed., *German Federalism: Past, Present, Future* (Basingstoke: Palgrave, 2002); Abigail Green, "The Federal Alternative? A New View of Modern German History," *Historical Journal* 46 (2003): 187–202.

22. See the relationship between "conflict" and "consensus" discussed in Siegfried Weichlein, *Nation und Region: Integrationsprozesse im Bismarckreich* (Düsseldorf: Droste, 2004), especially 34. Though primarily concerned with regional differences, Weichlein's account also has points on Catholic integration into the nation during the *Kulturkampf*. See 231–232, 284, 290, 372. Though more informative on Ireland than Germany, a notable contribution from outside the field of history on this idea is Kimberly Cowell-Meyers, *Religion and Politics in the Nineteenth Century: The Party Faithful in Ireland and Germany* (Westport, CN: Praeger, 2002).

23. Wolfgang Altgeld only mentions the post-1871 era briefly, but he does suggest that the *Kulturkampf* may have links to long-term integration as well: *Katholizismus, Protestantismus, Judentum*, 207.

24. For example, see Margaret Lavinia Anderson's, "The Kulturkampf and the Course of German History," *Central European History* 19 (1986): 82–115.

25. On the liberal viewpoint alone, of course, there have recently been two notable books: Michael B. Gross, *The War Against Catholicism: Liberalism and the Anti-Catholic Imagination in Nineteenth-Century Germany* (Ann Arbor: University of Michigan, 2005); Borutta, *Antikatholizismus: Deutschland und Italien im Zeitalter der europäischen Kulturkämpfe* (Göttingen: Vandenhoeck and Ruprecht, 2010).

26. Especially in older research, backing for government initiatives is equated with acceptance and support for the nation, suggesting a tendency in the literature to preference official or liberal visions that is still present at times in the newer research. On this point, also see Borutta, *Antikatholizismus*, especially 296.

27. Mergel discusses middle-class Catholics, for example, a small number of whom ultimately came to identify with liberalism and joined in actions against the Church: Mergel, *Zwischen Klasse und Konfession*, especially 253; Thomas Mergel, "Grenzgänger: Das katholische Bürgertum im Rheinland zwischen bürgerlichem und katholischem Milieu 1870–1914," in *Religion im Kaiserreich: Milieus—Mentalitäten—Krisen*, ed. Olaf Blaschke and Frank Michel Kuhlemann (Gütersloh: Chr. Kaiser, 1996), especially 174. For other examples, see Weber, *"Eine starke, enggeschlossene Phalanx"*, especially 42ff.; Gründer, "Rechtskatholizismus"; Heilbronner, "Die Besonderheit."

28. For the commonly cited statistics, see Johannes Schauff, *Das Wahlverhalten der deutschen Katholiken im Kaiserreich und in der Weimarer Republik: Untersuchungen aus dem Jahre 1928*, ed. Rudolf Morsey (Mainz: Matthias-Grünewald, 1975), 74. For a reanalysis, see Jonathan Sperber, *The Kaiser's Voters: Electors and Elections in Imperial Germany* (Cambridge, Cambridge University Press, 1997), 168.

29. Indeed, these have been addressed in terms of the divisive potential in political Catholicism specifically. See the older yet still helpful review of this as well as several other major issues of dispute that still affect how political Catholicism is viewed—such as how democratic or how liberal it was—by Winfried Becker, "Die Deutsche Zentrumspartei im Bismarckreich," in *Die Minderheit als Mitte: Die Deutsche Zentrumspartei in der Innenpolitik des Reiches 1871–1933*, ed. Winfried Becker (Paderborn: Schöningh, 1986), 9–45.

30. Even in an article on regionalism within Catholicism, Thomas Mergel nonetheless notes this unity on the whole: "Mapping Milieus," 82.

31. For more on this point, see the discussion below.

32. See, for example, Brian Vick on this point: *Defining Germany: The 1848 Frankfurt Parliamentarians and National Identity* (Cambridge, MA: Harvard University Press, 2002), 8. After all, the purpose of many of the laudable recent efforts to break down groups into smaller units—in certain cases telling nonnational narratives—is to uncover voices and visions that have not been heard in traditional accounts. On recent efforts in this trend, see Blackbourn and Retallack, *Localism, Landscape, and the Ambiguities*; Niel Gregor, Nils Roemer, and Mark Roseman, eds., *German History from the Margins* (Bloomington, IN: Indiana University Press, 2006). Even transnational narratives are not unconnected to nation-building: David Blackbourn, "Das Kaiserreich transnational: Eine Skizze," in *Das Kaiserreich Transnational: Deutschland in der Welt 1871–1914* (Göttingen: Vandenhoeck & Ruprecht, 2004), 304–305.

Konrad Jarausch and Michael Geyer also note that efforts to move beyond
the traditional narrative would still mean speaking about the nation in
some cases, but it would be the visions and constructions by minorities
and other marginalized groups: *Shattered Past: Reconstructing German
Histories* (Princeton: Princeton University Press, 2003), especially 59–60,
223, 228. Of course there is a more general, philosophical debate concerning the viability of larger narratives that goes beyond attempting to
respond to the particular needs of the current historiography. See also
Helmut Walser Smith, *The Continuities of German History: Nation,
Religion, and Race across the Long Nineteenth Century* (Cambridge:
Cambridge University Press, 2008), especially 4–6; Krijn Thijs, "The
Metaphor of the Master: 'Narrative Hierarchy' in National Historical
Cultures of Europe," in *The Contested Nation: Ethnicity, Class, Religion
and Gender in National Histories*, ed. Stefan Berger and Chris Lorenz,
(Basingstoke: Palgrave, 2008), especially 61–62.

33. This is not meant to suggest that nations are complete constructions
or total "inventions." See Miroslav Hroch, *Das Europa der Nationen:
Die moderne Nationsbildung im europäischen Vergleich* (Göttingen:
Vandenhoeck & Ruprecht, 2005), especially 8, 23–24, 39; John Breuilly,
"Introduction," in *Nations and Nationalism*, 2nd ed., Ernest Gellner
(Ithaca: Cornell University Press, 2008), 1; Bernd Estel, *Nation und
Nationale Identität: Versuch einer Rekonstruktion* (Weisbaden:
Westdeutscher Verlag, 2002), especially 14–15; Geoff Eley, "How and
Where is German History Centered?" in *German History from the
Margins*, ed. Neil Gregor, Nils H. Roemer, and Mark Roseman
(Bloomington, IN: Indiana University Press, 2006), 271.

34. For more on this point, see the discussion linked to the press below. But
also consider that it might have had particular relevance for this period, as
Pius IX's saying "One must give words their meaning back" was often
referenced in Catholic arguments that pointed to what they alleged was
liberal doubletalk. From this stemmed the tendency in Catholic arguments to expound on the true definition of words, distinguishing between
contemporary corruptions and the "best sense of the word." *Augsburger
Postzeitung*, February 20, 1872.

35. On the difficulty of defining "nation" and "nationalism," see Hroch,
Europa der Nationen, especially 11–13, 29, 33–35; Katherine Verdery,
"Whither 'Nation' and 'Nationalism'?," *Daedalus* 122 (1993): 38–39.
Chris Lorenz, drawing on the work of W. B. Gallie, suggests that the
idea of "essentially contested concepts" could also be applied to terms
such as these. See "Representations of Identity: Ethnicity, Race, Class,
Gender and Religion. An Introduction to Conceptual History," in *The*

Contested Nation: Ethnicity, Class, Religion and Gender in National Histories, ed. Stefan Berger and Chris Lorenz (Basingstoke: Palgrave, 2008), 30, 33.

36. This is in reference, of course, to the often cited quote by Massimo d'Azeglio: "We have made Italy: now we must make Italians."

37. On the use of "alternative" more generally, the word quickly brings to mind Vernon Lidtke's study. Yet Lidtke uses the term to suggest a force potentially destabilizing to the state or counter to the nation. Lidtke, *The Alternative Culture: Socialist Labor in Imperial Germany* (New York: Oxford University Press, 1985), especially 6–7. Many scholars of nations and nationalism also use *alternative* in this sense. See, for example, Homi K. Bhabha, "Introduction: Narrating the Nation," in *Nation and Narration,* ed. Homi K. Bhabha (London: Routledge, 1990), especially 3; Phillip Spencer and Howard Wollman, *Nationalism: A Critical Introduction* (London: SAGE, 2002), especially 50, 149, 170, 199. Here, however, *alternative* is used in reference to what Bismarck or the liberals were on the whole offering as a definition of Germanness in the 1870s, not to the nation itself. In this sense, see Katherine Verdery's use of *alternative*: "Whither 'Nation'," 39.

38. On the importance of newspaper sources generally, see Wilhelm Mommsen's 1926 article for *Archiv für Politik und Geschichte,* reprinted in "Die Zeitung als historische Quelle," in *Das Institut für Zeitungsforschung in Dortmund: 1926: Eine Disziplin nimmt Gestalt an; Festschrift zum 80jährigen Jubiläum,* ed. Gabriele Toepser-Ziegert and Karen Peter (Dortmund: Insitut für Zeitungsforschung, 2006), especially 56, 58, 64; Astrid Blome's article by partly the same name as Mommsen's: "Die Zeitung als historische Quelle. Ein Beispiel aus dem petrinischen Rußland," in *Zeitung, Zeitschrift, Intelligenzblatt und Kalender: Beiträge zur historischen Presseforschung,* ed. Astrid Blome (Bremen: Lumière, 2000), 161–176.

39. See Christopher Clark and Wolfram Kaiser, drawing on the ideas of Margaret Anderson as well: "Introduction: The European Culture Wars," in *Culture Wars: Secular-Catholic Conflict in Nineteenth-Century Europe,* ed. Chris Clark and Wolfram Kaiser (Cambridge: Cambridge University Press, 2003), 5; Manuel Borutta specifically poses the media itself as an "actor" in the conflict: *Antikatholizismus,* especially 25, 43, 155–158.

40. Contrast this with older accounts focusing on the Catholic press that largely use the reportage as a source for basic facts and general Center Party stances: Klemens Löffler, *Geschichte der katholischen Presse Deutschlands* (M. Gladbach: Volksvereins-Verlag, 1924); Hans Joachim

Reiber, *Die katholische deutsche Tagespresse unter dem Einfluß des Kulturkampfes* (Görlitz: Hoffmann & Reiber, 1930); Josef Lange, *Die Stellung der überregionalen katholischen deutschen Tagespresse zum Kulturkampf in Preußen (1871–1878)* (Frankfurt a.M.: Peter Lang, 1974).

41. On an overestimation of the power of the press, see, for example, Michael Parenti, *Inventing Reality: The Politics of News Media* (New York: St. Martin's, 1986).

42. On this point, see Peter Fritzsche, *Reading Berlin 1900* (Cambridge, MA: Harvard University Press, 1996), especially 2, 3, 6, 10. On the influence of the press on public opinion, also see, Thomas Nipperdey, *Deutsche Geschichte 1800–1866: Bürgerwelt und starker Staat* (Munich: Beck, 1983), 589–590; Kurt Koszyk, *Deutsche Presse im 19. Jahrhundert*, Teil II (Berlin: Colloquium, 1966), 24; Otto Groh, *Die unerkannte Kulturmacht: Grundlegung der Zeitungswissenschaft*, 7 vols. (Berlin: de Gruyter, 1960–1972), especially vols. 1 and 7. A contemporary of the late nineteenth century concluded, "Whenever the history of the origin and growth of public opinion shall be written, the history of the newspaper will be found to constitute its most important chapter." In Frank Taylor, *The Newspaper Press as a Power Both in the Expression and Formation of Public Opinion* (Oxford: Blackwell, 1898), 1.

43. Again, see Fritzsche, *Reading Berlin*, especially 2, 3, 6, 10.

44. On Catholics and representation in the production of scholarly historical texts, see Berger, *Search for Normality*, especially 11, 32. On Catholic marginalization in the construction of monuments, see also Hiort, "Negotiated Identities," 7. Furthermore, there are important limits to what has survived in the archival record itself, which is missing, for example, the wealth of information of the Centrum's main records for the *Kaiserreich* or the files of an organization like the Verein der deutschen Katholiken. Contrarily, the rather plentiful documents on Catholic daily conflicts often shed relatively little light on the issue of national identity by themselves.

45. Letter to Frau Professor Kleinschrod, June 4, 1872. Janssen repeated the sentiments in a letter to Fräulein Johanna Pastor, July 18, 1872. In *Johannes Janssens Briefe*, Band 1, 427, 430. On cohesion, including many references to the press in this respect, see Reiber, *Tagespresse*, 1; Lange, *Die Stellung*, 303; Nipperdey, *Deutsche Geschichte*, vol. 1, 443; Nipperdey, *Deutsche Geschichte*, vol. 2, 342–343; Mergel, "Mapping Milieus," 82; Jonathan Sperber, "Roman Catholic Religious Identity in Rhineland-Westphalia, 1800–70: Quantitative Examples and Some

Political Implications," *Social History* 7 (1982): 315ff.; Amine Haase, *Katholische Presse und die Judenfrage: Inhaltsanalyse katholischer Periodika am Ende des 19. Jahrhunderts* (Pullach: Verlag Dokumentation, 1975), 48–49. The Augustinus-Verein was established in 1878 to help coordinate the various press outlets, formalizing what had already been taking place throughout the 1870s. See Wilhelm Kisky, *Der Augustinus-Verein zur Pflege der katholischen Presse von 1878 bis 1928* (Düsseldorf: Verlag des Augustinus-Vereins, 1928). Observations of unity could cut both ways, as a government report from 1876 suggests. Even before all the actual reports from the various districts came in, the *Regierungspräsident* went ahead and formed his conclusions based on the "known Ultramontane beliefs" of the majority in his area. June 1, 1876, Staatsarchive Münster, OP 1601,3.

46. Bishop Ketteler of Mainz, for example, believed the founding of a central newspaper that all Catholics could look to would be "one of the most fortunate occurrences" in the process of overcoming disunity. See the letter to Archbishop Joseph Othmar Rauscher from February 14, 1862, Dom- und Diözesanarchiv Mainz, C7.3,2. Ketteler retained a particular interest in press activities, as his correspondence with Paul Majunke, head editor of *Germania*, suggests: see letters from September 20 and 22, 1874. Several years of conflict had, not surprisingly, done nothing to lessen estimations of the press's importance for keeping the Catholic community unified. In a letter to Christoph Moufang, who administered the bishopric after Ketteler's death, the papal nuncio to Germany stressed the importance of the Catholic newspapers also reporting on the sentiments beginning to take hold among the community in response to a recent event so that the further spread of the opinion could be aided. Letter from September 21, 1878, Dom- und Diözesanarchiv Mainz, D5.3, Nr. 2. In addition to many leading Catholics who wrote for the newspapers, Windthorst—who did not pen pieces directly—influenced the press via his contacts with key members of the industry: Ellen Lovell Evans, *The German Center Party 1870–1933: A Study in Political Catholicism* (Carbondale, IL: Southern Illinois University Press, 1981), 71. The development of the Catholic press was a topic of concern at all yearly *Katholikentage* meetings during the *Kulturkampf* as well. See also Borutta, *Antikatholizismus*, especially 157–159; Reiber, *Tagespresse*, 1–2; Lange, *Stellung*, 303: Hubert Jedin, "Freiheit und Aufstieg des deutschen Katholizismus zwischen 1848 und 1870," in *Kirche des Glaubens, Kirche der Geschichte: Ausgewählte Aufsätze und Vorträge*, ed. Hubert Jedin (Freiburg: Herder, 1966), 477.

47. The initial organizational announcement of the Verein der deutschen Katholiken, for example, included a segment on the issue of treatment Catholics received in the general press. See the copy in the Landeshauptarchiv Koblenz, 403, Nr. 6695. See also, Borutta, *Antikatholizismus*, especially 157–159. This concern had a long-standing history by the 1870s: Zalar, "Catholic Reading," 139, n. 24. It was not merely an issue for Catholics, however, as Karl August Mühlhäusser's tract for Protestants indicates: *Christentum und Presse* (Frankfurt a.M.: Zimmer, 1876).

48. Nipperdey suggests even other publications being included in measuring the importance of the Catholic press, finding their influence to have been "considerable." See Reiber, *Tagespresse*, 134ff.; Lange, *Stellung*, 2; Nipperdey, *Deutsche Geschichte*, vol. 1, 443.

49. Abigail Green also discusses the inherent difficulty of connecting various examples of identity construction with their actual reception: *Fatherlands*, 20.

50. Nancy R. Reagin, "Review: Recent Work on German National Identity: Regional? Imperial? Gendered? Imaginary?" *Central European History* 37 (2004): 286–288. For similar sentiments, see Heinz-Gerhard Haupt, "Religion and Nation in Europe in the 19th Century: Some Comparative Notes," *Estudos Avançados* 22 (2008): 89.

51. *Verhandlungen der einundzwanzigsten Generalversammlung der katholischen Vereine Deutschlands zu Mainz am 10., 11., 12.,13. Und 14. September 1871* (Mainz: Kirchhein, 1871), 261. The *Augsburger Postzeitung* asserted, "The press is a force." In "Die Tagespresse und die katholische Partai," September 27, 1871. After years of bitter struggle, *Tremonia* concluded that newspapers were one of the "most important factors of public life" in the appropriately titled article, "Der Einfluß der Presse auf das religiöse Leben der Gegenwart," from May 1, 1877.

52. Letter from September 9, 1871, StAM OP 1601,1. Such concerns led to various governmental limitations or outright bans in sensitive areas of the *Reich* like the newly acquired Alsace-Lorraine. See, for example, Reiber, *Tagespresse*, 11; Lange, *Stellung*, 2, 29; Anderson, *Practicing Democracy*, 113, n. 29. On government use of press outlets to its own ends, see Eberhard Naujoks, "Bismarck und die Organisation der Regierungspresse," *Historische Zeitschrift* 205 (1967): 46–80; Stewart A. Stehlin, "Bismarck and the Secret Use of the Guelph Fund," *Historian* 33 (1970): 21–39; Abigail Green, "Intervening in the Public Sphere: German Governments and the Press, 1815–1870," *The Historical Journal* 44 (2001): 155–175.

53. Though focusing more on clerical leaders, Anderson noted the "democratization and laicization" of Catholicism stemming from the *Kulturkampf*,

which meant that even "directives" were "more often reflective of the views of the 'Catholic people,'" than simply top-down pronouncements. See Anderson, "Kulturkampf," 113.

54. Reiber includes a particularly telling example of this regarding the readership cautioning the *Schlesische Volkszeitung* against causing dissent among Catholics: *Tagespresse*, 77. On the need for newspapers to be responsive to the readership more generally, see Troy Paddock (who is drawing upon Groh's *Die unerkannte Kulturmacht*) in *Creating the Russian Peril: Education, the Public Sphere, and National Identity in Imperial Germany, 1890–1914* (Rochester, NY: Camden House, 2010), 9.

55. Mommsen, "Zeitung," 60. On the idea of Catholic rhetoric as barefaced attempts to conceal the truth, see Weber, *"Eine starke, enggeschlossene Phalanx,"* especially 13. Yet August Reichensperger considered the newspapers accurate enough that he often referred his wife to various articles for more information on particular issues he was involved with in Berlin. See, for example, letters dated April 3, May 27, and December 18, 1871, Landeshauptarchiv Koblenz, 700,138, Nr. 4.

56. Morsey, "Streiflichter," 188. On the centrality of these meetings, see also Weber, *"Eine starke, enggeschlossene Phalanx,"* 131.

57. As the general history of the event has been dealt with in other accounts, this book refrains from a more extensive general narrative.

58. On this point, see Altgeld, *Katholizismus, Protestantismus, Judentum,* 207. While there is reason to question whether this was a "refounding of the *Reich*," as some have termed it, especially as this interpretation encompasses far more than just the role of the Center Party, the phrase nonetheless captures the significant shift in the position of Catholics and the party after the end of the *Kulturkampf.* For an overview, see Kenneth D. Barkin, "1878–1879: The Second Founding of the Reich, a Perspective," *German Studies Review* 10 (1987): 219–235. On the idea of the failure of the dominant version of the liberals, see, for example, Confino, *The Nation as a Local Metaphor.*

1. The German Question and Religion

1. On Görres, see Jon Vanden Heuvel, *A German Life in the Age of Revolution: Joseph Görres, 1776–1848* (Washington D.C.: Catholic University of America Press, 2001), especially Chapters 1–7. Heuvel points out that this change of opinion was rather understandable, as Görres had always seen French rule as merely a means to the much more important end, in his mind, of greater liberty. Only this could justify the difficulties that "the German national character" of those in the Rhineland would experience

in the face of French rule (p. 53). On the general decline of sympathy with republicanism in the Rhineland, see T. C. W. Blanning, *The French Revolution in Germany: Occupation and Resistance in the Rhineland, 1792–1802* (New York: Oxford University Press, 1983).

2. Nipperdey, *Deutsche Geschichte, 1800–1866*, 301–302.

3. Dieter Düding, "The Nineteenth-Century German Nationalist Movement as a Movement of Societies," in *Nation-Building in Central Europe*, ed. Hagen Schulze (Leamington Spa: Berg, 1987), 23.

4. Stefan Berger, *Germany* (London: Arnold, 2004), 29.

5. Düding, "Nationalist Movement," 40.

6. See, for example, Michael Jeismann, *Das Vaterland der Feinde: Studien zum nationalen Feindbegriff und Selbstverständnis in Deutschland und Frankreich, 1792–1918* (Stuttgart: Klett-Cotta, 1992).

7. Nipperdey, *Deutsche Geschichte 1800–1866*, 305; Düding, "Nationalist Movement," 25–26, 36; Berger, *Germany*, 43ff.; Anthony Steinhoff, "Christianity and the Creation of Germany," in *The Cambridge History of Christianity: World Christianities*, vol. 8, ed. Sheridan Gilley and Brian Stanley (Cambridge: Cambridge University Press, 2006), 283. Steinhoff's article provides an informative overview of many issues related to religion and nationalism.

8. Martin Kitchen, *A History of Modern Germany* (Malden, MA: Blackwell, 2006), 52ff.

9. Ibid., 64ff.

10. Berger, *Germany*, 45, 50.

11. David Blackbourn, *The Fontana History of Germany 1780–1918: The Long Nineteenth Century* (Hammersmith: Fontana, 1997), 135.

12. Nipperdey, *Deutsche Geschichte 1800–1866*, 189–191, 202, 307.

13. Blackbourn, *The Fontana History of Germany*, 248–252.

14. Altgeld, *Katholizismus, Protestantismus, Judentum*, 67, 79; Rudolf Lill, "Katholizismus und Nation bis zur Reichsgründung." in *Katholizismus, nationaler Gedanke und Europa seit 1800*, ed. Albrecht Langner (Paderborn: Schöningh, 1985), 58–59.

15. Sperber, *Popular Catholicism*, 60.

16. Lill, "Katholizismus," 59.

17. Stambolis, "Nationalisierung trotz Ultramontanisierung," 59; Charlotte Tacke, *Denkmal im sozialen Raum: Nationale Symbole in Deutschland und Frankreich im 19. Jahrhundert* (Göttingen: Vandenhoeck & Ruprecht, 1995), 39, 216–217. The monument commemorated Hermann of the Cherusci and his total defeat of Roman soldiers in a battle situated in the Teutoburg Forest in AD 9. For more, see Chapter 7.

18. Christopher Clark, *Iron Kingdom: The Rise and Downfall of Prussia, 1600–1947* (Cambridge, MA: Harvard University Press, 2008), 437; Walter Bußmann, *Zwischen Preußen und Deutschland: Friedrich Wilhelm IV. Eine Biographie* (Berlin: Siedler, 1990), 114, 294–295.

19. Bußmann, *Friedrich Wilhelm IV,* 174ff.

20. Altgeld emphasizes the dominance of these trends in *Katholizismus, Protestantismus, Judentum.*

21. Ibid., 55; Christel Köhle-Hezinger, *Evangelisch, Katholisch: Untersuchungen zu konfessionellem Vorurteil und Konflikt im 19. und 20. Jahrhundert vornehmlich am Beispiel Württembergs* (Tübingen: Tübinger Vereinigung für Volkskunde, 1976).

22. Steinhoff, "Creation of Germany," 282.

23. Ibid., 282, 286; Clark, *Iron Kingdom,* 419; Sperber, *Popular Catholicism,* Chapters 1 and 2.

24. On the conflict, see Clark, *Iron Kingdom,* 420–421; Bußmann, *Friedrich Wilhelm IV,* 159ff.; Friedrich Keinemann, *Das Kölner Erieignis, Sein Widerhall in der Rheinprovinz und in Westfalen*, Teil 1 (Münster: Aschendorf, 1974); Rudolf Amelunxen, *Das Kölner Erieignis* (Essen: Ruhrländische Verlagsgesellschaft, 1952).

25. Altgeld, *Katholizismus, Protestantismus, Judentum,* 152.

26. Bußmann, *Friedrich Wilhelm IV,* 162.

27. Ibid., 129; Adolf M. Birke, "German Catholics and the Quest for National Unity," in *Nation-Building in Central Europe,* ed. Hagen Schulze (Leamington Spa: Berg, 1987), 55.

28. Altgeld, *Katholizismus, Protestantismus, Judentum,* 125.

29. Ibid., 158; Steinhoff, "Creation of Germany," 283.

30. Kevin Cramer, "The Cult of Gustavus Adolphus: Protestant Identity and German Nationalism," in *Protestants, Catholics, and Jews, 1800–1914,* ed. Helmut Walser Smith (Oxford: Berg, 2001), 97–120.

31. Lill, "Katholizismus," 53, 59; Nipperdey, *Deutsche Geschichte 1800–1866,* 408; Buschmann, "Konfession und Nationalismus," 342.

32. Lill, "Katholizismus," 57.

33. Nipperdey, *Deutsche Geschichte 1800–1866,* 306.

34. Of interest given the feminine imagery of the nation employed by Catholics during the *Kulturkampf* is the inclusion of some women among these greats as well. On both of Ludwig's monuments, see Hans A. Pohlsander, *National Monuments and Nationalism in 19th Century Germany* (Bern: Lang, 2008), Chapter 6. On Saint Boniface, see Becker, "Konfessionelle Nationsbilder," 405.

35. Nipperdey, *Deutsche Geschichte 1800–1866,* 611.

36. Steinhoff, "Creation of Germany," 288.
37. Blackbourn, *Fontana History of Germany*, 159, 165.
38. Steinhoff, "Creation of Germany," 285.
39. Clark, *Iron Kingdom*, 438; Steinhoff, "Creation of Germany," 287.
40. Altgeld, *Katholizismus, Protestantismus, Judentum*, 146, 198.
41. This liberal claim even appears, sarcastically included, in a piece by the Bishop of Mainz, Wilhelm Emmanuel von Ketteler: *Der Culturkampf gegen die kathol. Kirche und die neuen Kirchengesetzentwürfe für Hessen* (Mainz: Kirchheim, 1874), 14. Concerning Gerlach, Gustav Kramer specifically addressed this claim and firmly rebutted the idea that the politician had either converted or even could have come close to doing so given his entrenched Protestant beliefs: *Die Stellung des Präsidenten Ludwig von Gerlach zum politischen Katholizismus* (Breslau: Marcus, 1931), especially 33, 35, 47. For the opposing view, see Christoph Weber, who suggests Gerlach, "de facto a crypto-Catholic," as well as many other individuals involved with the Center Party—both those openly and others secretly Catholics—were fundamentally deceptive about their real religious beliefs: *"Eine starke, enggeschlossene Phalanx"*, especially 36.
42. Buschmann, "Konfession und Nationalismus," especially 334, 343, 344, 347, 349, 368.
43. On liberal Catholics, see Mergel, *Zwischen Klasse*.
44. Sperber, *Popular Catholicism*, 52ff.; Steinhoff, "Creation of Germany," 289.
45. For more on the events in Baden, see Julius Dorneich, *Franz Josef Buss und die katholische Bewegung in Baden* (Freiburg: Herder, 1979), 330ff.
46. Nipperdey, *Deutsche Geschichte 1800–1866*, 409ff.; Steinhoff, "Creation of Germany," 290–291.
47. Lill, "Katholizismus," especially 61. See also Mergel, *Zwischen Klasse*.
48. On these stances and the lead up to the war, see Nipperdey, *Deutsche Geschichte 1800–1866*, especially 782–783; Clark, *Iron Kingdom*, especially 542–543; Blackbourn, *The Fontana History of Germany*, 225–259. On the Protestant churches' position, see Steinhoff, "Creation of Germany," 292.

2. The Beginning of the German Epoch

1. Ruldolf Lill has stressed that Austrian leadership already looked less likely at the beginning of the 1860s. See "Grossdeutsch und kleindeutsch im Spannungsfeld der Konfessionen," in *Probleme des Konfessionalismus in Deutschland seit 1800*, ed. Anton Rauscher (Paderborn: Schöningh, 1984), 41; "Katholizismus und Nation bis zur Reichsgründung," in *Katholiz-*

ismus, nationaler Gedanke und Europa seit 1800, ed. Albrecht Langner (Paderborn: Schöningh, 1985), 52. See also Edmund Jörg's own telling letter to August Reichensperger from May 25, 1864. In Dieter Albrecht, ed., *Joseph Edmund Jörg Briefwechsel 1846–1901* (Mainz: Matthias-Grünewald, 1988), 267.

2. Nipperdey, *Deutsche Geschichte,* vol. 1, 455. On Catholic grief, see Gross, *War Against Catholicism,* 115.

3. Nipperdey, *Deutsche Geschichte,* vol. 1, 455; Nipperdey, *Deutsche Geschichte,* vol. 2, 340; Nikolaus Buschmann, "Auferstehung der Nation? Konfession und Nationalismus vor der Reichsgründung in der Debatte jüdischer, protestantischer und katholischer Kreise," in *Nation und Religion in der deutschen Geschichte,* ed. Heinz-Gerhard Haupt and Dieter Langewiesche (Frankfurt a.M.: Campus, 2001), especially 386–387; Stefan Berger, *Germany* (London: Arnold, 2004), 86; Winfried Becker, "Die Deutsche Zentrumspartei im Bismarckreich," in *Die Minderheit als Mitte: Die Deutsche Zentrumspartei in der Innenpolitik des Reiches 1871–1933,* ed. Winfried Becker (Paderborn: Schöningh, 1986), especially 29.

4. Wilhelm Emmanuel von Ketteler, *Deutschland nach dem Kriege von 1866* (Mainz: Kirchheim, 1867).

5. Ibid., 9. Ketteler returns to this point on page 68. For more on Ketteler and his early support for acceptance of Prussian leadership after 1866, see Nipperdey, *Deutsche Geschichte,* vol. 2, 340; Becker, "Zentrumspartei," 29; Morsey, "Nationalstaat," 32; Lothar Roos, "Wilhelm Emmanuel Frhr. von Ketteler," in *Zeitgeschichte in Lebensbildern: aus dem deutschen Katholizismus des 19. und 20. Jahrhunderts,* ed. Jürgen Aretz et.al. (Mainz: Matthias-Grünewald, 1980), 30; Bachem, *Zentrumspartei,* 6.

6. Morsey, "Nationalstaat," 33; Buschmann, "Auferstehung," 387; Augustin Kurt Huber, *Kirche und deutsche Einheit im 19. Jahrhundert: Ein Beitrag zur österreichisch-deutschen Kirchengeschichte* (Königstein: Königsteiner Institut für Kirchen- und Geistesgeschichte der Sudetenländer, 1966), 76.

7. Wilhelm Emmanuel von Ketteler, *Die Katholiken im Deutschen Reiche* (Mainz: Kirchheim, 1873), 122.

8. Ibid., vi. The original manuscript received a new forward and one additional chapter upon its publication in 1873.

9. Lill, "Katholizismus und Nation," 52. Nipperdey, for example, also specifically mentions the "beginning integration" at this time: *Deutsche Geschichte,* vol. 1, 455. Like Lill, both Horst Gründer and Ernst Deuerlein reject the notion of Catholic integration during the

Kulturkampf but affirm Catholics' full acceptance of unification. See Horst Gründer, "Nation und Katholizismus im Kaiserreich," in *Katholizismus, nationaler Gedanke und Europa seit 1800*, ed. Albrecht Langner (Paderborn: Schöningh, 1985), 65; Deuerlein, "Bekehrung," 436. Christoph Weber is one of the few who appears to dispute this idea. See "*Eine starke, enggeschlossene Phalanx*".

10. Ernst Deuerlein, "Die Konfrontation von Nationalstaat und national bestimmter Kultur," in *Reichsgründung 1870/71*, ed. Theodor Schieder and E. Deuerlein (Stuttgart: Seewald Verlag, 1970), especially 258; Nipperdey, *Deutsche Geschichte*, vol. 2, 251–252; Erich Schmidt-Volkmar, *Der Kulturkampf in Deutschland 1871–1890* (Göttingen: Musterschmidt, 1962), 57–58.

11. Ketteler, *Katholiken im Deutschen Reiche*, vii.

12. See Schauff's commonly cited statistics: *Das Wahlverhalten*, especially 74. More recently, see Sperber, *Kaiser's Voters*, 83. He also indicates the same significantly lower support for the Center in 1871 from Catholics.

13. Weber also makes much of the relatively weak support for the Center Party in the 1871 election, but to very different ends. See "*Eine starke, enggeschlossene Phalanx*".

14. Morsey, "Nationalstaat," 33; Buschmann, "Auferstehung," 387; Huber, *Kirche und Deutsche Einheit*, 76; Bachem, *Zentrumspartei*, 121.

15. Letter from August 19, 1870. In *Janssens Briefe*, vol. 1, 401.

16. "Weltlage," *Germania*, March 5, 1871. It is impossible to determine authorship of almost all articles. In addition to the more general lack of archival records for many of the papers is also the fact that records of authorship were in some cases intentionally destroyed to protect individual writers from legal cases. See Lange, *Die Stellung*, 3, 87; Peter Bruno Max Wolfframm, *Die deutsche Außenpolitik und die großen deutschen Tageszeitungen, 1871–1890* (Zeulenroda: B. Sporn, 1936), 17. More generally, see Groh, *Unerkannte Kulturmacht*, vol. 1, 258ff.

17. "Das deutsche Kaiserthum," *Germania*, January 25, 1871.

18. "Zum Feste," *Germania*, June 16, 1871.

19. *Kölnische Volkszeitung*, April 5, 1871.

20. *Kölnische Volkszeitung*, March 29, 1871.

21. "Das deutsche Kaiserthum, III," *Germania*, January 24, 1871.

22. "Das deutsche Kaiserthum, IV," *Germania*, January 25, 1871.

23. "Deutschland und Rußland," *Schlesische Volkszeitung*, February 2, 1872. It is difficult to compare this with an initial reaction right after unification. The *Schlesische Volkszeitung* only formally began in July 1871, though it did appear under another title previously. In addition to

the title alteration, the organization of the paper underwent multiple changes, making comparison across the divide of July 1871 problematic. See Reiber, *Tagespresse*, 23–24. On the German "mission," see Chapter 9.

24. On this theme more generally, see Jeismann, *Vaterland*, 274–275.

25. On the improvement in the Church's position, see Jedin, "Freiheit und Aufstieg"; Bachem, *Zentrumspartei*, vol. 3, 44; Philip Dwyer, *Modern Prussian History 1830–1947* (New York: Longman, 2001), 14.

26. Hans-Georg Aschoff, *Rechtsstaatlichkeit und Emanzipation: Das politische Wirken Ludwig Windthorsts* (Sögel: Verlag der Emsländischen Landschaft für die Landkreise Emsland und Grafschaft Benheim, 1988), 67; Becker, "Konfessionelle Nationsbilder," 399; Dieter Riesenberger, "Katholische Militarismuskritik im Kaiserreich," in *Militarismus in Deutschland 1871 bis 1945: Zeitgenössiche Analysen und Kritik*, ed. Wolfram Wette (Münster: Lit, 1999), 101.

27. Bishop Peter Joseph Blum to Savigny, October 19, 1866. In Willy Real, ed., *Katholizismus und Reichsgründung: Neue Quellen aus dem Nachlaß Karl Friedrich Savignys* (Paderborn: Schöningh, 1988), 51. See also page 23.

28. The word *Kleinstaaterei* denotes the parochialism and inefficiency linked to the existence of a multiplicity of small states. Eugen Theodor Thissen to Savigny, October 15/16, 1866. In Real, *Katholizismus und Reichsgründung*, 51. See also pages 17, 22.

29. *Germania*, April 2, 1871.

30. "Zum deutschen Reichstage, II," *Kölnische Volkszeitung*, January 29, 1871. This article referenced Catholics in Baden. In a letter to Jörg, a contributor to the *Historisch-Politische Blätter* even asserted Bavaria could benefit, arguing that a recent regulation affecting confessional schooling there would never have passed in Prussia. See the letter from March 16, 1869, in Albrecht, *Jörg Briefwechsel*, 312.

31. "Bismarck und der Liberalismus," *Augsburger Postzeitung*, January 26, 1871.

32. See, for example, the *Reichstag* speech by Windthorst that was reprinted in *Germania* on February 4, 1872. See also "Die confessionelle Parität in frührer Zeit," *Kölnische Volkszeitung*, December 28, 1872.

33. Focus on the role of the monarch, of course, also allowed for a complete disavowal of any notion that revolutionary action in 1848 had actually precipitated change for the good.

34. The *Augsburger Postzeitung* obviously reported heavily on the issue, but the Patriots' opposition was a frequent topic of newspapers outside of

Bavaria as well, though often presented with a different slant. For example, see "Zum deutschen Reichstage, II," *Kölnische Volkszeitung,* January 29, 1871.

35. *Germania* shared in the more general role of the press in shaping Catholic opinion during the 1870s. The timing of its establishment coinciding with unification as well as both the "patriotic name" and the interest in a close rapport with its readership are discussed by Haase, *Katholische Presse,* 49, 62, 195, n. 188. Ketteler, for example, also voiced his hopes that *Germania* would be a unifying force among Catholics. See Reiber, *Tagespresse,* 7. From Ketteler's earlier correspondence, it is clear he did not consider, at least at that time, the *Kölnische Blätter* (the earlier name of the *Kölnische Volkszeitung*) able to fulfill the role of the central Catholic newspaper. See the letter to Archbishop Joseph Othmar Rauscher from February 14, 1862, "Dom- und Diözesanarchiv Mainz," C7.3,2.

36. *Germania,* January 8, 1871.

37. "Vom deutschen Reichstage," *Germania,* January 28, 1871.

38. "Weltage," *Germania,* March 21, 1871.

39. "Frieden," *Germania,* June 18, 1871.

40. "Annehmen oder Ablehnen?" *Augsburger Postzeitung,* January 10, 1871. It repeated this point again on January 18. The estimation must be taken cautiously, however, given that it served the paper's own stance.

41. Friedrich Hartmannsgruber, *Die Bayerische Patriotenpartei 1868/1887* (Beck: Munich, 1986), especially 194; Hans-Michael Körner, *Geschichte des Königreichs Bayern* (Beck: Munich, 2006), 134–135. None of the other south German states expressed as much opposition to entry into the *Reich* as Bavaria. See Karl Bosl, "Die Verhandlungen über den Eintritt der süddeutschen Staaten in den Norddeutschen Bund und die Entstehung der Reichsverfassung," in *Reichsgründung 1870/71,* ed. Theodor Schieder and E. Deuerlein (Stuttgart: Seewald Verlag, 1970), 152.

42. *Augsburger Postzeitung,* January 23, 1871.

43. "Katholiken habt Acht!" *Augsburger Postzeitung,* March 28, 1871.

44. *Augsburger Postzeitung,* January 1, 1872.

45. The paper called the day so "definitive" for the "favor of Germany" that it should "live on in our and later generations' memory." *Augsburger Postzeitung,* September 2, 1872. For more on Sedan Day, see Chapter 7.

46. Interestingly, Jörg's own estimation of his fellow Bavarians' attitude suggests they may have had less far to go in realigning themselves with Catholics throughout the rest of the *Reich* than the stance of the hardened Patriots themselves might have indicated when he wrote of "the public" in Bavaria being "drunk from success" in the Franco-Prussian

War. Letter to Georg Friedrich Kolb, September 29, 1870. In Albrecht, *Jörg Briefwechsel,* 354.

47. See, for example, "Zum deutschen Reichstage," *Germania,* January 13, 1871 or "Zum deutschen Reichstage, II," *Kölnische Volkszeitung,* January 29, 1871. The two were separate series despite sharing the same title. These papers also adopted some of the rhetoric of South German publications. A telling example is the theme of militarism. Initially *Germania* largely discounted the fears over Prussian militarism. See, for example, January 31, 1871. Yet criticism of militarism would soon become a major theme not just in the South but more generally, including in the pages of *Germania.* See Chapter 7.

48. Letters from January 22, 27, and 31, 1871. August Reichensperger not only sent a letter about this again a couple of weeks later (February 16), but his brother Peter had already written earlier (December 19, 1870) in an attempt to convince Jörg to vote alongside the moderate Patriots for Bavarian entry into the *Reich* as a show of unity. In Albrecht, *Jörg Briefwechsel,* 358–359, 362–364, 366–368.

49. Hartmannsgruber, *Patriotenpartei,* 194. Again, on the interplay between conflict and the transition from regional to national integration, see Weichlein, *Nation und Region,* especially 34, 231, 284. See also Chapter 6.

50. *Augsburger Postzeitung,* March 9, 1871.

51. "Was werden die Katholiken thun," *Augsburger Postzeitung,* July 21, 1871.

52. Jörg in a letter to Franz Binder, February 13, 1874. In Albrecht, *Jörg Briefwechsel,* 410.

53. Christoph Weber is right in this particular case to highlight the diversity among Catholic voters and question accounts like those of Karl Bachem, which suggest greater unity at this point than existed. See *"Eine stark enggeschlossene Phalanx",* especially 42, 112.

54. Landeshauptarchiv Koblenz, Nachlass A. Reichensperger 700,138, Nr. 4, March 27, 1871.

55. Landeshauptarchiv Koblenz, Nachlass A. Reichensperger 700,138, Nr. 4, April 3, 1871.

56. The document was reprinted and spread in newspapers. See both *Germania* and the *Kölnische Volkszeitung* on July 22, 1872.

57. The renaming of Old Catholics as "New Protestants" that commonly appeared in papers was a very concrete example of trying to displace such concerns for internal division onto the other confession. For example, see "Die Usurpation des katholischen Namens durch die Neuprotestanten," *Germania,* September 28, 1873.

58. Letter to Hermann Cardauns, October 29, 1875. Bundesarchiv (Koblenz), "Nachlass Hertling", N 1036/52.

59. Take, for example, August Reichensperger's "dark feeling of being unsatisfied" in response to a particular synopsis he read in the *Kölnische Volkszeitung*, despite his status as a leading Center politician in a time when the Catholic press had largely unified itself around the Center Party and included many articles written by deputies. Letter to Heinrich Freiherr von Langwert von Simmern, December 25, 1872. Landeshauptarchiv Koblenz, Nachlass Reichensperger 700,138, Nr. 43. Sometimes individual disagreements were even starker, as indicated by Hertling's admission to his wife Anna that in a recent vote he had acted not according to his own "innermost opinion" but according to the view of the "majority of the fraction." Bundesarchiv (Koblenz), Nachlass Hertling N 1036/10, letter from May 23, 1876.

60. Loth, "Soziale Bewegungen." This issue ties into the larger milieu debate, which is beyond the scope of the present argument. See M. Rainer Lepsius, "Parteiensystem und Sozialstruktur: Zum Problem der Demokratisierung der deutschen Gesellschaft," in *Deutsche Parteien vor 1918*, ed. Gerhard A. Ritter (Cologne, 1973), 56–80; Karl Rohe, *Wahlen und Wählertraditionen in Deutschland: kulturelle Grundlagen deutscher Parteien und Parteiensysteme im 19. und 20. Jahrhundert* (Frankfurt am Main, 1992); Gangolf Hübinger, *Kulturprotestantismus und Politik: zum Verhältnis von Liberalismus und Protestantismus im wilhelminischen Deutschland* (Tübingen: J.C.B. Mohr, 1994); Olaf Blaschke and Frank Michel Kuhlemann, eds., *Religion im Kaiserreich: Milieus—Mentalitäten—Krisen* (Gütersloh: Chr. Kaiser, 1996); Dietmar von Reeken, *Kirchen im Umbruch zur Moderne: Milieubildungsprozesse im nordwestdeutschen Protestantismus, 1849–1914* (Chr. Kaiser: Gütersloh, 1999); Othmar Nikola Haberl and Tobias Korenke, eds., *Politische Deutungskulturen: Festschrift für Karl Rohe* (Baden-Baden: Nomos, 1999); Johannes Horstmann and Antonius Liedhegener, eds., *Konfession, Milieu, Moderne. Konzeptionelle Positionen und Kontroversen zur Geschichte von Katholizismus und Kirche im 19. und 20. Jahrhundert* (Schwerte: Katholische Akademie Schwerte, 2001); Dietrich, *Konfession im Dorf*.

61. Letter to Frau Professor Kleinschrod, June 4, 1872. Janssen repeated the sentiments in a letter to Fräulein Johanna Pastor, July 18, 1872. In *Johannes Janssens Briefe*, vol. 1, 427, 430.

62. This was also reflected in areas like the choice of which regions to highlight. See Chapter 6.

63. "Vom deutschen Reichstag," *Germania*, January 14, 1871. Again, Bavarian appeals also took this stance. Consider the electoral program for the Patriot Party in Swabia that stated, "we also want to place ourselves on the new foundation [of the *Reich*]. . . . We want to take part in the national and state life of the German *Reich* as active and fully-entitled members." Reprinted in the *Augsburger Postzeitung*, February 13, 1871.

64. "Ermahnung an Unseren vielgeliebten Clerus," *Germania*, February 22, 1871. Weber provides some examples in which confessional differences were played upon in election campaigning to suggest that the Center Party dismissed both cross-confessional cooperation and drew votes from people hoping to benefit the Church to the exclusion of the *Reich*. Though certainly there were examples of using confessional differences to get votes, even material he provides in the appendix from Center campaigns suggests confession was not as important more generally and that voters were urged to participate for the good of both *Reich* and Church. See *"Eine stark enggeschlossene Phalanx,"* especially 81–82, 141. Anderson characterizes such interpretations as "reductionism" and also argues they are anachronistic, as in the beginning "Catholics, though uneasy, were still hopeful about the recognition of their interests in the new empire." In *Windthorst*, 136.

65. Schauff indicates that Catholics were 29.9 percent of those entitled to vote, yet they cast 34.1 percent of all votes. *Wahlverhalten*, 74. Sperber notes 62 percent of Catholics voted, compared to 43 percent of Protestants: *Kaiser's Voters*, 163.

66. Certainly this had much to do with how the pope and bishops guided Catholics regarding participation in elections, promoting voting in the German case and prohibiting it in the Italian one. Nipperdey, *Deutsche Geschichte*, vol. 2, 347; Becker, "Zentrumspartei," 28; Rudolf Morsey, "Der Kulturkampf," in *Der soziale und politische Katholizismus: Entwicklungslinien in Deutschland 1803–1963*, vol. 1, ed. Anton Rauscher (Munich: Günter Olzog Verlag, 1981), 105; Weichlein, *Nation und Region*, 290.

67. Schauff, *Wahlverhalten*, 74. Sperber also indicates a diversity of votes cast in 1871: *Kaiser's Voters*, 83.

68. On the stance of those influential from the very beginning in the Centrum, see Anderson, *Windthorst*, 136–138.

69. For an account that considers acts such as voting to be separate from efforts to define the nation, see Becker, "Konfessionelle Nationsbilder."

70. Becker, "Zentrumspartei," 28; Morsey, "Nationalstaat," 162. In this particular instance, Morsey compares the activity of the Center to the different course taken at times by the Social Democrats.

71. For an argument asserting the absence of any Catholic attempt to construct a national memory or alternate version of unification's meaning and national identity, see Becker, "Konfessionelle Nationsbilder."

72. On the opposing account, see Dwyer, *Prussian History*, especially 14. Also, see Chapter 7. Of course, reference to this much more extensive lineage of the new *Reich* was not exclusive to Catholic accounts. Consider, for example, the connection made in the official proclamation ceremony by the use of Henry III's chair. See Aschoff, *Rechtsstaatlichkeit*, 63.

73. "Das Deutsche Kaiserthum, I," *Germania*, January 21, 1871.

74. The phrasing served multiple purposes, as the exclusion of Joseph II and Leopold II also stemmed from their "Enlightenment" tendencies. Reichensperger's April 1 speech was reprinted in *Germania* on April 2, 1871.

75. "Die 'Vaterlandslosigkeit' der Katholiken," *Germania*, December 3, 1871. Such statements also alluded to the role ascribed to Saint Boniface. See Becker, "Konfessionelle Nationsbilder," 405. This intertwining of the new German empire with the Church not only placed Catholics squarely back in the foundation of the nation, it also served the much more specific goal of soliciting aid for the pope. See, for example, an early article that posits an inextricable link between the papacy and the new German nation while at the same time seeing unified Italy as completely illegitimate. "Italien und das Kaiserthum," *Germania*, December 28, 1870.

76. Morsey, "Deutschen Katholiken," 33.

77. *Verhandlungen der einundzwanzigsten Generalversammlung der katholischen Vereine Deutschlands zu Mainz am 10., 11., 12., 13. und 14. September 1871* (Mainz: Kirchheim, 1871), 20.

78. Ibid., 93. The meeting included speakers from other foreign countries as well.

79. *Verhandlungen der XXII. General=Versammlung der Katholiken Deutschlands zu Breslau am 8., 9., 10., 11., und 12. September 1872* (Breslau: G.P. Aderholz' Buchhandlung, 1872), 25, 28.

80. Similar to Janssen, the article also considered the sins of 1866 "atoned for." "Das Jahr 1871 und das deutsche Reich," *Westfälischer Merkur*, December 31, 1871.

81. "Unsere Stellung zum Reich," *Augsburger Postzeitung*, September 10, 1872; "Oesterreich und Deutschland, IV," *Schlesische Volkszeitung*, September 6, 1872.

82. On the unifying function of the *Kaiser*, see Nipperdey, *Deutsche Geschichte*, vol. 2, 259; Morsey, "Deutschen Katholiken," 36.

83. "Zur Geburtsfeier des deutschen Kaisers," *Schlesische Volkszeitung*, March 22, 1872.

84. "Zum 22. März," *Kölnische Volkszeitung*, March 22, 1872.

85. "Zum Kaisers Geburtstag," *Germania*, March 22, 1872.

86. See also Hiort, "Constructing," 28.

87. *Kölnische Volkszeitung*, March 27, 1872.

88. *Augsburger Postzeitung*, March 24, 1871. See also *Germania*, March 29, 1871.

89. For an example of stressing the *Kaiser*'s words on another occasion—this time about the dismissal of Minister Mühler—see the *Augsburger Postzeitung*, January 22, 1872.

90. See, for example, "Zeitläufe," *Historisch-Politische Blätter* 75 (1875), 710.

91. Pontus Hiort also asserts, "Catholics actively opposed the attempts to construct national identity along confessional lines." See "Constructing," 19.

92. "Zum 22. März," *Kölnische Volkszeitung*, March 22, 1872. This was not only rhetoric. Even in a letter to Jörg expressing concerns over the views of the larger Protestant populace in 1866, Bishop Heinrich Förster clearly separated out Wilhelm and his consort Augusta. Letter from October 9, 1866, in Albrecht, *Jörg Briefwechsel*, 291–292.

93. *Kölnische Volkszeitung*, January 25, 1871. See also chief editor Bachem's *Die Sünden des Liberalismus*.

94. "Das Jahr 1871 und das deutsche *Reich*," *Westfälischer Merkur*, December 31, 1871.

95. For particular pointed examples of this dichotomy, see "Bismarck und der Liberalismus," *Augsburger Postzeitung*, January 26, 1871; "Zur Lage," *Schlesische Volkszeitung*, February 11, 1872.

96. Hans Joachim Reiber, for example, singles out the moderation of the *Kölnische Volkszeitung* on Protestants. Reiber, *Tagespresse*, 39.

97. Lange, *Die Stellung*, 32, 84–85; Reiber, *Tagespresse*, 8; Löffler, *Geschichte*, 54; Schmolke, *Schlechte Presse*, 182–183; Mergel, *Zwischen Klasse und Konfession*, 205–208; Mergel, "Grenzgänger," 179; Ross, *Failure*, 160; Aschoff, *Rechtsstaalichkeit*, 139.

98. Bachem, *Zentrumspartei*, vol. 3, 131. Of course, there is a larger debate over whether or not the Center ultimately was a Catholic party after all. Certainly, men who were the leading influences in the founding of it did not have such intensions. Furthermore, their goals always covered the protection of both confessions, though their particular concern for Catholicism was obvious. On the other hand, it is hard to overlook the actual voters and who they elected, both of which were groups of almost exclusively Catholics. Hence, answering this question appears largely to depend upon which aspect of the Center one is considering. For more on

this, see, for example, Weber, *"Eine starke, enggeschlossene Phalanx"*, especially 128–133; Becker, "Zentrumspartei," 30–32.

99. "Die Katholiken und das deutsche Reich, II," *Germania*, January 16, 1872. Kirchner also notes the glee some Catholics felt over Protestant difficulties. Hubert Kirchner, *Das Papsttum und der deutsche Katholizismus 1870–1958* (Leipzig: Evangelische Verlagsanstalt, 1992), 51.

100. "Der Kampf gegen die katholische Kirche beginnt," *Germania*, April 15, 1871. The point of the article actually completely overturned the title that suggested the Church alone was the target of the struggle.

101. "Confession und Politik," *Germania*, May 21, 1871. The article invoked the idea of a larger Christian civilization, which was in turn inherently linked in Catholic ideas with Germany and Germanness itself. For more, see Chapter 9.

102. "'Der Kampf gegen Rom'," *Germania*, June 15, 1872.

103. Lange, *Die Stellung*, 87. Lange indicates that some of the articles were also authored by "Dr. Rudolf Mayer," though he must mean Rudolf Meyer, a conservative journalist largely concerned with the social question. Gerlach's work and that of other conservative Protestants was often discussed in other papers too. See, for example, *Augsburger Postzeitung*, August 10, 1871, as well as the day's *Beilage*.

104. "Einige Bemerkungen über Maßhaltung in confessionellen Differenzen: Von einem Protestanten," *Germania*, November 13, 1872.

105. In "Weshalb treiben Protestanten ihr Wesen in katholischen Zeitungen?" the author specifically addresses the issue of *Germania*'s treatment of Protestants, concluding "If, for example, *Germania* were to treat the Protestant confession with derision or disgracefully, it would be improper for a Protestant Christian to remain associated with the newspaper." He distinguishes this from "suitable" disagreement, which he finds acceptable and also evident within Protestantism itself. From October 17, 1872. Both Gerlach and Windthorst took this idea of cross-confessional cooperation to heart. See, for example, a letter from Windthorst to Gerlach dated September 26, 1872. In Hans-Georg Aschoff and Heinz-Jörg Heinrich, eds., *Ludwig Windthorst Briefe 1834–1880* (Paderborn: Schöningh, 1995), 325.

106. "Zur Stellung der Conservativen, Von einem Protestanten," *Germania*, January 4, 1872; "Die Auflösung der conservativen Partei," *Germania*, May 26, 1872. An article in the *Kölnische Volkszeitung*, for example, explained the support liberals were receiving from conservatives as a case of "better elements" that had nonetheless "lost their balance" recently. In "Zum neuen Jahr, II," January 3, 1872. The *Augsburger Postzeitung* referred to conserva-

tives as "undermined" by "current politics." On August 10, 1871. Similarly, Bachem referred to the conservatives as "split" and no longer a group significant enough to receive "attention." *Sünden des Liberalismus*, 33.

107. *Verhandlungen 1871*, 35; *Verhandlungen 1872*, 47.

108. *Verhandlungen 1871*, 299.

109. *Verhandlungen 1872*, 255.

110. Becker, "Zentrumspartei," 30–32; Morsey, "Ludwig Windthorst," 149, 152; Aschoff, *Rechtsstaatlichkeit*, 141; Lothar Roos, "Wilhelm Emmanuel Frhr. von Ketteler," in *Zeitgeschichte in Lebensbildern: Aus dem deutschen Katholizismus des 19. und 20. Jahrhunderts*, vol. 4, ed. Jürgen Aretz and Rudolf Morsey (Mainz: Matthias-Grünewald, 1980), 30.

111. The details can be found in StAM LRA Dortmund 834, February 16, May 5, June 4, June 9, June 10, 1852, May 28, May 30, May 31, August 10, September 23, October 7, 1872; Dortmund Stadtarchiv 5, 1.5, Acte 9, June 9, 1851.

112. StAM OP 2047, 1, September 12, 1873. The term was not specific to this case but more generally used.

113. Dietrich, *Konfession im Dorf*, especially 255–261. The several files reporting on many decades for another small community named Warstein, for example, also do not reflect heightened tensions during the 1870s. See Landeskirchliches Archiv der Evangelischen Kirche von Westfalen, 4,91. More generally, Clark and Kaiser also note that outright conflict was often "muted" in communities as well, full of "compromises" between the confessions: *Culture Wars*, 5–6.

114. Karin Schambach, *Stadtbürgertum und Industrieller Umbruch: Dortmund, 1780–1870* (Munich, 1996), 340–341; Christopher Beckmann, "Lambert Lensing (1889–1965), Zeitungsverleger, Mitgründer der CDU, Landesvorsitzender der CDU Westfalen-Lippe," *Historisch-Politische Mitteilungen: Archiv für Christlich-Demokratische Politik* 14 (2007): 154.

115. For the election statistics, see Schambach, *Dortmund,* 340. On Catholic voting, see Schauff, *Wahlverhalten*; Sperber, *Kaiser's Voters.*

116. For example, portrayals often focused on the liberal professor. See Chapter 8.

117. See Chapter 4.

118. On the debate over plausibility of a common Christian party, see W. Becker, "Zentrumspartei," especially 30–32; Weber, *"Eine starke, enggeschlossene Phalanx"*, 128–133. On revival, see Sperber, *Popular Catholicism*, especially Chapter 2; Gross, *War Against Catholicism*, especially Chapter 1; Michael B. Gross, "Catholic Missionary Crusade and the Protestant Revival in Nineteenth-Century Germany," in *Protestants,*

Catholics, and Jews, 1800–1914, ed. Helmut Walser Smith (Oxford: Berg, 2001: 245–265. Gross's article is especially enlightening on the cross-fertilization between the confessions during religious revival. On secularization, see especially Antonius Liedhegener, *Christentum und Urbanisierung: Katholiken und Protestanten in Münster und Bochum 1830–1933* (Paderborn: Schöningh, 1997).

119. This was particularly important just at the end of the decade when it became one of the pillars of argumentation for the continued relevance of the Center Party as the *Kulturkampf* ended. See, especially, Chapter 5.

120. "Zum neuen Jahr," *Kölnische Volkszeitung,* January 3, 1872.

121. "Das Jahr 1871 und das deutsche Reich," *Westfälischer Merkur,* December 31, 1871.

122. "Das Jahr 1871," *Germania,* January 3, 1872.

123. *Augsburger Postzeitung,* January 1, 1872.

124. "Jahres=Bilance," *Schlesische Volkszeitung,* December 31, 1871. On the paper's divergence, see also Reiber, *Tagespresse,* 25.

125. "Zum neuen Jahr, II," *Kölnische Volkszeitung,* January 3, 1872.

126. Here one must also consider the final approval for organization of the Verein der Deutschen Katholiken (Mainzer Verein) in early 1872 and its public announcement of July 8, 1872, as indications of this recognition. For background on the *Verein,* see Herbert Gottwald, "Mainzer Katholikenverein," in *Lexikon zur Parteiengeschichte: die bürgerlichen und kleinbürgerlichen Parteien und Verbände in Deutschland (1789–1945),* vol. 3, ed. Dieter Fricke (Leipzig: VEB Bibliographisches Institut Leipzig, 1985), 274. For a brief overview of the variety of scholarly opinion on when the *Kulturkampf* began, see Lange, *Die Stellung,* 16–18.

127. See, again, "Zum 22. März," *Kölnische Volkszeitung,* March 22, 1872; "Zum Kaisers Geburtstag," *Germania,* March 22, 1872. The *Westfälischer Merkur* had already asserted nothing would touch its "unshakable loyalty" when recapping the previous year and discussing what Catholics should do for the next. "Was sollen die Katholiken jetzt thun?" December 19, 1871.

128. *Augsburger Postzeitung,* June 19, 1872.

129. Letter from May 16–17, 1872, Staatsarchiv Münster, OP 1601,1.

130. "Zum 22 März," *Kölnische Volkszeitung,* March 22, 1872.

131. "Das Papstfeier am 16. Juni," *Germania,* June 22, 1872.

132. "Das Jahr 1871," *Germania,* January 3, 1871. Writing to Gerlach, Windthorst similarly reasoned that only efforts to show the government and liberals the error of their ways could lead people back to the harmo-

nious ideals of Friedrich Wilhelm IV. These, the Center leader concluded, "are the only ones that can lead to Germany's and Prussia's well being." Letter from September 26, 1872. In *Windthorst Briefe*, 325.

3. The Limits of Loyalty Tested

1. Kißling, for example, entitles a section covering roughly 1874 to 1875 "Der Höhepunkt des parlamentarischen Kulturkampfes im Reichstage": Johannes Baptist Kißling, *Geschichte des Kulurkampfes im Deutschen Reiche*, vol. 3, (Freiburg: Herder, 1911–1916), 1ff.; Bachem does the same for a chapter covering 1873 to 1878, entitled "Die Höhezeit des Kulturkampfes": *Zentrumspartei*, 267ff.; Sperber includes a section on 1874 to 1878 called "The *Kulturkampf* at its High Point": *Popular Catholicism*, 222; Ross writes of a point in May 1875 as the "height of the *Kulturkampf*": *Failure*, 77. Specifically discussing the content of the Catholic press, Reiber similarly noted the more "aggressive" tone of the press in 1874: *Tagespresse*, 86.
2. Several accounts of *Kulturkampf* legislation exist. A good summary of the following can be found in Sperber's *Popular Catholicism*, 209–210, 223. A more detailed account is in Bachem, *Zentrumspartei*, 269ff.
3. Even the 1872 law, however, only became fully developed in April 1873, as the orders categorized along with the Jesuits proper expanded to also include others like the Sisters of the Sacred Heart and the Redemptorists. On the Jesuit Law and its application, see Healy, *The Jesuit Specter in Imperial Germany* (Boston: Brill, 2003), especially 75. See also Michael B. Gross, "Kulturkampf and Unification: German Liberalism and the War against the Jesuits," *Central European History* 30 (1997): 545–566. Indeed, evidence that contemporaries often saw these dissolutions as part of the onslaught of 1873 is found in files like the one in the Staatsarchiv Münster (OP 2114) entitled "Ausführung der neuen kirchenpolitischen Gesetze zur Vorbildung und Anstellung der Geistlichen, 1873–1887," which also includes complaints from the fallout of closures.
4. On this law, see especially Marjorie Lamberti, *State, Society, and the Elementary School in Imperial Germany* (New York: Oxford University Press, 1989), 43ff.
5. See, for example, the complaints filed by mayors beginning in 1873 to report on the intransigence of priests and parishioners in their towns: Landeshauptarchiv Koblenz, 403 Nr. 10804.
6. Bachem, *Zentrumspartei*, 273. See also Ross, *Failure*, 36ff. Old Catholics and their Bishop Reinkens were widely denounced in the Catholic press.

7. Ross, *Failure*, 35–36.

8. In his account, Kißling attempts to defend the pope's wording by citing the canonical correctness of the statement and the theological incorrectness of part of the *Kaiser's* reply. Nonetheless, it is hard to see how such an inclusion made rapprochement more likely given the heightened tensions. The sensation created when the government released the documents was added to by withholding part of the correspondence. *Geschichte des Kulturkampfes*, 331–332. On the reaction among Protestants, see also Gross, *War Against Catholicism*, 233.

9. Bachem, *Zentrumspartei*, 278–279. For the raw statistics on the Prussian and national parliaments, see Thomas Kühne, *Handbuch der Wahlen zum Preussischen Abgeordnetenhaus 1867–1918: Wahlergebnisse, Wahlbündnisse und Wahlkandidaten* (Düsseldorf: Droste, 1994), 55; Gerhard Ritter and Merith Niehuss, *Wahlgeschichtliches Arbeitsbuch: Materialien zur Statistik des Kaiserreichs 1871–1918* (Munich: Beck, 1980), 54–55.

10. Bachem, *Zentrumspartei*, 294.

11. Ross, *Failure*, 146. See also Paul Majunke, *Geschichte des "Culturkampfes" in Preußen-Deutschland* (Paderborn: Schöningh, 1886), 131.

12. Landeshauptarchiv Koblenz, Nachlaß A. Reichensperger 700,138 Nr. 43, letter from July 26, 1874.

13. In his chronicle of the meetings, Joseph May indicates the first meeting was not held because of the cholera outbreak and the one for 1874 had an "unlucky star" hanging over it: *Geschichte der Generalversammlungen der Katholiken Deutschlands (1848–1902)* (Cologne: Bachem, 1903), 220.

14. On the jailing of Church leaders, see Rudolf Lill, "The *Kulturkampf* in Prussia and in the German Empire until 1878," in *The Church in the Industrial Age*, ed. Hubert Jedin, Roger Aubert, and John Dolan, trans. Margit Resch (London: Crossroad, 1981), 40.

15. Kirchner, *Das Papsttum*, 49.

16. Bachem, *Zentrumspartei*, 269. Manuel Borutta points out, however, that the term used in this sense had an earlier genesis outside of the more narrow *Reich* context in Switzerland in 1840: *Antikatholizismus*, 11.

17. "Zum neuen Jahre," *Schlesische Volkszeitung*, January 1873.

18. "Confiscirt!" *Germania*, January 1, 1873. On press controls and confiscations during the 1870s more generally, see Christian Heidrich, *Katholische Neusser Presse und Vereine im Kulturkampf* (Neuss: Stadtarchiv Neuss, 1994).

19. "Zum neuen Jahr!" *Germania*, January 1, 1873.

20. Majunke, *Geschichte des "Culturkampfes"*, 87.

21. "Die Würfel sind gefallen," and "Die 'Motive' zu dem Entwurfe eines Gesetzes über die Vorbildung und Anstellung der Geistlichen," *Germania*, February 5, 1873.

22. Erwin Gatz, ed., *Akten der Fuldaer Bischofskonferenz,* vol. 1 (Mainz: Matthias-Grünewald, 1977), 270. The document is only dated Spring 1873.

23. *Germania,* March 23, 1873.

24. See *Schlesische Volkszeitung,* March 22 and May 12, 1872 and March 22 and May 13, 1873.

25. "Zum neuen Jahr," *Germania,* Janaury 1, 1874.

26. "Wählet und wählet gut," *Schlesische Volkszeitung,* December 10, 1873.

27. "Zur Sedanfeier," *Central-Volksblatt,* August 30, 1873.

28. *Kölnische Volkszeitung,* September 3, 1873.

29. "Gneist's Rede über die Eigenart des preußischen Staats, II," *Germania,* January 10, 1874. On the extensive use of examples from Ireland—crafted to be more about German than Irish reality—see Chapter 9.

30. For a typical example from 1871, see *Kölnische Volkszeitung*'s statement about "modernen Heiden," from July 21. Consider also, for example, August Reichensperger's reference to a *Neuheidenthum* in architecture, which he placed in conflict with that of a German medieval style. In the parliamentary speech by Reichensperger reprinted in "In welchem Style sollen wir bauen?," *Zeitschrift für praktische Baukunst* 12 (1852): 291–304.

31. See, for example, Daniel Boyarin, *Dying for God: Martyrdom and the Making of Christianity and Judaism* (Stanford: Stanford University Press, 1999), 116; Michael Gaddis, *There is No Crime for Those Who Have Christ: Religious Violence in the Christian Roman Empire* (Berkeley: University of California Press, 2005), 36, 43.

32. Wilfried Nippel, "'Rationeller Fortschritt' auf dem 'antiquarischen Bauplatz'—Mommsen als Architekt des 'Römischen Staatsrechts,'" in *Theodor Mommsen: Wissenschaft und Politik im 19. Jahrhundert,* ed. Alexander Demandt et. al. (Berlin: Walter de Gruyter, 2005), 255; Alexander Demandt, "Introduction," *A History of Rome Under the Emperors,* Theodor Mommsen, ed. Barbara Demandt and Alexander Demandt, trans. Clare Krojzl, English edition ed. Thomas Wiedemann (London: Routledge, 1996), 29; Heinrich Schlange-Schöningen, "Konstantin der Große und der 'Kulturkampf': Bemerkungen zur Bewertung des ersten christlichen Kaisers in Theodor Mommsens Römischer Kaisergeschichte," *Gymnasium* 104 (1997): especially 393, 397. See also Suzanne Marchand, *Down from Olympus: Archeology and Philhellenism in Germany, 1750–1970* (Princeton: Princeton University Press, 1996), 108.

33. Demandt, "Introduction," 45, 477; Schlange-Schöningen, "Konstantin," 390–391, 396.

34. Gatz, *Akten*, letter from January 14, 1873, 199.

35. Ibid., letter from May 2, 1873, 285.

36. This is the first of its kind during the *Kulturkampf* run in the *Schlesische Volkszeitung* that I have found. For this specific quote, see December 20, 1872.

37. In this particular article, Nero was mentioned by name alongside Julian. "Unsere Lage," *Schlesische Volkszeitung*, February 8, 1873.

38. It appears in *Germania* that the increased attention to ancient Roman persecution picked up beginning with this reference. "Die Würfel sind gefallen," *Germania*, February 5, 1873.

39. "Zwei Ministeransprüche," *Germania*, May 31, 1873; "Seit den Tagen eines Diocletians!" *Germania*, September 2, 1873. It is quite possible that *Germania*'s editor Paul Majunke had a particular interest in Diocletian that also contributed to the frequency with which the emperor appeared in the paper. One of the few documents that has survived in Majunke's almost nonexistent *Nachlaß* located in Wroclaw is an undated essay detailing the character and actions of Diocletian alongside some references to other emperors. It is likely the essay was part of his studies at the University of Breslau, as in another handwriting the word "average" appears! Archiwum Archidiecezjalne we Wroclawiu, Nachlaß Paul Majunke.

40. Josef Lange notes in a few places the use of martyrdom and persecution in Catholic rhetoric of the press. Yet he does not attempt to specify its importance any further for symbolism or temporal implications. Likewise, he does not discuss any distinctions between the references to Roman times and persecution during the French Revolution or under the Russian Tsars, for example. *Die Stellung*, for example, 71, 92, 303.

41. The name of Bolanden's novel expressed the link to contemporary events even better: Conrad von Bolanden [Joseph Bischoff], *Die Reichsfeinde* (Mainz: Kirchheim, 1874); Wilhelm Molitor, *Des Kaisers Günstling* (Mainz: Kirchheim, 1874). On Bolanden, see Chapter 9.

42. This translation was also published in Mainz by the Kirchheim press.

43. "Der Schulzwang, ein Stück moderner Tyrannei," *Schlesische Volkszeitung*, December 19, 1872.

44. "Die Jesuiten und die Lehre von Tyrannenmord," *Augsburger Postzeitung*, July 28, 1871.

45. See, for example, the article "Der Jesuit Mariana und seine Lehre vom Tyrannenmord," by M. Kirchner in *Deutsche Blätter : Eine Monatsschrift für Staat, Kirche und sociales Leben* (1874), 555. The editors added that the topic in the article, which was initially given as a lecture, had attracted

a lot of attention recently. As always, other Protestants tried to reconcile the devout of both confessions as having more in common than not. Heinrich Wilhelm Josias Thiersch, for example, argued that similar sentiments to those of Mariana could be found among notable Protestants' writings too: *Ueber den christlichen Staat* (Basel: Schneider, 1875), 192–193.

46. The *Augsburger Postzeitung* felt the need to reprint this parliamentary speech in its *Beilage*. See "Die politische Gewalt von Gott—die Lehre vom 'Tyrannenmord'—Bedeutung des kirch. Patronats," June 3, 1874. The specific Jesuit's teachings in question this time were those of Robert Bellarmine.

47. Julius Bachem, *Erinnerungen eines alten Publizisten und Politikers* (Cologne: Bachem, 1913), 133; Otto von Bismarck, *Bismarck: The Man and Statesman*, vol. 2, trans. A. J. Butler (New York: Cosimo, 2007), 137; William II, *My Early Life*, trans. from the German (New York: Doran, 1971), 215.

48. On Julian in Christian tradition, see Gaddis, *There Is No Crime*, 90–92, 97.

49. See, for example, "Beneidenswerthe Freiheiten der ersten Christen im alten römischen Reiche," Germania, November 9, 1874.

50. Scholars have no definitive answer as to who threw the spear that killed Julian on the battlefield. This uncertainty was reflected in earlier writings alongside the Christian interpretations. See, Gaddis, *There Is No Crime*, 97; Giuseppe Ricciotti, *Julian the Apostate*, trans. Joseph Costelloe (Milwaukee: Bruce, 1960), 255; G. W. Bowersock, *Julian the Apostate* (Cambridge: Harvard University Press, 1978), 2, 9.

51. Pat Southern, *The Roman Empire from Severus to Constantine* (London: Routledge, 2001), 168; W. H. C. Frend, *The Rise of Christianity* (Philadelphia: Fortress, 1984), 456. It is important to recognize that despite Galerius holding the title of *Caesar*, from which the German word *Kaiser* develops, the two offices were not only quite distinct but also described as such in the Catholic and non-Catholic publications of the 1870s. See, for example, "Die Verfolgung der katholischen Kirche unter dem Kaiser Diocletian," *Germania*, July 17, 1874; Theodor Mommsen, *Römisches Staatsrecht*, vol. 2 (Leipzig: Hirzel, 1875), 1044–1046.

52. Indeed, Gregory of Nazianzus, who was often the main source for early Christian narratives of Julian, appears as a character in Molitor's play, uttering his well-known condemnation of the emperor's character, which allegedly was apparent from childhood. Wilhelm Molitor, *Julian der Apostate* (Mainz: Kirchheim, 1866), 21.

53. Conrad von Bolanden [Joseph Bischoff], *Urdeutsch: Historischer Roman* (Munich: A & B Schuler, 1908), 24. Originally published in 1875 by Kirchheim in Mainz.

54. On Lactantius and the characterization of Galerius, see, for example, Bolanden, *Reichsfeinde*, 15. On this summary of Molitor's play, see the review by J. B. Diel in *Stimmen aus Maria-Laach* 7(1874), 347.

55. Molitor, *Des Kaisers Günstling*, 55, 160.

56. This balancing act is also portrayed in Bolanden's novel, where subversion—of a strictly nonviolent nature—is both raised but also rejected. The story's hero Marcellin rashly tears down a persecutory law posted in the name of the *Kaiser*. His fellow Christians chide him for this act that could potentially be interpreted as "rebellion." Marcellin agrees that he should not have done it. But he just could not help himself given the situation. See Bolanden, *Reichsfeinde*, especially 340–341.

57. Kißling, *Geschichte*, vol. 2, 334–335.

58. *Germania*, March 28, 1874. Recall, they had largely laid the blame at the foot of ministers in the 1873 message. Reiber indicates a similar report questioning Wilhelm's involvement with the laws coming in the *Kölnische Volkszeitung* slightly earlier in February: Reiber, *Tagespresse*, 88–89.

59. *Germania*, May 23, 1874.

60. *Germania*, March 22, 1875.

61. "Culturpolitik," *Germania*, January 15, 1875.

62. Nipperdey notes the integrative power of the pope among Catholics, including his identity as a "martyr" as well as "prisoner" during the 1870s: *Deutsche Geschichte*, vol. 1, 435. Yet the reference more specifically to Roman persecution of Christians and "martyrdom" generally—as likewise distinct from an emphasis on sacrifice that pervaded the Catholic rhetoric of the *Kulturkampf*—is quite linked to this particular phase of the conflict.

4. The Real Threat Emerges

1. Scholars have proposed several explanations for the outburst of anti-Semitic rhetoric during the 1870s. Most of them are not necessarily exclusive of each other, though arguments usually highlight one or two of them as particularly applicable to the events of the decade and much debate exists on the ultimate explanation of the outburst. For the argument that cooperation with Protestants lay at the heart of the ferocity of Catholic anti-Semitic rhetoric during the *Kulturkampf*, see Ernst Heinen, "Antisemitische Strömungen im politischen Katholizismus während des Kulturkampfes," in *Geschichte in der Gegenwart: Festschrift*

für Kurt Kluxen, ed. Ernst Heinen and Hans J. Schoeps (Paderborn: Schöningh, 1972), especially 268, 272, 297; Hermann Grieve, "Die gesellschaftliche Bedeutung der christlich-jüdischen Differenz: Zur Situation im deutschen Katholizismus," in *Juden in Wilhelminischen Deutschland, 1890–1914* (Tübingen: Mohr, 1976), especially 355. While Olaf Blaschke has also noted this as a reason, he has mainly emphasized the long-standing anti-Semitism among German Catholics, anger over the *Kulturkampf* seen as a Jewish-led campaign, and especially opposition to Jews as an integrative cement within Catholicism. See *Offenders or Victims? German Jews and the Causes of Modern Catholic Antisemitism* (Lincoln: University of Nebraska Press, 2009), especially 51; *Katholizismus und Antisemitismus im Deutschen Kaiserreich* (Göttingen: Vandenhoeck & Ruprecht, 1999), especially 25, 30–31, 36, 61, 63, 136ff. David Blackbourn has also emphasized the integrative potential of anti-Semitism within political Catholicism: "Roman Catholics, the Centre Party and Anti-Semitism in Imperial Germany," in *Nationalist and Racialist Movements in Britain and Germany before 1914*, ed. Paul M. Kennedy and Anthony J. Nicholls (London: Macmillan, 1981), especially 114–115.

2. Unlike others, especially Ernst Heinen, who see this tactic as having worked both in the short and the long term, Helmut Smith has focused not so much on the reason for the outburst but on identifying the problems that prevented a rallying around anti-Semitism as becoming an effective solution for various divisions. See "Religion and Conflict: Protestants, Catholics, and Anti-Semitism in the State of Baden in the Era of Wilhelm II," *Central European History* 27 (1994): 310; "The Learned and the Popular Discourse of Anti-Semitism in the Catholic Milieu of the Kaiserreich," *Central European History* 27 (1994): 328.

3. On the importance of anti-socialism over anti-Semitism more generally for Catholics and across the confessional divide, see Steinhoff, "Creation of Germany," 299–300.

4. For examples of such generalizing assessments, see Blaschke, *Katholizismus und Antisemitismus*, 67; Grieve, "Bedeutung," 355; Blackbourn, "Roman Catholics," 106–107; 111; Uwe Mazura, *Zentrumspartei und Judenfrage 1870/71–1933: Verfassungsstaat und Minderheitenschutz* (Mainz: Matthias-Grünewald, 1994), 45; Uriel Tal, *Christians and Jews in Germany: Religion, Politics, and Ideology in the Second Reich, 1870–1914* (Ithaca: Cornell University Press, 1975), 90.

5. Heinen's article focuses on the *Kulturkampf* and does make some differentiations for the later years of the 1870s. Nonetheless, he largely sees the early years of the period as connected to the anti-Semitic

outburst: "Antisemitische Strömungen." Josef Lange briefly notes the prominence of anti-Semitism in the particular year of 1875 for *Germania*, at least, but gives no further explanation: *Die Stellung*, 124. Marcel Stoetzler notes 1875 as a point of ascendency for anti-Semitism as a "modern political discourse," not suggesting the subsequent drop off in Catholic rhetoric: *The State, the Nation, & the Jews: Liberalism and the Antisemitism Dispute in Bismarck's Germany* (Lincoln: University of Nebraska Press, 2008), 214.

6. See, for example, an article speaking of moral decline in society and the assertion that "Jewification" was quite appropriate to describe events. Interestingly, this article did come right on the heels of the 1873 collapse, though the content largely focused on more general religious themes of difference between Jews and Christians: "Moralische Feigheit," *Kölnische Volkszeitung*, July 8, 1873. Also of a different nature from both the general anti-Semitism of the period and the specific outburst in 1875 was an emphasis in Catholic rhetoric on Germany as a Christian *Reich*, which was commonly made without any reference to Jews. Of course it could contain an implicit anti-Semitism, but it need not have necessarily. For more on the importance of Germany as a Christian *Reich*, see Chapter 9.

7. Blaschke, *Katholizismus und Antisemitismus*, especially 20.

8. On the more general opposition of Catholicism to Freemasonry, see Sperber, *Popular Catholicism*, 29, 152–153, 230; Smith, *German Nationalism*, 105; Michael Langer, *Zwischen Vorurteil und Aggression: Zum Judenbild in der deutschsprachigen katholischen Volksbildung des 19. Jahrhunderts* (Freibrug: Herder, 1994), 51, 305. On Jews in Freemasonry, see Stefan-Ludwig Hoffmann, "Brothers or Strangers? Jews and Freemasons in Nineteenth-century Germany," *German History* 18 (2000): 143–161.

9. "Nationalliberalismus und Commune," *Germania*, May 6, 1871.

10. "Gründer und Gesetzmacherei," *Germania*, February 11, 1873.

11. "Der Börsenschwindel," *Germania*, October 12, 1873.

12. "Zum neuen Jahr," *Germania*, January 1, 1874.

13. For an example from after the collapse, see "'Seit den Tagen eines Diocletian!'," *Germania*, September 2, 1873. Even as late as March 27, 1875, *Germania* could focus on this religiously-pointed hate, as it did in its review of the week. *Der Talmudjude*—whose sole purpose was to promote anti-Semitic rhetoric—also fit in with this more religious-based opposition to Jews, beginning in 1871 when its first edition appeared. Indeed, the book was based on a collection of misrepresentations of the Talmud in an

earlier text from the eighteenth century entitled *Entdecktes Judentum* by Johann Eisenmenger. Only in a later edition in the second half of the decade did the text come closer to a more "modern" anti-Semitism. August Rohling, *Der Talmudjude: Zur Beherzigung für Juden und Christen aller Stände*, 4th ed. (Münster: Adolf Russel, 1872). On this transition, also see Blaschke, *Katholizismus und Antisemitismus*, 60. See also, Bruce F. Pauley, *From Prejudice to Persecution: A History of Austrian Anti/Semitism* (Chapel Hill: University of North Carolina Press, 1992), 50.

14. On Majunke, see Blackbourn, "Roman Catholics," 125, n. 15. On Cremer, see Mazura, *Zentrumspartei*, 42ff; Anderson, *Windthorst*, 248, 257.

15. Even the case for the clearly anti-Semitic *Historisch-Politische Blätter* is shaky at best for the earlier years of the *Kulturkampf*. In his much cited article, Ernst Heinen notes the strong anti-Semitism expressed in the pages of the journal, drawing in particular on evidence—as part of his discussion of the fierce anti-Semitism of the decade—from a two-part article run in 1873. Yet, while the first part certainly makes anti-Semitic references, they are rather limited. The over forty-page article, including the second part, includes only a few references of any type to Jews. Indeed, the quotes drawn by Heinen from the first article as evidence of this heightened anti-Semitism largely fail to make any specific connection to Jews. Instead, the text's focus is—as the title suggests—the stock market and socialism. Heinen asserted that these had an explicitly anti-Semitic content largely because he argued that such attacks against modern developments always carried with them attacks against the Jews. Much like the earlier articles of other undoubtedly anti-Semitic outlets, however, the strident anti-Semitism that the *Kulturkampf* became known for, which is really the phenomenon that historians attempt to explain for the period, is not there. For the original article, see "Börsianismus und Socialismus," *Historisch-Politische Blätter* 71 (1873), 122–139, 173–200. See Heinen, "Antisemitische Strömungen," 260.

16. Blackbourn, "Roman Catholics," 106, 109, 121; Mazura, *Zentrumspartei*, 10. See also, Anderson, *Windthorst*.

17. "Die Aera Bleichröder=Delbrück=Camphausen und die neudeutsche Wirtschaftspolitik," *Schlesische Volkszeitung*, July 2, 1875.

18. "The Schmarotzerpflanzen in der Geschäftswelt," *Germania*, September 18, 1875.

19. On the more general context of this dichotomy, see Blaschke, *Katholizismus und Antisemitismus*, Chapter 4.

20. J. W. Schröder, *Nicht Judenhatz—aber Christenschutz! Ein Beitrag zur 'Judenfrage.'*, 3rd ed. (Paderborn: Bonifacius, 1875).

21. Though the argument here is largely concerned with the rhetorical outburst, the real violence that could be associated with anti-Semitism should not be overlooked. Thomas Mergel notes that there were some examples during the *Kulturkampf* of Catholic "mass militancy" against Jews, among other groups, by which apparently physically violent conflicts are meant. It is unclear what, if any, temporal progression there was to these attacks. See *Zwischen Klasse*, 260.

22. "Die Judenfrage," which continued on throughout the rest of August 1875.

23. "Zur Judenfrage," was an unnumbered series that began on September 4.

24. "Judenthum und Börse" appeared on September 13, 14, and 15.

25. "Unmotivierte Freude in Israel" ran over several days in the middle of October.

26. "Freimaurer und Juden," August 25; "Juden und Militär," December 11.

27. "Die Judenfrage," appeared beginning on September 10 in the *Beilage* of the paper.

28. "Katholicismus, Protestantismus und—Judenthum," began on August 20, 1875.

29. "Die Judenstadt in Amsterdam," *Deutscher Hausschatz*, vol. 1 (1874–1875), 708–710. This article was in no. 45, which meant it likely appeared sometime in August 1875 as well. The particular interest in the Jewish community of Amsterdam as a sore spot was not unique to the *Deutscher Hausschatz*. *Germania*, for example, also singled out the Netherlands, noting that the "masses of the Jews" almost exclusively existed in the East aside from "the exception of Holland." See "Die Judenfrage, VI," August 23, 1875.

30. Many scholars have explained the extreme anti-Semitism of the period as a Catholic reaction to the alleged responsibility of Jews for the *Kulturkampf*, the collapse of 1873, or both. While certainly such beliefs added fuel to the fire, they do not explain why such forms of anti-Semitism flooded onto the pages of Catholic publications specifically in 1875, not earlier. For a few examples outside of the literature already noted in this chapter, see also Blaschke, "Wider die 'Herrschaft des modern-jüdischen Geistes': Der Katholizismus zwischen traditionellem Antijudaismus und modernem Antisemitismus," in *Deutscher Katholizimus im Umbruch zur Moderne*, ed. Wilfried Loth (Stuttgart: Kohlhammer, 1991), 247; Haase, *Katholische Presse*, 33; Rudolf Lill, "Die deutschen Katholiken und die Juden in der Zeit von 1850 bis zur Machtübernahme

Hitlers," in *Kirche und Synagoge: Handbuch zur Geschichte von Christen und Juden*, vol. 2, ed. Karl Heinrich Rengstorf and Siegfried von Kortzfleisch (Stuttgart: Klett, 1970), especially 380–381, 392.

31. The articles began on June 29, 1875. Other scholars have noted the connection to the *Kreuzzeitung* series. Given the more generalized sense of the timing of anti-Semitism during the *Kulturkampf*, however, it is often not given the central role it is here. See, for example, Blaschke, *Katholizismus und Antisemitismus*, 62–63.

32. "'Die Kreuzzeitung' und die Judencamarilla in Preußen," *Germania*, August 4, 1875.

33. "Die Aera Bleichröder=Delbrück=Camphausen und die neudeutsche Wirtschaftspolitik," *Schlesische Volkszeitung*, July 2, 1875. Indeed, even what *Germania* ran on August 4 was actually a reprint of a *Historisch-Politische Blätter* article. On the idea that the *Schlesische Volkszeitung* followed *Germania*'s lead, see the often cited point by Heinen in "Antisemitische Strömungen," 272.

34. It appeared under the title series "Politik und Börse" beginning on September 14, 1875.

35. See, for example, the pamphlet *Nicht Judenhatz—aber Christenschutz!* that goes no further than two sentences before mentioning the "welcome" articles of the *Kreuzzeitung*.

36. On the tendency to associate anti-Semitism with Protestantism instead of Catholicism, see Blaschke, *Katholizismus und Antisemitismus*, 14–15.

37. "Die Judenfrage, I," August 17, 1875. The reference would be made several times in the coming months.

38. See, for example, Smith, "Discourse of Anti-Semitism," 320; Blaschke, *Katholizismus und Antisemitismus*, 27–28; Mazura, *Zentrumspartei*, 3; Haase, *Katholische Presse*, 79ff.

39. "Die Judenfrage, IV," *Germania*, August 20, 1875; "'Die Kreuzzeitung' und die Judencamarilla in Preußen," *Germania*, August 4, 1875; "Die Judenfrage, V," *Germania*, August 21, 1875. Not surprisingly, the latter article at that point was speaking of the rather traditional trope of "exploitation of our farmers through Jewish usurers."

40. "Die Judenfrage, VI," *Germania*, August 23, 1875.

41. As the pamphlet *Nicht Judenhatz—aber Christenschutz!* alleged, Jews could not be counted on to lose one drop of blood for the nation where they were born or lived a long time, as "they at bottom have no Fatherland!" (p. 20). See also, for example, "Zur Judenfrage," *Germania*, September 11, 1875.

42. "Unser Kronprinz," *Germania*, September 1, 1875.

43. "Die Judenfrage, VII," *Germania*, August 24, 1875.

44. See, for example, repeated references in the August 1875 *Germania* series "Die Judenfrage." Given his status among some, at least, as a founding father of German nationalism, the words of Fichte also appeared as "evidence" of Jewish unsuitability for Germanness in *Nicht Judenhatz— aber Christenschutz!*, 19. Of course the choice of these individuals was also a calculated effort on the part of the Catholic writers to cite figures well-acknowledged in the national canon largely determined by Protestants. See also Stoetzler, *The State*, 215. On the canon, see Smith, *German Nationalism*, 22–26.

45. "Zur Judenfrage," *Germania*, September 11, 1875.

46. "Die Judenfrage, I," *Germania*, August 17, 1875.

47. "Ursprung und Charakter unserer Judenartikel," *Germania*, October 7, 1875.

48. Bachem, *Zentrumspartei*, vol. 3, 278–279. For the raw statistics on the Prussian and national parliaments, see Thomas Kühne, *Handbuch der Wahlen zum Preussischen Abgeordnetenhaus 1867–1918: Wahlergebnisse, Wahlbündnisse und Wahlkandidaten* (Düsseldorf: Droste, 1994), 55; Gerhard Ritter and Merith Niehuss, *Wahlgeschichtliches Arbeitsbuch: Materialien zur Statistik des Kaiserreichs 1871–1918* (Munich: Beck, 1980), 54–55.

49. Sperber, *Kaiser's Voters*, 165–166.

50. "Das Bekenntniß unsers Kaisers," *Schlesische Volkszeitung*, February 9, 1875.

51. James Sheehan, *German Liberalism in the Nineteenth Century* (Chicago: University of Chicago, 1978), 137.

52. "Das Bekenntniß unsers Kaisers," *Schlesische Volkszeitung*, February 9, 1875.

53. On anti-Semitism as a product of insecurity, see Blaschke, *Katholizismus und Antisemitismus*, 61; Blackbourn, "Roman Catholics," 111; Grieve, "Bedeutung," 355ff. Though Grieve suggests this motive during the *Kulturkampf*, he also notes the general possibility for anti-Semitism to come from rising fortunes (p. 388).

54. See, for example, Bachem, *Zentrumspartei*, vol. 3, 314ff.

55. "Die Aera Bleichröder=Delbrück=Camphausen und die neudeutsche Wirthschaftspolitik," *Schlesische Volkszeitung*, July 3, 1875.

56. "Es dämmert," *Germania*, September 25, 1875.

57. "Die Liberalen haben Angst," *Germania*, October 22, 1875.

58. "Unser Kronprinz," *Germania*, September 1, 1875.

59. "Die Juden und die Militärdienstpflicht," *Germania*, March 28, 1876.

60. This is based on reading the paper beginning in 1877. The year 1876 of *Tremonia* appears to no longer be extant, as even the collections of the Institut für Zeitungsforschung (in Dortmund) and the Stadtarchiv Dortmund do not have it.

61. Heinen also notes the "notable reserve" on the "Jewish Question" after 1875. He suggests the void reflects editors being otherwise engaged than any problems caused by anti-Semitic rhetoric. "Antisemitische Strömungen," 279.

62. See the discussion of this in the Introduction.

63. Contrary to this point, one of Blaschke's main claims is that Ultramontanism "homogenized the discourse" among Catholics: *Katholizismus und Antisemitismus*, 31. Helmut Walser Smith, dealing mainly with the *Kaiserreich* period—especially the latter part—more generally, however, asserts that a great diversity of opinion existed among Catholics on the issue of anti-Semitism. See "Religion and Conflict," 310; "Discourse of Anti-Semitism," 327. On the significance of anti-Semitism for Catholics and the Center Party, David Blackbourn also supports its high importance, much like Blaschke does: "Roman Catholics."

64. On *Der Katholik*, see Blaschke, *Katholizismus und Antisemitismus*. On Stolz, see also Smith, *German Nationalism*, 64.

65. On the leader's disavowal of anti-Semitism, see, of course, the classic biography *Windthorst* by Anderson. Smith suggests that the Center Party's aversion to anti-Semitism also made an impact on the local level as well: "Religion and Conflict," 308.

66. "Freimaurer und Juden," *Germania*, August 25, 1875; "Zuschriften über die Judenfrage," *Germania*, August 30, 1875. Heinen also notes the varied responses: "Antisemitische Strömungen," 266, 270.

67. *Verhandlungen der XXIII. Generalversammlung der Katholiken Deutschlands zu Freiburg im Breisgau am 31. August, 1.2.3. und 4. September 1875* (Freiburg: Herder, 1875).

68. Heinen, like those who have drawn on his work, presents the conflict rather differently. This appears to stem largely from relying on *Germania*'s report of the event as not so much an expression of their side but as an accurate account of how the conflict developed. The original articles in the *Schlesische Volkszeitung* that were selectively quoted by *Germania*, however, tell a rather different story: "Antisemitische Strömungen," especially 271–272. Importantly, the Breslau paper's "Jewish articles" appear to have been those from August, which appeared before the blowup, not after.

69. "Ursprung und Charakter unserer Judenartikel," *Germania*, October 6, 1875.

70. "Katholizismus, Protestantismus—und Judenthum," *Schlesische Volkzeitung*, beginning on August 20, 1875.

71. "Ursprung und Charakter unserer Judenartikel," *Germania*, October 7, 1875.

72. Even though Blaschke emphasizes homogeneity among Catholics on the issue of anti-Semitism, he also notes the general distance to more racially-based anti-Semitism. This, of course, was the direction *Germania* and its followers were taking. On the distance of Catholics to racial anti-Semitism, see "Wider die 'Herrschaft'," 256; *Offenders*, 39.

73. Blackbourn, *Fontana History of Germany*, 223.

74. "Die Socialdemokratie" made its first appearance on August 10, 1875.

75. "Die katholische Presse und die Socialdemokratie," *Germania*, December 18, 1875.

76. "Katholicismus und Socialismus, I," *Germania*, September 30, 1876.

77. Sperber, *Popular Catholicism*, 60.

78. See, for example, "Juden und Militär," *Germania*, December 11, 1875.

79. See, for example, "Der Socialismus in der Kaserne," *Germania*, May 29, 1876.

80. "Ist Notstand im Lande?" *Germania*, February 10, 1876.

81. "Zur protestantischen Bewegung," *Germania*, March 28, 1876. See also "Die Sprengung der 'großen liberalen Partei'," *Germania*, December 23, 1876. In part, this differentiation among liberals drew on the idea in Catholic rhetoric that the liberal parties as a whole no longer espoused true liberalism, which is often why the articles placed the term liberal in scare quotes. Instead, the Catholic position argued it was actually defending true liberalism in the church-state conflict.

82. Blackbourn, "Roman Catholics," 119–120; Mergel, *Zwischen Klasse*, 259.

83. On Catholic workers and the Center Party, see Anderson, *Practicing Democracy*, 105; Sperber, *Kaiser's Voters*, 64ff.

84. Indeed, Windthorst had just recently brought the issue up in the *Reichstag*, an article reported, "to bring acknowledgement in sufficient manner to the existence of a crisis" concerning the average people's living standards: "Ueber den Nothstand," *Germania*, February 15, 1876. On Ketteler and the "social question" see Martin O'Malley, *Wilhelm Ketteler and the Birth of Modern Catholic Social Thought: A Catholic Manifesto in Revolutionary 1848* (Munich: Utz, 2008), 66–67.

85. On the distinction between the individuals and socialism as a whole, see, for example, the sympathetic treatment of workers so plagued by "hunger and misery" that they are left often seemingly with no good choices: "Ist Nothstand im Lande?" *Germania*, February 10, 1876.

86. Anderson, *Windthorst*, 207ff. On the other hand, August Reichensperger and a few dozen other Center Party deputies supported passage of exceptional laws against socialists (p. 320).

87. "Die Socialdemokratie bei Studenten und Soldaten," *Germania*, July 24, 1877.

88. "Freie Kirche und Gewissensfreiheit, VI," *Germania*, October 27, 1876. On this development, see also "Ein kräftiger, tüchtiger Stoß gegen den echten, frischen, fröhlichen, einträchtigen 'Culturkampf'," *Germania*, October 23, 1876; "Ueber die beklagenswerthe, ihren christlichen Charakter in Frage stellende Lage der altpreußischen evangelischen Landeskirche gegeüber der Civilehe," *Germania*, October 26, 1876.

89. "Die Bewegungen innerhalb der protestantischen Landeskirche Preußens und der 'Culturkampf'," *Germania*, June 26, 1877. On the Hoßbach affair, see Schmidt-Volkmar, *Kulturkampf*, 215–216.

90. "Zu Spät?" *Germania*, June 28, 1877.

91. "Wie steht der Kaiser und wie stehen die 'Liberalen' zum 'Culturkampf?'" *Germania*, July 4, 1877.

92. *Verhandlungen der XXIV katholischen Generalversammlung Deutschlands zu München am 11., 12., 13. und 14. September 1876* (Munich: Herder, 1876), 67.

93. Suggesting the unifying potential of anti-socialism, it was only the socialist threat in the 1890s that prompted Catholics in Alsace-Lorraine to unify more closely at least on the regional level: Dan P. Silverman, "Political Catholicism and Social Democracy in Alsace-Lorraine, 1871–1914," *The Catholic Historical Review* 52 (1966). On how few Catholics voted for the socialists, see Sperber, *Kaiser's Voters*, 64ff.

5. The Search for Continued Relevance

1. "Zur Lage des 'Culturkampfes'," *Germania*, September 10, 1877. Renan, "What is a Nation?," in *Nationalism in Europe 1815 to the Present*, ed. Stuart Woolf (London: Routledge, 1996), especially 50.

2. On the Bismarck cult, see Richard E. Frankel, *Bismarck's Shadow: The Cult of Leadership and the Transformation of the German Right, 1898–1945* (Oxford: Berg, 2005); Thomas Weber, *Our Friend "the Enemy": Elite Education in Britain and Germany before World War I* (Stanford: Stanford University Press, 2008), 114.

3. Bachem, *Zentrumspartei*, vol. 3, 322–323; Kißling, *Geschichte*, 203.

4. This came on the heels of a separate assassination attempt in the previous month. Bachem, *Zentrumspartei*, vol. 3, 344–345; Reiber, *Tagespresse*,

100; Anderson, *Windthorst*, 205–206; Schmidt-Volkmar, *Kulturkampf*, 225, 228.

5. Bachem, *Zentrumspartei*, vol. 3, 346.

6. For emphasis on this line of thought, see Anderson, *Windthorst*, 217, 234–235. From the standpoint of the lingering effects on communities in terms of parish vacancies and such, a rather longer view of the span of the *Kulturkampf* is appropriate. See, for example, the conditions described in Ludwig Ficker, *Der Kulturkampf in Münster*, ed. Otto Hellinghaus (Münster: Aschendorff, 1928).

7. "Das katholische Volk und der Culturkampf," *Schlesische Volkszeitung*, October 12, 1877.

8. Windthorst, *Briefe*, 308, letter to Christoph Moufang on December 29, 1877.

9. Anderson, *Windthorst*, 219, 228; Bachem, *Zentrumspartei*, vol. 3, 365–366.

10. Lamberti, *State, Society, and the Elementary School*, 81.

11. *Germania*, March 16, 1878. The article specifically singled out a recent court ruling that upheld the rights of some monks in face of government repression.

12. Most clearly on this larger point, see Sperber, *Kaiser's Voters*, 83, 173, 332–333. Sperber indicates that the decline in turnout among Catholics amounted to a 10 percent drop from 1874 to the elections later in the decade, with the Center receiving even fewer votes in 1878 than 1877. In his classic and often-cited study, Schauff, who used different calculations for his findings, indicates no drop off in the percentage of Catholics going to the polls who gave their vote to the Center between 1874 and 1877, but does register a decline in 1878: *Wahlverhalten*, 74. Despite maintaining its share of the deputies in the *Reichstag*, the Center percentage of votes received when calculated based on all voters declined from 1874 to 1877 and again in 1878: Ritter, *Wahlgeschichtliches*, 54–55.

13. Hartmannsgruber, *Patriotenpartei*, 122, 131ff.

14. Anderson, *Windthorst*, 209; Sperber, *Popular Catholicism*, 263.

15. Anderson, *Windthorst*, 215, 273ff.

16. One article, for example, suggested three main variations among Catholics on how the *Kulturkampf* should be ended: "Nochmals: Friede zwischen Rom und Berlin?" *Germania*, August 12, 1878. On the press generally, see Reiber, *Tagespresse*, 101.

17. Anderson, *Windthorst*, 206.

18. Bachem, *Zentrumspartei*, vol. 3, 342; Anderson, *Windthorst*, 218.

19. Given the fears of fragmentation, it is not surprising that the Augustinus-Verein for the promotion of unity in the Catholic press began in 1878. On the association, see Kisky, *Der Augustinus-Verein*.

20. "Zur Lage in Baiern," *Germania*, July 31, 1877.

21. "Nochmals: Friede zwischen Rom und Berlin?" *Germania*, August 12, 1878.

22. See also Bachem, *Zentrumspartei*, vol. 3, 331; Anderson, *Windthorst*, 217.

23. Ludwig Windthorst, *Ausgewählte Reden des Staatsministers a.D. und Parlimentariers Dr. Ludwig Windthorst, gehalten in der Zeit von 1851–1891*, vol. 2 (Osnabrück: Bernhard Wehberg, 1902), 154.

24. *Germania*, June 15, 1878.

25. "Die positive Thätigkeit der katholischen Kirche und der Centrumspartei auf socialem Gebiete, II," *Germania*, October 25, 1878.

26. "Die Vereinigungsbestrebungen der Bergleute im rheinisch=westfälischen Kohlenrevier," *Tremonia*, January 25, 1878. On Dortmund as an industrial center, see Friedrich Wilhelm Saal, "Die katholische Kirche in Dortmund und die Industrialisierung im Ruhrgebiet," in *Seelsorge und Diakonie in Berlin*, ed. Kasper Elm and Hans-Dietrich Loock (Berlin, de Gruyter, 1990), 136–143.

27. "Versammlung des kathol.=polit. Volkes=Vereins für den Stadt= und Landkreis Dortmund," *Tremonia*, May 17, 1878.

28. May gives no indication of why the city was chosen, however, beyond being a magnificent, "truly Catholic imperial city": *Geschichte der Generalversammlungen*, 253.

29. *Verhandlungen der XXVI. Generalversammlung der Katholiken Deutschlands zu Aachen am 8., 9., 10., und 11. September 1879* (Aachen: Jacobi & Co., 1879), 185.

30. Ibid., 186.

31. Ibid.

32. Ibid., 188.

33. Anderson, *Windthorst*, 217.

34. "Die Centrumspartei—die wahrhaft liberale Partei," *Schlesische Volkszeitung*, July 24, 1878. A couple of months later the paper even ran an article with the simple title, "Das Centrum eine politische Partei," October 13, 1878.

35. "Die Haltung des Centrums," *Germania*, September 6, 1878.

36. "Wähler und Gewählte der Centrumspartei," *Germania*, October 10, 1878. See also, for example, "Die 'Particularisten' im Centrum," *Germania*, November 25, 1878; April 5, 1879, *Germania*.

37. *Kölnische Volkszeitung*, August 7, 1878.

38. Though Windthorst once claimed the Center would disband if the *Kulturkampf* was ended, Noel D. Cary rightly points out how unlikely this was: *The Path to Christian Democracy: German Catholics and the Party*

System from Windthorst to Adenauer (Cambridge: Harvard University Press, 1996), 17.

39. Windthorst, *Briefe,* to Onno Klopp on September 23, 1879, 424.

40. *Verhandlungen 1879,* 55.

41. On middle-class Catholics and liberalism, see especially Mergel, *Zwischen Klasse.*

42. For just one example, see "Zur protestantischen Bewegung," *Germania,* March 28, 1876. August Reichensperger included a lengthy entry in his book *Phrasen und Schlagwörter* under "Liberal, Liberalismus," pointing out just how inappropriate this word was for what *Kulturkämpfer* promoted: *Phrasen und Schlagwörter. Ein Noth und Hülfsbüchlein für Zeitungsleser,* 3rd edition (Paderborn: Schöningh, 1872), 68–82.

43. "Die Centrumspartei—die wahrhaft liberale Partei," *Schlesische Volkszeitung,* July 24, 1878. Of course, the Center's opposition to the Socialist Law should be connected to this idea. For the seminal interpretation of the Center as a liberal party, see Anderson, *Windthorst.*

44. "Versammlung des katho.=polit. Volks=Vereins für den Stadt= und Landkreis Dortmund," *Tremonia,* May 17, 1878. On Dortmund, see Schambach, *Stadtbürgertum,* 340–341; Beckmann, "Lambert Lensing," 154.

45. *Germania,* April 5, 1879. See also, for example, the same play on words on July 6, 1878.

46. On whether or not 1878/79 was a "refounding" of the *Reich,* see Barkin, "1878–1879." See also Bachem, *Zentrumspartei,* vol. 3, Chapter 8; Sperber, *Popular Catholicism,* 251.

47. "Ultramontane Politik," *Tremonia,* April 29, 1878; *Schlesische Volkszeitung,* June 23, 1878.

48. *Germania,* July 19, 1879.

49. Anderson notes that following Pius IX's death, Windthorst told fellow Center deputies to refrain from attacking Bismarck: *Windthorst,* 205–206. This appears to have left its mark on the rhetoric surrounding the *Kulturkampf* more generally as well.

50. "Friedenspolitik," *Germania,* August 19, 1878.

51. See also Anderson, *Windthorst,* 216–217.

52. As Anderson has asserted, the Center's parliamentary efforts to have articles 15, 16, and 18 of the Constitution reinstated in December 1878 represented an effort to bring the conflict back into an arena where the party could act: *Windthorst,* 218. The same goal appears to have motivated the attempts to present the conflict as one Catholics could not just leave up to the papacy to settle.

53. On the issue of class interests and how effectively they were met by the Center, see the useful discussion in Becker, "Die Deutsche Zentrum-spartei," 35ff. Including a diversity of class interests should perhaps not be seen as exceptional to the Center as it commonly has been. Jonathan Sperber's fascinating statistics regarding who voted for the Social Democrats suggest the non-worker segment of support for the party was substantial, making it far more than a class-based entity: *Kaiser's Voters*, especially 63ff.

54. Windthorst, *Briefe*, letter to Eduard von Ungern-Sternberg on December 29, 1880, 518.

55. Anderson also notes Windthorst's concerns over a potential decline in support for the Center Party as a result of negotiations between Berlin and Rome, though she suggests a somewhat different cause: *Windthorst*, 294.

56. On the long-term support for the Center Party, see Sperber, *Kaiser's Voters*, 79ff.

6. Mapping Germany from the Borders to Berlin

1. "Die confessionellen Hetzereien," *Germania*, November 6, 1872.

2. Ibid.

3. Even after the greater immigration to the city upon becoming the capital, statistics for 1880 indicate that Catholics only comprised 7 percent of the inhabitants, or 80,616 out of the 1,122,330 people living in Berlin. Richard Dietrich, "Berlins Weg zur Industrie- und Handelsstadt," in *Berlin: Zehn Kapitel seiner Geschichte*, ed. Richard Dietrich (Berlin: Gruyter, 1981), 170.

4. "Nothwendigkeit der Ruhe für Deutschland," *Germania*, March 18, 1871.

5. David Blackbourn and James Retallack point more generally to the connection between identity, geographic perceptions, and mental mapping: "Germans used a variety of strategies both to experience their emotional home as a place on a map and to imagine their chosen place as a natural home." "Introduction," *Localism, Landscape, and the Ambiguities of Place: German-Speaking Central Europe, 1860–1930*, ed. Blackbourn and Retallack (Toronto: University of Toronto, 2007), 4. An especially good overview of the variety of fields and contexts important for considering geographical perceptions is Frithjof Benjamin Schenk, "Mental Maps. Die Konstruktion von geographischen Räumen in Europa seit der Aufklärung," *Geschichte und Gesellschaft* 28 (2002): 493–514. See also Berger, *Germany*, 35; David Hooson, ed., *Geography and*

National Identity (Cambridge, MA: Blackwell, 1994); Mark Bassin, "Imperialer Raum/Nationaler Raum: Sibirien auf der kognitiven Landkarte Rußlands im 19. Jahrhundert," *Geschichte und Gesellschaft* 28 (2002): 378–403.

6. On Catholics grasping membership in a region more easily than the nation directly, see Mergel, "Mapping Milieus, 94.

7. For example, see Retallack, ed., *Saxony in German History*; Blackbourn and Retallack, eds., *Localism*. For a more general overview of the renewed interest in regions, see Celia Applegate, "A Europe of Regions: Reflections on the Historiography of sub-national places in modern times," *American Historical Review* 104 (1999): 1157–1182.

8. Mergel, "Mapping Mileius," 82. Mergel specifies he is speaking of the "German variety," which explains the absence of some places on his list, such as Posen.

9. See, for example, Heilbronner, "Besonderheit," especially 230–236, 257; Oded Heilbronner, "Wohin verschwand das katholische Bürgertum? Der Ort des katholischen Bürgertums in der neueren deutschen Historiographie," *Zeitschrift für Religions und Geistesgeschichte* 47 (1995).

10. Applegate, *A Nation of Provincials*. More recently the term has also been applied to the integration of individuals living outside the nation-state into a greater sense of Germanness. See Krista O'Donnell, Nancy Reagin, and Renate Bridenthal (eds), *The* Heimat *Abroad: The Boundaries of Germanness* (Ann Arbor: University of Michigan, 2005).

11. Siegfried Weichlein's *Nation und Region* is a notable exception.

12. Confino, *The Nation as a Local Metaphor*, especially 8, 98, 103ff.

13. As Confino writes, "The *Heimat* idea was a common denominator of variousness." "Federalism and the *Heimat* idea in Imperial Germany," in *German Federalism*, 78. On the difficulty of pinning down a precise definition of *Heimat*, see Applegate, *A Nation of Provincials*, 3ff.; Gunther Gebhard et. al., "Heimatdenken: Konjunkturen und Konturen. Staat einer Einleitung," in *Heimat. Konturen und Konjunkturen eines umstrittenen Konzepts*, ed. Gunther Gebhard et. al. (Bielefeld: Transcript, 2007), 9–56.

14. Green, *Fatherlands*. For a different long-term context beginning much earlier, see Maiken Umbach, "Reich, Region und Föderalismus als Denkfiguren in *politischen Diskursen* der Frühen und der Späten Neuzeit," in *Die Föderative Nation: Deutschlandkonzepte von der Reformation bis zum Ersten Weltkrieg*, ed. D. Langewiesche and G. Schmidt (Münich: Oldenbourg, 2000), especially 192, 203.

15. Green, *Fatherlands*, especially 19, 21, 287, 319, 330; Weichlein, *Nation und Region*, especially 13, 34, 231, 371–372.

16. Confino, *The Nation as a Local Metaphor*, 158. See also Weichlein, *Nation und Religion*, 372.

17. An early article spoke pointedly of the "tremendous importance" of representation in "the daily press of the present national capital," concluding that "the existence of a Catholic newspaper in Berlin is an irrefutable necessity, about which everyone can only be in agreement now." "In eigener Angelegenheit," *Germania*, 18 June, 1871. See also Reiber, *Tagespresse*, 8. The rush to found a newspaper in the new capital was not limited to Catholics alone but spurred a more general rise in Berlin's publication lists. See Dietrich, "Berlins Weg," 190–191.

18. This was an advantage *Germania* enjoyed even more so after its chief editor, Paul Majunke, became a parliamentary deputy in 1874. Reiber, *Tagespresse*, 31, 113.

19. In the early 1860s, Bishop Ketteler of Mainz and Archbishop Rauscher of Vienna discussed the need for founding a "major" Catholic newspaper for "all of Germany," though the situation at the time prompted the suggestion of Vienna, not Berlin. Dom- und Diözesanarchiv Mainz C7.3,2 January 29, 1862; February 14, 1862.

20. Lange, *Die Stellung*, 84; Reiber, *Tagespresse*, 6; Löffler, *Geschichte*, 52.

21. Catholic publications were quite aware of this imbalance: "Die confessionellen Hetzereien," *Germania*, November 6, 1872.

22. "Die Angst vor den 'Ultramontanen'," *Germania*, April 1, 1871.

23. Indeed, in a letter to Savigny after the founding of *Germania*, Gerlach still reminded the former of not only how important but also how difficult an undertaking like the Berlin newspaper would be. Letter from July 18, 1871 in Real, *Katholizismus und Reichsgründung*, 281–282.

24. "Die confessionellen Hetzereien," *Germania*, November 6, 1872.

25. The number of Jews living in Berlin did increase vastly during the 1870s, with almost three times more living in the capital by 1880 as compared to just a couple of decades earlier. See David Clay Large, *Berlin* (New York: Basic Books, 2000), 9, 13, 23–26. Anti-Semitism also played a role in such statements. For more on anti-Semitism, see Chapter 4.

26. October 31 is celebrated as the beginning of the Reformation, the day Martin Luther posted his 95 Theses in Wittenberg. Early November is also notable for commemorations of Luther's birth, which occurred on the tenth of the month in 1483.

27. "Eine 'christliche' Synode," *Germania*, November 2, 1877. Note the use of scare quotes in the original around the word "Christian."

28. Johann Heinrich Kurtz, *Church History*, Vol. 3, trans. John Macpherson (New York: Funk & Wagnalls, 1890), 188–189; Friedrich Michael Schiele,

"Apostolikumstreit," *Die Religion in Geschichte und Gegenwart,* 1st ed., vol. 1 (Tübingen: Mohr Siebeck, 1909), 601–605. Reprinted in Markus Vinzent, *Der Ursprung des Apostolikums im Urteil der kritischen Forschung* (Göttingen: Vandenhoeck & Ruprecht, 2006), 88–91; Friedrich Wilhelm Bautz, "Theodor Hoßbach," in *Biographisch-Bibliographisches Kirchenlexikon,* Vol. 2 (Hamm: T. Bautz, 1990), 1076–1078. On the Deutscher Protestantenverein, see also Claudia Lepp, *Protestantisch-liberaler Aufbruch in die Moderne: Der deutsche Protestantenverein in der Zeit der Reichsgründung und des Kulturkampfes* (Gütersloh: Chr. Kaiser, 1996).

29. "Eine 'christliche' Synode," *Germania,* November 2, 1877. For a longer discussion of the Hoßbach case in a contemporary Catholic publication, see *Historisch-Politische Blätter,* vol. 81 (1878), 714–717.

30. "Die wachsende Unsittlichkeit in Berlin," *Germania,* November 9, 1871; "Wie kann der zunehmenden Unsittlichkeit gestenert [sic] werden? " *Germania,* November 10, 1871; "Der Börsenschwindel," *Germania,* October 12, 1873; "Wucherer und Rückkaufshändler in Berlin," *Germania,* May 7, 1878. The designation "city of intelligence" also had a confessional coding, linked to the dominance of Protestants in education, which Catholic publications likewise challenged by placing the phrase in scare quotes. For more on education, see Chapter 8.

31. "Die Berliner Kirchensteuer," *Germania,* September 27, 1876.

32. Large, *Berlin,* xviii, xxi, 2, 5, 6, 12, 21; Wolfgang Ribbe and Jürgen Schmädeke, *Kleine Berlin-Geschichte,* 3rd ed. (Berlin: Stapp, 1994), 108–109.

33. Hans Jürgen Brandt rightly cautions, however, against applying the idea of Catholic anti-modernism too widely to the various positions held by the Church membership. In particular, he asserts that the general Catholic position on urbanization and the modern metropolis did not necessarily lead to negative evaluations of big cities. Brandt, "Katholische Kirche und Urbanisation im deutschen Kaiserreich," *Blätter für deutsche Landesgeschichte* 128 (1992): 221–239.

34. "Wie kann der zunehmenden Unsittlichkeit gestenert [sic] werden?" *Germania,* November 10, 1871.

35. *Germania,* January 12, 1872.

36. "Die kirchlichen Processionen," *Germania,* May 24, 1875.

37. The view of such buildings and events as confessional "conquests" becomes particularly evident in the full description of processions, which the article also calls "triumphal processions," whose "brilliance and splendor" might dismay non-Catholics when displayed in such a public manner. Descriptions of processions in archival files also suggest such

events could be used to stake Catholics' claim on public space in a given community. See, for example, a well documented case from Dortmund: StAM LRA Dortmund 834, February 16, May 5, June 4, June 9, June 10, 1852, May 28, May 30, May 31, August 10, September 23, October 7, 1872; Dortmund Stadtarchiv 5, 1.5, Acte 9, June 9, 1851. The desire to parade in front of Protestants, specifically, during celebrations has statistical corroboration in the details of a case from the community of Herne. In 1911 the route passed 1,350 houses, of which 918 were Protestant. Hence, 70 percent of houses passed belonged to Protestants, although the town had a Catholic majority. StAM OP 2047, 2, August 11, 1911. More generally on the symbolic significance of processions, see Robert Darnton, *The Great Cat Massacre and Other Episodes in French Cultural History* (New York: Vintage, 1985), especially 120, 124; Mary Ryan, *Civic Wars: Democracy and Public Life in the American City during the Nineteenth Century* (Berkeley: University of California Press, 1997), especially 229–230. On the claiming of urban space via buildings, see Anthony Steinhoff, *Gods of the City: Protestantism and Religious Culture in Strasbourg, 1870–1914* (Leiden: Brill, 2008), 113–116.

38. "Nothwendigkeit der Ruhe für Deutschland," *Germania*, March 18, 1871.

39. "Weltlage," *Germania*, March 17, 1871. This promotion of Berlin occurred even as *Germania*'s articles had already begun taking a more oppositional stance to the government.

40. On these earlier estimations of Berlin, see Walter Erhart, "Written Capitals and Capital Topography: Berlin and Washington in Travel Literature," in *Berlin-Washington, 1800–2000: Capital Cities, Cultural Representation, and National Identities*, ed. Andreas Daum and Christof Mauch (Cambridge: Cambridge University Press, 2005), 59–60.

41. "Die wachsende Unsittlichkeit in Berlin," *Germania*, November 9, 1871. For the same argument in other papers, see "Nothstände in Berlin," *Augsburger Postzeitung*, October 26, 1871. This article was reprinted from the original in the *Kölnische Volkszeitung*.

42. Amazingly, the population of Catholics in Berlin did grow to 400,000, becoming the second largest in absolute numbers (after Cologne) in Germany on the eve of World War I. Given the size of the metropolis, however, Catholics were still highly outnumbered. See Brandt, "Katholische Kirche und Urbanisation," 226–227; Dietrich, "Berlins Weg," 169–170.

43. According to the two subscription lists published by *Germania* to show the "wide distribution" of their paper, almost 1,000 separate communities outside of Berlin received copies of the publication. While the capital had the largest concentration of subscribers in any one place, the total orders

throughout the *Reich* dwarfed the local readership. The list of other cities with high subscription numbers is, not surprisingly, topped with Catholic locations like Munich, Cologne, and Münster. See *Germania* editions for December 24, 1871 and March 31, 1872.

44. Again, many groups other than Catholics felt this way. For the 1870s, see, for example, Green, *Fatherlands*; Applegate, *A Nation of Provincials*; Large, *Berlin*, especially xxi, xxv, 2, 5, 6.

45. Mergel, "Mapping Milieus," 82–83.

46. This issue is more fully discussed in Chapter 2. See also Sperber, *Kaiser's Voters*, 163–164; Windell, *The Catholics and German Unity*, 175.

47. Arbeitskreis für Kirchliche Zeitgeschichte, Münster, "Konfession und Cleavages im 19. Jahrhundert: Ein Erklärungsmodell zur regionalen Enstehung des katholischen Milieus in Deutschland," *Historisches Jahrbuch* 121 (2000): 386; Anderson, *Windthorst*, 141; Anderson, *Practicing Democracy*, 103.

48. Anderson, *Windthorst*, 130, 136–138, 145.

49. Witold Molik, "Assimilation der polnischen Intelligenz im preußischen Teilungsgebiet durch Bildung 1871–1914," *Archiv für Sozialgeschichte* 32 (1992): 82–83; Nipperdey, *Deutsche Geschichte*, vol. 2, 267, 279–280. Silesia was also less than ideal given the strong presence of "state Catholics" in the region: Gründer, *Rechtskatholizismus*, 109ff.

50. Arbeitskreis für kirchliche Zeitgeschichte, Münster, "Konfession und Cleavages," 385; Richard Blanke, *Prussian Poland in the German Empire (1871–1900)* (Boulder: East European Monographs, 1981), 28–29, 31; Anderson, *Practicing Democracy*, 141–142; Evans, *German Center Party*, 109; Windell, *Catholics and German Unity*, 80. For later developments among Polish Catholics, not always in the nationalist direction, see James E. Bjork, *Neither German Nor Pole: Catholicism and National Indifference in a Central European* Borderland (Ann Arbor: University of Michigan, 2008). For more on the Polish Question in Catholic arguments of the period, see Chapter 9.

51. Blanke, *Prussian Poland*, 24, 30; Evans, *German Center Party*, 48–49; Anderson, *Windthorst*, 145.

52. Rudolf Buchner, *Die elsässische Frage und das deutsch-französische Verhältnis im 19. Jahrhundert* (Darmstadt: Wissenschaftliche Buchgesellschaft, 1969), 26; Hermann Hiery, *Reichstagswahlen im Reichsland: ein Beitrag zur Landesgeschichte von Elsass-Lothringen und zur Wahlgeschichte des Deutschen Reiches, 1871–1918* (Düsseldorf: Droste, 1986), 64; Anderson, *Windthorst*, 145; Evans, *German Center Party*, 48–49.

53. Hiery, *Reichstagswahlen*, 46, 62–63, 69, 171; Buchner, *Die elsässiche Frage*, 27; Sperber, *Kaiser's Voters*, 75; Nipperdey, *Deutsche Geschichte, 1866–1918*, vol. 2, 284.

54. Hiery, *Reichstagswahlen*, 92, 139, 176.

55. Mergel, "Mapping Milieus," 82–83.

56. Heilbronner, "Besonderheit," especially 232, 235.

57. Ellen Lovell Evans, *The Cross and the Ballot: Catholic Political Parties in Germany, Switzerland, Austria, Belgium, and the Netherlands, 1785– 1985*, 100. (Boston: Humanities Press, 1999).

58. On the pace of development, see Anderson, *Practicing Democracy*, 104; Hans-Jürgen Kremer, Michael Caroli, and Jörg Schadt, *Mit Gott für Wahrheit, Freiheit und Recht : Quellen zur Organisation und Politik der Zentrumspartei und des politischen Katholizismus in Baden, 1888–1914* (Stuttgart: Kohlhammer, 1983).

59. Kurt Düwell, "Selbstreflexion und Sicht im Rheinland auf das Ruhrgebiet: Einführung," in *Das Ruhrgebiet in Rhienland und Westfalen: Koexistenz und Konkurrenz des Raumbewusstseins im 19. und 20. Jahrhundert*, ed. Karl Ditt and Klaus Tenfelde (Paderborn: Schöningh, 2007), 19–21. Jonathan Sperber, for example, concentrated on Westphalia and the northern part of the Rhine Province in his seminal study *Popular Catholicism*. The provinces had differences, nonetheless. The Italian-born papal nuncio in Munich, Gaetano Aloisi Masella, asked Christoph Moufang to brief him on the differences between the populations of the Rhineland and Westphalia concerning religion and politics. Dom- und Diözesanarchiv Mainz, D.5.3; Nr. 2, letter from Munich, May 21, 1879.

60. Anderson, *Practicing Democracy*, 97–98. For statistical analysis of voting in these areas, see also Sperber, *Popular Catholicism*, especially 253–260.

61. Wilhelm Kohl, *Kleine Westfälische Geschichte* (Düsseldorf: Patmos, 1994), 229; Heilbronner, "Besonderheit," 237, 252; Sperber, *Popular Catholicism*, Chapter 5; Ross, *Failure*, 108–111.

62. Yonke, "Problems," 267; Mergel, "Mapping Milieus," 93; Bußmann, *Friedrich Wilhelm IV*, 162.

63. Yonke, "Problems," 265, 279; Ernst Heinen, "Aufbruch-Erneuerung-Politik," *Rheinische Vierteljahrsblätter* 64 (2000): 282, 287; Mergel, "Grenzgänger," especially 175; Heilbronner, "Besonderheit," 232. Anderson, *Windthorst*, 136–137.

64. Ketteler was Bishop of Mainz but hailed from Westphalian nobility.

65. Mergel, "Grenzgänger," 176. More generally, see Nipperdey, *Deutsche Geschichte, 1866–1918*, vol. 2, 340.

66. For example, Christoph Moufang, Center parliamentarian and unofficial head of the Bishopric of Mainz after Ketteler's death, filed suit in 1871 against the editor of a newspaper claiming the priest had travelled south to the Hapsburg lands to preach a union of Austria with France against Germany. The court ruled in favor of Moufang. Dom- und Diözesanarchiv Mainz D 6.2; Nr. 6 "Urteil gegen Edelmann," July 29, 1871.

67. On these individual cases, see Lill, "The *Kulturkampf* in Prussia," 40; Joachim Köhler, "Die katholische Kirche," in *Geschichte Schlesiens*, vol. 3, ed. Josef Joachem Menzel (Stuttgart: Thorbecke, 1999), 226–228.

68. Nipperdey, *Deutsche Geschichte 1800–1866*, 9ff.; Mergel, "Mapping Milieus," 83; Sperber, *Popular Catholicism*, 7. Emphasizing the importance of the Rhineland and Westphalia was not limited to Catholic inhabitants. In 1909, Protestant Francis Kruse, born in Cologne and acting as Düsseldoff *Regierungspräsident* at the time, asserted that "the Prussian monarchy is not a circle with a center but an ellipse with two focal points. The one is Berlin and its suburbs, the other the *cluster of Rhenish-Westphalian cities.*" Original source unclear. Quoted, with italics added, in Düwell, "Selbstreflexion," 19.

69. Etienne François, "Regionale Unterschiede der Lese- und Schreibfähigkeit in Deutschland im 18. und 19. Jahrhundert," *Jahrbuch für Regionalgeschichte* 17 (1990): 156–158.

70. Consider, for example, the two destinations of most immigrants from Silesia: Berlin and the Ruhr. Konrad Fuchs, *Gestalten und Ereignisse aus Schlesiens Wirtschaft, Kultur and Politik* (Dortmund: Forschungsstelle Ostmitteleuropa, 1992), 98.

71. See also Mergel, *Zwischen Klasse*, especially 15. On references to Cologne as the "German Rome," see, for example, "Die Papstfeier am 16. Juni," *Germania*, June 22, 1872.

72. Anderson, *Practicing Democracy*, 97–98; Heinen, "Aufbruch," 287.

73. See, for example, "Die Simultanschule vor dem Lantage," *Germania*, August 10, 1876; "Zur Frage der *missio canonica* für Elementarlehrer," *Germania*, May 2, 1877; "Ein unerklärlicher Zwiespalt," *Germania*, December 4, 1877.

74. "'Culturkampf' und freiwillige Krankenpflege im Felde," *Germania*, August 18, 1876. Indeed, the effort at the end of the century by many Protestant communities in the West to found hospitals suggests an awareness of the greater availability of Catholic sick care in the area. See, for example, LHAK OP 403, Nr. 15834, newspaper clipping from *Kölnische Volkszeitung* (July 31, 1893), undated leaflet entitled 'Dringende

Bitte,' newspaper clipping from *Saar und Mosel Zeitung* (August 8, 1893); Ernst Brinkmann, *Evangelische Kirche im Dortmunder Raum in der Zeit von 1815 bis 1945* (Dortumd: Historischer Verein, 1979), 53–54. On the confessional disparity and tensions regarding sick care in Germany more generally, see Armin Müller-Dreier, *Konfession in Politik, Gesellschaft und Kultur des Kaiserreichs: Der Evangelische Bund 1886–1914* (Gütersloh: Chr. Kaiser, 1998), 358–376; Healy, *Jesuit Specter,* 146; Liedhegener, *Christentum und Urbanisierung,* 170; Bennette, "Confessional Conflict in the Rhine Province and Westphalia during the Nineteenth Century," *German History* 26 (2008): 190–193.

75. For example, *Germania,* April 18, 1874; "Der Verein christlicher Mütter," *Germania,* May 12, 1874; *Germania,* July 25, 1874, which all dealt with efforts by women.

76. Mergel, "Mapping Milieus," 93.

77. The argument played out over several articles, including those quoted here: "Die Papstfeier am 16. Juni," *Germania,* June 22, 1872; "Eine neue Epoch des Papsthums," *Germania,* February 3, 1874; "Eine päpstliche Denkschrift von 1839 als Leitartikel für unsere Tage," *Germania,* May 26, 1874; *Germania,* March 20, 1875; "Ein Bekenner Christi," *Germania,* February 1, 1876.

78. "Unser Kronprinz," *Germania,* September 1, 1875.

79. "Die cultusministerielle Vergnügungsreise," *Germania,* June 30, 1875; "Unser Kronprinz," *Germania,* September 1, 1875.

80. "Katholisches Leben und Treiben," *Germania,* February 12, 1876. The article also alluded to the debate over railway centralization, widely reported on in the Catholic press of the latter 1870s. On the great extent to which the railway did connect the various regions of the *Reich,* see Weichlein, *Nation und Region,* 100; Dietrich, "Berlins Weg," 179–180.

81. "Der 'Culturkampf' aus der Nähe gesehen," *Germania,* April 23, 1878; "Die Hohenzollern und die katholischen Rheinlande," *Germania,* September 27, 1878. Note the use of "mainly" to describe the Protestant areas and "purely" for those where Catholics lived.

82. See again "Die confessionellen Hetzereien," *Germania,* November 6, 1872.

83. "Das neue deutsche Reich, III," *Germania,* August 10, 1871. As the emphasis on the larger unity of the *Reich* indicates, this initial use of "particularism" in this quote should not be equated with the more specifically political use linked with particularists, also noted separately in the original article. It was closer to our modern understanding of "regionalism," which was not a term in use at the time. For more on the

differences between the two in current scholarly use, see Dan S. White, "Regionalism and Particularism," in *Imperial Germany: A Historiographical Companion*, ed. Roger Chickering (Westport, CT: Greenwood, 1996), 131–133.

84. Mergel has also noted the extent to which religious and regional cultures were linked in the Catholic case. See "Mapping Milieus," 95.

85. On liberals' preference for consensus, see Weichlein, *Nation und Region*, 372.

86. "Baiern," *Germania*, July 1, 1871.

87. "Von dem Versuchsfeld des deutschen Reiches," *Germania*, December 14, 1871.

88. "Die Papstfeier am 16. Juni," *Germania*, June 22, 1872.

89. "Zum deutschen Reichstage, I," *Kölnische Volkszeitung*, January 27, 1871,

90. "Die kirchlichen Verhältnisse in Deutschland vor und während der Zeit der Kölner Wirren: Eine Beleuchtung für unsere Tage, II," *Schlesische Volkszeitung*, December 8, 1872.

91. "Pro Rheno," *Historisch-Politische Blätter für das katholische Deutschland*, 77(1876), 661–664. For yet another example of the general argument emphasizing diversity as both a positive and quintessentially German trait, see Jesuit priest H. J. Fugger's explanation of Germany's leading role in Europe: "Patriotische Briefe," *Stimmen aus Maria-Laach* 8 (1875): especially 273–280.

92. *Augsburger Postzeitung*, February 23, 1871.

93. "Das neue Deutschland, II," *Augsburger Postzeitung*, April 9, 1872.

94. Indeed, most *Augsburger Postzeitung* articles addressing the issue of diversity appear to be based on non-Bavarian, non-Catholic sources, as the above examples are. See also Chapter 2.

95. Even considering regional differences, Mergel nonetheless emphasizes Catholicism's "impressive homogeneity." See "Mapping Milieus," 82, 86. On increasing similarity among publications over time as well as individual cases of variation, see Reiber, *Tagespresse*, especially 25, 41–43, 60ff., 76–77. For more on the closeness of the Catholic community during the *Kulturkampf*, see both the Introduction and Chapter 2.

96. Josef Lange is also careful to qualify his statements on the influence of the *Kölnische Volkszeitung* on the West, indicating its regional basis. See Lange, *Die Stellung*, 33, 80.

97. See, for example, "Verbrecherthum in Berlin," *Kölnische Volkszeitung*, May 7, 1872.

98. For more on this theme, see Chapter 7.

99. The event in Moabit played a formative role in the foundation of *Germania*. Lange, *Die Stellung*, 84; Reiber, *Tagespresse*, 6; Löffler, *Geschichte*,

52. On violent resistance in the West, see Sperber, *Popular Catholicism*, 229–231; Elaine Glovka Spencer, *Police and the Social Order in German Cities: The Düsseldorf District, 1848–1914* (DeKalb: Northern Illinois Press, 1992), 55, 77. Ross also includes several detailed examples from these areas in Chapter 7 of *Failure*.

100. Indeed, Josef Bachem's dislike of Majunke's acrid style led to the latter's quick departure from the staff of the *Kölnische Volkszeitung* in 1870. He went on to head *Germania*, for which his style was viewed as better suited. Lange, *Die Stellung*, 32, 84–85; Reiber, *Tagespresse*, 8; Löffler, *Geschichte*, 54; Michael Schmolke, *Die schlechte Presse. Katholiken und Publizistik zwischen "Katholik" und "Publik" 1821–1968* (Münster: Regensberg, 1971), 182–183; Mergel, *Zwischen Klasse*, 205–208.

101. Sperber, *Popular Catholicism*, 5. On greater Catholic confidence in certain regions, see Bennette, "Confessional Conflict"; Mergel, "Mapping Milieus," especially 94. Mergel's investigation of the Rhineland also suggests other possible contributing factors to the more moderate tone of the *Kölnische Volkszeitung*. See Mergel, *Zwischen Klasse*, especially 259–263. Even considering regional differences, the distinctions were not hard and fast. A wide variety of publications beyond newspapers captured a national audience. Moreover, *Germania* itself was widely read in the West, with inhabitants of Cologne ordering the third largest number of subscriptions from any one place in the *Reich*. See "Abonnenten-Liste der 'Germania,'" *Germania*, December 24, 1871 and March 31, 1872.

102. Wilhelm Emmanuel von Ketteler, *Katholiken im Deutschen Reiche*, Mainz: Kirchheim, 1873, 19.

103. Weichlein, *Nation und Region*, especially 20; Mergel, "Mapping Milieus," 94.

104. On the connection between federalism and *Heimat*, see Applegate, *A Nation of Provincials*, 13; Umbach, "Introduction," especially 5, 7, 8; Confino, "Federalism and the *Heimat* Idea." Another interesting connection between Catholic arguments in the 1870s and the later emphasis on *Heimat* is the connection some *Heimat* proponents made between it and anti-militarism. Karl Ditt, "Regionalbewußtsein und Regionalismus in Westfalen vom Kaiserreich bis zur Bundesrepublik," *Comparativ* 13 (2003): 19–20. For more on Catholic anti-militarism, see Chapter 7. Catholic arguments during the *Kulturkampf* concerning geographic perceptions may also have helped long-term integration by highlighting as quintessentially Catholic an area that ultimately became associated with moderation and modernization within Catholicism itself, as suggested by the appellation "Cologne Line" used to describe the interconfessional stance supported by Karl Bachem and others around him, including many

from the Rhenish *Bürgertum*. Indeed, Thomas Mergel notes that it was the circumstances of the *Kulturkampf* itself that allowed so many prominent middle-class Catholics, especially from the Rhineland, to rise in the ranks of the Center Party during the 1870s and exercise far more control over the direction of political Catholicism than members of the clergy did. Ultimately, this produced a new generation of political leaders in the Center who cut their teeth during the *Kulturkampf* but nonetheless also had connections to the liberal heritage of the Rhenish middle class. Such leadership undoubtedly suggested more possibilities for the integration of Catholics long term. See Mergel, "Grenzgänger," especially 180, 182–183, 189–190; Mergel, *Zwischen Klasse*, especially 273, 276–280; Margaret Lavinia Anderson, "Interdenominationalism, Clericalism, Pluralism: The Zentrumsstreit and the Dilemma of Catholicism in Wilhelmine Germany," *Central European History* 21 (1988): 350–378.

7. Femininity and the Debate over the Guiding Principle of the Nation

1. Letter from April 30, 1874. In *Johannes Janssens Briefe*, vol. 2, 6. Shortly after finishing his habilitation in Münster in 1854, Janssen moved to Frankfurt upon receiving a position at the *Gymnasium* there as an instructor of history and remained in the city save a short stint in Berlin as a member of Prussian parliament in the 1870s. Ludwig von Pastor, "Johannes Janssen," in *Allgemeine Deutsche Biographie*, vol. 50 (Leipzig: Dunker & Humblot, 1905), 733–774.

2. Letter to Josephine and Maria Fronmüller, May 2, 1875, *Johannes Janssens Briefe*, vol. 2, 20.

3. Johannes Janssen, *Geschichte des deutschen Volkes seit dem Ausgang des Mittelalters,* 8 vols., (Freiburg: Herder, 1876–1894). The last two volumes were published posthumously, edited by Ludwig von Pastor.

4. Ludwig von Pastor, *Johannes Janssen: Ein Lebensbild, vornehmlich nach den ungedruckten Briefen und Tagebüchern desselben* (Freiburg: Herder, 1892), 2; Ludwig von Pastor, "Johannes Janssen," in *Allgemeine Deutsche Biographie*, vol. 50 (Leipzig: Dunker & Humblot, 1905), 734, 737. The first half of the initial volume was published in 1876, and the full edition appeared in 1878. The second volume came out in 1879.

5. On the confessional divide in historical scholarship during the nineteenth century, see, for example, Holger Th. Gräf, "Reich, Nation und Kirche in der gross- und kleindeutschen Historiographie," *Historisches Jahrbuch*, vol. 116 (1992): 367–394; Augustin Kurt Huber, *Kirche und Deutsche Einheit im 19. Jahrhundert: Ein Beitrag zur österreichisch-*

deutschen Kirchengeschichte (Königstein: Königsteiner Institut für Kirchen- und Geistesgeschichte der Sudetenländer, 1966), 69; Stefan Berger, *The Search for Normality: National Identity and Historical Consciousness in Germany since 1800* (Oxford: Berghahn, 1997), especially 31–32.

6. Johannes Janssen, "Vorwort," *Geschichte des deutschen Volkes*, vol. 1, 6th ed. (Freiburg: Herder, 1880). The forward was penned in 1879.

7. Indeed, Janssen notes initial problems already arising under the Hohenstaufens, who broke with tradition not only by trying to follow the caesaropapism of ancient Roman law but also, not coincidentally, by making the *Reich* less German through gains in Sardinia. *Geschichte des deutschen Volkes*, vol. 1 (1880), 428–429.

8. Janssen appears to have been very mindful of not heightening confessional tensions unnecessarily. Nonetheless, the cross-confessional praise became less common after Janssen's third volume (1881), which highlighted the problems resulting from the Reformation. Ludwig von Pastor, *Johannes Janssen: Ein Lebensbild*, 75, 99, 112–114; Ludwig von Pastor, "Johannes Janssen," in *Allgemeine Deutsche Biographie*, vol. 50, (Leipzig: Dunker and Humblot, 1905), 738.

9. Janssen, *Geschichte des deutschen Volkes*, vol. 1., (1880), xxi, 483.

10. Ibid., 469, 497.

11. On the impact of the Franco-Prussian war experience, see Dieter Riesenberger, "Katholische Militarismuskritik im Kaiserreich," in *Militarismus in Deutschland 1871 bis 1945: Zeitgenössiche Analysen und Kritik*, ed. Wolfram Wette (Münster: Lit, 1999), 102.

12. This was the title given to one of the articles discussing the Thirty Years' War. "Eine Lehre der Geschichte," *Germania*, August 25, 1876. There are many other instances of this, of course. For example, Ketteler also presents the developments of history in the same basic manner. See *Die Katholiken im Deutschen Reiche*, 31. See also *Kölnische Volkszeitung*, December 28, 1871.

13. *Germania*, May 13, 1876.

14. *Germania*, January 23, 1875.

15. "Eine Lehre der Geschichte," *Germania*, August 25, 1876. Depending on the confession of the scholar, the Thirty Years' War also received disparate characterizations in the nineteenth-century historiography. See Kevin Cramer, *The Thirty Years' War and German Memory in the Nineteenth Century* (Lincoln: University of Nebraska, 2007).

16. *Germania*, May 13, 1876.

17. Ibid.

18. *Germania*, January 23, 1875.

19. This could be translated as "new heathendom" or "neopaganism." *Germania*, May 13, 1876.

20. Of course, in these terms, the end of the *Reich* started centuries before its *de facto* dissolution.

21. On these Catholic evaluations of the other groups, see Chapters 2 through 5.

22. Many of these works are cited throughout the chapter, though the treatment of these issues in Gross's *War Against Catholicism* merits particular mention here. A notable addition that focuses on femininity in the German nation more generally is Nancy R. Reagin, *Sweeping the German Nation: Domesticity and National Identity in Germany, 1870–1945* (Cambridge: Cambridge University Press, 2007).

23. The two authors closest to this topic are Margaret Anderson and Michael Gross. See Anderson, *Practicing Democracy*, especially 127; Gross, *War Against Catholicism,* 225. Angelika Schaser has remarked on the general lack of integration between the study of gender history in religion and in nationalism. See "The Challenge of Gender: National Historiography, Nationalism, and National Identities," in *Gendering Modern German History: Rewriting Historiography*, ed. Karen Hagemann and Jean H. Quataert (Oxford: Berg, 2007), 54.

24. Wolfgang Altgeld, "Religion, Denomination and Nationalism in Nineteenth-Century Germany," in *Protestants, Catholics, and Jews in Germany, 1800–1914*, ed. Helmut Walser Smith (Berg: Oxford, 2001), 51.

25. David Blackbourn, for example, writes that "the universities, the bureaucracy, and the army and of course the Hohenzollern dynasty of the expanding Prussian state all bore a powerful Protestant imprint." In "Liberals, Catholics and the State in Bismarck's Germany," in *Populists and Patricians*, ed. David Blackbourn (Allen & Unwin: London, 1987), 143. See also Jonathan Sperber, "Festivals of National Unity in the German Revolution of 1848–9," *Past and Present*, 136 (1992): 121. Nonetheless, it is important not to forget that there was regional variation within Prussia and significant areas of Catholic preponderance. Indeed the large population of Prussia meant even its Catholic minority constituted a more sizable group in absolute numbers than its coreligionists in any other state. See Blackbourn, *Fontana History of Germany*, 261.

26. Blackbourn, "Progress and Piety," 143.

27. Jakob Vogel, "Zwischen protestantischen Herrscherideal und Mittelaltermystik. Wilhelm I. und die 'Mythomotorik' des Deutschen Kaiserreichs," in *"Gott mit uns": Nation, Religion und Gewalt im 19. und frühen 20.*

Jahrhundert, ed. Gerd Krumeich and Hartmut Lehmann (Vandenhoeck & Ruprecht: Göttingen, 2000), 213–214.

28. Sperber, *Popular Catholicism*, 225.

29. Claudia Lepp, "Protestanten Feiern Ihre Nation—Die Kulturprotestant-ischen Ursprünge des Sedantages," *Historisches Jahrbuch* 118 (1998).

30. Green, *Fatherlands*, 313; Lepp, "Protestanten Feiern Ihre Nation," 219.

31. The Catholic opposition to, and Protestant support of, Sedan Day is the most obvious division. Of course, there were also additional groups that remained distant to Sedan Day for other reasons. See, for example, Confino, *The Nation as Local Metaphor*, and Green, *Fatherlands*.

32. Lepp, "Protestanten Feiern Ihre Nation," 220; Sperber, *Popular Catholicism*, 225–226; Confino, *The Nation as Local Metaphor*, 75; Berger, *Germany*, 102. The *Kölnische Volkszeitung* reprinted an interesting poem encapsulating the denigration of Catholics in the new *Reich* that Sedan Day had come to symbolize for them. See "Bei Sedan," September 3, 1876.

33. Confino, *The Nation as a Local Metaphor*, 58, 75; Altgeld, *Katholizismus, Protestantismus, Judentum*, 203; Altgeld, "Religion, Denomination and Nationalism," 53.

34. Lepp, "Protestanten Feiern Ihre Nation"; Confino, *The Nation as a Local Metaphor*.

35. Lepp, "Protestanten Feiern Ihre Nation," especially 219; Confino, *The Nation as a Local Metaphor*. For an example of this assessment in the contemporary Catholic press, see *Westfälischer Merkur*, September 3, 1873.

36. Even the toned-down (militarily speaking) celebrations by liberals in Württemberg that Confino describes included a reenactment of the Sedan battle. In *The Nation as Local Metaphor*, 45–46. Furthermore, Sperber suggests greater military emphasis in Rhenish and Westphalian celebrations. In *Popular Catholicism*, 226.

37. On the *Kaiserparaden*, see Green, *Fatherlands*, 319; Jakob Vogel, "Militärfeiern in Deutschland und Frankreich als Rituale der Nation (1871–1914)," in *Nation und Emotion. Deutschland und Frankreich im Vergleich. 19. und 20. Jahrhundert*, ed. Étienne François, Hannes Siegrist, and Jakob Vogel (Göttingen: Vandenhoeck and Ruprecht, 1995), especially 199–200. On monuments, see Berger, *Germany*, 83; Wolfgang Hardtwig, "Bürgertum, Staatssymbolik und Staatsbewußtsein im Deutschen Kaiserreich 1871–1914," in *Nationalismus und Bürgerkultur in Deutschland 1500–1914: Ausgewählte Aufsatze*, ed. Wolfgang Hardtwig (Göttingen: Vandenhoeck and Ruprecht, 1994).

38. Hardtwig, "Bürgertum, Staatssymbolik und Staatsbewußtsein"; Berger, *Inventing the Nation*, 101, 103; Blackbourn, *Fontana History of Germany*, 375–376. Wolfram Wette, *Militarismus in Deutschland: Geschichte einer kriegerischen Kultur* (Frankfurt a.M.: Fischer, 2008), 45–47.

39. Michael Jeismann, *Das Vaterland der Feinde. Studien zum nationalen Feind-Begriff und Selbstverständnis in Deutschland und Frankreich, 1792–1918* (Stuttgart: Klett-Cotta, 1992), 242. Quoted in Rudy Koshar, *From Monuments to Traces: Artifacts of German Memory, 1870–1990* (Berkeley; University of California Press, 2000), 19.

40. Karen Hagemann, *"Männlicher Muth und Teutsche Ehre": Nation, Militär und Geschlecht zur Zeit der Antinapoleonischen Kriege Preußens* (Paderborn: Schöningh, 2002); Karen Hagemann, "Of 'Manly Valor' and 'German Honor': Nation, War, and Masculinity in the Age of the Prussian Uprising Against Napoleon', *Central European History*, 30 (1997): 187–220; Karen Hagemann, "A Valorous *Volk* Family: the Nation, the Military, and the Gender Order in Prussia in the Time of the Anti-Napoleonic Wars, 1806–1815," in *Gendered Nations: Nationalisms and Gender Order in the Long Nineteenth Century*, ed. Ida Blom, Karen Hagemann, and Catherine Hall (Oxford: Berg, 2000), 179–205.

41. Indeed, Ernst Deuerlein's article on the Catholic switch to support for the nation in later decades assumed the role of militarism was so integral that he gauged the development of this "conversion" by the willingness of the *Zentrum* to support military increases in parliament. As implied in his choice of title, Deuerlein's portrayal also suggested that during the *Kulturkampf*, Catholics were largely distant to the nation. "Die Bekehrung des Zentrums zur nationalen Idee," *Hochland* 62 (1970): 432–449.

42. Werner Conze, "Militarismus," in *Geschichtliche Grundbegriffe: historisches Lexikon zur politisch-sozialen Sprache in Deutschland*, vol. 4, ed. Otto Brunner, Werner Conze, and Reinhart Koselleck (Stuttgart: Klett, 1978), 1–47; Volker Berghahn, *Militarismus: Die Geschichte einer internationalen Debatte* (Leamington Spa: Berg, 1986), 14. Riesenberger, "Katholische Militarismuskritik." Though the term militarism often has a negative connotation, this is not inherent in its definition. Certainly, supporters of the militarism in German national memory did not view it that way. See, for example, Wolfram Wette, *Militarismus in Deutschland: Geschichte einer kriegerischen Kultur* (Frankfurt a.M.: Fischer, 2008), 14. Furthermore, as George Mosse has asserted, it is important to recall that masculinity in the nineteenth century increasingly incorporated bourgeois elements into it, which also affected military ideals: "Masculinity cannot

be reduced to the sole exercise of raw power in the empire, society or family, or nation; it was never so one-dimensional. Instead, modern masculinity contained a whole series of attributes that . . . did not conflict with virtues such as fair play, harmony, and order, which an undue display of power must not disrupt." In *The Image of Man: The Creation of Modern Masculinity* (New York: Oxford University Press, 1996), 7, 15, 20–21. See also Karen Hagemann, "German Heroes: The Cult of the death for the Fatherland in Nineteenth-Century Germany," in *Masculinities in Politics and War: Gendering Modern History*, ed. Stefan Dudink, Karen Hagemann, and John Tosh (Manchester: Manchester University Press, 2004), 117. Of course, Catholics interpreted it differently, as did other critics of the state. On non-Catholic criticism, see also Wette, *Militarismus*, especially 64ff and 86ff; David Blackbourn, *Marpingen: Apparitions of the Virgin Mary in Nineteenth-Century Germany* (New York: Knopf, 1994), 266; Blackbourn, *Fontana History of Germany*, 374; Hardtwig, "Bürgertum, Staatssymbolik und Staatsbewußtsein," 204.

43. Letter to Benjamin Herder, November 1871. In Pastor, *Johannes Janssens Briefe*. Quoted in Gräf, "Reich, Nation und Kirche," 385. Not surprisingly, Bavaria did not adopt the *Pickelhaube* for military dress until much later in 1887. For more on anti-Semitism, see Chapter 4.

44. For more on the connection between the military and masculinity, see Mosse, *The Image of Man*, 20, 50; Ida Blom, "Gender and the Nation in International Comparison," in *Gendered Nations*, 15; Hagemann, *"Mannlicher Muth und Teutsche Ehre"*; Hagemann, "Of 'Manly Valor' and 'German Honor' "; Hagemann, "A Valorous *Volk* Family"; Vogel, "Militärfeiern," 203; Hagemann, "German Heroes," 128–129; Karen Hagemann, "Military, War, and the Mainstreams: Gendering Modern German Military History," in *Gendering Modern German History: Rewriting Historiography*, ed. Karen Hagemann and Jean H. Quataert (Oxford: Berg, 2007), 69.

45. Quote from Koshar, *From Monuments to Traces*, 70. On women's inclusion, see Hagemann, "Of 'Manly Valor' and 'German Honor,' " 205–206. Berger's account also indicates this reason for exclusion with a discussion of how certain women attempted to argue for greater rights by asserting that motherhood was tantamount to military service. In *Germany*, 95.

46. Karin Hausen, "Die Polarisierung der 'Geschlechtscharaktere'—Eine Spiegelung der Dissoziation von Erwerbs- und Familienleben," in *Sozialgeschichte der Familie in der Neuzeit Europas. Neue Forschungen*, ed. Werner Conze (Stuttgart: Klett, 1976), 363–393; Nira

Yuval-Davis, "Gender and Nation," in *Women, Ethnicity and Nationalism: The Politics of Transition*, ed. Rich Wilford and Robert L. Miller (London: Routledge, 1998); Sylvia Paletschek, "Religiöser Dissens um 1848: Das Zusammenspiel von Klasse, Geschlecht und anderen Differenzierungslinien," *Geschichte und Gesellschaft*, 18(1992): 175; Mosse, *Image of Man*.

47. George Mosse, *Nationalism and Sexuality: Middle-Class Morality and Sexual Norms in Modern Europe* (Madison: University of Wisconsin Press, 1985), 17; Mosse, *Image of Man*, 7; Hagemann, "Of 'Manly Valor' and 'German Honor'"; Hagemann, "A Valorous *Volk* Family," 185, 195; Vogel, "Militärfeiern," 210; Elizabeth Harvey, "Pilgrimages to the 'Bleeding Border': Gender and Rituals of Nationalist Protest in Germany, 1919–39," *Women's History Review* 9 (2000): 203; Koshar, *From Monuments to Traces*, 70.

48. On monuments, see Koshar, *From Monuments to Traces*, 70–71. On literature, see Brent O. Peterson, "The Fatherland's Kiss of Death: Gender and Germany in Nineteenth-Century Historical Fiction," in *Gender and Germanness: Cultural Productions of the Nation*, ed. Patricia Herminghouse and Magda Mueller (Providence: Berghahn, 1997), 82–97; Todd Kontje, *Women, the Novel, and the German Nation, 1771–1871: Domestic Fiction in the Fatherland* (Cambridge: Cambridge University Press, 1998), xii–xiii; John Horne, "Masculinity in Politics and War in the Age of Nation-States and World Wars, 1850–1950," in *Masculinities in Politics and War: Gendering Modern History*, ed. Stefan Dudink, Karen Hagemann and John Tosh (Manchester: Manchester University Press, 2004), 27–28, 41.

49. Blackbourn, "Progress and Piety," 149; Smith, *German Nationalism*, 54; Blom, "Gender and Nation," 43.

50. Mosse, *The Image of Man*, 55, 70; Hagemann, "Of 'Manly Valor' and 'German Honor,'" 194.

51. Berger, *Germany*, 85; Gross, *War Against Catholicism*, 201–204; Blackbourn, "Progress and Piety," 150; Smith, *German Nationalism*, 54; Róisín Healy, "Anti-Jesuitism in Imperial Germany: The Jesuit as Androgyne," in *Protestants, Catholics and Jews in Germany, 1800–1914*, ed. Helmut Smith (Oxford and New York: Berg, 2001), 159, 163, 166; Healy, *Jesuit Specter*. This feminine gendering of Catholicism as a reflection of its unworthiness for inclusion in the nation was able to coexist with the view of Ultramontane aggression and Jesuit militarism. See Anderson, *Practicing Democracy*, 80–81, 117, 128–129.

52. Colin Wells, *The Roman Empire*, 2nd ed. (Cambridge, MA: Harvard University Press, 1992), 75–76; Simon Schama, *Landscape and Memory*

(New York: Knopf, 1995), 87–89; Jeismann, *Vaterland der Feinde,*
59–60.

53. Berger, *Germany,* 18, 83; Jeismann, *Vaterland der Feinde,* 59.

54. Schama, *Landscape and Memory,* 109; Hardtwig, "Bürgertum,
Staatssymbolik und Staatsbewußtsein," 201; Werner M. Doyé, "Arminius,"
in *Deutsche Erinnerungsorte,* vol. 3 (Munich: Verlag C.H. Beck, 2001), 596.

55. Hardtwig, "Bürgertum, Staatssymbolik und Staatsbewußtsein," 201;
Schama, *Landscape and Memory,* 111; Koshar, *From Monuments to
Traces,* 36.

56. Barbara Stambolis, "Nationalisierung trotz Ultramontanisierung oder:
'Alles für Deutschland. Deutschland aber für Christus': Mentalitätsleit-
ende Wertorientierung deutscher Katholiken im 19. und 20. Jahrhundert,"
Historische Zeitschrift 269 (1999): 59. Charlotte Tacke, *Denkmal im
sozialen Raum: Nationale Symbole in Deutschland und Frankreich im 19.
Jahrhundert* (Göttingen: Vandenhoeck & Ruprecht, 1995), 39, 216–217.

57. Berger, *Germany,* 83; Wolfgang Burgdorf, " 'Reichsnationalismus' gegen
'Territorialnationalismus': Phasen der Intensivierung des nationalen
Bewußtseins in Deutschland seit dem Siebenjährige Krieg," in *Föderative
Nation,* ed. Dieter Langewiesche and Georg Schmidt (München:
Oldenbourg Wissenschaftsverlag GmbH, 2000), 165–166.

58. Doyé, "Arminius," 587–588; Michael Werner, "Die 'Germania,'" in
Deutsche Erinnerungsorte, 575. Schama, *Landscape and Memory,*
92–95. Schama suggests that Luther himself prompted the switch from
calling the hero by his Latin name, Arminius, to using the German
equivalent, Hermann. See Schama, *Landscape and Memory,* 95. Yet, the
question of the origin of the switch remains debated. Doyé highlights the
role of Luther's contemporary, Johannes Aventinus: "Arminius," 590.

59. George Mosse, *The Nationalization of the Masses: Political Symbolism
and Mass Movements in Germany from the Napoleonic Wars through the
Third Reich* (New York: Fertig, 1975), 61; Koshar, *From Monuments to
Traces,* 38; Berger, *Germany,* 83.

60. Schama, *Landscape and Memory,* 109–110.

61. Ibid., 110–112; Koshar, *From Monuments to Traces,* 38; Mosse, *Nation-
alism and Sexuality,* 59. On the specific attention and meaning contempo-
rary descriptions gave to Hermann's sword, see Andreas Dörner,
*Politischer Mythos und symbolische Politik: Der Hermann-mythos zur
Entstehung des Nationalbewußtseins der Deutschen* (Reinbek bei
Hamburg: Rowohlt, 1996), 190–191.

62. Hardtwig, "Bürgertum, Staatssymbolik und Staatsbewußtsein"; Berger,
Inventing the Nation, 83.

63. Koshar, *From Monuments to Traces,* 44.

64. Kenneth C. Schellhase, *Tacitus in Renaissance Political Thought* (Chicago, 1976), 47. Quoted in Schama, *Landscape and Memory,* 95.

65. Mosse, *Nationalism and Sexuality,* 18; Koshar, *From Monuments to Traces,* 71.

66. Koshar, *From Monuments to Traces,* 48.

67. Schama, *Landscape and Memory,* 112.

68. Confino, *The Nation as a Local Metaphor*; Confino, *Germany as a Culture of Remembrance: Promises and Limits of Writing History* (Chapel Hill: University of North Carolina Press, 2006).

69. Patricia Herminghouse and Magda Mueller, "Introduction: Looking for Germania," in *Gender and Germanness,* ed. Patricia Herminghouse and Magda Mueller (Providence: Berghahn Books, 1997), 2.

70. Hagemann, "Of 'Manly Valor' and 'German Honor' "; Hagemann, "A Valorous *Volk* Family," 195.

71. Carola Lipp, "Bräute, Mütter, Gefährtinnen. Frauen und politische Öffentlichkeit in der Revolution 1848," in *Grenzgängerinnen: Revolutionäre Frauen im 18. und 19. Jahrhundert. Weibliche Wirklichkeit und männliche Phantasien,* ed. Helga Grubitzsch, Hannelore Cyrus, Elke Haarbusch (Düsseldorf: Schwann, 1985), 71–92; Mosse, *The Image of Man,* 8; Confino, *The Nation as Local Metaphor,* 170; Berger, *Germany,* 95–96.

72. Hausen, "Die Polarisierung."

73. Lipp, "Bräute, Mütter, Gefährtinnen"; Roger Chickering, " 'Casting Their Gaze More Broadly': Women's Patriotic Activism in Imperial Germany," *Past and Present* 118 (1988): 156–185; Sylvia Paletschek, *Frauen und Dissens: Frauen im Deutschkatholizismus und in den freien Gemeinden 1841–1852* (Göttingen: Vandenhoeck & Ruprecht, 1990); Paletschek, "Religiöser Dissens,"; Douglas J. Cremer, "The Limits of Maternalism: Gender Ideology and the South German Catholic Workingwomen's Associations, 1904–1918," *Catholic Historical Review* 87 (2001): 428–452; Jean H. Quataert, *Staging Philanthropy: Patriotic Women and the National Imagination in Dynastic Germany, 1813–1916* (Ann Arbor: University of Michigan Press, 2001); Karen Hagemann, "Female Patriots: Women, War and the Nation in the Period of the Prussian-German Anti-Napoleonic Wars," *Gender and History* 16 (2004): especially 406, 408–409, 413. Among the instances noted, however, there is variation. In the cases discussed by Lipp and Paletschek, there is some suggestion that these women may also have attempted to affect ideas and, hence, imagery about women's role in Germany. In her case study, Elizabeth Harvey argues that women were reformulating the nationalist imagery, and Heide

Fehrenbach discusses how the imagery changed to give women a more equal role. Not surprisingly, both of these scholars focus on periods after the Second *Reich*. See, Harvey, "Pilgrimages"; Fehrenbach, "Rehabilitating Fatherland: Race and German Remasculinization," *Signs* 24 (1998):107–127. This can be fit into a larger debate over the extent to which women's increased activities in the public sphere that nonetheless continued to support the traditional gendering of roles allowed for emancipation.

74. Confino, *Germany as a Culture of Remembrance*, 51; Confino, *The Nation as a Local Metaphor*, 184–185.

75. Hagemann, "A Valorous *Volk* Family," 195.

76. Mosse, *Nationalism and Sexuality*, 21–23, 92–97.

77. Blackbourn, *Marpingen*, 13; Gross, *War Against Catholicism*, 217; Ruth Harris, *Lourdes: Body and Spirit in the Secular Age*, (New York: Viking, 1999), 78–79.

78. Marina Warner, *Alone of All Her Sex: The Myth and the Cult of the Virgin Mary* (New York: Knopf, 1976), 286, 288; Bill Hart, " 'The Kindness of the Blessed Virgin': Faith, Succour, and the Cult of Mary among Christian Hurons and Iroquois in Seventeenth-Century New France," in *Spiritual Encounters: Interactions between Christianity and Native Religions in Colonial America*, ed. Nicholas Griffiths and Fernando Cervantes (Birmingham: University of Birmingham Press, 1999), 68.

79. Sperber, *Popular Catholicism*, 64–65, 75.

80. Blackbourn, *Marpingen*, 20; Smith, *German Nationalism*, 45.

81. On discrimination against Catholics see, among others, Blackbourn, "Progress and Piety," 143.

82. StAM, Regierungsbezirk Arnsberg II E 424, Siegen, February 21, 1833.

83. Friedrich Hermann Fonk, *Das staatliche Mischehenrecht in Preußen vom allgemeinen Landrecht an: Eine rechtsgeschichtliche Untersuchung* (Bielefeld: Gieseking, 1961).

84. Heinrich Schörs, "Hermesianische Pfarrer," in *Annalen des Historischen Vereins für den Niederrhein*, 103 (1919): 164. Letter to the Archbishop of Cologne dated December 7, 1825. Quoted in Fonk, *Staatliche Mischehenrecht*, 97.

85. Antonius Liedhegener concurs that grooms really were more commonly Protestant in Münster, the area he studied. In *Christentum und Urbanisierung*, 114. Smith, more generally, suggests the opposite. In *German Nationalism*, 97. The resonance of such gendering of communal conflicts likely varied from place to place, providing a pool of experiences from which a feminine gendering could be drawn upon in certain areas, like

the significant western provinces of Prussia, but not in others. See also Chapter 6.

86. Georg Nowottnick, *Geburt, Hochzeit, Tod in Sitte, Brauch und Volks- dichtung* (Berlin, Wiedmannische Buchhandlung, no date), 8.

87. Staatsarchiv Münster, Regierungsbezirk Arnsberg E 422, newspaper excerpt included in file.

88. See, for example, the cases included in Staatsarchiv Münster, Landratsamt Dortmund 839.

89. Staatsarchiv Münster, Oberpräsidium 1867,1, Münster, February 16, 1864.

90. Blackbourn, *Marpingen*, 30–31; Norbert Busch, "Die Feminisierung der Frömmigkeit," in *Wunderbare Erscheinungen: Frauen und katholische Frömmigkeit im 19. und 20. Jahrhundert*, ed. Irmtraud Götz von Olenhusen (Paderborn: Schöningh, 1995), 203–219; Norbert Busch, *Katholische Frömmigkeit und Moderne: die Sozial- und Mentalitätsgeschichte des Herz-Jesu-Kultes in Deutschland zwischen Kulturkampf und Erstem Weltkrieg* (Gütersloh: Chr. Kaiser, 1997), 119, 269; Smith, *German Nationalism*, 89, 92; Ann Douglas, *The Feminization of American Culture* (London: Papermac, 1996); Gross, *War Against Catholicism*, 209–217. Sylvia Paletschek includes an interesting counter to this tendency. In *Frauen und Dissens*, 248–249.

91. Gross, *War Against Catholicism*, 215.

92. Blackbourn, *Marpingen*, 4.

93. Gross, *War Against Catholicism*, 213, 215. Gross is drawing on the work of Relinde Meiwes: *'Arbeiterinnen des Herrn': Katholische Frauenkongregationen im 19. Jahrhundert* (Frankfurt: Campus, 2000); "Religiosität und Arbeit als Lebensform für katholische Frauen: Kongregationen im 19. Jahrhundert," in *Frauen unter dem Patriarchat der Kirchen: Katholikinnen und Protestantinnen im 19. und 20. Jahrhundert*, eds. Irmtraud Götz von Olenhusen et al. (Stuttgart: Kohlhammer, 1995), 69–88.

94. Altgeld, *Katholizismus, Protestantismus, Judentum*, 153; Liedhegener, *Christentum und Urbanisierung*; Berger, *Germany*, 86.

95. Conze, "Militarismus," 26–31; Berghahn, *Militarismus*, 14; Wette, *Militarismus*, 64ff, 86ff; Riesenberger, "Katholische Militarismuskritik"; Blackbourn, *Fontana History of Germany*, 374; Horst Gründer, "Nation und Katholizismus im Kaiserreich," 67; Green, "The Federal Alternative," 201; Nicholas Stargardt, *The German Idea of Militarism: Radical and Socialist Critics, 1866–1914* (Cambridge: Cambridge University Press, 1994), especially 19–32.

96. Conze, "Militarismus," 28. Catholics also identified other violent conflicts during the late 1860s that delegitimized Prussian policy. See Gräf, "Reich, Nation und Kirche," 383, 393.

97. Conze, "Militarismus," 28–29; Berghahn, *Militarismus*, 15; Riesenberger, "Katholische Militarismuskritik"; Blackbourn, *Fontana History of Germany*, 374–375. As the Jesuit and political theorist Georg Pachtler observed, "Government power, even though not obvious, has the character of military force." See *Historisch-Politische Blätter* 1869, 196. Quoted in Conze, "Militarismus," 29.

98. Conze, "Militarismus."

99. While the geographic meaning is older, the feminine iconography was already extant by the eighteenth century. For more on the intertwined meaning of *Germania* as both geographic descriptor and female icon, see Lothar Gall, "Die Germania als Symbol nationaler Identität im 19. und 20. Jahrhundert," in *Bürgertum, liberale Bewegung und Nation*, ed. Lothar Gall (Munich: Oldenbourg, 1996), 13. It is unclear how exactly the founders of the newspaper understood the meaning of the title. In his study, Löffler vaguely suggests connection to geographic meaning, though the accounts by Reiber and Lange make no such mention. See Löffler, *Geschichte*, 54; Reiber, *Tagespresse*; Lange, *Die Stellung*. Nonetheless, a telling indication of how deeply ingrained and gendered contemporaries' views of even mythical figures like Germania were is Bismarck's dislike of the monument erected in the Niederwald in 1883. The chancellor asserted that "a woman *(weibliches Wesen)* with a sword in this aggressive posture is unnatural. Every officer will feel the same way as I do about this." Quoted in Frank B. Tipton, *A History of Modern Germany since 1815* (Berkeley: University of California Press, 2003), 134.

100. For discussions of the representations of Germania in the nineteenth century, see Mosse, *Nationalism and Sexuality;* Lothar Gall, *Germania: Eine deutsche Marianne?* (Bonn: Bouvier, 1993); Hardtwig, "Bürgertum, Staatssymbolik und Staatsbewußtsein"; Marie-Louise von Plessen, ed., *Marianne und Germania 1789–1889: Frankreich und Deutschland: Zwei Welten—Eine Revue: Eine Ausstellung der Berliner Festspiele GmbH im Rahmen der ›46. Berliner Festwochen 1996‹ als Beitrag zur Städtepartnerschaft Paris-Berlin im Martin-Gropius-Bau, Stresemannstraße 110 vom 15. September 1996 bis 5. Januar 1997* (Berlin: Argon, 1996); Herminghouse and Mueller, "Introduction"; Esther-Beatrice von Bruchhausen "Das Zeichen im Kostümball—Marianne und Germania in der politischen Ikonographie," Dr. phil. Diss., Martin-Luther-Universität Halle-Wittenberg, 2000.

101. *Germania*, September 2, 1871. On the name dispute, see also Löffler, *Geschichte*, 54. For more on the linguistic origins of the word *Deutschland* see Werner Conze, "'Deutschland' und 'deutsche Nation' als historische Begriffe," in *Die Rolle der Nation in der deutschen Geschichte und Gegenwart: Beiträge zu einer internationalen Konferenz in Berlin (West) von 16. bis 18. Juni 1893,* ed. Otto Büsch and James Sheehan (Berlin: Colloquium, 1985), 24.

102. See, for example, "Rückblick auf das Jahr 1870, I," *Augsburger Postzeitung,* January 1, 1871.

103. "Das neue Deutschland, II," *Augsburger Postzeitung,* April 9, 1872.

104. For an example of *Germania's* initial outlook, see January 31, 1871. For more of this change in *Germania's* position, see Chapter 2.

105. "Nochmals die Kreuzzeitung und das Centrum, II," *Germania,* July 8, 1871. This article responded to what is sometimes identified as the beginning of the *Kulturkampf,* the publication of an article in the *Kreuzzeitung* that many Catholics took as a "semi-official declaration of war against the Center Party." See the first article in the series, which appeared in *Germania* on July 7, 1871.

106. *Germania*, December 10, 1871.

107. "Das Neue Deutsche Reich," *Germania,* February 23, 1872. On the idea of the war turned inward, also see, for example, *Kölnische Volkszeitung,* June 19, 1872. On the police and gendarmes as the internal arm of militarism, see: Annuarius Osseg [Georg Pachtler], *Der Europäische Militarismus* (Amberg: Habbel, 1876).

108. *Germania*, June 18, 1871. The phrase "bis auf's Messer," which appears to have been initially used by an opponent, found repetition throughout the Catholic press in describing the conflict. For example, "Inneres und eben deshalb Wichtiges," *Schlesische Volkszeitung,* August 11, 1872; "Berlins öffentliche Sittenlosigkeit und sociales Elend," *Historisch-Politische Blätter* 69 (1872), 273; "Berliner Leben," *Stimmen aus Maria-Laach* 3 (1872), 188.

109. *Germania*, June 27, 1871.

110. "Nochmals die Kreuzzeitung und das Centrum," *Germania,* July 7, 1871. See also, for example, *Germania,* June 22, 1871; *Kölnische Volkszeitung,* March 20, 1872; and a parliamentary speech of Paul Majunke's reprinted in *Germania* on September 17, 1871.

111. Underlined in the original. Bistumsarchiv Trier, BIII 11,10, Band 3, newspaper clipping from *Germania,* August 2, 1873.

112. "Ausschriben des Bischofs von Mainz," reprinted in *Germania,* August 24, 1874.

113. Anderson, *Practicing Democracy*, 94.

114. Osseg, *Europäische Militarismus*, 10. Advertisements for the book were run in daily papers like *Germania*. See February 18, 1876. Not surprisingly, criticism by Pachtler of spreading militarism also appeared in the periodical *Stimmen aus Maria-Laach*, which he became chief editor of in 1871. See, for example, Pachtler's "Der moderne Staat als Vorläufer der Socialdemokratie," *Stimmen aus Maria-Laach* 14 (1878), 480. Riesenberger also discusses Pachtler's work. See "Katholische Militarismuskritik."

115. Osseg, *Europäische Militarismus*, especially 166ff.

116. Ibid., especially 187ff.

117. Ibid., especially 232–248.

118. Ibid., 17.

119. Ibid., especially 21.

120. As noted previously, no records detailing individual authorship of articles in *Germania* remain.

121. On Janssen's view of Prussia, see Pastor, "Johannes Janssen," 737.

122. A more limited publication, not surprisingly, Pachtler's account critiqued the Reformation much more harshly than Janssen's first two volumes did and served as a more encompassing condemnation of war in general than the articles that appeared in the pages of *Germania* ever did.

123. Certainly this was the reason why articles in *Germania* attempted to both praise certain Hohenzollern traditions but also stress that the German nation equaled more than Prussia writ larger. The difficult task of muting divisions that any editor of a truly national paper for German Catholics would have was already recognized by Bishop Ketteler a decade earlier. See Dom- und Diözesanarchiv Mainz, C7.3,2, Mainz, February 14, 1862.

124. *"Faustrecht"* can be translated as "fist rule" or the "rule of force." For examples, see Pachtler, *Europäische Militarismus*, 13; "Die Atomisierung der Gesellschaft durch den Liberalismus," *Stimmen aus Maria-Laach* 6 (1874), 107; "Kirche und Liberalismus," *Historisch-Politische Blätter* 76 (1875), 360–361. *Kölnische Volkszeitung*, March 18, 1874; "Zur Jahreswende," *Augsburger Postzeitung*, January 1, 1872. An article in *Germania* already warned of how near the *Reich* was coming to being ruled by *"Faustrecht"* in an August 8, 1871, piece entitled, "Das neue deutsche Reich." Writing a work on the Middle Ages, Janssen tended to use *Faustrecht* in a more specific historical sense in connection with *Fehderecht*. Nonetheless, he also notes the rise of *Faustrecht* in connection with the decline of the empire. See, for example, p. 434. Progovernment publications also rejected *Faustrecht*, of course, but emphasized it as a characteristic of the Middle Ages, not the nineteenth century. See, for example, Paul Röhde's article, "Ueber das Schöffeninstitut nach der

Carolina und dessen weitere Ausbildung in Deutschland," *Preußische Jahrbücher* 39 (1877), 347. Nonetheless, Stefan Berger asserts that the devaluation of morality in light of the wars of unification did occur in the dominant historical scholarship of the period: "Bismarck's violent unification of Germany had an important impact on how historians committed to the national paradigm, from Heinrich von Sybel to Hans-Peter Schwarz, have consistently used the category of 'success' to legitimise or delegitimise historical developments. A historical action was not justified by its moral credibility but by its success. . . . All this is the foundation of a historiography of victors, in which losers have no place. Values and actions are relative to their success." In *The Search for Normality*, 29–30.

125. "Recht und Moral," *Germania*, December 30, 1871.

126. "Zur Geschichte der politischen Moral in Deutschland," *Germania*, February 21, 1874; "Phrasen und Schlagwörter," *Germania*, July 28, 1872; "Thron und Altar," *Germania*, August 18, 1874.

127. Using this martial language concerning the legal system, Georg Hertling wrote to his wife about a law being debated in parliament that would add "new weapons in the battle against Ultramontanes." Bundesarchiv (Koblenz), N 1036, Nr. 9, Berlin, December 3, 1875. See also, "Der Kampf gegen die Kirche in Baden," *Germania*, October 22, 1874.

128. "'Liberalle' Begriffe von religiöser Freiheit," *Germania*, February 7, 1872.

129. "Thron und Altar," *Germania*, August 18, 1874.

130. "Reichsrecht oder Gewalt des Stärkeren," *Germania*, July 12, 1875.

131. Osseg, *Europäische Militarismus*, 18–19. A piece in the *Schlesische Volkszeitung*, for example, contended that passive resistance backed up by the moral high ground had "the enviable advantage" of being "victorious" every time: "Inneres und eben deshalb Wichtiges," August 11, 1872.

132. "Die religiöse Lage Deutschlands und die Centrumsfraction im deutschen Reichstag, Schluß," *Germania*, September 29, 1871.

133. See, for example, "Die religiöse und sittliche Verwilderung im Gefolge des 'Culturkampfes' zeigt sich bis jetzt nur auf protestantischem Boden, auf katholischer Seite sind die letzten Jahre Jahre der Erneuerung und Erfrischung gewesen," *Germania*, June 1, 1876.

134. "Die religiöse Lage Deutschlands und die Centrumsfraction im deutschen Reichstag, Schluß," *Germania*, September 29, 1871. See also, for example, "Eine Lehre der Geschichte," *Germania*, August 25, 1876.

135. Riesenberger also notes this as a point made in Ketteler's writing. See "Katholische Militarismuskritik," 99. Of course, this was a reference to and rejection of the claim often made by opponents that Jesuits believed in the motto "the ends justify the means." Catholic arguments asserted

that it was the amoral actions of the aggressors in the *Kulturkampf* that displayed such a belief. See, for example, *Augsburger Postzeitung*, May 20, 1872; June 19, 1875. For another example, see Ketteler, *Die Katholiken im Deutschen Reiche*, 11.

136. Other assertions stressed this as well. Ketteler, for example, emphasized the lows to which the government had fallen in these same terms by referring to its use not of "spiritual weapons" but of "violent oppression" in the *Kulturkampf*. In *Die Katholiken im Deutschen Reiche*, 122.

137. "Die Unterscheidung von kirchlicher und staatlicher Gewalt im christlichen Alterthum," *Germania*, March 31, 1874.

138. "Katholisches Leben und Treiben," *Germania*, February 12, 1876.

139. "Die Papstfeier am 16. Juni," *Germania*, June 22, 1872.

140. Hausen, "Die Polarisierung."

141. Hagemann, "A Valorous *Volk* Family," 191.

142. Mosse, *Nationalism and Sexuality*, 98.

143. *Verhandlungen der XXVI. Generalverssamlung der Katholiken Deutschlands zu Aachen am 8., 9., 10., und 11. September 1879* (Aachen: Jacobi, 1879), 366.

144. Again, it is important to note that opponents of Catholics certainly did not agree with this view. Indeed, soldiers and morality had just recently been harmoniously paired in the propaganda of the Franco-Prussian War. Central to the German understanding was the belief that they were waging a moral war against the immoral French, and both traits were seen as nationally defined characteristics. See Jeismann, *Vaterland der Feinde*, 248–252, 277–279. Furthermore, despite the emphasis on considering issues from the standpoint of morality during the 1870s, an earlier article written in the wake of 1866 in the Catholic *Historisch-Politische Blätter* apparently considered the usefulness of war against France from the standpoint of its potential benefits to the losers of the Austro-Prussian War. See Nikolaus Buschmann, "Volksgemeinschaft und Waffenbruderschaft: Nationalismus und Kriegserfahrung in Deutschland zwischen 'Novemberkrise' und 'Bruderkrieg,'" in *Föderative Nation: Deutschlandkonzepte von der Reformation bis zum Ersten Weltkrieg*, ed. Dieter Langewiesche and Georg Schmidt (Münich: Oldenbourg, 2000), 108–109.

145. Sperber, *Popular Catholicism*, 231.

146. One of the files listed in the register of the holdings in the Dom- und Diözesanarchiv Mainz is "Konferenz vom 29. IV.1873." Though the file itself is no longer extant, the listing notes that this conference included a "Beschluß: Passiver Widerstand" against the laws, listing in particular a few of the most recently passed by the government. See file listing for

C.7.2, 4f. "Passiver Widerstand" was further expounded upon greatly in numerous editions of *Germania,* as well as other papers. See, for example, "Inneres und eben deshalb Wichtiges," *Schlesische Volkszeitung,* August 11, 1872.

147. Dom- und Diözesanarchiv Mainz D.6,1b, undated letter (probably 1874 or 1875). For more on German Catholics' views of O'Connell and his success in Ireland, see Chapter 9.

148. Morsey, "Die Deutschen Katholiken," 35; Sperber, *Popular Catholicism,* 229–331; Blackbourn, "Progress and Piety," 152; Blackbourn, *Marpingen,* 239; Gross, *War Against Catholicism,* 224. Gross tends to emphasize both active and passive resistance, while Blackbourn emphasizes the dominance of the latter most heavily. Indeed, in a personal letter to Guelph party member Heinrich Langwert von Simmern, August Reichensperger indicated how Kullmann's assassination attempt on Bismarck, bringing with it so many accusations against Catholics in general, "truly dazed" him. Landeshauptarchiv Koblenz, 700,138, Nr. 43, July 26, 1874.

149. Hausen, "Die Polarisierung"; Confino, *The Nation as a Local Metaphor,* 212.

150. Previously, liberals had undertaken passive resistance against Bismarck during the conflicts of the 1860s. See Thomas Parent, *"Passiver Widerstand" im preußischen Verfassungskonflikt: die Kölner Abgeordnetenfeste* (Cologne: DME-Verlag, 1982).

151. On literature, see Patricia Herminghouse, "The Ladies' Auxiliary of German Literature: Nineteenth-Century Women Writers and the Quest for a National Literary History," in *Gender and Germanness,* ed. Patricia Herminghaus and Magda Mueller (Providence: Berghahn Books, 1997), 148; Sperber, *Popular Catholicism,* 228; Blackbourn, "Progress and Piety," 152–153; Blackbourn, *Marpingen,* 241.

152. Blackbourn refers to such choices as "highly developed iconographical forms": Blackbourn, "Progress and Piety," 152–153. See also Blackbourn, *Marpingen,* 241; Sperber, *Popular Catholicism,* 228; Gross, *War Against Catholicism,* 224.

153. Gross, *War Against Catholicism,* 225. From the literature I have considered, Gross comes closest, particularly in this quote, to the ideas being argued in this chapter. He draws this conclusion from the significant participation of women in both Church activities and in demonstrations. For his instructive discussion of this topic, see Gross, *War Against Catholicism,* 201–225. While drawing upon this activity, this chapter places more emphasis on the imagery of Catholic opposition and its linkage with the creation of a competing construction of Germanness.

154. "Der Verein Christlicher Mütter," *Germania*, May 12, 1874.

155. *Germania*, July 11, 1874.

156. Anderson, *Practicing Democracy*, 127. This is also noted in Gross, drawing on the work of Anderson in this case. In *War Against Catholicism*, 224–225.

157. *Germania*, September 21, 1871.

158. "Ehret die Frauen!" *Germania*, October 26. 1874. For more on the view of events in Spain, see Chapter 9.

159. For example, see "Kampf, nicht Friede," *Germania*, December 12, 1878. Even when discussing orders not being dissolved, articles were certain to contrast the meekness of those women involved with the actions of the authorities, such as placing the nuns under "special police surveillance." See "Die sociale Noth und die barmherzigen Schwestern, I," *Tremonia*, December 19, 1877. Sick care in nineteenth-century Germany also played into *Germania*'s portrayal of the militaristic state versus a feminine Catholicism. As Catholic religious orders were being labeled "dangerous to the state," an article on March 5, 1872 pointed out the importance of such groups in nursing. While it noted that men had also been important in such capacities, it focused on the Sisters of Charity and their dedicated service to Germany. Playing on the idea that the military was so important to the state, the article ended with the sarcastic question and answer, "Who would care for the sick during a later war? These liberal gentlemen certainly not!" This theme was the topic of countless *Germania* articles during the 1870s. Catholic strength in sick care was well known and a concern among Protestants. Though for a later date, the estimate of the relative deficiency in Protestant to Catholic female staff providing sick care made by the Protestant League in 1908 places the deficiency in more concrete terms. According to their calculations, there was a ratio of one Protestant *Diakonisse* for every 1,720 Protestants versus one Catholic *Krankenschwester* for every 670 Catholics in Germany. See Armin Müller-Dreier, *Konfession in Politik, Gesellschaft und Kultur des Kaiserreichs: Der Evangelische Bund 1886–1914*, (Gütersloh: Chr. Kaiser, 1998), 370. Even adjusting for the difference in size of the two confessions in Germany, these statistics indicate that Catholics had an advantage in absolute numbers too.

160. *Germania*, July 11, 1874.

161. Blackbourn, "Progress and Piety," 156–157; Blackbourn, *Marpingen*, 204–205, 239, 263; Smith, *German Nationalism*, 45.

162. *Historisch-Politische Blätter* (1879), 517–526. Cited in Smith, *German Nationalism*, 45. On the earlier themes in the journal, see Kevin Cramer,

"The Cult of Gustavus Adolphus: Protestant Identity and German Nationalism," in *Protestants, Catholics and Jews, 1800–1914*, ed. Helmut Walser Smith (Oxford: Berg, 2001), 111; Conze, "Militarismus." Indeed, reports about the Marpingen case generally highlighted the use of violence. See, for example, the discussion in the Prussian diet that was reprinted as "Die Affare Marpingen im Abgeordnetenhause," *Tremonia*, January 21, 22, and 23, 1878.

163. Blackbourn, "Progress and Piety," 156.

164. For just one of many examples, see Landeshauptarchiv Koblenz 441, Nr. 17231, letter written in Molsberg, July 10, 1873.

165. Staatsarchiv Münster, OP 2114 "Ausführung der neuen kirchenpolitischen Gesetze zur Vorbildung und Anstellung der Geistlichen, 1873–1887," letter from October 13, 1873.

166. Yuval-Davis, "Gender and Nation," 29. Beyond rape specifically, the importance of sexuality for nationalism has been discussed by Yuval-Davis and also Mosse in *Nationalism and Sexuality*.

167. Ulinka Rublack, "Wench and Maiden: Women, War and the Pictorial Function of the Feminine in German Cities in the Early Modern Period," *History Workshop Journal*, 44 (1997): 4.

168. Hagemann, "'Of Manly Valor' and 'German Honor'," 216–217. The imagery of defeated and humiliated Germany after World War I also included the trope of wartime rape. Harvey describes a nationalist image depicting a naked woman representing Germany being threatened by a bear representing Poland. Notably, the bear is "pawing her thighs." In "Pilgrimages," 211. On the symbolism of rape during wartime, see also John Horne and Alan Kramer, *German Atrocities, 1914: A History of Denial* (New Haven: Yale University Press, 2001), especially 196–204.

169. Smith, *German Nationalism*, 47.

170. *Germania*, June 18, 1871.

171. "Zur Lage, IV," *Schlesische Volkszeitung*, February 11, 1872.

172. "Die Hermannsschlacht," *Germania*, April 20, 1875.

173. "Die Lage der barmherzigen Schwestern nach dem Klostergesetz," *Germania*, May 10, 1875.

174. "Wie kann der zunehmenden Unsittlichkeit gestenert [sic] werden," *Germania*, November 10, 1871; "Die Stellung der Frau im Heidenthum," *Germania*, October 27, 1872, Schluß"; *Germania*, June 20, 1874. "Die Verfolgung der katholischen Kirche unter dem Kaiser Diokletian," *Germania*, July 17, 1874; "Die Majestät des Papsthums," *Germania*, June 8, 1877. This undoubtedly tied in to the gendering of many

communal conflicts and ideas of soldiers' immoral behavior, like in Pachtler's critique of militarism discussed above. Again emphasizing the moral salvation offered by the feminine, Pachtler asserted that the few exceptions to the general moral debauchery of soldiers were the "wonders of godly grace, fruits of the prayers of a pious mother, of a tender sister." In *Europäische Militarismus*, 241.

175. In Alban Stoltz, *Gesammelte Werke,* vol. 10 (Freiburg: Herder, 1875), 13–14. This context also added to the Catholic disgust expressed when progressive Protestant clergy would deny the virgin birth of Jesus Christ, especially for men like Stolz. "Die abermalige Wahl eines heidnischen Predigers an einer grossen christlichen Gemeinde zu Berlin," *Germania,* June 1, 1877. On Stolz's views of sexuality, see Herzog, *Intimacy and Exclusion,* 30–32.

176. Indeed, both public and private Catholic writings highlight the importance of sacrifice and the willingness to suffer, whether it be as victims of state aggression or merely from the privations of the tough times. See, for example, a letter by August Reichensperger to his wife in the Landeshauptarchiv Koblenz, 700, 138, Nr. 4, Berlin, October 30, 1871; letters to Moufang from his niece in the Dom- und Diözesanarchiv Mainz, D, 6, 1a, Amiens, August 17, 1873 and London, October 29, 1873; *Germania,* July 11, 1874; July 25, 1874.

177. Altgeld, *Katholizimus, Protestantismus, Judentum*; Altgeld, "Religion, Denomination and Nationalism."

178. Such an explanation is suggested by Norbert Busch's article on feminine piety, "Die Feminisierung der Frömmigkeit."

179. Michel Foucault addresses this issue in *History of Sexuality, Volume I: An Introduction.* He makes the point most explicitly in the example of homosexuality: "There is no question that the appearance in nineteenth-century psychiatry, jurisprudence, and literature of a whole series of discourses on the species and subspecies of homosexuality, inversion, pederasty, and 'psychic hermaphrodism' made possible a strong advance of social controls into this area of 'perversity'; but it also made possible the formation of a 'reverse' discourse: homosexuality began to speak in its own behalf, to demand that its legitimacy or 'naturality' be acknowledged, often in the same vocabulary, using the same categories by which it was medically disqualified." In *The History of Sexuality, Volume I: An Introduction,* trans. Robert Hurley (New York: Vintage, 1990), 101. Emphasis added. Ruth Roach Pierson also suggests the application of Foucault to gender and nationalism, though without specific emphasis on the importance of the discourse being reversed. Pierson, "Nations:

Gendered, Racialized, Crossed with Empire," in *Gendered Nations: Nationalism and Gender Order in the Long Nineteenth Century*, ed. Ida Blom, Karen Hagemann, and Catherine Hall (Oxford: Berg, 2000), 43.

180. Indeed, on the issue of Marian veneration among Catholics, at least, Norbert Busch suggests the high esteem given to the Virgin Mary made attainment of similar status by women more difficult, as they could never live up to their model's image. *Katholische Frömmigkeit*, 128–129.

181. On the other hand, some elements of the Catholic argument persisted. On the critique of militarism, for example, see, Riesenberger, "Katholische Militarismuskritik."

182. Busch, "Die Feminisierung der Frömmigkeit."

183. Confino, *The Nation as a Local Metaphor.*

184. Describing the fate of liberalism, *Germania* concluded: "nothing remains other than the violated name and the empty pretense." August 23, 1879.

185. Other works have noted the ability of crisis situations to impact issues of gender boundaries. See, for example, Hagemann, "Female Patriots," 415.

8. The Battle over Schools and Scholarship

1. Reichensperger was also an art historian, staunchly advocating the neo-gothic over the neo-classical style. See Hanno-Walter Kruft, *Geschichte der Architekturtheorie*, 5th ed. (Munich: C.H. Beck, 2004), 361–363.

2. A second edition had been published in 1863. Reichensperger, *Phrasen und Schlagwörter*, iii.

3. Ibid., viii–ix.

4. Ibid., vii.

5. Ibid., iii.

6. Ludwig Pastor, *August Reichensperger. Sein Leben und sein Wirken auf dem Gebiet der Politik, der Kunst, und der Wissenschaft*, vol. 2 (Freiburg im Breisgau: Herder, 1899), 85. The reprinting of tantalizing excerpts in newspapers likely helped sales. See, for example, *Germania* July 28, 30 and August 4, 1872.

7. Reichensperger, *Phrasen und Schlagwörter*, ix.

8. Ibid.

9. Ibid., 170.

10. Ibid.

11. Ibid., 170–171.

12. For example, see Nipperdey, *Deutsche Geschichte*, vol. 1, 531; Marjorie Lamberti, *State, Society, and the Elementary School in Imperial Germany* (New York: Oxford, 1989).

13. Christoph Weber, "Der deutsche Katholizismus und die Herausforderung des protestantischen Bildungsanspruchs," in *Bildungsbürgertum im 19. Jahrhundert, Teil II: Bildungsgüter und Bildungswissen*, ed. Reinhart Koselleck (Stuttgart: Klett-Cotta, 1990), 161.

14. This is connected to Georg Hertling, discussed later in this chapter. On *Heimat*, see Applegate, *A Nation of Provincials*; Confino, *The Nation as a Local Metaphor*.

15. See, for example, Nipperdey, *Deutsche Geschichte*, vol. 1, 445; Jeffrey Zalar, "The Process of Confessional Inculturation: Catholic Reading in the 'Long Nineteenth Century'," in *Protestants, Catholics, and Jews in Germany, 1800–1914*, ed. Helmut Walser Smith (Oxford: Berg, 2001); Dieter Langewiesche, "Vom Gebildeten zum Bildungsbürger? Umrisse eines katholischen Bildungsbürgertum im wilhelminischen Deutschland," in *Liberalismus und Sozialismus: Gesellschaftsbilder-Zukunftsvisionen-Bildungskonzeptionen*, ed. Friedrich Lenger (Bonn: Dietz, 2003), especially 192; Gross, *The War Against Catholicism*, 227.

16. See, for example, Martin Baumeister, *Parität und katholische Inferiorität*.

17. Baumeister, *Parität und katholische Inferiorität*, 16. See also Gangolf Hübinger, "Confessionalism," in *Imperial Germany: A Historiographical Companion*, ed. Roger Chickering (Westport, CT: Greenwood, 1996), 173.

18. David Blackbourn, for example, writes that "in a reversal of the trend that dominated at the beginning of the nineteenth century, Catholicism traded on its closeness to the 'people' and 'popular' beliefs. The new attention paid to children, now confirmed at an earlier age and even accepted as potential visionaries, was one sign of this emphasis on simplicity rather than learning, the heart rather than the head." Blackbourn, *Fontana History of Germany*, 302. See also, Weber, "Der deutsche Katholizismus," 165; Nipperdey, *Deutsche Geschichte*, vol. 1, 431–432.

19. Hübinger, "Confessionalism," 174.

20. For examples of statistics on students and professors broken down by confession, see Fritz Ringer, "A Sociography of German Academics, 1863–1938," *Central European History* 25 (1992): 276; Konrad Jarausch, *Deutsche Studenten 1800–1970* (Frankfurt am Main: Suhrkamp, 1984), 28; Thomas Mergel, *Zwischen Klasse und Konfession: Katholisches Bürgertum im Rheinland 1794–1914* (Göttingen: Vandenhoeck & Ruprecht, 1994), 391. For a nuanced discussion of what these statistics represent, see Michael Klöcker, "Das katholische Bildungsdefizit in Deutschland: Eine historische Analyse," *Geschichte in Wissenschaft und Unterricht* 32 (1981): 79–83.

21. The most notable work on the Catholic Bürgertum is Thomas Mergel's study of the Rhineland. Though also stressing the complexity of the case,

his findings confirm the general picture of a Catholic educational lag. See *Zwischen Klasse.*

22. Nipperdey, *Deutsche Geschichte, 1800–1866,* 451.

23. Ibid., 452.

24. James Albisetti, "Education," in *Imperial Germany: A Historiographical Companion,* ed. Roger Chickering (Westport, CT: Greenwood, 1996), 244.

25. Statistics and evaluations for determining literacy differ. Nipperdey notes that three-fourths of the populace was literate by 1871. Wolfgang von Ungern-Sternberg provides this figure and the more recent estimation of 87 percent. Frank-Michael Kuhlemann also gives the latter statistic. See Nipperdey, *Deutsche Geschichte 1800–1866,* 587; Ungern-Sternberg, "Medien," in *Handbuch der deutschen Bildungsgeschichte,* Band III, ed. Karl-Ernst Jeismann and Peter Lundgreen, (Munich: C.H. Beck, 1987), 386–387; Kuhlemann, "Niedere Schulen," in *Handbuch der deutschen Bildungsgeschichte,* vol. 4, ed. Christa Berg (Munich: C.H. Beck, 1991), 193. On the limits of schooling, see Lamberti, *State, Society, and the Elementary School,* 6.

26. Rüdiger vom Bruch, "The Academic Disciplines and Social Thought," in *Imperial Germany: A Historiographical Companion,* ed. Roger Chickering (Westport, CT: Greenwood, 1996), 344.

27. Albisetti, "Education," 257; Nipperdey, *Deutsche Geschichte 1800–1866,* 416; Thomas Ellwein, *Die deutsche Universität: Vom Mittelalter bis zur Gegenwart* (Königstein: Athenäum, 1985), 115; Thomas Albert Howard, *Protestant Theology and the Making of the Modern German University* (Oxford: Oxford University Press, 2006), 5; Georg Bollenbeck, *Bildung und Kultur: Glanz und Elend eines deutschen Deutungsmusters,* (Frankfurt a. M.: Insel, 1994), 224. Woodruff D. Smith, *Politics and the Sciences of Culture in Germany, 1814–1920* (New York: Oxford University Press, 1991), 72.

28. Blackbourn, *Fontana History of Germany,* 275.

29. Howard, *Protestant Theology,* 1–5.

30. Less influential reforms also occurred in earlier centuries. John E. Craig, *Scholarship and Nation Building: The Universities of Strasbourg and Alsatian Society, 1870–1939* (Chicago: University of Chicago Press, 1984), 7, 12–13; Howard, *Protestant Theology,* 141.

31. Howard, *Protestant Theology,* 12.

32. Philip Schaff, *Germany: Its Universities, Theology, and Religion* (Edinburgh: T and T Clark, 1857), 63. Quoted in Howard, *Protestant Theology,* 12.

33. Bruch, "The Academic Disciplines," 357; Nipperdey, *Deutsche Geschichte*, vol. 1, 602.

34. Blackbourn, *Fontana History of Germany*, 275; Paul Julian Weindling, *Darwinism and Social Darwinism in Imperial Germany: The Contribution of the Cell Biologist Oscar Hertwig (1849–1922)* (Stuttgart: Fischer, 1991), 22.

35. Bruch, "The Academic Disciplines," 345.

36. Ibid., 350.

37. Howard, *Protestant Theology*, 141–142; Schelling, "Über das Wesen deutscher Wissenschaft" (1811), in *Schellings Werke*, vol. 4, ed. Manfred Schröter (Munich: Beck, 1927). Quoted in Howard, *Protestant Theology*, 142.

38. Berger, *Germany*, 52.

39. Albisetti, "Education," 244; Angela Schwarz, *Der Schlüssel zur modernen Welt: Wissenschaftspopularisierung in Großbritanien und Deutschland im Übergang zur Moderne (ca. 1870–1914)* (Stuttgart: Steiner, 1999), 332, 337–338.

40. Masako Shibata, "Controlling National Identity and Reshaping the Role of Education," *History of Education* 33 (2004): 83.

41. Nipperdey, *Deutsche Geschichte 1800–1866*, 455; Assmann, *Arbeit am nationalen Gedächtnis*, 65; Bollenbeck, *Bildung und Kultur*, 244.

42. Nipperdey, *Deutsche Geschichte 1800–1866*, 475; Ellwein, *Die deutsche Universität*, 125.

43. Nipperdey, *Deutsche Geschichte 1800–1866*, 475; see also Lisa Swartout, "Culture Wars: Protestant, Catholic, and Jewish Students at German Universities, 1890–1914," in *Religion und Nation, Nation und Religion: Beiträge zu einer unbewältigten Geschichte*, ed. Michael Geyer and Hartmut Lehmann (Göttingen: Wallstein, 2004): 157–175.

44. Nipperdey, *Deutsche Geschichte 1800–1866*, 480. The identification with nationalism appears only to have become stronger by the century's end. See Konrad Jarausch, *Students, Society, and Politics in Imperial Germany: The Rise of Academic Illiberalism* (Princeton: Princeton University Press, 1982), 178.

45. Berger, *Germany*, 50, 70; Nipperdey, *Deutsche Geschichte 1800–1866*, 480.

46. Berger, *Germany*, 33–34; Howard, *Protestant Theology*, 141; Frank Michael Kuhlemann, "Das Kaiserreich als Erziehungsstaat," *Geschichte in Wissenschaft und Unterricht* 49 (1998): 730.

47. Friedrich Schiller and Johann Wolfgang von Goethe, *Xenien*. Quoted in Berger, *Germany*, 3.

48. Katharine D. Kennedy, "A Nation's Readers: Cultural Integration and the Schoolbook Canon in Wilhelmine Germany," *Padagogica Historica* 33:2 (1997): 460; Berger, *Germany*, 81.

49. Lamberti, *State, Society, and the Elementary School*, 109.

50. Craig, *Scholarship and Nation Building*, especially 23–24, 29–30, 55–56, 80, 83; Steinhoff, *Gods of the City*, 92–93.

51. Kuhlemann, "Das Kaiserreich als Erziehungsstaat"; Craig, *Scholarship and Nation Building*, especially 102–105.

52. Bruch, "The Academic Disciplines," 357; Weindling, *Darwinism and Social Darwinism*.

53. Nipperdey, *Deutsche Geschichte*, vol. 1, 633; Stefan Berger, *The Search for Normality: National Identity and Historical Consciousness in Germany Since 1800* (Providence: Berghahn, 1997); Holger Th. Gräf, "Reich, Nation und Kirche in der gross- und kleindeutschen Historiographie," *Historisches Jahrbuch* 116 (1996): 367–94; Gangolf Hübinger, "Geschichte als leitende Orientierungswissenschaft im 19. Jahrhundert," *Berichte zur Wissenschaftsgeschichte* 11 (1988): 149–158; Ulrich Wyrwa, "Heinrich von Treitschke. Geschichtsschreibung und öffentliche Meinung im Deutschland des 19. Jahrhunderts," *Zeitschrift für Geschichtswissenschaft* 51 (2003): 781–792; Assmann, *Arbeit am nationalen Gedächtnis*, 110; Brent O. Peterson, *History, Fiction, and Germany: Writing the Nineteenth-Century Nation* (Detroit: Wayne State Press, 2005), see especially 9, 13, 32.

54. For overviews of the topic that discuss the causes, see: Klöcker, "Das katholische Bildungsdefizit"; Werner Rösener, "Das katholische Bildungsdefizit im deutschen Kaiserreich—ein Erbe der Säkularisation vom 1803?" *Historisches Jahrbuch der Görres-Gesellschaft* 112 (1992): 104–127.

55. Charles E. McClelland, "Structural Change and Social Reproduction in German Universities, 1870–1920," *History of Education* 15 (1986): 180; Fritz Ringer, "Higher Education in Germany in the Nineteenth Century," *Journal of Contemporary History* 2 (1967): 132–134.

56. Rösener, "Das katholische Bildungsdefizit," 119–120; Hübinger, "Confessionalism," 167.

57. Jarausch, *Students, Society, and Politics in Imperial Germany*, 81. Ringer, "Higher Education," 135. Michael Klöcker, "Katholizismus und Bildungsbürgertum: Hinweise zur Erforschung vernachlässigter Bereiche der deutschen Bildungsgeschichte im 19. Jahrhundert," in *Bildungsbürgertum im 19. Jahrhundert, Teil 2: Bildungsgüter und Bildungswissen*, ed. Reinhart Koselleck (Stuttgart: Klett-Cotta, 1990), 119.

58. Klöcker, "Das katholische Bildungsdefizit," 83, 88; McClelland, "Structural Change," 180.

59. Rösener, "Das katholische Bildungsdefizit," 121.

60. Reinhart Koselleck, "*Bildungsbürgertum im 19. Jahrhundert, Teil II: Bildungsgüter und Bildungswissen* (Stuttgart: Klett-Cotta, 1990), 11–12; Jarausch, *Students, Society, and Politics*, 85.

61. On the limited nature of a Catholic bourgeoisie and its tense relationship with education see Mergel, *Zwischen Klasse*; Nipperdey, *Deutsche Geschichte*, vol. 1, 429; Gross, *The War Against Catholicism*, 120. On the search for a Catholic bourgeoisie more generally, see Heilbronner, "Wohin verschwand das katholische Bürgertum?"

62. Weber, "Der deutsche Katholizismus," 142; Hübinger, "Confessionalism," 174.

63. Raymond Geuss, "Kultur, Bildung, Geist," *History and Theory* 35 (1996): 154. On the difficulty of translation, see Koselleck, *Bildungsbürgertum*, 13–14; Jarausch, *Students, Society, and Politics*, 9.

64. Bollenbeck, *Bildung und Kultur*, 223; Assmann, *Arbeit am nationalen Gedächtnis*, 9.

65. Jarausch, *Students, Society, and Politics*, 9; Nipperdey, *Deutsche Geschichte*, vol. 1, 590; Fritz Ringer, "Comparing Two Academic Cultures," *History of Education* 16 (1987); Ellwein, *Die deutsche Universität*, 124–125; Margit Szöllösi-Janze, "Science and Social Space," *Minerva* 43 (2005).

66. Andreas Daum, "Science, Politics, and Religion: Humboldtian Thinking and the Transformation of Civil Society in Germany, 1830–1870," *Osiris* 17 (2002): 112; Manfred Hettling and Stefan-Ludwig Hoffmann, "Der bürgerliche Wertehimmel: Zum Problem individueller Lebensführung im 19. Jahrhundert," *Geschichte und Gesellschaft* 23(1997): 335–336; Hans-Dieter Nägelke, "Gelehrte Gemeinschaft und wissenschaftlicher Großbetrieb: Hochschulbau als Spiegel von Wissenschaftsidee und –praxis im 19. und frühen 20. Jahrhundert," *Berichte zur Wissenschaftsgeschichte* 21 (1998).

67. See, for example, Nipperday, *Deutsche Geschichte 1800–1866*, especially 403–404; 440–451.

68. Blackbourn, *Fontana History of Germany*, 284; Nipperdey, *Deutsche Geschichte 1800–1866*, 473–474. Of course, this was not always the case, even for Catholics. See David Berger, "Ratio Fidei fundamenta demonstrat. Fundamentaltheologisches Denken zwischen 1870 und 1960," in *Die katholisch-theologischen Disziplinen in Deutschland 1870–1962: Ihre Geschichte, ihr Zeitbezug*, ed. Hubert Wolf (Paderborn: Schöningh, 1999), 95–127.

69. On secularization, see Liedhegener, *Christentum und Urbanisierung*.

70. Koselleck, *Bildungsbürgertum*, 24.

71. Howard, *Protestant Theology*, 8–9.

72. Ibid., 33–34, 62.

73. Howard, *Protestant Theology*; Hermann Timm, "Bildungsreligion im deutschsprachigen Protestantismus—eine grundbegriffliche Perspektiverung," in *Bildungsbürgertum im 19. Jahrhundert, Teil II: Bildungsgüter und Bildungswissen*, ed. Reinhart Koselleck (Stuttgart: Klett-Cotta, 1990), 57.

74. George S. Williamson, *The Longing for Myth: Religion and Aesthetic Culture from Romanticism to Nietzsche* (Chicago: Chicago University Press, 2004), especially 8; Suzanne Marchand, *Down from Olympus: Archaeology and Philhellenism in Germany* (Princeton: Princeton University Press, 1996), especially xxiii.

75. Swartout, "Culture Wars."

76. Weber, "Der deutsche Katholizismus," 142.

77. Jarausch, *Students, Society, and Politics*, 138–139; Howard, *Protestant Theology*, 134–135.

78. Weber, "Der deutsche Katholizismus," 154. On the marginalization of dissenting historians, see Hubert Wolf, "Der Historiker ist kein Prophet. Zur theologischen (Selbst-) Marginalisierung der katholischen deutschen Kirchengeschichtsschreibung zwischen 1870 und 1960," in *Die katholisch-theologischen Disziplinen in Deutschland 1870–1962*, ed. Hubert Wolf with Claus Arnold (Paderborn: Schöningh, 1999), 71–93.

79. Weber, "Der deutsche Katholizismus," 156; Zalar, "Catholic Reading." Weber stresses effectiveness; Zalar emphasizes limits.

80. Ringer, "Comparing Two Academic Cultures," 185; Fritz Ringer, "Bildung: The Social and Ideological Context of the German Historical Tradition," *History of European Ideas* 10 (1989), 193–195.

81. See the detailed analysis by Gross, *The War Against Catholicism*, especially 23.

82. Nipperdey, *Deutsche Geschichte*, vol. 1, 531.

83. Such disputes are ubiquitous in archival records. See, for example, Bistumsarchiv Trier BIII 9,7 Band 10; LHAK, 441 Nr. 3516; 442 Nr. 2202; LAEKW, 0,0, sig. 172b; BSA, LA 270; StAM, OP 2166.

84. Member loss was linked not only to confessional schooling but other issues, such as mixed marriages more generally and adult conversions. While both sides feared this decline, Catholic losses tended to be greater. Given regional variation in confessional composition, however, certain

locales could exhibit the opposite trend. Ross, *Failure*, 17; Dietrich Höroldt, "Mischehe und konfessionelle Kindererziehung im Bereich der rheinischen Landeskirche seit 1815," *Rheinische Vierteljahrsblätter* 39 (1975): 147–188. On secularization compared between Catholics and Protestants, see Antonius Liedhegener, *Christentum und Urbanisierung.*

85. For example, the teacher's confession and the lesson reader's character both became issues in the Medard *Simultanschule* dispute: LHAK, 441 Nr. 26927. See also Anderson, *Windthorst*, 106.

86. LHAK 441, Nr. 10608. Though the dispute came to a head in the early 1880s, the file includes copies of background letters from earlier years (August 10, 1877).

87. Alfred Kelley, "The Franco-Prussian War and Unification in German History Schoolbooks," in *German Unifications and the Change of Literary Discourse*, ed. Walter Pape (Berlin: Walter de Gruyter, 1993), 41; Stephen L. Harp, *Learning to be Loyal: Primary Schooling as Nation Building in Alsace and Lorraine 1850–1940* (Dekalb: Northern Illinois Press, 1998), xi.

88. Anderson, *Windthorst*, 134; Evans, *The German Center Party*, 39–41.

89. Anderson, *Windthorst*, 60–1.

90. Sperber, *Popular Catholicism*, 184. Anderson, *Windthorst*, 135; Windell, *The Catholics and German Unity*, 278–279.

91. Wilhelm Mommsen, *Deutsche Parteiprogramme* (Munich: Isar, 1960), 217; Herbert Lepper, *Volk, Kirche und Vaterland. Wahlaufrufe, Aufrufe, Satzungen und Statuten des Zentrums 1870–1933: Eine Quellensammlung zur Geschichte insbesondere der Rheinischen und Westfälischen Zentrumspartei* (Düsseldorf: Droste, 1998), 141; Ludwig Bergsträßer, *Der politische Katholizismus: Dokumente seiner Entwicklung, II (1871–1914)* (Munich: Drei Masken, 1923), 27.

92. Lamberti, "State, Church, and the Politics of School Reform"; Lamberti, *State, Society, and the Elementary School*; Ross, *Failure*; 6.

93. Lamberti, "State, Church, and the Politics of School Reform"; Lamberti, *State, Society, and the Elementary School*; Sperber, *Popular Catholicism*, 209–210.

94. For example, the School Supervision Law succeeded partly because of some Conservative support in the legislature. Anderson, *Windthorst*, 159–160. Though accounts generally suggest that Protestant protest was less, there is disagreement over to what extent. See also Ross, *The Failure of Bismarck's Kulturkampf*, 31–32; Lamberti, *State, Society, and the Elementary School*, especially 44, 59, 61, 75; Kuhlemann, "Das Kaiserreich als Erziehungsstaat," 734–735.

95. These issues were also central to the complaints found in archival files.

96. "Cujus regio, ejus religio im Jahre der Gnade 1871," *Germania,* June 10, 1871.

97. "Confessionslose Schulen und confessionelle Bücher," *Germania,* June 22, 1871.

98. For a detailed account, see Harp, *Learning to be Loyal.*

99. In Alsace and Lorraine, this meant a sizable increase in the number of school inspectors; in heavily Polish areas, the School Supervision Law was applied with particular alacrity. Harp, *Learning to be Loyal,* 52–53; Lamberti, *State, Society, and Elementary School,* 109–112.

100. Harp, *Learning to be Loyal,* especially 60–62.

101. "Was hat Elsaß-Lothringen Deutschland seit drei Jahren zu danken?," *Germania,* October 31, 1873.

102. Articles portrayed the educational changes as un-German by another route as well. Given the importance attached to Prussia's educational system for turning out military recruits capable of producing a victory in the Franco-Prussian War, Catholic arguments posed changes to the traditional, confessional education system as changes that would ultimately weaken the *Reich.* See, for example, "Die Confessionslosen in Frankreich," *Germania,* November 7, 1871; *Germania,* January 19, 1873. On the importance attributed to Prussian education for military victory, see Ellwein, *Die deutsche Universität,* 115.

103. See, for example, "Petition der katholischen Familienväter Allensteins und der Umgegend," *Germania,* January 14, 1872.

104. This was not Catholic victory, however, as Falk also found the Bishop of Ermland faulty in excommunicating Wollmann without considering how that would affect his position as a state employee, highlighting again what liberals saw as the inability of Catholics to serve both Church and country. On the Braunsberg conflict, see Evans, *The German Center Party,* 51–52, 59–60; Anderson, *Windthorst,* 167, 171; Rudolf Lill, "The *Kulturkampf* in Prussia and in the German Empire until 1878," in *The Church in the Industrial Age,* ed. Roger Aubert et. al., trans. Margit Resch, 31–32.

105. Windell, *The Catholics and German Unity,* 8–9, n. 22.

106. Harald Dickerhof, "Die katholischen Universitäten im Heiligen Römischen Reich deutscher Nation des 18. Jahrhunderts" in *Universitäten und Aufklärung,* ed. Notker Hammerstein (Göttingen: Wallstein-Verlag, 1995), 161. A close accounting of the damages to higher education from secularization is in Laetitia Boehm, "Katholizismus, Bildungs- und Hochschulwesen nach der Säkularisation," in *Katholizismus, Bildung und Wissenschaft im 19. Jahrhundert,* ed. Anton Rauscher (Paderborn: Schöningh, 1987).

107. Dickerhof, "Katholischen Universitäten," 160, n. 11.

108. Wilhelm Emmanuel von Ketteler, *Das Recht und der Rechtschutz der katholischen Kirche in Deutschland* (Mainz: Kirchheim, 1854), 16.

109. Joseph Hansen, *Die Rheinprovinz, 1815–1915. Hundert Jahre preußischer Herrschaft am Rhein*, vol. 1, (Bonn: A. Marcus and E. Weber, 1917), 797. Quoted in translation in Windell, *The Catholics and German Unity*, 8–9, n. 22.

110. Wilhelm Spael, *Die Görres Gesellschaft, 1876–1941* (Paderborn: Schöningh, 1957), 8–11; Windell, *The Catholics and German Unity*, 35–38.

111. Franz Joseph Buß, *Der Unterschied der katholischen und protestantischen Universitäten Teutschlands,* (Freiburg: Herder, 1846), 365ff. Quoted in Dickerhof, "Katholischen Universitäten," 162, n. 19. See also Harald Dickerhof, "Staatliches Bildungsmonopol: Die Idee einer katholischen Universität und die Schulen der katholischen Theologie im 19. Jahrhundert," in *Archiv für Kulturgeschichte* 66 (1984): 210.

112. On parents' wishes, see Dickerhof, "Katholischen Universitäten," 162, n. 19.

113. Dickerhof particularly emphasizes the importance of Catholics' different educational ideas. Ibid., especially 162, 172.

114. *Historisch-Politische Blätter* 54 (1864), 540ff. Quoted in Dickerhof, "Staatliches Bildungsmonopol," 208. See also Richard Schaefer, "Program for a New Catholic *Wissenschaft*: Devotional Activism and Catholic Modernity in the Nineteenth Century," *Modern Intellectual History* 4 (2007): 433–462.

115. "Gedanken über die Begründung einer katholischen Wissenshchaft," *Historisch-politische Blätter* 21 (1848). Quoted in Schaefer, "Program for a new Catholic *Wissenschaft*, 449.

116. Dickerhof, "Katholischen Universitäten," especially 162, 172. Hans Jürgen Brandt offers a more detailed examination of efforts for a Catholic university, discussing this viewpoint as well as opposing ones: *Eine katholische Universität in Deutschland?: das Ringen der Katholiken in Deutschland um eine Universitätsbildung im 19. Jahrhundert* (Cologne: Böhlau, 1981).

117. *Germania*, September 15, 1877.

118. The difficulties faced by Catholics in the university system is highlighted in Heribert Raab, " 'Katholische Wissenschaft,'—Ein Postulat und seine Variationen in der Wissenschafts- und Bildungspolitik deutscher Katholiken während des 19. Jahrhunderts," in *Katholizismus, Bildung und Wissenschaft im 19. Jahrhundert*, ed. Anton Rauscher (Paderborn: Schöningh, 1987), especially 72–77. He concludes that far

from withdrawing from university life, Catholics were "driven out." See also, Dickerhof, "Katholischen Universitäten," 173.

119. Given the rarity of believing Christians in university positions, he concluded that the current situation meant "the Catholic Church in Germany is even lacking the protection of scholarship. . . . If only the Church had its institutions in order to battle a scholarship, which now boasts of a victory over Christianity, because Christianity's mouth is closed." Ketteler, *Das Recht und der Rechtschutz*, 15. Part of this is also quoted in Raab, "Katholische Wissenschaft," 73.

120. Wilhelm Emmanuel von Ketteler, *Deutschland nach dem Kriege von 1866* (Mainz: Kirchheim, 1867), vi, 195. Ketteler emphasized this in his private correspondence too. See his letter to Archbishop Melchers, December 23, 1868. Reproduced in Brandt, *Eine katholische Universität*, 489–490.

121. Heinrich Fels, *Martin Deutinger* (Munich: Köstel-Pustet: 1938), 141–142. Quoted in Raab (though with an incorrect page number) " 'Katholische Wissenschaft'," 81. Deutinger died in 1864 before the *Kulturkampf*.

122. These comments were written in 1864 to Hertling's friend, Theodor Stahl, later editor of *Germania* in the 1880s. Adolf Dyroff, *Reden, Ansprachen, und Vorträge des Grafen Georg von Hertling mit einigen Erinnerungen an ihn* (Cologne: Bachem, 1929), 218, 223. Also quoted in Spael, *Görres-Gesellschaft*, 9.

123. "Die religiöse Lage Deutschlands und die Centrumsfraction im deutschen Reichstage, II," *Germania*, September 28, 1871.

124. See, for example, Blackbourn, *Fontana History of Germany*, 302.

125. Nipperdey is quick to note, however, the limited impact of the Syllabus in reality. *Deutsche Geschichte, 1800–1866*, 413–414.

126. Weber, "Der deutsche Katholizismus" especially 165; Nipperdey, *Deutsche Geschichte, 1800–1866*, 414; Mergel, *Zwischen Klasse*, especially 162–167; Mergel, "Grenzgänger."

127. In an 1897 speech, Hertling gave an explicit definition, which he began by stating that Catholic *Wissenschaft* is "the scholarship of learned Catholics." He continued to note Catholic *Wissenschaft*'s accordance with "general scholarly methods," allowing, however, that in areas not "purely scholarly" the researcher's confession could play a role. See "Gibt es eine katholische Wissenschaft?" in Dyroff, *Reden, Ansprachen und Vorträge*, 25–26. Even current day usage of the phrase by scholars suggests a great deal of variation in how it is understood. Consider the variation among the following scholars: Dickerhof, "Katholischen Universitäten"; Schaefer, "Program for a New Catholic *Wissenschaft*," especially 451; and Raab, " 'Katholische Wissenschaft'."

128. Wilhelm Emmanuel von Ketteler, *Die moderne Tendenz-Wissenschaft. Beleuchtet am Exempel des Herrn Professor Dr. Emil Friedberg* (Mainz: Kirchheim, 1873).

129. On the dangers of *Tendenzwissenschaft* among legal scholars close to the government, see also "Ein Kanonist der Gegenwart," *Historisch-Politische Blätter* 78 (1876), 358–359. More generally, see *Der Katholik: Zeitschrift für katholische Wissenschaft und kirchliches Leben,* 33 (1875), 337.

130. Wilhelm Emmanuel von Ketteler, *Die preußischen Gesetzentwürfe über die Stellung der Kirche zum Staat* (Mainz: Kirchheim, 1873).

131. Ketteler, *Tendenz-Wissenschaft,* 5.

132. See, for example, ibid., 23, 24, 25, 31.

133. See, for example, ibid., 8, 15, 17, 30.

134. Ibid., 6.

135. Ibid., especially 5, 13, 15.

136. Ibid., 15.

137. Ibid., 22–23. See also, "Intelligenz," in Reichensperger, *Phrasen und Schlagwörter,* 60–62.

138. Ketteler, *Tendenz-Wissenschaft,* 25.

139. Nipperdey notes Ketteler as one who questioned liberal claims to a "monopoly claim on humanity, reason, and culture" more generally: *Deutsche Geschichte,* vol. 1, 452.

140. The criticism was published anonymously: *Nationalität und Freiheit. Eine Widerlegung des Buches: Deutschland nach dem Kriege von 1866. Von Wilhelm Emmanuel v. Ketteler, Bischof von Mainz* (Landsberg a.d.W.: Schäffer, 1867), especially 166–168.

141. The specific Ketteler-Friedberg debate was also discussed in newspapers. See, for example, "Geistige Corruption," *Kölnische Volkszeitung,* May 30, 1873.

142. "Das deutsche Kaiserthum, II," *Germania,* January 22, 1871.

143. "Das deutsche Kaiserthum, IV," *Germania,* January 25, 1871. Ideas of the new *Reich* as the German epoch are discussed in Chapter 2.

144. For example, "Das gebildetste Volk der Erde," *Germania,* November 19, 1871; "Die päpstliche Encyclica vom 8. December 1864 und der elsaß=lothringische Antrag auf Volksabstimmung," *Germania,* March 3, 1874; *Germania,* March 7, 1874; "'Liberale' Unwissenheit in kirchlichen Dingen," *Germania,* February 9, 1875; "'Gartenlaube'," *Germania,* February 10, 1875.

145. "Die päpstliche Encyclica," March 3, 1874.

146. See Gross, *The War Against Catholicism.* One could also read the comment in another vein, suggesting that Catholic scholars had no part in this mockery of "German scholarship."

147. "Liberale Ignoranz," *Kölnische Volkszeitung*, December 10, 1873.

148. Given the paucity of Catholics in higher education, however, the accounts often had to resort to discussing earlier centuries. For example, see "Derselbe Weg—dasselbe Ziel," *Germania*, August 26, 1871; *Germania*, March 7, 1874; "Die Ohnmacht der modernen naturwissenschaftlichen 'Forschung'," *Germania*, December 19, 1875. While other newspapers defended Catholic scholarship as well, they never addressed the issue as often as *Germania*. One can also view works like Janssen's first volume of *Geschichte des deutschen Volkes* as attempts to highlight Catholic intellectual activity.

149. "Die gestrige Debatte über den 'Marpinger Antrag'," *Germania*, January 17, 1878. On Protestant views of Catholic belief in miracles, see Ross, *Failure*, 18–19. For another example of the attempt to scientifically support miracles, see Paul Majunke, *Louise Lateau, ihr Wunderleben und ihre Bedeutung im deutschen Kirchenconflicte* (Berlin: Verlag der Germania, 1874). Indeed, both Majunke and Virchow gave lectures, though naturally with very different viewpoints, on the stigmatic Lateau. The *Augsburger Postzeitung* described the details of Virchow's investigation into Lateau and summed up its assessment of the liberal professor's process by asserting, "But that is certainly not scientific." *Beilage* from October 22, 1874.

150. "Döllinger einst und jetzt," *Germania*, May 2, 1871.

151. "Derselbe Weg—dasselbe Ziel," *Germania*, August 26, 1871.

152. "Gneist's Rede über die Eigenart des preußischen Staats, II," *Germania*, January 10, 1874.

153. "Die 'deutsche Wissenschaft' vor dem preußischen Abgeordnetenhause," *Germania*, November 27, 1873.

154. See, for example, "Die Wahrheit und die Ministerbank," *Germania*, April 5, 1875; "Herr Professor Hinschius als Belehrer der 'Culturkämpfer'," *Germania*, November 8, 1875.

155. "'Liberale' Unwissenheit in kirchlichen Dingen," *Germania*, February 9, 1875.

156. "Die päpstliche Encyclica vom 8. December 1864 und der elsaß=lothringische Antrag auf Volksabstimmung," *Germania*, March 3, 1874.

157. "Gneist's Rede über die Eigenart des preußischen Staats, I," *Germania*, January 9, 1874.

158. In this case the problem came not from the liberal camp but from conservative Protestantism, represented by the paper *Der Reichsbote*. Though the article noted that conservative Protestants often had better

sense about the *Kulturkampf*, it also realized "from time to time it [the *Reichsbote*] needed to vent its Protestant feelings" against Catholics. This article expressed more specifically Catholic-Protestant animosity than most, which mainly considered liberal shortcomings: "Ein Kathechismuslection," *Germania*, September 10, 1875.

159. "'Liberale' Unwissenheit in kirchlichen Dingen," *Germania*, February 9, 1875.

160. "Unwissenheit—oder Lüge?" *Germania*, February 18, 1872.

161. "Die 'deutsche Wissenschaft' vor dem preußischen Abgeordnetenhause," *Germania*, November 27, 1873.

162. "Ein neues Attentat auf die Freiheit der Kirche und eine neue Bewährung der 'politischen Heuchelei," *Germania*, November 14, 1876. Also on Latin translation problems, see "Die päpstliche Allocution vom 23. December," *Kölnische Volkszeitung*, December 30, 1872.

163. "Döllinger über Luther, V," *Germania*, May 12, 1872. The article also referenced Döllinger, as it attempted to use the scholar's earlier historical research on the Reformation to discredit his opposition to papal infallibility.

164. Marchand, *Down from Olympus*, especially 6, 152, 156, 159; Williamson, *The Longing for Myth*, especially 8, 297–299.

165. Wilfried Stroh, *Latein ist tot, es lebe Latein!: kleine Geschichte einer großen Sprache* (Berlin: List, 2007), 260–261, 263–264; Ellwein, *Die deutsche Universität*, 128.

166. Of course, in reality the vast majority of Catholics did not understand the Latin originals. Writers for *Germania* were also not above including Greek in their own articles to further buttress their claims to education. See, for example, "Der Frosch," *Germania*, April 19, 1875; "Die Naturwissenschaften als 'Erziehungsgrundlage'," *Germania*, August 13, 1877. In other instances, Catholic papers included Latin text for more religiously symbolic reasons. Take, for example, the *Augsburger Postzeitung*'s reprinting of a papal allocution in Latin on December 27, 1872. A translation was only offered in the following day's paper.

167. "Unrichtigkeiten der Bismarckschen Papstwahldepesche in Bezug auf die Lehre und das Recht der katholischen Kirche," *Germania*, February 12, 1875.

168. "Aus dem Abgeordnetenhause," *Germania*, January 19, 1871.

169. "Bildung!" *Germania*, May 10, 1871. Reichensperger also took liberals to task for mistaking appearance (*Schein*) for reality (*Sein*) in his book. *Phrasen und Schlagwörter*, 26.

170. Koselleck, *Bildungsbürgertum*, 30.

171. Of course, the scholarly validity of infallibility also received attention beyond its connection with Döllinger. See, for example, "Die lehramtliche Unfehlbarkeit des Papstes und die theologische Wissenschaft in Deutschland," *Beilage*, November 1, 1871, *Augsburger Postzeitung.*

172. "Döllinger einst und jetzt, I," *Germania*, May 2, 1871.

173. "Unrichtigkeiten der Bismarckschen Papstwahldepesche in Bezug auf die Lehre und das Recht der katholischen Kirche, (Fortsetzung)" *Germania*, February 13, 1875; "Unrichtigkeiten der Bismarckschen Papstwahldepesche in Bezug auf die Lehre und das Recht der katholischen Kirche, (Schluß)" *Germania*, February 16, 1875.

174. "Unrichtigkeiten der Bismarckschen Papstwahldepesche in Bezug auf die Lehre und das Recht der katholischen Kirche, (Schluß)" *Germania*, February 16, 1875.

175. "Döllinger und Luther," *Germania*, April 29, 1871.

176. "Döllinger einst und jetzt, I," *Germania*, May 2, 1871.

177. "'Liberale' Unwissenheit in kirchlichen Dingen," *Germania*, February 9, 1875.

178. "Die Marienerscheinungen in Marpingen," *Germania*, July 29, 1876.

179. Blackbourn, *Fontana History of Germany*, 282. Andreas Daum cautions against seeing the conflict as a foregone conclusion, instead emphasizing that there were also attempts to harmonize Darwinism with religion during the larger time span he studies. See *Wissenschaftspopularisierung*, especially 13–14, 79–80; "Science, Politics, and Religion," especially 114 ff. See also, Schwarz, *Der Schlüssel zur modernen Welt*, 286 ff.

180. Andreas Daum, *Wissenschaftspopularisierung im 19. Jahrhundert: Bürgerliche Kultur, naturwissenschaftliche Bildung und die deutsche Öffentlichkeit, 1848–1914* (Munich: Oldenbourg, 2002), 3, 5, 9, 12, *Daum*, "Science, Politics, and Religion," 134–135; Smith, *Politics and the Sciences*, 91.

181. "Der Frosch," *Germania*, April 19, 1875. On *Die Gartenlaube* and science, see Alfred Kelley, *The Descent of Darwin: The Popularization of Darwinism in Germany, 1860–1914* (Chapel Hill: University of North Carolina Press, 1981), 15; Daum, *Wissenschaftspopularisierung*, 339. On the publication more generally, see Kirsten Belgum, *Popularizing the Nation: Audience, Representation, and the Production of Identity in Die Gartenlaube, 1853–1900* (Lincoln: University of Nebraska Press, 1998). One should not take this parody out of context. Indeed, established as an alternative to *Die Gartenlaube*, the Catholic *Deutscher Hausschatz* also included quite detailed articles on recent scientific developments. See, for

example, the series entitled "Mikroskopische Unterhaltungen," which included various scientific drawings of substances as they appeared under magnification. *Deutscher Hausschatz* 2 (1875–76), nos. 14 and 15. Of course, it also included a series critiquing Darwinism, repeating many of the same claims about the topic as featured in the more wittily and sharply written *Germania* articles. See Karl Scheidenmacher, "Ueber den Darwinismus," *Deutscher Hausschatz* 2 (1875–76), nos. 22–26.

182. "Der Frosch," *Germania*, April 19, 1875.

183. Schwarz notes opponents criticizing the "Unwissenschaftlichkeit" of Darwin more generally. See, *Der Schlüssel zur modernen Welt*, 286.

184. "Die Ohnmacht der modernen naturwissenschaftlichen 'Forschung'. Studien aus Büchner und Darwin, VI" *Germania*, January 23, 1876; Paul Majunke, *Die Ohnmacht der modernen naturwissenschaftlichen "Forschung": Studien aus Büchner und Darwin* (Berlin: Verlag der Germania, 1876), 17. This book was a collection of newspaper articles. It is important to note that "the powerlessness of modern natural science research" was not posed generally, but referred to the issue of disproving religious belief.

185. "Die Naturwissenschaften als 'Erziehungsgrundlage'," *Germania*, August 13, 1877.

186. "Die Ohnmacht der modernen naturwissenschaftlichen 'Forschung'. Studien aus Büchner und Darwin, VI," *Germania*, January 23, 1876.

187. "Die Ohnmacht der modernen naturwissenschaftlichen 'Forschung'. Studien aus Büchner und Darwin, VII," *Germania*, January 30, 1876.

188. Paul Majunke, *Die Ohnmacht*, 3, 15.

189. Daum, *Wissenschaftspopularisierung*, 66–71.

190. "Janssen's 'Geschichte des deutschen Volkes'," *Germania*, May 24, 1877.

191. On the confessional divide in historical scholarship, see, for example, Gräf, "Reich, Nation und Kirche"; Berger, *The Search for Normality*, especially 31–32.

192. "Die Aufgaben des neuen Culturministers, III," *Germania*, March 2, 1872.

193. "Zur 'ultramontanen Conflictsperiode' im preußischen Abgeordneten-hause," *Germania*, February 14, 1872.

194. Ibid. Reichensperger also decried the "rule of constantly changing fashion" on the ideas of "trendy scholars" and "trendy philosophers": *Phrasen und Schlagwörter*, 26. On following the latest fashion, see also: "Die Naturwissenschaften," *Germania*, August 11, 1877.

195. "Die Naturwissenschaften," *Germania*, August 11, 1877; "Die Naturwissenschaften als 'Erziehungsgrundlage'," *Germania*, August 13, 1877.

196. Though Virchow was a noted opponent of Darwin's ideas, *Germania* made little distinction in these articles between support for increased emphasis on the natural sciences and support for Darwinism. On Virchow and Darwinism, see Daum, *Wissenschaftspopularisierung*, 65; Smith, *Politics and the Sciences*, 92–94. Here again, skepticism concerning greater inclusion of the natural sciences more generally was not found among Catholics alone. Liberal Emil Du Bois-Reymond also found the natural sciences important but opposed the "Americanisation" of German education that their wholesale introduction into the curriculum would herald. Daum, *Wissenschaftspopularisierung*, 69.

197. *Scheinbildung* can be translated as sham or pseudoeducation. In this sense, *Scheinpapieren* referred to worthless papers, or stock certificates. "Bildung!, I," *Germania*, May 10, 1871. Given the Catholic assessment of Döllinger's scholarship, the same connection could be expressed by article titles like "Döllingerschwindel und Börsenschwindel" from *Germania*'s May 7, 1871 issue. The *Kölnische Volkszeitung* implied the connection as well with phrases like "scholarly bankruptcy." See "Wissenschaftliche Mamelucken," March 12, 1874.

198. For more on Catholic arguments concerning liberals and economics, see Chapter 4.

199. Catholic criticism of liberals' mercurial loyalties is discussed in the first part of the book.

200. Bruch, "The Academic Disciplines," 348.

201. Ibid., 349.

202. Certainly there were elements of class and urban-rural conflict tied to disputes over education, with Catholics often championing the less privileged. Likewise, it is unmistakable that Catholic views of education often emphasized the ability of simple people, including children and women, to understand more about life than those with book learning. Yet that line of argumentation is in the background in the battle over *Bildung* and German *Wissenschaft*. Catholic arguments denigrated these liberal professors not because of their scholarly attainments but because of a purported lack of them. On the class and urban-rural elements of the *Kulturkampf*, see Gross, *The War Against Catholicism*, 125; Smith, *German Nationalism and Religious Conflict*, 35, 85, 108; Raab, "'Katholische Wissenschaft'," 175–176. On the idea of practical over book learning among Catholics, see Weber, "Der deutsche Katholizismus," 145–146.

203. "Gneist's Rede über die Eigenart des preußischen Staats, II," *Germania*, January 10, 1874.

204. "Geschichtliche Studie über den Geschichtsbaumeister v. Sybel," *Germania*, February 25, 1874. Similarly, see the *Beilage* of the *Augsburger Postzeitung*, June 3, 1874; "Der macht die Citate," *Kölnische Volkszeitung*, June 19, 1874.

205. "Unwissenheit oder Lüge," *Germania*, February 18, 1872.

206. "Die Aufgaben des neuen Cultusministers, II," *Germania*, March 1, 1872; Reichensperger, *Phrasen und Schlagwörter*, 170. Conrad von Bolanden wrote a novel around this theme: *Die Unfehlbaren* (Mainz: Kirchheim, 1871). See also, *Beilage, Augsburger Postzeitung*, June 24, 1871.

207. On the importance of being bias free to liberal ideas of scholarship and the criticism of Catholic scholars on this account, see Howard, *Protestant Theology*, 29.

208. On liberals and convent atrocity stories, see Gross, *The War against Catholicism*, Chapter 3. On the moral implications of *Bildung* for liberals, see Howard, *Protestant Theology*, 140; Geuss, "Kultur, Bildung, Geist," 162.

209. "Beiträge zur confessionellen Statistik," *Germania*, February 9 1873.

210. "Der kirchliche Frieden und die Centrumspartei, II," *Germania*, November 15, 1878. The Center Party posited that education needed to be based on "the mind and on the soul" but that liberals had ignored the latter part of this, the "*Bildung* of the heart." "Bildung!," *Germania*, May 12, 1871.

211. *Germania*, November 24, 1877.

212. "Die Selbstmordmanie der Gegenwart," August 4, 1877. On suicide and statistics, see also "Die moderne Selbstmordmanie," *Beilage, Augsburger Postzeitung*, August 25, 1875; "Selbstmord und Confession," *Kölnische Volkszeitung*, September 21, 1877.

213. For example, see *Germania*, April 21, 1874; "Zur Judenfrage," *Germania*, September 4, 1875; "Eine doppelte Antwort der 'Schles. Volksztg'," *Germania*, October 9, 1875; "Zur Statistik der letzten Reichstagswahlen," *Germania*, June 11, 1877; "Das statische Bureau in Amerika und die deutsche Einwanderung," *Schlesische Volkszeitung*, July 26, 1872; "Die Judenfrage, VI," *Beilage, Augsburger Postzeitung*, October 12, 1875. On the interest for statistics among scholars during the 1870s, see Nipperdey, *Deutsche Geschichte, 1866–1918*, 512.

214. J. Adam Tooze, *Statistics and the German State, 1900–1945: The Making of Modern Economic Knowledge* (Cambridge: Cambridge University Press, 2001), 1–2; Herald Westergaard, *Contributions to the History of Statistics* (London: P.S. King & Son, Ltd., 1932), 2–3, 187; Stuart Woolf, "Statistics and the Modern State," *Comparative Studies in Society and History* 31 (1989): 590, 594–595.

215. Mohammed Rassem and Justin Stagl, "Zur Geschichte der Statistik und Staatsbeschreibung in der Neuzeit," *Zeitschrift für Politik* 24 (1977): 82; Alain Desrosieres, *The Politics of Large Numbers: A History of Statistical Reasoning,* trans. Camille Naish (Cambridge: Harvard, 1998), 182.

216. Woolf, "Statistics," 594.

217. See, for example, "Die wachsende Unsittlichkeit in Berlin," *Germania,* November 9, 1871; "Berliner sociale Züstände," *Augsburger Postzeitung,* November 16, 1871. For similar comments by Julius Bachem, see Mergel, *Zwischen Klasse,* 258. On the importance of *Kultur* for German national identity, see, for example, Geuss, "Kultur, Bildung, Geist," 163.

218. This article specifically questioned Heinrich von Treitschke's ideas: "Die Aufgaben des neuen Culturministers, II," *Germania,* March 11, 1872. The *Augsburger Postzeitung,* for example, posed exactly the same dichotomy between a "constitutional state" and a "prison state." See "Der Staat der Zukunft," December 28, 1871.

219. This ties back into the arguments discussed in the previous chapter.

220. "Der nationale Wohlstand und die nationale Bildung," *Germania,* April 5, 1876. The use of *Cadavergehorsam* (blind obedience) to characterize such officials turned the allegation of Catholics' blind obedience to the pope around to characterize liberals.

221. "Das neue Deutschland, I," *Augsburger Postzeitung,* April 8, 1872.

222. "Die lehramtliche Unfehlbarkeit des Papstes und die theologische Wissenschaft in Deutschland," *Beilage, Augsburger Postzeitung,* November 1, 1871.

223. The connection between scholarship and truth often appeared in Catholic arguments. For newspaper articles, see for example: "Unwissenheit oder Lüge," *Germania,* February 18, 1872; "'Liberale' Unwissenheit in kirchlichen Dingen," *Germania,* Feburary 9, 1875.

224. On the role of truth in the bourgeois ideal of *Bildung,* see Ellwein, *Die deutsche Universität,* 124. Of course, the relationship between scholarship and truth is mediated by a number of factors. See, for example, Timothy Lenoir, *Politik im Tempel der Wissenschaft: Forschung und Machtausübung im deutschen Kaiserreich* (Frankfurt: Campus, 1992).

225. The society's full name was Görres-Gesellschaft zur Pflege der Wissenschaft im katholischen Deutschland. On the importance of the *Kulturkampf* for the society's founding as well as more general information on its establishment, see Spael, *Görres-Gesellschaft,* especially 7–13. On the difficulties of Catholic scholars to advance in the university system and its

importance for the founding of the society, see Winfried Becker, *Georg von Hertling 1843–1919, Band I: Jugend und Selbstfindung zwischen Romantik und Kulturkampf* (Mainz: Matthias-Grünewald, 1981), 10, 264. The difficulties experienced by founding members themselves is well documented. See, for example, Georg von Hertling, *Erinnerungen aus meinem Leben,* vol. 1 (München: J. Kösel, 1919) especially 175ff; letter from Johannes Janssen to Georg von Hertling, December 1, 1875, in Ludwig von Pastor, *Johannes Janssens Briefe,* vol. 2 (Freiburg: Herder, 1920), 30–31. Hertling discussed the purpose of the society at the 1876 *Katholikentag,* repeatedly asking rhetorically if Catholics "should just stand by" as their scholars were discriminated against and forced out of academia: "Rede des Abgeordneten Dr. Freiherrn von Hertling," *Jahresbericht der Görres=Gesellschaft für das Jahr 1876* (Cologne: Bachem, 1877), 43.

226. *Verhandlungen der XXV. Generalversammlung der Katholiken Deutschlands zu Würzburg am 10., 11., 12. und 13. September 1877* (Würzburg, 1877), 128. Haffner went on to become Bishop of Mainz in 1886.

227. "Der wissenschaftliche Verein in Brüssel und das Bedürfniß der katholischen Wissenschaft in Deutschalnd," *Kölnische Volkszeitung,* September 30, 1875.

228. Bundesarchiv (Koblenz), Nachlaß Hertling, N1036/58: Letter from Hertling to Cardauns, Berlin, October 29, 1875.

229. Hermann Cardauns, *Die Görres-Gesellschaft 1876–1901. Denkschrift zur Feier ihres 25jährigen Bestehens nebst Jahresbericht für 1900* (Cologne: Bachem, 1901), 4–11.

230. *Germania,* January 7, 1876.

231. *Germania,* January 29, 1876.

232. Spael, *Görres-Gesellschaft,* 14, 53.

233. From an 1876 letter of the society's executive committee. Quoted in Becker, *Georg von Hertling,* 266.

234. "Der wissenschaftliche Verein in Brüssel und das Bedürfniß der katholischen Wissenschaft in Deutschland," *Kölnische Volkszeitung,* September 30, 1875.

235. Hertling felt that his religion had been central to the rejection. Spael, *Görres-Gesellschaft,* 8, 14. Indeed, Hertling received a professorship (*extraordinarius*) at Bonn in 1880 only with the help of Minister Puttkamer and against the wishes of the faculty. A similar process played out in Munich, where Hertling later became professor *ordinarius.* See Rudolf Morsey, "Georg Graf v. Hertling," in *Zeitgeschichte in Lebensbildern: Aus*

dem deutschen Katholizismus des 20. Jahrhunderts, ed. Rudolf Morsey (Mainz: Grünewald, 1973), 45.

236. Baumeister, *Parität,* especially 50–59; Boehm, "Katholizismus, Bildungs- und Hochschulwesen," 20–21; Jeffrey T. Zalar, " 'Knowledge is Power': The *Borromäusverein* and Catholic Reading Habits in Imperial Germany," *Catholic Historical Review* 86 (2000): 38–39; Zalar, "Knowledge and Nationalism." A similar emphasis is also implied, though only through very brief mention of Hertling, in Hübinger, "Confessionalism," 173; Schaefer, "Program for a New Catholic *Wissenschaft,*" 461. In part, this emphasis on Hertling's later efforts is possibly linked to the existence of more of his speeches and writings from that era. On the other hand, brief discussions of Hertling and the Görres-Gesellschaft by Brandt and Klöcker do suggest recognition of such efforts already in 1876: *Eine katholische Universität,* especially 350; Klöcker, "Das katholische Bildungsdefizit," 88.

237. Dyroff, *Reden, Ansprachen, und Vorträge,* 223.

238. Bundesarchiv (Koblenz), Nachlaß Hertling, N1036/45: Letter from Brentano to Hertling, Aschaffenburg, October 25, 1870.

239. On Hertling's book, see Becker, *Georg von Hertling,* 162ff.

240. Zalar, who uses the term "modernizing", emphasizes the limits of this step: "Knowledge and Nationalism in Imperial Germany," 157.

241. While we have letter exchanges and many longer treatises by Hertling specifically addressing this viewpoint from later decades, less is extant for the *Kulturkampf* period itself, which is underrepresented in his Nachlaß. In the collection of letters exchanged with Franz Brentano (Bundesarchiv Koblenz, N1036/45), for example, the letters run dry by 1871 and do not pick up again until long after the end of the *Kulturkampf.* Nonetheless, nothing suggests Hertling wavered from his basic position that he already held in the 1860s.

242. Cardauns, *Görres-Gesellschaft,* 96.

243. "Der deutsche Katholizismus und die Wissenschaft," a speech given in Konstanz in 1896. In Dyroff, *Reden, Ansprachen, und Vorträge,* 6–7.

244. Though not to posit an equivalence between Catholics and liberals, neither the scholarship of the latter nor their political actions always lived up to their expressed ideals either. See, for example, Gross, *War Against Catholicism.*

9. The Moral Geography of Europe and Beyond

1. Conrad von Bolanden [Joseph Bischoff], *Urdeutsch: Historischer Roman* (Mainz: Kirchheim, 1875).

2. Rainer Kipper, *Der Germanenmythos im deutschen Kaiserreich: Formen und Funktionen historischer Selbstthematisierung* (Göttingen: Vandenhoeck & Ruprecht, 2002), especially 166–168, 179, including quotations originally from Franz Brümmer, *Deutsches Dichter-lexikon: Biographische und bibliographische Mittheilungen über deutsche Dichter aller Zeiten* (Eichstätt: H. Hugendubel, 1886–87), 64.

3. Conrad von Bolanden [Joseph Bischoff], *Urdeutsch: Historischer Roman* (Munich, A & B Schuler, 1908), 3. Subsequent citations are also from this twentieth-century printing.

4. For a brief overview of the Hermann myth, see Doyé, "Arminius," 587–602. For more, see Chapter 7.

5. Bolanden, *Urdeutsch*, 494.

6. Ibid., 7.

7. Ibid., 5.

8. Ibid., 497.

9. "Weltlage," *Germania*, December 20, 1870.

10. "Das deutsche Kaiserthum, V," *Germania*, January 26, 1871.

11. "Zum neuen Jahr, II," *Kölnische Volkszeitung*, January 3, 1873.

12. "Patriotische Briefe: Sechster Brief.—Germanomanie," *Stimmen aus Maria-Laach*, vol. 8 (1875), 274.

13. Anderson, *Practicing Democracy*, 103; Sperber, *Kaiser's Voters*, 75; Nipperdey, *Deutsche Geschichte*, vol. 2, 284.

14. Frank J. Coppa, *Politics and the Papacy in the Modern World* (Westport, CT: Greenwood, 2008), especially 33–53.

15. On the tendency to associate Catholics with universalism in opposition to nationalism, see Buschmann, "Auferstehung der Nation," 337.

16. For example, see the general account by Stefan Berger in *Germany* (London: Arnold, 2004), especially 83–87.

17. A good example is Becker, "Konfessionelle Nationsbilder." Max Vögler suggests the same by posing Ultramontanism as a case of nationalism focused on the papacy itself, not a particular home country. In "Similar Paths, Different 'Nations'?: Ultramontanism and the Old Catholic Movement in Upper Austria, 1870–71," in *Different Paths to the Nation: Regional and National Identities in Central Europe and Italy, 1830–70,* ed. Laurance Cole (Basingstoke: Palgrave, 2007). Of course, opponents at the time harbored concerns about German Catholics allying with co-religionists in other countries in a coalition against the *Reich*. On Bismarck and this issue, see Bachem, *Zentrumspartei*, vol. 3, 213–215.

18. Nipperdey, *Deutsche Geschichte*, vol. 2, 258.

19. Again, the distinctions between various words based on the root "national" that often become blurred need to be kept in mind. For more on this issue, see the Introduction.

20. Nipperdey, *Deutsche Geschichte*, vol. 2, 257; Berger, *Germany*, 53; Rudolf Jaworski, "Zwischen Polenliebe und Polenschelte" in *Das Bild 'des Anderen': Politische Wahrnemung im 19. und 20. Jahrhundert*, ed. Birgit Aschmann and Michel Salewski (Stuttgart: F. Steiner, 2000), 82; Adam Galos, "Image of a Pole in 19th Century Germany" *Polish Western Affairs* 19(1978): 177.

21. Nipperdey, *Deutsche Geschichte*, vol. 2, 258.

22. Mark Hewitson, *National Identity and Political Thought in Germany: Wilhelmine Depictions of the French Third Republic, 1890–1914* (Oxford: Oxford University Press, 2000), 17.

23. "Das deutsche Kaiserthum, V," *Germania*, January 26, 1871.

24. "Zum neuen Jahr, II," *Kölnische Volkszeitung*, January 3, 1873. For more on this point, see Hiort, "Constructing," 28–29.

25. "Patriotische Briefe," *Stimmen aus Maria-Laach*, 274.

26. On the tendency to equate early Germanic tribes with modern-day Germans, see Heinrich Beck et. al., eds., *Zur Geschichte der Gleichung "germanisch-deutsch": Sprache und Namen, Geschichte und Institutionen* (Berlin: De Gruyter, 2004).

27. Bolanden, *Urdeutsch*, 19.

28. Ibid., 491.

29. Ibid., 20.

30. Ibid., *Urdeutsch*, 41, 54.

31. Ibid., 291.

32. Ibid., 497.

33. Ibid., 7.

34. Both could be translations for the word "*urdeutsch*." Reagin, *Sweeping the Nation*; on associational life, see, for example, Keith H. Pickus, *Constructing Modern Identities: Jewish University Students in Germany 1815–1914* (Detroit: Wayne State University Press, 1999), 86; Gerald D. Feldman, *The Great Disorder: Politics, Economics, and Society in the German Inflation 1914–1924* (Oxford: Oxford University Press, 1997), 17. Of course, the abundance of associational life could also lead to its devaluation, seen in such terms as *Vereinsmeierei*. See David Blackbourn, "The Discreet Charm of the Bourgeoisie: Reappraising German History in the Nineteenth Century," in *The Peculiarities of German History: Bourgeois Society and Politics in Nineteenth-Century Germany*, ed. David Blackbourn and Geoff Eley (Oxford: Oxford University Press, 1984), 227.

35. "*Kultur*" and "*Zivilisation*" were used similarly. The opposition between the two terms only became commonplace much later. See Jörg Fisch, "Zivilisation, Kultur" in *Geschichtliche Grundbegriffe: historisches Lexikon zur politisch-sozialen Sprache in Deutschland*, vol. 7, ed. Otto Brunner, Werner Conze, and Reinhart Koselleck (Stuttgart: Klett-Cotta, 1992), 681, 722, 725, 739, 740, 746, 760.

36. On the role of assigning values to other places of the world as part of defining one's own position, see, for example, Schenk, "Mental Maps," especially 498, 514; Larry Wolff, *Inventing Eastern Europe: The Map of Civilization on the Mind of the Enlightenment* (Stanford: Stanford University Press, 1994), especially 6–7.

37. On the general European assertion of cultural superiority linked to the opposition between civilization and barbarism, see Fisch, "Zivilisation, Kultur," especially 681, 743, 745.

38. "Zum neuen Jahr, II," *Kölnische Volkszeitung*, January 3, 1873.

39. "Türkische und russische Grausamkeiten," *Germania*, August 24, 1876.

40. On the usage of "England," see Arnd Bauerkämper and Christiane Eisenberg, "Introduction: Perceptions of Britain in Germany—Approaches, Methods and Analytical Dimensions," in *Britain as a Model of Modern Society? German Views*, ed. Arnd Bauerkämper and Christiane Eisenberg (Augsburg: Wissner-Verlag, 2006), 7.

41. Peter Wende, "Models of Britain for Nineteenth-Century Germany," in *Britain as a Model*, 33; Berger, *Germany*, 53; Geraldine Grogan, *The Noblest Agitator: Daniel O'Connell and the German Catholic Movement, 1830–1850* (Dublin: Veritas, 1991), especially 106.

42. Raymond James Sontag, *Germany and England: Background of Conflict, 1848–1894* (New York: D. Appleton-Century, 1938), ix, 87–90, 96; Wende, "Models of Britain," 32; Julia Angster, "'The Older and Stronger Firm': German Perceptions of Britain as a World Trading and Imperial Nation," in *Britain as a Model*, 140.

43. "Die Neutralität Englands," *Germania*, January 10, 1871.

44. "Social Verhältnisse," *Germania*, January 6, 1871.

45. Sontag, *Germany and England*, 88. See also Angster, "German Perceptions," 140.

46. "Ein english=protestantisches Urtheil über das Jesuitengesetz," *Germania*, July 17, 1872. See also, for example, "Die 'Times' über die Kirchenpolitik Bismarcks," *Germania*, March 6, 1874; "Stimmen des Auslandes über die preußisch=deutsche Kirchenpolitik," *Kölnische Volkszeitung*, June 17, 1874. Quotations from British publications also made it beyond the Catholic daily press and into stand-alone books like Peter Reichensperger's

Kulturkampf oder Friede in Staat und Kirche (Berlin: Springer, 1876), 67–68.

47. "No popery!" *Kölnische Volkszeitung*, December 6, 1873.

48. *Germania*, October 17, 1874. See also, for example, *Germania*, February 5, 1876.

49. On the reality in Britain, see D. G. Paz, *Popular Anti-Catholicism in Mid-Victorian England* (Stanford: Stanford University Press, 1992).

50. Ludwig Windthorst, *Ausgewählte Reden des Staatsministers a.D. und Parlimentariers Dr. Ludwig Windthorst, gehalten in der Zeit von 1851–1891*, Band II (Osnabrück: Bernhard Wehberg, 1902), speech of March 23, 1873, 56.

51. On liberal contacts and Bismarck's intensions, see Berger, *Germany*, 53–54; Sontag, *Germany and England*, 140. Catholic arguments also highlighted the shared "German" (*deutsch*) heritage with the English. See, for example, "Englisches Recht und englische Unduldsamkeit," *Kölnische Volkszeitung*, March 22, 1874, an article in which Britain is said to be largely free from "Roman law" and instead benefitting from "German law."

52. Windthorst, *Reden*, 56–57.

53. See, for example, *Germania*, June 9 and June 16, 1877. Colin Barr, "An Irish Dimension to a British *Kulturkampf*?" *Journal of Ecclesiastical History* 56 (2005): 475–476.

54. "Ein christlich=sociales Programm," *Germania*, March 6, 1877."

55. *Germania*, May 13, 1876. See also, for example, "England und die Orientkrisis," *Germania*, February 22, 1878. Earlier in the decade, descriptions of English reticence to intervene could still be tinged with allegations of the country's moral shortcomings from being more interested in trade than anything else. See, for example, "Die Christenverfolgung in Japan," *Germania*, April 3, 1872. On British foreign involvement, see John F. Beeler, *British Naval Policy in the Gladstone-Disraeli Era 1866–1880* (Stanford: Stanford University Press, 1997), 8–10; Alan Cassels, *Ideology and International Relations in the Modern World* (London: Routledge, 1996), 117.

56. Grogan, *Noblest Agitator*, 160; Andreas Hüther, "A Transnational Nation-Building Process: Philologists and Universities in Nineteenth-Century Ireland and Germany," in *Ireland and Europe in the Nineteenth Century*, ed. Leon Litvack and Colin Graham (Dublin: Four Courts, 2006), 102.

57. "Vom 'Befreier' Irlands, O'Connell," *Germania*, March 13, 1874.

58. *Kölnische Volkszeitung*, November 4, 1873. On O'Connell in the Rhineland, see Grogan, *Noblest Agitator*, especially 28–29.

59. The *Schlesische Volkszeitung* began a series on January 10, 1875. *Deutscher Hausschatz* did so in no. 50 of their first volume (1874–75).

60. Dom- und Diözesanarchiv Mainz D.6,1b, undated letter (probably 1874 or 1875). *Kölnische Volkszeitung*, August 12, 1875; *Germania*, July 22, 1875. Grogan, *Noblest Agitator*, especially 103. On O'Connell and nonviolence, see also Chapter 7.

61. Rudolf Morsey, "Streiflichter zur Geschichte der deutschen Katholikentage 1848–1932," in *Von Windthorst bis Adenauer: Ausgewählte Aufsätze zu Politik, Verwaltung und politischem Katholizismus im 19. und 20. Jahrhundert*, ed. Ulrich von Hehl, Hans Günter Hockerts, Horst Möller, and Martin Schumacher (Paderborn: Schöningh, 1997), 191; Grogan, *Noblest Agitator*, 11.

62. For example, "Zur Säcularfeier des Geburtstages Daniel O'Connells," *Germania*, August 6, 1875.

63. *Germania*, March 30, April 5, and April 17, 1875.

64. Grogan suggests this in her analysis of early century reportage on Ireland: *Noblest Agitator*, especially 104. On this process more generally, see Dietmar Hüser, "Selbstfindung durch Fremdwahrnehmung in Kriegs- und Nachkriegszeiten. Französische Nation und deutscher Nachbar seit 1870," in *Das Bild*, 55–79; Hubert Orlowski, *"Polnische Wirtschaft": Zum deutschen Polendiskurs der Neuzeit* (Wiesbaden: Harrassowitz, 1996), especially 155–189; Joep Leerssen, "As Others See, Among Others, Us: The Anglo-German Relationship in Context," in *As Others See Us: Anglo-German Perceptions*, ed. Harald Husemann (Frankfurt a.M: Peter Lang, 1994), 69–79; Kaelble, "Die vergessene Gesellschaft im Westen?: Das Bild der Deutschen von der französischen Gesellschaft, 1871–1914," *Revue d'Allemagne* 21 (1989): 181; Bernhard Struck, *Nicht West—Nicht Ost: Frankreich und Polen in der Wahrnehmung deutscher Reisender zwischen 1750 und 1850* (Göttingen: Wallstein, 2006), 18.

65. *Germania*, June 9, 1877.

66. "Jahres=Rundschau, II" *Germania*, January 7, 1878.

67. Horst Dippel, "Deutsches Reich und Französische Revolution. Politik und Ideologie in der deutschen Geschichtsschreibung, 1871–1945," especially 99–101. See also Jeismann, *Vaterland der Feinde*; Berit Pleitner, *Die 'vernünftige' Nation: zur Funktion von Stereotypen über Polen und Franzosen im deutschen nationalen Diskurs 1850 bis 1871* (Frankfurt a.M: Peter Lang, 2001).

68. *Verhandlungen der einundzwanzigsten Generalversammlung der katholischen Vereine Deutschlands zu Mainz am 10. 11. 12. 13. Und 14. September 1871* (Mainz: Kirchheim, 1871), 308.

69. "Das neue Deutschland," *Augsburger Postzeitung*, April 9, 1872.

70. In addition to the *Augsburger Postzeitung*, for example, see "Die nation-alen Vorurtheile," *Schlesische Volkszeitung*, January 6, 1872; "Die Kirchenverfolgung unter Napoleon I," *Kölnische Volkszeitung*, July 30, 1874; "Die katholische Kirche und die französische Revolution. 1789–93," *Germania*, November 14, 1875. The latter was part of the longer series.

71. "Die katholische Kirche und die französische Revoluion. 1789–1793," *Germania*, May 7, 1876.

72. "Die katholische Kirche und die französische Revoluion. 1789–1793," *Germania*, April 23, 1876.

73. *Kölnische Volkszeitung*, June 24, 1874.

74. *Germania*, January 8, 1877.

75. "Weltlage," *Germania*, January 3, 1871; see also "Das Jahr 1871," *Germania*, January 3, 1872.

76. "Das Jahr 1871," *Germania*, January 3, 1872.

77. *Germania*, January 20, 1877.

78. *Kölnische Volkszeitung*, May 23, 1877.

79. Smith, *German Nationalism*, 61–63. Though stressing Catholics' distance to the *Reich*, even Frank Becker suggests this second point in part. See "Konfessionelle Nationsbilder," especially 402. Of course, there were exceptions of individual Catholics who left Germany as a sign of denying the new *Reich*. Lill, "Reichsgründung," 356.

80. Lill, *Reichsgründung*, 349–350; Berger, *Germany*, 86; Morsey, "Nationalstaat," 159–160; Bachem, *Zentrumspartei*, especially 5–12.

81. Noting it had come from an earlier conservative newspaper piece, one article alluded to this point, adding that the alternative to Germany and Austria was an alliance of France and Russia that would be unstoppable against unallied opponents. *Germania*, December 22, 1879. Yet the idea had long been around in Catholic circles too. See, for example, the *Augsburger Postzeitung* on January 21, 1871.

82. The *Germania* article "Ein 'großdeutsches' Programm," March 24, 1874, for example, specifically notes the unwillingness to comment on a specific program.

83. For an overview of this changing relationship, see, for example, in *Germania* "Vom deutschen Reichstage," January 14, 1871; "Bismarckische Politik," March 10, 1874; "Ein Rückblick und Umblick beim Jahreswechsel, II," January 4, 1876; "Ein 'großdeutsches' Programm" March 24, 1874; "Zur 'Culturkampfs'stimmung im 'liberalen' und officiösen Lager," September 23, 1876; July 7, 1877. On Bismarck and German isolation, see Imanuel Geiss, *German Foreign Policy, 1871–1914* (London: Routledge, 1976), 29; Schmidt-Volkmar, *Kulturkampf*, 152ff.

84. "Gegen das Wiener Vaterland," *Schlesische Volkszeitung,*
    May 23, 1877.
85. "Die orientalische Frage vor dem deutschen Reichstage," *Germania,*
    February 20, 1878. On this point more generally, see also Morsey,
    "Nationalstaat," 159.
86. "Deutschland und Oesterreich in dauernden völkerrechtlichen Bunde,"
    Germania, September 24, 1879. On problems between Austrian and
    German Catholics, see, for example, "Die Oesterreicher und wir,"
    Germania, March 21, 1876; Aschoff and Heinrich, eds., *Ludwig
    Windthorst Briefe,* letters from April 23, 1876 and November 13, 1876.
    On the Dual Alliance as the fulfillment of Catholic efforts for a closer
    connection to Austria, see Bachem, *Zentrumspartei,* 118; Lill,
    "Reichsgründung," 349.
87. Nipperdey, *Deutsche Geschichte,* vol. 2, 252–253, 442.
88. "Caesaropäpismus, II," *Kölnische Volkszeitung,* January 29, 1873.
89. *Germania,* May 13, 1876. In 1870, the Catholic *Westfälisches Volksblatt*
    had already published and supported the conclusion of Bavarian Franz
    Hoffmann, who saw 1866 as exemplifying the inability of Austria to lead
    and "win Germany its lost position in the world." From December 24,
    1870. Quoted in Bachem, *Zentrumspartei,* 12. Even the *Augsburger
    Postzeitung* could not help pointing out in 1871 that any contest
    between Germany and Austria was "hopeless" for the latter. From
    the January 21 paper.
90. *Tremonia,* March 6, 1878.
91. The article referred specifically in this case to the Hapsburg position on
    Christians in Turkey. "Ein Rückblick und Umblick beim Jahreswechsel,
    III," *Tremonia,* January 5, 1876. See also *Germania,* January 8, 1876;
    "Oesterreich=Ungarn im Jahre 1875," *Kölnische Volkszeitung,*
    January 6, 1876.
92. "Oesterreich=Ungarn im Jahre 1877," *Kölnische Volkszeitung,*
    Janaury 5, 1878.
93. "Schweden und Norwegen," *Germania,* August 9, 1875.
94. "Die Lage Italiens und sein Verhältnis zu den übrigen europäischen
    Staaten, I," *Germania,* April 9, 1873.
95. M. Pachtler, "Zur neusten Geschichte der italienischen Freimaurerei,"
    Stimmen aus Maria-Laach 6 (1874): 340.
96. *Germania,* October 6, 1877.
97. "Die Lage Italiens," *Germania,* October 22, 1873.
98. *Germania,* September 14, 1873.
99. "Das Jahr 1877," *Schlesische Volkszeitung,* January 3, 1878.
100. Lill, "Katholizismus," 62.

101. "Das Jahr 1871," *Germania*, January 3, 1872.
102. *Germania*, January 23, 1875; February 26, 1876; June 2, 1877.
103. "Patriotische Briefe: Sechster Brief.—Germanomanie," *Stimmen aus Maria-Laach* 8 (1875), 274, 282.
104. Bolanden, *Urdeutsch*, 58.
105. *Germania*, May 13, 1876. Given that the Center recognized, at least "tacitly," that resolving the papal issue might require military force, Catholic ridicule of Italy is especially indicative of this. On acceptance of a possible war with Italy, see Anderson, *Windthorst*, 147.
106. The *Schlesische Volkszeitung* spoke of Germany's "mission" to lead the "Occident," for example. See "Deutschland und Rußland," February 2, 1872. For the opposition's views of the "German mission," which encompassed many different facets on each side, see Cramer, *Thirty Years' War*, especially 59, 63, 81, 88; Friedrich Meinecke, *The Age of German Liberation, 1795–1815*, trans. Peter Paret and Helmut Fischer (Berkeley: University of California Press, 1977), 125; David Blackbourn, "Progress and Piety: Liberalism, Catholicism and the State in Imperial Germany," *History Workshop Journal* 26 (1988): 72; Stefan-Ludwig Hoffmann, *The Politics of Sociability: Freemasonry and German Civil Society, 1840–1918*, trans. Tom Lampert (Ann Arbor: University of Michigan Press, 2007), 255. Of course, Catholics also believed they now had an internally directed mission as well to rid the new *Reich* of all non-German elements in its law and customs that had "hindered the German nationality." "Weltlage," *Germania*, March 5, 1871.
107. "Das deutsche Kaiserthum, V," *Germania*, January 26, 1871.
108. "Das Jahr 1871," *Germania*, January 3, 1872; "Das deutsche Kaiserthum, III," *Germania*, January 24, 1871.
109. "Zum neuen Jahr: Aus dem neuen Reich und der ewigen Kirche, I," *Kölnische Volkszeitung*, January 1, 1872.
110. Indeed, the way in which internal and external relations were conducted was presented as inseparable. For more on this topic, see Chapter 7.
111. Of course, Bismarck, aware of the waves Germany's unification had caused throughout Europe, also wanted to avoid another war. Nipperdey, *Deutsche Geschichte*, 257, 427, 431; Klaus Hildebrand, "Great Britain and the Foundation of the German Reich," in *German Foreign Policy from Bismarck to Adenauer: The Limits of Statecraft*, ed. Klaus Hildebrand, trans. Louise Willmot (London: Unwin, 1989), 27–28; Geiss, *German Foreign Policy*, 25; Volker Berghahn, *Imperial Germany 1871–1918: Economy, Society, Culture and Politics* (Providence: Berghahn, 1994), 263. Nonetheless, Catholic opinion presented the Chancellor's *Realpolitik*

as the cause for Germany's vulnerable position versus potential alliances among other powers. See, for example, "Die Bedrohung des Weltfriedens," *Germania*, April 7, 1875.

112. Both the *Kölnische Volkszeitung* and *Germania* included running commentary on the pope's situation in Italy during the early years of the *Kulturkampf.*

113. Bachem, *Zentrumspartei*, 193–197.

114. See, for example, the *Kölnische Volkszeitung* June 18, 1875; May 23, 1877; "Panslavische Strebungen," June 2, 1877; from *Germania* see "Rußland und Europa," August 16, 1871; "Ein Rückblick und Umblick beim Jahreswechsel, III," January 5, 1876; "Kreuz und Halbmond," July 6, 1877.

115. For a concise example of the connection, see "Zum neuen Jahr, II," *Kölnische Volkszeitung*, January 3, 1873.

116. It engendered suspicion as Austria had been the leading force in the Holy Roman Empire. See Bachem, *Zentrumspartei,* vol. 1. See also Schieder, "Das deutsche Reich," 424. The Holy Roman Empire was also linked to the preference for federalism. See Buschmann, "Auferstehung der Nation?" 336. More generally, liberals saw in the new *Reich* a new nation-state as opposed to the dynastic empire of the old one. Of course, more recent historiography has questioned whether the difference between the two entities—in so far as their potential for being the object of nationalist aspirations—was as great as has often been suggested. See, for example, Dieter Langewiesche and Schmidt, *Föderative Nation;* Abigail Green, "The Federal Alternative: A New View of Modern German History," *The Historical Journal* 46 (2003): 187–202; Berger, *Germany,* 16, 19.

117. *Germania,* March 24, 1872.

118. See, for example, "Ein Rückblick und Umblick beim Jahreswechsel, III" *Germania,* January 5, 1876; "Zum neuen Jahr," *Kölnische Volkszeitung,* January 3, 1873. Opting for *Real-* versus *Idealpolitik,* as Catholic portrayals presented discounting the example of the old *Reich* and instead supporting such things as nonintervention, was seen as going hand-in-hand with instigating a dicey international situation, Germany's endangered status, and the promotion of Prussian militarism believed to be necessary to provide the *Reich* with even a chance of survival in such a climate. Including an excerpt from Reichensperger's *Phrasen und Schlagwörter,* an article in *Germania* (August 4, 1872) informed readers that nonintervention really meant something quite different than it sounded, giving stronger governments the right to do whatever they

wanted "provided that an army of a corresponding number of bayonets stands behind [it]." In the book proper, Reichensperger built upon this idea of a rejection of true civilization that the old *Reich* represented leading instead to the "modern" definition of it that made militarism essential: "As one of the most outstanding achievements of modern civilization the skill to kill as many people from nation to nation as quickly and securely as possible is to be especially noted." Reichensperger, *Phrasen und Schlagwörter*, 21. For another invocation of the old *Reich*, see "Neujahrs=Erscheinungen," *Historisch-Politische Blätter* 75 (1875), especially 6. While more arms and soldiers might protect them for the moment, Germany could not keep up this mode of existence for long, Catholic arguments contended. In a letter to Wilhelm von Hammerstein, Windthorst dejectedly concluded the likelihood of a bloody conflict in the near future to be great: "The next war that we, providing we live ten more years, can still take part in will be a global conflagration, and it will make the present war pale in comparison like child's play." Letter from October 22, 1870 in *Windthorst Briefe*.

119. Johannes Janssen, *History of the German People at the Close of the Middle Ages*, trans. M. A. Mitchell and A. M. Christie (New York: AMS Press, 1966), 190.

120. Conrad von Bolanden, [Joseph Bischoff], *Altdeutsch: historischer Roman* (Mainz: Kirchheim, 1881).

121. "Weltlage," *Germania*, December 28, 1870. On some of these same themes discussed in German Catholic mentality post-World War I, see Martin Menke, "Thy Will Be Done: German Catholics and National Identity in the Twentieth Century," *Catholic Historical Review* 91 (2005): 300–20.

122. "Zum neuen Jahr, II," *Kölnische Volkszeitung*, January 3, 1873.

123. "Urdeutsch," *Stimmen aus Maria-Laach* 10 (1876), 234. Spillmann was born in Zug, Switzerland, but moved to Germany while still a boy. Upon the expulsion of the Jesuits from Germany, he moved to Britain. On Spillmann, see Blackbourn, *Fontana History of Germany*, 392; A. Baumgartner, "Erinnerungen an P. Joseph Spillmann, S.J.," *Stimmen aus Maria-Laach* 69 (1905), 1–22.

124. See, for example, Janssen, *History of the German People*, 118.

125. The several-installment series began on January 21, 1871.

126. *Germania*, January 23, 1875.

127. "Das deutsche Kaiserthum," *Germania*, January 22, 1871.

128. On *Wissenschaft* see Chapter 8. Reporting on Alsace-Lorrain, for example, the *Reichsland* was being ruled by "'liberalism' stemming from

France," not a "German spirit" more in line with "Christian Germany." See *Germania*, March 10, 1877. Though references almost always stressed Christianity in general, certain cases did stress a German affinity to Catholicism specifically, reversing the claim opponents made of a connection to Protestantism. See, for example, H. J. Fugger, "Patriotische Briefe," *Stimmen aus Maria-Laach* 8 (1875), 288–89.

129. *Verhandlungen 1871*, 308.

130. For the initial quote, see "Der Amerikaner: wie sich die deutschen Dinge von außen ansehen?" *Historisch-Politische Blätter* 74 (1874), 489. On the Center leader, see Windthorst, *Ausgewählte Reden*, vol. 2, 61. Such claims exemplify the more general practice Anderson notes of political factions appealing to the records of other nations assumed to be "civilized" to bolster their own positions. *Practicing Democracy*, 92, 136, 149.

131. *Germania*, January 23, 1875; February 26, 1876.

132. *Germania*, January 23, 1875.

133. *Kölnische Volkszeitung*, May 23, 1877.

134. "Zeitläufe. Neuester Fortgang des 'Culturkampfes' in Preußen," *Historisch-Politische Blätter* 75 (1875), 623. Of course, some believed that the *Reich* was so powerful that even if it continued going in the wrong direction there would nonetheless be a fleeting period in which it would still enjoy the "imitation" of other countries. See *Germania*, June 2, 1877.

135. *Germania*, April 19, 1879.

136. "Zeitläufe," *Historisch-Politische Blätter*, 642.

137. *Augsburger Postzeitung*, February 20, 1872.

138. On the ability of the Holy Roman Empire to incorporate many nationalities, see, for example, "Ein Rückblick und Umblick beim Jahreswechsel, III," *Germania*, January 5, 1876.

139. On this theme, see Nipperdey, *Deutsche Geschichte*, vol. 2, 257, 269–270; Galos, "Image," 177ff., 194–195; Jaworski, "Polenliebe und Polenschelte," especially 82–83; Richard Blanke, *Prussian Poland in the German Empire (1871–1900)* (Boulder: East European Monographs, 1981), especially 2, 26.

140. *Germania*, October 5, 1873.

141. Blanke, *Prussian Poland*, especially 28–29; Bachem, *Zentrumspartei*, vol. 3, 148; Arbeitskreis Münster, "Konfession und Cleavages," 385; Anderson, *Windthorst*; Anderson, *Practicing Democracy*, 141–142

142. See, for example, "Zur 'polnischen' Frage," *Germania*, October 4, 1877. See also Lill, "Windthorst," 324. Additionally, Anderson notes that not only did the Center not support any goals of Polish nationalism contra to the German constitution but also provides other historical examples of

parties that were both "national and still appeal[ing] explicitly to the interests of a variety of (often mutually hostile) religious and ethnic minorities." *Windthorst,* 145, 193.

143. "Fragen und Gegenfragen," *Germania,* March 13, 1874.

144. Speech in the *Abgeordnetenhaus* of April 20, 1876. Quoted along with the added parenthetical information in Blanke, *Prussian Poland,* 28. Blanke also notes the ambiguity of this statement. Similarly, a two-part newspaper article entitled "Germanismus und Polonismus in Westpreußen," actually asserted that areas commonly thought to be Polish in West Prussia really had German roots after all, which could be reawakened. *Germania,* October 4 and 5, 1872. To add yet another layer of ambiguity on the issue, a week later the paper published a long response apparently sent in to the paper asserting the falsity of the assertion that West Prussia was originally German: *Germania,* October 13, 1872. On Windthorst's actions on behalf of Poles, see Anderson, *Windthorst.*

145. Berit Pleitner's analysis also suggests this point more generally in *Die "vernünftige" Nation: zur Funktion von Sterotypen über Polen und Franzosen im deutschen nationalen Diskurs 1850 bis 1871* (Frankfurt a.M.: Lang, 2001), 339ff. An article in *Germania* took aim at both Polish and Russian culture by rhetorically asking what did the latter have to offer the former other than a "Russian economy," playing on the idea of a figurative "Polish economy," the shorthand for Poland's inferiority, simply being replaced by an undesirable one from Russia. "Russische Wirthschaft in Polen," July 4, 1876. On the connotations of "Polish economy" see Hubert Orlowski, *"Polnische Wirtschaft": Zum deutschen Polendiskurs der Neuzeit* (Wiesbaden: Harrassowitz, 1996). On liberals' view of German versus Polish culture, see Nipperdey, *Deutsche Geschichte,* vol. 2, 269–270.

146. For pointed examples of this dichotomy, see "Rückschau und Ausschau beim Jahreswechsel," *Germania,* January 4, 1875; Majunke, *Louise Lateau,* 109.

147. On the general hold of this dichotomy in contemporaries' minds, see Fisch, "Zivilisation, Kultur," especially 740, 744. For an earlier period, also see Urs Bitterli, *Die "Wilden" und die "Zivilisierten": Grundzüge einer Geistes- und Kulturgeschichte der europäisch-überseeischen Begegnung* (Munich: C.H. Beck, 1976).

148. See at the beginning, for example, "Zum Kirchenstreit in Brasilien," February 28 and March 1, 1874. On the church-state conflict in Brazil, see Roderick J. Barman, *Citizen Emperor: Pedro II and the Making of Brazil, 1825–1891* (Stanford: Stanford University Press, 1999), 254ff.

149. *Germania*, April 13, 1878. Brazil was not alone, as the quote suggests. See, for example, reportage on "Der Culturkampf in Buenos=Ayres," *Schlesische Volkszeitung*, April 7, 1875. On other "barbarities" in Latin America see, for example, *Germania*, January 12, 1878.

150. *Germania*, August 4, 1877.

151. "Amerikanisches Raisonnment über den deutschen Liberalismus," *Kölnische Volkszeitung*, July 21, 1872.

152. Windthorst, *Ausgewählte Reden*, speech of May 15, 1876, 107. A more clearly negative mention of America occurred in an article on civil marriage. Despite the stretch, an article in the *Historisch-Politische Blätter* linked civil marriage to ultimately having to allow such things like polygamy, "if tomorrow the Mormons . . . move from the Salt Lake to Europe." Clearly such an example smacked of "barbarism," they concluded. "Die Civilehe und der Rechtsstaat," 69 (1872), 524. Though outlawed in the 1860s, polygamy still remained an issue before the Supreme Court, which only ruled it to not be a matter of religious freedom in 1878.

153. "Amerikanisches Raisonnment über den deutschen Liberalismus," *Kölnische Volkszeitung*, July 21, 1872.

154. "Das Reich der Mitte," *Historisch-Politisch Blätter* 75 (1875), 718–719.

155. *Germania*, June 27, 1874 and September 30, 1876.

156. *Germania*, June 27, 1874. For more on the debate over German *Wissenschaft*, see Chapter 8.

157. "Die Christenverfolgung in Japan," *Germania*, April 3, 1872. Also on Japan, see "Der moderne Staat nach liberalem Zuschnitt und die katholische Kirche," *Schlesische Volkszeitung*, November 9, 1872.

158. For more on the Oriental Question, see Klaus Hildebrand, *Das vergangene Reich: Deutsche Außenpolitik von Bismarck bis Hitler 1871–1945* (Stuttgart: Deutsche-Verlags Anstalt, 1995), 34–64; Geiss, *German Foreign Policy*, 31ff. For a history of German affairs in the region focusing on later decades, see Gregor Schöllgen, *Imperialismus und Gleichgewicht: Deutschland, England und die orientalische Frage 1871–1914* (Munich: Oldenbourg, 2000).

159. Suzanne Marchand is undoubtedly right that approaches based on Said's Orientalism paint the picture of European views of others too starkly. Indeed, Catholic publications could also include positive references to the Orient, especially given the importance of the Holy Land. For the period in question and the arguments dealing with national identity, however, the overwhelming Catholic portrayal of areas like Turkey were quite negative, as the quotes above suggest. See Marchand, *German Orientalism in the*

Age of Empire: Religion, Race, and Scholarship (Washington D.C.: German Historical Institute; New York: Cambridge University Press, 2009), especially xxii. The limits of Said's Orientalism are also discussed in Margaret Lavinia Anderson, "Down in Turkey, Far Away: Human Rights, the Armenian Massacres, and Orientalism in Wilhelmine Germany," *Journal of Modern History* 79 (2007).

160. *Germania*, November 7, 1874 and April 28, 1877. On the far more encompassing use of the East and the Orient see, for example, Anderson, "Down in Turkey," especially 85–86, 110–111; Wolff, *Inventing Eastern Europe*, 6–7.

161. *Germania*, August 12, 1875.

162. "Ein Rückblick und Umblick beim Jahreswechsel," *Germania*, January 5, 1876.

163. In accordance with such ideas, an article that agreed with the opinion sent in by a Turkish individual could only square the circle by stressing that he "sounded very Christian" and probably drew such conclusions from "intelligence other than Turkish intelligence." "Eine—türkische Stimme über den 'Culturkampf,'" *Germania*, March 16, 1876.

164. "Türkische und russische Grausamkeiten," *Germania*, August 24, 1876.

165. On Bismarck's attitude to Russia and foreign policy, see Peter Bruno Max Wolfframm, *Die deutsche Außenpolitik und die großen deutschen Tageszeitungen, 1871–1890* (Zeulenroda: Bernard Sporn, 1936), 48–50; Walter Laqueur, *Russia and Germany; A Century of Conflict* (New Brunswick, NJ: Transaction Publishers, 1990), 26; Martin, *Der katholische Weg*, 90; Vejas Gabriel Liulevicius, *War Land on the Eastern Front: Culture, National Identity, and German Occupation in World War I* (Cambridge: Cambridge University Press, 2000), 23. On the particular opposition of Catholics to Russia, see Martin, *Der katholische Weg*, 90.

166. "Frieden," *Germania*, June 18, 1871.

167. For example, see *Kölnische Volkszeitung*, August 13, 1872 and June 18, 1875; *Germania*, June 20, 1871 and May 25, 1875.

168. *Germania*, June 20, 1871; "Pro Rheno," *Historisch-Politische Blätter* 77(1876), 662.

169. "Gewaltsame Bekehrung der Griechish-Unierten im Königreiche Polen zur russischen Staatskirche," *Germania*, April 15, 1874. Similar statements abound in the papers of the day. For more examples, see *Augsburger Postzeitung*, May 13, 1875; "Zur Orientfrage. Rußlands nächste Pläne im Süd=Osten Europas," *Tremonia*, May 16, 1877; "Die Greuel des Krieges," *Tremonia*, August 28, 1877; "'The Russian revolver has missed fire!'", *Schlesische Volkszeitung*, January 19, 1877; "Russische Grausamkeit und

deren Bestrafung," *Schlesische Volkszeitung*, March 15, 1878. Though negative portrayals, quite common among liberal critics of Russia earlier in the century, often grouped Poles among Slavs as well, Catholic rhetoric tended to see the former as distinct. See Liulevicius, *War Land*, 25; Galos, "Image of a Pole," 186; Pleitner, *Die vernünftige Nation*, 339ff. On early liberal attitudes to Russia, see Struck, *Nicht West, nicht Ost*, 176; Günther Stökl, *Osteuropa und die Deutschen: Geschichte und Gegenwart einer spannungsreichen Nachbarschaft*, 3rd. edition (Stuttgart: Hirzel, 1982), 124. On perceptions of the Russian threat leading up to World War I more generally, see Paddock, *Russian Peril*.

170. "Rußland und Europa, I," *Germania*, August 16, 1871.

171. "Der Amerikaner," *Historisch-Politische Blätter* 74 (1874), 487.

172. *Kölnische Volkszeitung*, June 10, 1874. "Eine objective Studie" (November 16, 1875) in *Germania* posed the past and present trajectory in the same manner.

173. "Ein Rückblick und Umblick beim Jahreswechsel, II," *Germania*, Janaury 4, 1876.

174. "An die Gewehre!!" *Tremonia*, January 9, 1877.

175. *Kölnische Volkszeitung*, May 23, 1877. Such heightened expressions of national shame *vis-à-vis* Russia were hardly isolated. Other instances, for example, spoke of Germany having "to beg" as well as the *Reich* being "forced" to undertake certain actions in foreign policy in light of Russia's dominance. See "Der Amerikaner," *Historisch-Politische Blätter*, 487; "Eine objective Studie," *Germania*, November 16, 1875.

176. From the beginning, articles in the *Kölnische Volkszeitung* expressed greater hesitancy at calling for intervention, most likely already having the larger consequences of Russian intervention in a region portrayed by the Rhenish paper from the very beginning as "ailing." "Cäsaropapismus," *Kölnische Volkszeitung*, January 29, 1873.

177. "Ein Rückblick und Umblick beim Jahreswechsel, III," *Germania*, Janaury 5, 1876; "Kreuz und Halbmond," *Germania*, July 6, 1877.

178. See, for example, "Russland und das Völkerrecht," *Kölnische Volkszeitung*, September 16, 1876.

179. On "standing by our German brothers in the Baltic provinces," see, for example, *Kölnische Volkszeitung*, May 23, 1877. See also the concern over stripping people there of their "German past." In "Zur Russisierung der baltischen Provinzen," *Schlesische Volkszeitung*, May 25, 1877. For the situation of Baltic Germans, see Rogers Brubaker, *Nationalism Reframed: Nationhood and the National Question in the New Europe* (Cambridge: University of Cambridge Press, 1996), 115; Liulevicius, *War Land*, 24.

180. *Kölnische Volkszeitung*, September 30, 1876.
181. "Die Interpellation der 'Reichstreuen' in der Orientfrage," *Germania*,
     February 11, 1878; See also, for example, "Aphorismen über russische
     Zustände und Parteien, III. Der Panslavismus und die Slavophilen,"
     Historisch-Politische Blätter 79 (1877), 642–659; *Kölnische Volkszeitung*,
     May 23, 1877; "Der Panslavismus," *Schlesische Volkszeitung*, July 3, 4, 5,
     6, 7, 1877.
182. *Kölnische Volkszeitung*, May 23, 1877.
183. "Die Interpellation der 'Reichstreuen' in der Orientfrage," *Germania*,
     February 11, 1878. Though less often, arguments could also appeal to
     national economic interests as a way of presenting Russia, as well as other
     countries, as opponents. See, for example, *Kölnische Volkszeitung*,
     January 28, 1876 and May 23, 1877; *Germania*, September 27, 1876. Of
     course, grain tariffs did play a role in the increased Russian-German
     distance. See Berghahn, *Imperial Germany*, 264.
184. *Germania*, September 8, 1877; *Kölnische Volkszeitung*, February 2, 1876.
185. "Rußland und Europa, I," *Germania*, August 16, 1871. In this instance,
     socialism was also included in this charge of the biggest threat to Western
     civilization.
186. "Eine objective Studie," *Germania*, November 16, 1875. See also *Köl-
     nische Volkszeitung*, June 10, 1874.
187. Catholic rhetoric portrayed *Kulturkämpfer* as internal barbarians through
     a number of ways. Given the association of Christianity with civilization,
     for example, the reference to liberals as the new pagans suggested this.
     The view that Russia had little to offer in the development of true
     civilization paralleled the same assertions about liberals, whose *Kul-
     turkampf* was portrayed as bringing anything but culture. See, for
     example, the article "Stambul und Marpingen," which questions the
     ability of Russia to improve the situation in Turkey any more than
     Kulturkämpfer did in the case of the Marpingen miracle: *Germania*,
     January 23, 1877. Another edition of *Germania* reprinted a letter that
     referred to liberals as the modern-day threat to Europe replacing
     the allegedly barbarian Muslims of centuries ago: August 12, 1875.
     Blackbourn also notes the Center Party's referencing of nationalism,
     which of course liberals championed, as "modern Islam." *Fontana
     History of Germany*, 285. See also the *Augsburger Postzeitung*'s use of
     the term "civilized barbarians" on May 31, 1871. That the *Kulturkämpfer*
     were barbarians was also the implication of Mother Superior Auguste von
     Sartorius in her letter to the *Oberpräsident* of Westphalia when she
     concluded that even "non-civilized peoples and governments" would not

have forced her community of nuns to leave. StAM OP 2114, letter from October 13, 1873. Both highlighting Russian barbarism and associating it with the liberals in Germany continued to play a role in Catholic rhetoric. See, for example, the case of Father Habighorst from Altena. The local *Landrat* requested the priest's transfer after the latter gave a speech to local voters asserting that liberals "would treat Catholics like Russian Jews" if the Center Party were not there to protect them. The speech took place not long after the three-day Kishinev pogrom that left dozens of Jews dead, hundreds wounded, and still many more homeless, quickly ratcheting up emigration from Russia and becoming "emblematic" of anti-Semitic violence. Both the Kishinev pogrom itself as well as the incident involving Habighorst made the newspapers. Given the advances made by the Social Democrats, the speech also saw that party in cahoots with the liberals. StAM, OP 1925,1 letters from June 18 and August 11, 1903. On the Kishinev pogrom, see David Vital, *A People Apart: The Jews in Europe, 1789–1939* (Oxford: Oxford University Press, 1999), 310, 509–513.

188. See, for example, Berger, *Germany*, 92, 96; Jeismann, *Vaterland der Feinde*, especially 11, 14, 15, 16.

189. On foreign relations, including the changing approach to Russia, see Berghahn, *Imperial Germany*, especially 263ff.; Geiss, *German Foreign Policy*, 19, 33–35, Nipperdey, *Deutsche Geschichte*, vol. 2, especially 436–439.

190. David Blackbourn colorfully describes this approach of the *Reich* to Britain: "German statesmen behaved like abusive suitors who alternated between whispering endearments and issuing threats." See, *Fontana History of Germany*, 445.

191. Providing an overview of foreign policy, Jost Düffler notes for mainstream views more generally that "perceptions of a Russian threat originated in the 1880s, but they intensified thereafter to the point that expectations of conflict between 'Germandom' and 'Slavdom' were freighted with racist ideology." See "Foreign Policy," in *Imperial Germany: A Historiographical Companion*, ed. Roger Chickering (Westport, CT: Greenwood, 1996), 410.

192. The most obvious example is Deuerlein's idea of a "return" to the "national idea" in his 1970 article that is based on the Center's support for military bills (which were heavily interconnected to colonial politics as well). See Deuerlein, "Die Bekehrung." Even scholars like Morsey, who does not propose the same distance having come between Catholics and the nation in the preceding decades, nonetheless connects support for military and

colonial policies as an even greater indication of a "national" position. See, "Katholiken und der Nationalstaat," especially 175. For other examples, see Ulrich von Hehl, "Die Zentrumspartei—Ihr Weg von 'Reichsfeind' zur parlimentarischen Schlüsselstellung in Kaiserreich und Republik," in *Auf dem Weg zum modernen Parteienstaat: Zur Entstehung, Organisation und Struktur politischer Parteien in Deutschland und den Niederlanden*, ed. Hermann Walther von der Dunk and Horst Lademacher (Melsungen: Kasseler Forschungen zur Zeitgeschichte, 1986), 105; Gründer, "Rechtskatholizismus," 124–125; and more recently, Berger, *Germany*, 87.

193. On the significance for national identity, see, for example, Berger, *Germany*, especially 99–100; Nipperdey, *Deutsche Geschichte*, vol. 2, 263. As the title of Susanne Zantop's book suggests, such importance often relied on the views of self and other that colonialism enabled: *Colonial Fantasies: Conquest, Family, and Nation in Precolonial Germany, 1770–1870* (Durham, NC: Duke University Press, 1997).

194. Quoted in Morsey, "Katholiken und Nationalstaat," 175.

195. On this connection, see Becker, "Konfessionelle Nationsbilder," 408; Bachem, *Zentrumspartei*, vol. 5, especially 50–51; Hubert Mohr, *Katholische Orden und deutscher Imperialismus* (Berlin: Akademie Verlag, 1965). The last source is rather ideological and should, of course, be used with this in mind.

196. From documents reprinted in Bachem, *Zentrumspartei*, vol. 7, 457–458, 461–463.

197. Bachem, *Zentrumspartei*, vol. 7, 445–447. Bachem also emphasizes "thoughts of the world mission (*Weltaufgabe*) of general cultural development" in the Center's reasoning for supporting colonialism. Interestingly, he also is careful to balance the mention of "more highly cultured peoples" and "less cultured" ones with a mention of "the unity of the human race." See *Zentrumspartei*, vol. 7, 50–51.

198. Klaus Epstein, "Erzberger and the German Colonial Scandals, 1905–1910," *The English Historical Review* 74 (1959): especially 646, 648, 650, 663. More generally, see Bachem, *Zentrumspartei*, vol. 6, 59–60.

199. Becker, for example, stressing the continued distance of Catholics to the nation even later in the *Reich* largely explains their support for the government's military and colonial politics as tactical decisions made in hopes of gaining support for their own initiatives: "Konfessionelle Nationsbilder," 408. For a similar view, see Loth, "Zwischen autoritärer und demokratischer Ordnung."

200. Matthias Erzberger, *Kolonial-Berufe: Ratgeber für alle Erwerbsaus-sichten in den deutschen Schutzgebieten* (Berlin: Verlag der Germania, 1912), 76. Quoted in translation in Epstein, "Erzberger," 642. Interestingly, in one of the rare mentions of the still largely uncolonized continent during the 1870s, *Germania* situated the significance of missions to the "pagan peoples of inner Africa" in the larger context of liberals and the *Kulturkampf*, again pointing to long-term continuities between the fight against barbarism that Catholic rhetoric concerning the moral geography of the world posed as facing the new *Reich* after 1871 and later colonization activities supported by the Center Party.

201. The reference is, of course, to Deuerlein's 1970 article, "Die Bekehrung." As much as it held the Holy Roman Empire up as a model, Catholic rhetoric also asserted the new *Reich* could not simply pick up where the old one had left off.

Conclusion

1. Highlighting both morality and a retreat from a national identity revolving around it—at least from its most obvious expression in the form of a feminine Germany—coupled with the emphasis on both universalism and a clear hierarchy of civilized and barbaric nations in the Catholic construction of the nation suggest a lack of a clear cut distinction between ethnic and civic nationalism, as so much scholarship has indicated more recently. On the post-1945 tendency in the study of nationalism to differentiate between types dominant in Western Europe versus Germany (commonly associated with the work of Hans Kohn among others) and often concerned with divisions between "civic" and "ethnic" types, see overviews in Miroslav Hroch, *Das Europa der Nationen: Die moderne Nationsbildung im europäischen Vergleich* (Göttingen: Vandenhoeck & Ruprecht, 2005), 18ff.; Philip Spencer and Howard Wollman, eds., *Nationalism: A Critical Introduction* (London: SAGE, 2002), 94ff. See also, of course, the works of Kohn himself, for example *Nationalism. Its Meaning and History* (Princeton: Van Nostrand, 1955). On the more recent questioning of this distinction, see Rogers Brubaker, "Myths and Misconceptions in the Study of Nationalism," in *State of the Nation: Ernest Gellner and the Theory of Nationalism,* ed. John A. Hall (Cambridge: Cambridge University Press, 1998), 298–301; Erika Harris, *Nationalism: Theories and Cases* (Edinburgh: Edinburgh University Press, 2009), 28ff. For specific studies of Germany that question the distinction, see Jeismann, *Vaterland der Feinde*; Vick, *Defining Germany,* especially 205ff.

2. On the conflict of the *Kulturkampf*, despite its severity, still being fundamentally rooted in the system of a *Rechtsstaat*, see Blackbourn, *Marpingen*. Also, on the significance of the idea that Catholics and Protestants worked out their differences without literally killing each other, see Smith, *German Nationalism*, 235.

3. On the idea of "practicing," see Anderson, *Practicing Democracy*.

Bibliography

Archival Sources

Archiwum Archidiecezjalne we Wrocławiu (AAW)
Nachlaß Paul Majunke.

Bistumsarchiv Trier (BAT)
Abteilung BIII
9,7, Bd.10 Ehesakrament: Mischehen zwischen Katholiken und Militärpersonen, 1826–1894
11,10, Bd.3 Gottesdienstliche Bestimmungen: Feier des Sedantages, 1873–1875

Bochum Stadtarchiv (BSA)
LA 270 Religiöse Erziehung der Kinder aus gemischt konfessionellen Ehen, 1838–1841, 1852–1859

Bundesarchiv Koblenz (BAK)
N 1036 Nachlaß Hertling
(includes documents formerly cataloged as Nachlaß Cardauns)

Dom- und Diözesanarchiv Mainz (DDM)
C.7.2,4f Konverenz vom 29. IV. 1873: Beschluss: Passiver Widerstand gegen die Gesetze
C7.3,2 Verein zur Hebung katholischer Wissenschaft, Literatur und Presse
D5.3,2 Korrespondenz Moufangs mit der Nuntiatur, 1877–1886
D6.1a Moufang-Korrespondenz: Briefe von den Angehörigen, 1834–1884
D6.1b Briefe an Moufang, 1837–1888
D6.2,6 Urteil gegen Edelmann

Dortmund Stadtarchiv (DSA)
   5, 1.5, Acte 9 Abhaltung kirchlicher Prozessioner und Wallfahrten, 1851, 1891

Landeshauptarchiv Koblenz (LHAK)
   Bestand 403 Oberpräsidium der Rheinprovinz
      6695 Teilnahme der Lehrer und Beamten an staatsgefährdenden Ver-
         einen, 1872–1876
      10804 Durchführung des Gesetzes über die Vorbildung und Anstellung
         der Geistlichen vom 11. Mai 1873
      15834 Proselytenmachereÿ, 1840, 1865, 1893–1904
   Bestand 441 Regierungsbezirk Koblenz
      3516 Die gemischten Ehen, 1817–1854
      10608 Die Simultanschule in Niederkostenz, Kreis Simmern, 1880–1881
      26927 Das von den Katholiken in Medard beanspruchte Schulsimulta-
         neum, 1826–1893
      17231 Der in Mainz zusammengetretene sogen. Verein der deutschen
         Katholiken, 1872–1874
   Bestand 442 Regierungsbezirk Trier
      2202 Die Beschwerden wegen Störung des Unterrichts und Kränkungen
         der Schullehrer und Unterricht ertheilenden Pfarrer
   Bestand 700,138
   Nachlaß A. Reichensperger

Landeskirchliches Archiv der Evangelischen Kirche von Westfalen (LAEKW)
   Bestand 0
      0/ 172b Die gemischten Ehen (besonders in den Diaspora-Gebieten),
         Band I, 1824–1881
   Bestand 4
   91 Warstein

Staatsarchiv Münster (StAM)
   Oberpräsidium
      1601,1 Die Bildung eines Westfälischen Bauern Vereins und die Ueberwa-
         chung der politsch-religiösen Bewegung, 1871–1874
      1601,3 Die Bildung eines Westfälischen Bauern Vereins und die Ueberwa-
         chung der politsch-religiösen Bewegung, 1875–1876
      1867,1 Die Vornahme geistlichen Amtshandlungen an einen protestant-
         ischen Eingepfarrten durch einen katholischen Geistlichen und
         umgekehrt, 1849–1867
      1925,1 Beschwerden über katholische Geistliche, 1887–1906
      2047,1 Die Prozessionen, 1826–1878

2047,2 Die Prozessionen, 1879–1913

2114 Ausführung der neuen kirchenpolitischen Gesetze zur Vorbildung und Anstellung der Geistlichen, 1873–1887

2166 Religiöse Erziehung der Kinder aus Mischehen und unehelicher Kinder, 1831–1835, 1888–1921

Regierungsbezirk Arnsberg

E 422 Verfahren der katholischen Geistlichen bei gemischten Ehen, 1816–1924

Landratsamt Dortmund

834 Sonn-und Festtagsfeier und Lustbarkeiten bei katholischen Prozessionen, überhaupt Heilighaltung der Sonn- und Festtage, 1817–1896

839 Gegenseitige Verrichtungen von Parochialhandlungen von Geistlichen beider Religionspartheien, 1833–1846

Newspapers and Periodicals

Augsburger Postzeitung
Central-Volksblatt
Deutscher Hausschatz
Germania
Historisch-Politische Blätter
Der Katholik: Zeitschrift für katholische Wissenschaft und kirchliches Leben
Kölnische Volkszeitung
Schlesische Volkszeitung
Stimmen aus Maria-Laach
Tremonia
Westfälischer Merkur

Printed Primary Sources

Albrecht, Dieter, ed. *Joseph Edmund Jörg Briefwechsel, 1846–1901.* Mainz: Matthias-Grünewald, 1988.

Bachem, Julius. *Die Sünden des Liberalismus im ersten Jahre des neuen Deutschen Reichs.* Leipzig: Leuckart, 1872.

———. *Erinnerungen eines alten Publizisten und Politikers.* Cologne: Bachem, 1913.

Bergsträßer, Ludwig. *Der politische Katholizismus: Dokumente seiner Entwicklung, II 1871–1914.* Munich: Drei Masken, 1923.

Bismarck, Otto von. *Bismarck: The Man and Statesman.* Vol. 2, translated by A. J. Butler. New York: Cosimo, 2007.

Bolanden, Conrad von [Joseph Bischoff]. *Die Unfehlbaren*. Mainz: Kirchheim, 1871.

———. *Die Reichsfeinde*. Mainz: Kirchheim, 1874.

———. *Urdeutsch: Historischer Roman*. Mainz: Kirchheim, 1875.

———. *Altdeutsch: Historischer Roman*. Mainz: Kirchheim, 1881.

———. *Urdeutsch: Historischer Roman*. Munich: A & B Schuler, 1908.

Brümmer, Franz. *Deutsches Dichter-lexikon: Biographische und bibliographische Mittheilungen über deutsche Dichter aller Zeiten*. Eichstätt: H. Hugendubel, 1886–1887.

Buß, Franz Joseph. *Der Unterschied der katholischen und protestantischen Universitäten Teutschlands*. Freiburg: Herder, 1846.

Cardauns, Hermann. *Die Görres-Gesellschaft 1876–1901. Denkschrift zur Feier ihres 25 jährigen Bestehens nebst Jahresbericht für 1900*. Cologne: Bachem, 1901.

Dyroff, Adolf. *Reden, Ansprachen, und Vorträge des Grafen Georg von Hertling mit einigen Erinnerungen an ihn*. Cologne: Bachem, 1929.

Erzberger, Matthias. *Kolonial-Berufe: Ratgeber für alle Erwerbsaussichten in den deutschen Schutzgebieten*. Berlin: Verlag der Germania, 1912.

Ficker, Ludwig. *Der Kulturkampf in Münster*. Edited by Otto Hellinghaus. Münster: Aschendorff, 1928.

Gatz, Erwin, ed. *Akten der Fuldaer Bischofskonferenz*. Vol. 1. Mainz: Matthias-Grünewald, 1977.

Hertling, Georg von. "Rede des Abgeordneten Dr. Freiherrn von Hertling." In *Jahresbericht der Görres=Gesellschaft für das Jahr 1876*, 41–46. Cologne: Bachem, 1877.

———. *Erinnerungen aus meinem Leben*, Band I. München: J. Kösel, 1919.

Janssen, Johannes. *Geschichte des deutschen Volkes seit dem Ausgang des Mittelalters*. 8 vols. Freiburg: Herder, 1876–1894.

———. *History of the German People at the Close of the Middle Ages*. Translated by M. A. Mitchell and A. M. Christie. New York: AMS Press, 1966.

Ketteler, Wilhelm Emmanuel von. *Das Recht und der Rechtschutz der katholischen Kirche in Deutschland*. Mainz: Kirchheim, 1854.

———. *Deutschland nach dem Kriege von 1866*. Mainz: Kirchheim, 1867.

———. *Die Katholiken im Deutschen Reiche*. Mainz: Kirchheim, 1873.

———. *Die moderne Tendenz-Wissenschaft. Beleuchtet am Exempel des Herrn Professor Dr. Emil Friedberg*. Mainz: Kirchheim, 1873.

———. *Die preußischen Gesetzentwürfe über die Stellung der Kirche zum Staat*. Mainz: Kirchheim, 1873.

———. *Der Culturkampf gegen die kathol. Kirche und die neuen Kirchengesetzentwürfe für Hessen*. Mainz: Kirchheim, 1874.

Kirchner, M. "Der Jesuit Mariana und seine Lehre vom Tyrannenmord."
    Deutsche Blätter : Eine Monatsschrift für Staat, Kirche und sociales Leben
    (1874): 542–559.

Majunke, Paul. *Louise Lateau, ihr Wunderleben und ihre Bedeutung im
    deutschen Kirchenconflicte.* Berlin: Verlag der Germania, 1874.

———. *Die Ohnmacht der modernen naturwissenschaftlichen "Forschung":
    Studien aus Büchner und Darwin.* Berlin: Verlag der Germania, 1876.

———. *Geschichte des "Culturkampfes" in Preußen-Deutschland.* Paderborn:
    Schöningh, 1886.

Molitor, Wilhelm. *Julian der Apostate.* Mainz: Kirchheim, 1866.

———. *Des Kaisers Günstling.* Mainz: Kirchheim, 1874.

Mommsen, Theodor. *Römisches Staatsrecht.* Vol. II. Leipzig: Hirzel, 1875.

Mommsen, Wilhelm. *Deutsche Parteiprogramme.* Munich: Isar, 1960.

Mühlhäusser, Karl August. *Christentum und Presse.* Frankfurt a.M.: Zimmer,
    1876.

*Nationalität und Freiheit. Eine Widerlegung des Buches: Deutschland nach
    dem Kriege von 1866. Von Wilhelm Emmanuel v. Ketteler, Bischof von
    Mainz.* Landsberg a.d.W.: Schäffer, 1867.

Osseg, Annuarius [Georg Pachtler]. *Der Europäische Militarismus.* Amberg:
    Habbel, 1876.

Pastor, Ludwig von, ed. *Johannes Janssens Briefe.* 2 vols. Freiburg: Herder, 1920.

Real, Willy, ed. *Katholizismus und Reichsgründung: Neue Quellen aus dem
    Nachlaß Karl Friedrich von Savignys.* Paderborn: Schöningh, 1988.

Reichensperger, August. "In welchem Style sollen wir bauen?" *Zeitschrift für
    praktische Baukunst* 12 (1852): 291–304.

———. *Phrasen und Schlagwörter. Ein Noth und Hülfsbüchlein für Zeitungs-
    leser.* 3rd ed. Paderborn: Schöningh, 1872.

Reichensperger, Peter. *Kulturkampf oder Friede in Staat und Kirche.* Berlin:
    Springer, 1876.

Renan, Ernest. "What is a Nation?" In *Nationalism in Europe 1815 to the Present:
    A Reader.* Edited by Stuart Woolf, 48–60. London: Routledge, 1996.

Röhde, Paul. "Ueber das Schöffeninstitut nach der Carolina und dessen
    weitere Ausbildung in Deutschland." *Preußische Jahrbücher* 39 (1877):
    337–360.

Rohling, August. *Der Talmudjude: Zur Beherzigung für Juden und Christen
    aller Stände.* 4th ed. Münster: Adolf Russel, 1872.

Schaff, Philip. *Germany: Its Universities, Theology, and Religion.* Edinburgh:
    T and T Clark, 1857.

Schröder, J. W. *Nicht Judenhatz—aber Christenschutz! Ein Beitrag zur
    'Judenfrage.'* 3rd ed. Paderborn: Bonifacius, 1875.

Stoltz, Alban. *Gesammelte Werke.* Vol. 10. Freiburg: Herder, 1875.

Taylor, Frank. *The Newspaper Press as a Power Both in the Expression and Formation of Public Opinion.* Oxford: Blackwell, 1898.

Thiersch, Heinrich Wilhelm Josias. *Ueber den christlichen Staat.* Basel: Schneider, 1875.

Verhandlungen der einundzwanzigsten Generalversammlung der katholischen Vereine Deutschlands zu Mainz am 10., 11., 12., 13. und 14. September 1871. Mainz: Kirchheim, 1871.

Verhandlungen der XXII. General=Versammlung der Katholiken Deutschlands zu Breslau am 8., 9., 10., 11. und 12. September 1872. Breslau: G.P. Aderholz' Buchhandlung, 1872.

Verhandlungen der XXIII. Generalversammlung der Katholiken Deutschlands zu Freiburg im Breisgau am 31. August 1., 2., 3. und 4. September 1875. Freiburg: Herder, 1875.

Verhandlungen der XXIV katholischen Generalversammlung Deutschlands zu München am 11., 12., 13. und 14. September 1876. Munich: Herder, 1876.

Verhandlungen der XXV. Generalversammlung der Katholiken Deutschlands zu Würzburg am 10., 11., 12. und 13. September 1877. Würzburg, 1877.

Verhandlungen der XXVI. Generalversammlung der Katholiken Deutschlands zu Aachen am 8., 9., 10., und 11. September 1879. Aachen: Jacobi and Co., 1879.

Wilhelm II, Kaiser. *My Early Life.* New York: Doran, 1971.

Windthorst, Ludwig. *Ausgewählte Reden des Staatsministers a.D. und Parlimentariers Dr. Ludwig Windthorst, gehalten in der Zeit von 1851–1891.* Band II. Osnabrück: Bernhard Wehberg, 1902.

———. *Briefe 1834–1880.* Edited by Hans-Georg Aschoff and Heinz-Jörg Heinrich. Paderborn: Schöningh, 1995.

Secondary Literature

Altgeld, Wolfgang. *Katholizismus, Protestantismus, Judentum: über religiös begründete Gegensätze und nationalreligiöse Ideen in der Geschichte des deutschen Nationalismus.* Mainz: Matthias-Grünewald, 1992.

———. "Religion, Denomination and Nationalism in Nineteenth-Century Germany." In *Protestants, Catholics, and Jews in Germany, 1800–1914,* edited by Helmut Walser Smith, 49–65. Berg: Oxford, 2001.

Amelunxen, Rudolf. *Das Kölner Ereignis.* Essen: Ruhrländische Verlagsgesellschaft, 1952.

Anderson, Benedict. *Imagined Communities: Reflections on the Origins and Spread of Nationalism.* London: Verso, 1983.

Anderson, Margaret Lavinia. *Windthorst: A Political Biography.* Oxford: Clarendon, 1981.

———. "The Kulturkampf and the Course of German History." *Central European History* 19 (1986): 82–115.

———. "Interdenominationalism, Clericalism, Pluralism: The *Zentrumsstreit* and the Dilemma of Catholicism in Wilhelmine Germany." *Central European History* 21 (1988): 350–378.

———. *Practicing Democracy: Elections and Political Culture in Imperial Germany.* Princeton: Princeton University Press, 2000.

———. "Down in Turkey, Far Away: Human Rights, the Armenian Massacres, and Orientalism in Wilhelmine Germany." *Journal of Modern History* 79 (1) (2007): 80–111.

Angster, Julia. "'The Older and Stronger Firm': German Perceptions of Britain as a World Trading and Imperial Nation." In *Britain as a Model of Modern Society? German Views,* edited by Arnd Bauerkämper and Christiane Eisenberg, 133–146. Augsburg: Wissner-Verlag, 2006.

Applegate, Celia. *A Nation of Provincials: The German Idea of Heimat.* Berkeley: University of California Press, 1990.

———. "A Europe of Regions: Reflections on the Historiography of Sub-National Places in Modern Times." *American Historical Review* 104 (1999): 1157–1182.

Arbeitskreis für kirchliche Zeitgeschichte, Münster. "Konfession und Cleavages im 19. Jahrhundert: Ein Erklärungsmodell zur regionalen Enstehung des katholischen Milieus in Deutschland." *Historisches Jahrbuch* 121 (2000): 358–395.

Aschoff, Hans-Georg. *Rechtsstaatlichkeit und Emanzipation: Das politische Wirken Ludwig Windthorsts.* Sögel: Verlag der Emsländischen Landschaft für die Landkreise Emsland und Grafschaft Benheim, 1988.

Assmann, Aleida. *Arbeit am nationalen Gedächtnis: Eine kurze Geschichte der deutschen Bildungsidee.* Frankfurt a.M.: Campus, 1993.

Bachem, Karl. *Vorgeschichte, Geschichte und Politik der deutschen Zentrumspartei, zugleich ein Beitrag zur Geschichte der katholischen Bewegung, sowie zur allgemeinen Geschichte des neueren und neuesten Deutschland, 1815–1914.* 9 vols. Cologne: J.P. Bachem, 1927–1932.

Barkin, Kenneth D. "1878–1879: The Second Founding of the Reich, a Perspective." *German Studies Review* 10 (1987): 219–235.

Barman, Roderick J. *Citizen Emperor: Pedro II and the Making of Brazil, 1825–1891.* Stanford: Stanford University Press, 1999.

Barr, Colin. "An Irish Dimension to a British *Kulturkampf*?" *Journal of Ecclesiastical History* 56 (2005): 475–476.

Bassin, Mark. "Imperialer Raum/Nationaler Raum: Sibirien auf der kognitiven Landkarte Rußlands im 19. Jahrhundert." *Geschichte und Gesellschaft* 28 (2002): 378–403.

Bauerkämper, Arnd, and Christiane Eisenberg. "Introduction: Perceptions of Britain in Germany—Approaches, Methods and Analytical Dimensions." In *Britain as a Model of Modern Society? German Views*, edited by Arnd Bauerkämper and Christiane Eisenberg, 7–24. Augsburg: Wissner-Verlag, 2006.

Baumeister, Martin. *Parität und katholische Inferiorität: Untersuchungen zur Stellung des Katholizismus im Deutschen Kaiserreich*. Paderborn: Schöningh, 1987.

Bautz, Friedrich Wilhelm. "Theodor Hoßbach." In *Biographisch-Bibliographisches Kirchenlexikon*. Vol. II, edited by Friedrich Wilhelm Bautz, 1076–1078. Hamm: T. Bautz, 1990.

Beck, Heinrich, Dieter Geuenich, Heiko Steuer and Dietrich Hakelberg, eds. *Zur Geschichte der Gleichung "germanisch-deutsch": Sprache und Namen, Geschichte und Institutionen*. Berlin: Walter de Gruyter, 2004.

Becker, Frank. "Konfessionelle Nationsbilder im Deutschen Kaiserreich." In *Nation und Religion in der deutschen Geschichte*, edited by Heinz-Gerhard Haupt and Dieter Langewiesche, 389–418. Frankfurt and New York: Campus, 2001.

Becker, Winfried. *Georg von Hertling 1843–1919, Band I: Jugend und Selbstfindung zwischen Romantik und Kulturkampf*. Mainz: Matthias-Grünewald, 1981.

———. "Die Deutsche Zentrumspartei im Bismarckreich." In *Die Minderheit als Mitte: Die Deutsche Zentrumspartei in der Innenpolitik des Reiches 1871–1933*, edited by Winfried Becker, 9–45. Paderborn: Schöningh, 1986.

Beckmann, Christopher. "Lambert Lensing (1889–1965): Zeitungsverleger, Mitgründer der CDU, Landesvorsitzender der CDU Westfalen-Lippe." *Historisch-Politische Mitteilungen: Archiv für Christlich-Demokratische Politik* 14 (2007): 153–186.

Beeler, John F. *British Naval Policy in the Gladstone-Disraeli Era 1866–1880*. Stanford: Stanford University Press, 1997.

Belgum, Kirsten. *Popularizing the Nation: Audience, Representation, and the Production of Identity in Die Gartenlaube, 1853–1900*. Lincoln: University of Nebraska Press, 1998.

Bennette, Rebecca Ayako. "Confessional Mixing and Religious Differentiation in Nineteenth-Century Germany." PhD diss., Harvard University, 2002.

———. "Threatened Protestants: Confessional Conflict in the Rhine Province and Westphalia during the Nineteenth Century." *German History* 26 (2008): 168–194.

Berger, David. "Ratio Fidei fundamenta demonstrat. Fundamentaltheologisches Denken zwischen 1870 und 1960." In *Die katholisch-theologischen Disziplinen in Deutschland 1870–1962: Ihre Geschichte, ihr Zeitbezug*, edited by Hubert Wolf, 95–127. Paderborn: Schöningh, 1999.

Berger, Stefan. *The Search for Normality: National Identity and Historical Consciousness in Germany Since 1800.* Providence: Berghahn, 1997.

———. *Germany.* London: Arnold, 2004.

Berghahn, Volker. *Militarismus: Die Geschichte einer internationalen Debatte.* Leamington Spa: Berg, 1986.

———. *Imperial Germany 1871–1918: Economy, Society, Culture and Politics.* Providence: Berghahn, 1994.

Bhabha, Homi K. "Introduction: Narrating the Nation." In *Nation and Narration,* edited by Homi K. Bhabha, 1–7. London: Routledge, 1990.

Birke, Adolf M. "German Catholics and the Quest for National Unity." In *Nation-Building in Central Europe,* edited by Hagen Schulze, 51–63. Leamington Spa: Berg, 1987.

Bitterli, Urs. *Die "Wilden" und die "Zivilisierten": Grundzüge einer Geistes- und Kulturgeschichte der europäisch-überseeischen Begegnung.* Munich: C.H. Beck, 1976.

Bjork, James E. *Neither German Nor Pole: Catholicism and National Indifference in a Central European Borderland.* Ann Arbor: University of Michigan, 2008.

Blackbourn, David. "Roman Catholics, the Centre Party and Anti-Semitism in Imperial Germany." In *Nationalist and Racialist Movements in Britain and Germany before 1914,* edited by Paul M. Kennedy and Anthony J. Nicholls, 106–129. London: Macmillan, 1981.

———. "The Discreet Charm of the Bourgeoisie: Reappraising German History in the Nineteenth Century." In *The Peculiarities of German History: Bourgeois Society and Politics in Nineteenth-Century Germany,* edited by David Blackbourn and Geoff Eley, 159–292. Oxford: Oxford University Press, 1984.

———. "Liberals, Catholics and the State in Bismarck's Germany." In *Populists and Patricians: Essays in Modern German History,* edited by David Blackbourn, 143–167. London: Allen & Unwin, 1987.

———. *Marpingen: Apparitions of the Virgin Mary in Nineteenth-Century Germany.* New York: Knopf, 1994.

———. *The Fontana History of Germany 1780–1918: The Long Nineteenth Century.* London: Fontana, 1997.

———. "Das Kaiserreich transnational: Eine Skizze." in *Das Kaiserreich Transnational: Deutschland in der Welt, 1871–1914,* edited by Sebastian Conrad and Jürgen Osterhammel, 302–324. Göttingen: Vandenhoeck and Ruprecht, 2004.

Blackbourn, David, and James Retallack. "Introduction." In *Localism, Landscape, and the Ambiguities of Place: German-Speaking Central Europe, 1860–1930,* edited by David Blackbourn and James Retallack, 3–38. Toronto: University of Toronto Press, 2007.

Blanke, Richard. *Prussian Poland in the German Empire (1871–1900)*. Boulder: East European Monographs, 1981.

Blanning, T. C. W. *The French Revolution in Germany: Occupation and Resistance in the Rhineland, 1792–1802*. New York: Oxford University Press, 1983.

Blaschke, Olaf. "Wider die 'Herrschaft des modern-jüdischen Geistes': Der Katholizismus zwischen traditionellem Antijudaismus und modernem Antisemitismus." In *Deutscher Katholizismus im Umbruch zur Moderne*, edited by Wilfried Loth, 236–265. Stuttgart: Kohlhammer, 1991.

———. *Katholizismus und Antisemitismus im Deutschen Kaiserreich*. Göttingen: Vandenhoeck and Ruprecht, 1999.

———. *Konfessionen im Konflikt: Deutschland zwischen 1800 und 1970: ein zweites konfessionelles Zeitalter*. Göttingen: Vandenhoeck and Ruprecht, 2002.

———. *Offenders or Victims? German Jews and the Causes of Modern Catholic Antisemitism*. Lincoln: University of Nebraska Press, 2009.

Blaschke, Olaf, and Frank Michel Kuhlemann, eds. *Religion im Kaiserreich: Milieus—Mentalitäten—Krisen*. Gütersloh: Chr. Kaiser, 1996.

Blessing, Werner. *Staat und Kirche in der Gesellschaft: institutionelle Autorität und mentaler Wandel in Bayern während des 19. Jahrhunderts*. Göttingen: Vandenhoeck and Ruprecht, 1982.

Blom, Ida, Karen Hagemann, and Catherine Hall, eds. *Gendered Nations: Nationalism and Gender Order in the Long Nineteenth Century*. Oxford: Berg, 2000.

Blome, Astrid. "Die Zeitung als historische Quelle. Ein Beispiel aus dem petrinischen Rußland." In *Zeitung, Zeitschrift, Intelligenzblatt und Kalender: Beiträge zur historischen Presseforschung*, edited by Astrid Blome, 161–176. Bremen: Lumière, 2000.

Boehm, Laetitia. "Katholizismus, Bildungs- und Hochschulwesen nach der Säkularisation." In *Katholizismus, Bildung und Wissenschaft im 19. Jahrhundert*, edited by Anton Rauscher, 9–59. Paderborn: Schöningh, 1987.

Bollenbeck, Georg. *Bildung und Kultur: Glanz und Elend eines deutschen Deutungsmusters*. Frankfurt a. M.: Insel, 1994.

Borutta, Manuel. *Antikatholizismus: Deutschland und Italien im Zeitalter der europäischen Kulturkämpfe*. Göttingen: Vandenhoeck and Ruprecht, 2010.

Bosl, Karl. "Die Verhandlungen über den Eintritt der süddeutschen Staaten in den Nortdeutschen Bund und die Entstehung der Reichsverfassung." In *Reichsgründung 1870/71*, edited by Theodor Schieder and E. Deuerlein, 148–163. Stuttgart: Seewald Verlag, 1970.

Bowersock, G. W. *Julian the Apostate*. Cambridge: Harvard University Press, 1978.

Boyarin, Daniel. *Dying for God: Martyrdom and the Making of Christianity and Judaism*. Stanford: Stanford University Press, 1999.

Brandt, Hans Jürgen. *Eine katholische Universität in Deutschland?: das Ringen der Katholiken in Deutschland um eine Universitätsbildung im 19. Jahrhundert*. Cologne: Böhlau, 1981.

———."Katholische Kirche und Urbanisation im deutschen Kaiserreich." *Blätter für deutsche Landesgeschichte* 128 (1992): 221–239.

Breuilly, John. "Introduction." In *Nations and Nationalism*, 2nd ed., by Ernest Gellner. Ithaca: Cornell University Press, 2008.

Brinkmann, Ernst. *Evangelische Kirche im Dortmunder Raum in der Zeit von 1815 bis 1945*. Dortmund: Historischer Verein, 1979.

Brubaker, Rogers. *Nationalism Reframed: Nationhood and the National Question in the New Europe*. Cambridge: University of Cambridge Press, 1996.

———. "Myths and Misconceptions in the Study of Nationalism." In *State of the Nation: Ernest Gellner and the Theory of Nationalism*, edited by John A. Hall, 298–301. Cambridge: Cambridge University Press, 1998.

Bruch, Rüdiger vom. "The Academic Disciplines and Social Thought." In *Imperial Germany: A Historiographical Companion*, edited by Roger Chickering, 343–376. Westport, CT: Greenwood, 1996.

Bruchhausen, Esther-Beatrice von. "Das Zeichen im Kostümball—Marianne und Germania in der politischen Ikonographie." PhD diss., Martin-Luther-Universität, Halle-Wittenberg, 2000.

Buchner, Rudolf. *Die elsässische Frage und das deutsch-französische Verhältnis im 19. Jahrhundert*. Darmstadt: Wissenschaftliche Buchgesellschaft, 1969.

Burgdorf, Wolfgang. "'Reichsnationalismus' gegen 'Territorialnationalismus': Phasen der Intensivierung des nationalen Bewußtseins in Deutschland seit dem Siebenjährige Krieg." In *Föderative Nation*, edited by Dieter Langewiesche and Georg Schmidt, 157–190. München: Oldenbourg Wissenschaftsverlag GmbH, 2000.

Busch, Norbert. "Die Feminisierung der Frömmigkeit." In *Wunderbare Erscheinungen: Frauen und katholische Frömmigkeit im 19. und 20. Jahrhundert*, edited by Irmtraud Götz von Olenhusen, 203–219. Paderborn: Schöningh, 1995.

———. *Katholische Frömmigkeit und Moderne: die Sozial- und Metalitätsgeschichte des Herz-Jesu-Kultes in Deutschland zwischen Kulturkampf und Erstem Weltkrieg*. Gütersloh: Chr. Kaiser, 1997.

Buschmann, Nikolaus. "Auferstehung der Nation? Konfession und National-
    ismus vor der Reichsgründung in der Debatte jüdischer, protestantischer
    und katholischer Kreise." In *Nation und Religion in der deutschen
    Geschichte,* edited by Heinz-Gerhard Haupt and Dieter Langewiesche,
    333–388. Frankfurt a.M.: Campus, 2001.

Bußmann, Walter. *Zwischen Preußen und Deutschland: Friedrich Wilhelm IV.
    Eine Biographie.* Berlin: Siedler, 1990.

Cary, Noel D. *The Path to Christian Democracy: German Catholics and the
    Party System from Windthorst to Adenauer.* Cambridge: Harvard Univer-
    sity Press, 1996.

Cassels, Alan. *Ideology and International Relations in the Modern World.*
    London: Routledge, 1996.

Chickering, Roger. "'Casting Their Gaze More Broadly': Women's Patriotic
    Activism in Imperial Germany." *Past and Present* 118 (1988): 156–185.

Clark, Christopher. *Iron Kingdom: The Rise and Downfall of Prussia, 1600–
    1947.* Cambridge, MA: Harvard University Press, 2008.

Clark, Christopher, and Wolfram Kaiser, eds. *Culture Wars: Secular-Catholic
    Conflict in Nineteenth-Century Europe.* Cambridge: Cambridge University
    Press, 2003.

———. "Introduction: The European Culture Wars." In *Culture Wars:
    Secular-Catholic Conflict in Nineteenth-Century Europe,* edited by
    Christopher Clark and Wolfram Kaiser, 1–10. Cambridge: Cambridge
    University Press, 2003.

Confino, Alon. *The Nation as a Local Metaphor: Württemberg, Imperial
    Germany, and National Memory, 1871–1918.* Chapel Hill: University of
    North Carolina Press, 1997.

———. "Collective Memory and Cultural History: Problems of Method."
    American Historical Review 102 (1997): 1386–1403.

———. *Germany as a Culture of Remembrance: Promises and Limits of
    Writing History.* Chapel Hill: University of North Carolina Press, 2006.

Confino, Alon and Peter Fritzsche. *The Work of Memory: New Directions in
    the Study of German Society and Culture.* Urbana: University of Illinois
    Press, 2002.

Connerton, Paul. *How Societies Remember.* Cambridge: Cambridge University
    Press, 1989.

Conrad, Sebastian, and Jürgen Osterhammel, eds. *Das Kaiserreich Transna-
    tional: Deutschland in der Welt 1871–1914.* Göttingen: Vandenhoeck and
    Ruprecht, 2004.

Conze, Werner. "Militarismus." In *Geschichtliche Grundbegriffe: historisches
    Lexikon zur politisch-sozialen Sprache in Deutschland,* Vol. 4, edited by Otto
    Brunner, Werner Conze, and Reinhart Koselleck, 1–47. Stuttgart: Klett, 1978.

———. "'Deutschland' und 'deutsche Nation' als historische Begriffe." In *Die Rolle der Nation in der deutschen Geschichte und Gegenwart: Beiträge zu einer internationalen Konferenz in Berlin (West) von 16. bis 18. Juni 1983*, edited by Otto Büsch and James Sheehan, 3–20. Berlin: Colloquium, 1985.

Coppa, Frank J. *Politics and the Papacy in the Modern World*. Westport, CT: Praeger, 2008.

Cowell-Meyers, Kimberly. *Religion and Politics in the Nineteenth Century: The Party Faithful in Ireland and Germany*. Westport, CT: Praeger, 2002.

Craig, John E. *Scholarship and Nation Building: The Universities of Strasbourg and Alsatian Society, 1870–1939*. Chicago: University of Chicago Press, 1984.

Cramer, Kevin. "The Cult of Gustavus Adolphus: Protestant Identity and German Nationalism." In *Protestants, Catholics and Jews, 1800–1914*, edited by Helmut Walser Smith, 97–120. Oxford: Berg, 2001.

———. *The Thirty Years' War and German Memory in the Nineteenth Century*. Lincoln: University of Nebraska, 2007.

Cremer, Douglas J. "The Limits of Maternalism: Gender Ideology and the South German Catholic Workingwomen's Associations, 1904–1918." *Catholic Historical Review* 87 (2001): 428–452.

Dann, Otto. *Nation und Nationalismus in Deutschland, 1770–1990*. Munich: Beck, 1993.

Dann, Otto, and Miroslav Hroch. "Einleitung." In *Patriotismus und Nationsbildung am Ende des Heiligen Römischen Reiches*, edited by Otto Dann, Miroslav Hroch, and Johannes Koll. Cologne: SH-Verlag, 2003: 9–18.

Darnton, Robert. *The Great Cat Massacre and Other Episodes in French Cultural History*. New York: Vintage, 1985.

Daum, Andreas. "Science, Politics, and Religion: Humboldtian Thinking and the Transformation of Civil Society in Germany, 1830–1870." *Osiris* 17 (2002): 107–140.

———. *Wissenschaftspopularisierung im 19. Jahrhundert: Bürgerliche Kultur, naturwissenschaftliche Bildung und die deutsche Öffentlichkeit, 1848–1914*. Munich: Oldenbourg, 2002.

Demandt, Alexander. "Introduction." In *A History of Rome Under the Emperors*, by Theodor Mommsen and edited by Barbara Demandt and Alexander Demandt, English edition edited by Thomas Wiedemann and translated by Clare Krojzl, 1–35. London: Routledge, 1996.

Desrosieres, Alain. *The Politics of Large Numbers: A History of Statistical Reasoning*. Translated by Camille Naish. Cambridge: Harvard, 1998.

Deuerlein, Ernst. "Die Bekehrung des Zentrums zur nationalen Idee." *Hochland* 62 (1970): 432–449.

————. "Die Konfrontation von Nationalstaat und national bestimmter Kultur." In *Reichsgründung 1870/71*, edited by Theodor Schieder and E. Deuerlein, 226–258. Stuttgart: Seewald Verlag, 1970.

Dickerhof, Harald. "Staatliches Bildungsmonopol: Die Idee einer katholischen Universität und die Schulen der katholischen Theologie im 19. Jahrhundert." *Archiv für Kulturgeschichte* 66 (1984): 175–214.

————. "Die katholischen Universitäten im Heiligen Römischen Reich deutscher Nation des 18. Jahrhunderts." In *Universitäten und Aufklärung*, edited by Notker Hammerstein, 21–48. Göttingen: Wallstein-Verlag, 1995.

Dietrich, Richard. "Berlins Weg zur Industrie- und Handelsstadt." In *Berlin: Zehn Kapitel seiner Geschichte*, edited by Richard Dietrich, 159–198. Berlin: Gruyter, 1981.

Dietrich, Tobias. *Konfession im Dorf: Westeuropäische Erfahrungen im 19. Jahrhundert*. Cologne: Böhlau, 2004.

Dippel, Horst. "Deutsches Reich und Französische Revolution. Politik und Ideologie in der deutschen Geschichtsschreibung, 1871–1945." In *Frankreich und Deutschland im 18. Und 19. Jahrhundert im Vergleich*, edited by Matthias Middell, 97–111. Leipzig: Leipziger Univ.-Verl., 1992.

Ditt, Karl. "Regionalbewußtsein und Regionalismus in Westfalen vom Kaiserreich bis zur Bundesrepublik." *Comparativ* 13 (2003): 17–31.

Dorneich, Julius. *Franz Josef Buss und die katholische Bewegung in Baden*. Freiburg: Herder, 1979.

Dörner, Andreas. *Politischer Mythos und symbolische Politik: Der Hermannmythos zur Entstehung des Nationalbewußtseins der Deutschen*. Reinbek bei Hamburg: Rowohlt, 1996.

Douglas, Ann. *The Feminization of American Culture*. London: Papermac, 1996.

Doyé, Werner M. "Arminius." In *Deutsche Erinnerungsorte, Band III*, edited by Etienne François and Hagen Schultze, 587–602. Munich: Verlag C.H. Beck, 2001.

Düding, Dieter. "The Nineteenth-Century German Nationalist Movement as a Movement of Societies." In *Nation-Building in Central Europe*, edited by Hagen Schulze, 19–49. Leamington Spa: Berg, 1987.

Düffler, Jost. "Foreign Policy." In *Imperial Germany: A Historiographical Companion*, edited by Roger Chickering, 409–429. Westport, CT: Greenwood, 1996.

Düwell, Kurt. "Selbstreflexion und Sicht im Rheinland auf das Ruhrgebiet: Einführung." In *Das Ruhrgebiet in Rhienland und Westfalen: Koexistenz und Konkurrenz des Raumbewusstseins im 19. und 20. Jahrhundert*, edited by Karl Ditt and Klaus Tenfelde, 19–21. Paderborn: Schöningh, 2007.

Dwyer, Philip. *Modern Prussian History 1830–1947.* New York: Longman, 2001.

Eley, Geoff. "How and Where is German History Centered?" In *German History from the Margins,* edited by Neil Gregor, Nils H. Roemer, and Mark Roseman, 268–286. Bloomington, IN: Indiana University Press, 2006.

Ellwein, Thomas. *Die deutsche Universität: Vom Mittelalter bis zur Gegenwart.* Königstein: Athenäum, 1985.

Epstein, Klaus. "Erzberger and the German Colonial Scandals, 1905–1910." *The English Historical Review* 74 (1959): 637–663.

Erhart, Walter. "Written Capitals and Capital Topography: Berlin and Washington in Travel Literature." In *Berlin-Washington, 1800–2000: Capital Cities, Cultural Representation, and National Identities,* edited Andreas Daum and Christof Mauch, 51–78. Cambridge: Cambridge University Press, 2005.

Estel, Bernd. *Nation und nationale Identität: Versuch einer Rekonstruktion.* Weisbaden: Westdeutscher Verlag, 2002.

Evans, Ellen Lovell. *The German Center Party 1870–1933: A Study in Political Catholicism.* Carbondale, IL: Southern Illinois University Press, 1981.

Fehrenbach, Heide. "Rehabilitating Fatherland: Race and German Remasculinization." *Signs* 24 (1998): 107–127.

Feldman, Gerald D. *The Great Disorder: Politics, Economics, and Society in the German Inflation 1914–1924.* Oxford: Oxford University Press, 1997.

Fels, Heinrich. *Martin Deutinger.* Munich: Köstel-Pustet: 1938.

Fisch, Jörg. "Zivilisation, Kultur." In *Geschichtliche Grundbegriffe: historisches Lexikon zur politisch-sozialen Sprache in Deutschland,* Vol. 7, edited by Otto Brunner, Werner Conze, and Reinhart Koselleck, 679–774. Stuttgart: Klett-Cotta, 1992.

Fonk, Friedrich Hermann. *Das staatliche Mischehenrecht in Preußen vom allgemeinen Landrecht an: Eine rechtsgeschichtliche Untersuchung.* Bielefeld: Gieseking, 1961.

Foucault, Michel. *The History of Sexuality, Volume I: An Introduction,* translated by Robert Hurley. New York: Vintage, 1990.

François, Etienne. "Regionale Unterschiede der Lese- und Schreibfähigkeit in Deutschland im 18. und 19. Jahrhundert." *Jahrbuch für Regionalgeschichte* 17 (1990): 154–172.

Frankel, Richard E. *Bismarck's Shadow: The Cult of Leadership and the Transformation of the German Richt, 1898–1945.* Oxford: Berg, 2005.

Frend, W. H. C. *The Rise of Christianity.* Philadelphia: Fortress, 1984.

Fritzsche, Peter. *Reading Berlin 1900.* Cambridge, MA: Harvard University Press, 1996.

Fuchs, Konrad. *Gestalten und Ereignisse aus Schlesiens Wirtschaft, Kultur and Politik.* Dortmund: Forschungsstelle Ostmitteleuropa, 1992.

Gaddis, Michael. *There is No Crime for Those Who Have Christ: Religious Violence in the Christian Roman Empire.* Berkeley: University of California Press, 2005.

Gall, Lothar. *Germania: Eine deutsche Marianne?* Bonn: Bouvier, 1993.

———. "Die Germania als Symbol nationaler Identität im 19. und 20. Jahrhundert." In *Bürgertum, liberale Bewegung und Nation,* edited by Lothar Gall, 311–337. Munich: Oldenbourg, 1996.

Galos, Adam. "Image of a Pole in 19th Century Germany." *Polish Western Affairs* 19 (1978): 175–196.

Gebhard, Gunther, Oliver Geisler, and Steffen Schröter. "Heimatdenken: Konjunkturen und Konturen. Staat einer Einleitung." In *Heimat. Konturen und Konjunkturen eines umstrittenen Konzepts,* edited by Gunther Gebhard, Oliver Geisler, and Steffen Schröter, 9–56. Bielefeld: Transcript, 2007.

Geiss, Imanuel. *German Foreign Policy, 1871–1914.* London: Routledge, 1976.

Gellner, Ernest. *Nations and Nationalism.* Ithaca: Cornell University Press, 1983.

Geuss, Raymond. "Kultur, Bildung, Geist." *History and Theory* 35 (1996): 151–164.

Gillis, John R. "Memory and Identity: The History of a Relationship." In *Commemorations: The Politics of National Identity,* edited by John R. Gillis, 3–26. Princeton: Princeton University Press, 1994.

Gottwald, Herbert. "Mainzer Katholikenverein." In *Lexikon zur Parteiengeschichte: die bürgerlichen und kleinbürgerlichen Parteien und Verbände in Deutschland (1789–1945),* Band III, edited by Dieter Fricke, 274–276. Leipzig: VEB Bibliographisches Institut Leipzig, 1985.

Gräf, Holger Th. "Reich, Nation und Kirche in der gross- und kleindeutschen Historiographie." *Historisches Jahrbuch,* 116 (1992): 367–394.

Green, Abigail. *Fatherlands: State-Building and Nationhood in Nineteenth-Century Germany.* Cambridge: Cambridge University Press, 2001.

———. "Intervening in the Public Sphere: German Governments and the Press, 1815–1870." *The Historical Journal* 44 (2001): 155–75.

———. "The Federal Alternative? A New View of Modern German History." *Historical Journal* 46 (2003): 187–202.

Gregor, Niel, Nils Roemer, and Mark Roseman, eds. *German History from the Margins.* Bloomington, IN: Indiana University Press, 2006.

Grieve, Hermann. "Die gesellschaftliche Bedeutung der christlich-jüdischen Differenz: Zur Situation im deutschen Katholizismus." In *Juden in*

Wilhelminischen Deutschland, 1890–1914, edited by Werner Mosse, 349–388. Tübingen: Mohr, 1976.

Grogan, Geraldine. *The Noblest Agitator: Daniel O'Connell and the German Catholic Movement, 1830–1850.* Dublin: Veritas, 1991.

Groh, Otto. *Die unerkannte Kulturmacht: Grundlegung der Zeitungswissenschaft.* 7 vols. Berlin: Walter de Gruyter, 1960–72.

Gross, Michael B. "Kulturkampf and Unification: German Liberalism and the War against the Jesuits." *Central European History* 30 (1997): 545–566.

———. "Catholic Missionary Crusade and the Protestant Revival in Nineteenth-Century Germany." In *Protestants, Catholics, and Jews in Germany, 1800–1914,* edited by Helmut Walser Smith, 245–265. Oxford: Berg, 2001.

———. *The War Against Catholicism: Liberalism and the Anti-Catholic Imagination in Nineteenth-Century Germany.* Ann Arbor: University of Michigan, 2005.

Gründer, Horst. "Rechtskatholizismus im Kaiserreich und in der Weimarer Republik." *Westfälische Zeitschrift* 134 (1984): 107–155.

———. "Nation und Katholizismus im Kaiserreich." In *Katholizismus, nationaler Gedanke und Europa seit 1800,* edited by Albrecht Langner, 65–87. Paderborn: Schöningh, 1985.

Haase, Amine. *Katholische Presse und die Judenfrage: Inhaltsanalyse katholischer Periodika am Ende des 19. Jahrhunderts.* Pullach: Verlag Dokumentation, 1975.

Haberl, Othmar Nikola, and Tobias Korenke, eds. *Politische Deutungskulturen: Festschrift für Karl Rohe.* Baden-Baden: Nomos, 1999.

Hagemann, Karen. "Of 'Manly Valor' and 'German Honor': Nation, War, and Masculinity in the Age of the Prussian Uprising Against Napoleon." *Central European History* 30 (1997): 187–220.

———."A Valorous *Volk* Family: the Nation, the Military, and the Gender Order in Prussia in the Time of the Anti-Napoleonic Wars, 1806–15." In *Gendered Nations: Nationalisms and Gender Order in the Long Nineteenth Century,* edited by Ida Blom, Karen Hagemann, and Catherine Hall, 179–205. Oxford: Berg, 2000.

———. *"Mannlicher Muth und Teutsche Ehre": Nation, Militär und Geschlecht zur Zeit der Antinapoleonischen Kriege Preußens.* Paderborn: Schöningh, 2002.

———. "Female Patriots: Women, War and the Nation in the Period of the Prussian-German Anti-Napoleonic Wars." *Gender and History* 16 (2004): 397–424.

————. "German Heroes: The Cult of the Death for the Fatherland in Nineteenth-Century Germany." In *Masculinities in Politics and War: Gendering Modern History,* edited by Stefan Dudink, Karen Hagemann, and John Tosh, 116–134. Manchester: Manchester University Press, 2004.

Halbwachs, Maurice. *On Collective Memory.* Edited by Lewis A. Coser. Chicago: University of Chicago Press, 1992.

Hansen, Joseph. *Die Rheinprovinz, 1815–1915. Hundert Jahre preußischer Herrschaft am Rhein,* Vol. 1. Bonn: A. Marcus and E. Weber, 1917.

Hardtwig, Wolfgang. "Bürgertum, Staatssymbolik und Staatsbewußtsein im Deutschen Kaiserreich 1871–1914." In *Nationalismus und Bürgerkultur in Deutschland 1500–1914: Ausgewählte Aufsatze,* edited by Wolfgang Hardtwig, 191–218. Göttingen: Vandenhoeck and Ruprecht, 1994.

Harp, Stephen L. *Learning to be Loyal: Primary Schooling as Nation Building in Alsace and Lorraine 1850–1940.* Dekalb: Northern Illinois Press, 1998.

Harris, Erika. *Nationalism: Theories and Cases.* Edinburgh: Edinburgh University Press, 2009.

Harris, Ruth. *Lourdes: Body and Spirit in the Secular Age.* New York: Viking, 1999.

Hart, Bill. " 'The Kindness of the Blessed Virgin': Faith, Succour, and the Cult of Mary among Christian Hurons and Iroquois in Seventeenth-Century New France." In *Spiritual Encounters: Interactions Between Christianity and Native Religions in Colonial America,* edited by Nicholas Griffiths and Fernando Cervantes, 65–90. Birmingham: University of Birmingham Press, 1999.

Hartmannsgruber, Friedrich. *Die Bayerische Patriotenpartei 1868–1887.* Munich: Beck, 1986.

Harvey, Elizabeth. "Pilgrimages to the 'Bleeding Border'; Gender and Rituals of Nationalist Protest in Germany, 1919–39." *Women's History Review* 9 (2000): 201–229.

Hastings, Derek. "Fears of a Feminized Church: Catholicism, Clerical Celibacy, and the Crisis of Masculinity in Wilhelmine Germany." *European History Quarterly* 38 (2008): 34–65.

Haupt, Heinz-Gerhard. "Religion and Nation in Europe in the 19th Century: Some Comparative Notes." *Estudos Avançados* 22 (2008): 77–94.

Haupt, Heinz-Gerhard, and Dieter Langewiesche, eds. *Nation und Religion in der deutschen Geschichte.* Frankfurt and New York: Campus, 2001.

Hausen, Karin. "Die Polarisierung der 'Geschlechtscharaktere'—Eine Spiegelung der Dissoziation von Erwerbs- und Familienleben." In *Sozialge-*

schichte der Familie in der Neuzeit Europas. Neue Forschungen, edited by Werner Conze, 363–393. Stuttgart: Klett, 1976.

Healy, Róisín. "Anti-Jesuitism in Imperial Germany: The Jesuit as Androgyne." In *Protestants, Catholics and Jews in Germany, 1800–1914,* edited by Helmut Smith, 153–181. Oxford andNew York: Berg, 2001.

———. *The Jesuit Specter in Imperial Germany.* Boston: Brill, 2003.

Hehl, Ulrich von. "Die Zentrumspartei—Ihr Weg von 'Reichsfeind' zur parlimentarischen Schlüsselstellung in Kaiserreich und Republik." In *Auf dem Weg zum modernen Parteienstaat: Zur Entstehung, Organisation und Struktur politischer Parteien in Deutschland und den Niederlanden,* edited by Hermann Walther von der Dunk and Horst Lademacher, 97–120. Melsungen: Kasseler Forschungen zur Zeitgeschichte, 1986.

Heidrich, Christian. *Katholische Neusser Presse und Vereine im Kulturkampf.* Neuss: Stadtarchiv Neuss, 1994.

Heilbronner, Oded. "Wohin verschwand das katholische Bürgertum?—oder der Ort des katholischen Bürgertums in der neueren deutschen Historiographie." *Zeitschrift für Religions- und Geistesgeschichte* 47 (1995): 320–337.

———. "Regionale Aspekte zum katholischen Bürgertum. Oder Die Besonderheit des katholischen Bürgertums im ländlichen Süddeutschland." *Blätter für Deutsche Landesgeschichte* 131 (1995): 223–259.

———. "From Ghetto to Ghetto: The Place of German Catholic Society in Recent Historiography." *Journal of Modern History* 72 (2000): 453–495.

Heinen, Ernst. "Antisemitische Strömungen im politischen Katholizismus während des Kulturkampfes." In *Geschichte in der Gegenwart: Festschrift für Kurt Kluxen,* edited by Ernst Heinen and Hans J. Schoeps, 259–299. Paderborn: Schöningh, 1972.

———. "Aufbruch-Erneuerung-Politik," *Rheinische Vierteljahrsblätter* 64 (2000): 266–289.

Herminghouse, Patricia. "The Ladies' Auxiliary of German Literature: Nineteenth-Century Women Writers and the Quest for a National Literary History." In *Gender and Germanness,* edited by Patricia Herminghouse and Magda Mueller, 145–158. Providence: Berghahn Books, 1997.

Herminghouse, Patricia, and Magda Mueller. "Introduction: Looking for Germania." In *Gender and Germanness,* edited by Patricia Herminghouse and Magda Mueller, 1–18. Providence: Berghahn Books, 1997.

Hervieu-Léger, Danièle. *Religion as a Chain of Memory.* New Brunswick, NJ: Rutgers University Press, 2000.

Herzog, Dagmar. *Intimacy and Exclusion: Religious Politics in Pre-Revolutionary Baden.* Princeton: Princeton, 1996.

Hettling, Manfred, and Stefan-Ludwig Hoffmann. "Der bürgerliche Werte-himmel: Zum Problem individueller Lebensführung im 19. Jahrhundert." *Geschichte und Gesellschaft* 23(1997): 333–359.

Heuvel, Jon Vanden. *A German Life in the Age of Revolution: Joseph Görres, 1776–1848.* Washington D.C.: Catholic University of America Press, 2001.

Hewitson, Mark. *National Identity and Political Thought in Germany: Wilhelmine Depictions of the French Third Republic, 1890–1914.* Oxford: Oxford University Press, 2000.

Hiery, Hermann. *Reichstagswahlen im Reichsland: ein Beitrag zur Landesge-schichte von Elsass-Lothringen und zur Wahlgeschichte des Deutschen Reiches, 1871–1918.* Düsseldorf: Droste, 1986.

Hildebrand, Klaus. "Great Britain and the Foundation of the German Reich." In *German Foreign Policy from Bismarck to Adenauer: The Limits of Statecraft,* by Klaus Hildebrand, translated by Louise Willmot, 3–42. London: Unwin, 1989.

———. *Das vergangene Reich: Deutsche Außenpolitik von Bismarck bis Hitler 1871–1945.* Stuttgart: Deutsche-Verlags Anstalt, 1995.

Hiort, Pontus. "Constructing Another Kind of German: Catholic Commemora-tions of German Unification in Baden, 1870–1876." *Catholic Historical Review* 93 (2007): 17–46.

———. "Negotiating Identities: South German Catholics and the Formation of National Identity, 1871–1914." PhD. diss., Northern Illinois University, 2007.

Hobsbawm, Eric, and Terence Ranger, eds. *The Invention of Tradition.* Cambridge: Cambridge University Press, 1983.

Hoffman, Stefan-Ludwig. "Brothers or Strangers? Jews and Freemasons in Nineteenth-century Germany." *German History* 18 (2000): 143–161.

———. *The Politics of Sociability: Freemasonry and German Civil Society, 1840–1918.* Translated by Tom Lampert. Ann Arbor: University of Mich-igan Press, 2007.

Hooson, David, ed. *Geography and National Identity.* Cambridge, MA: Blackwell, 1994.

Horne, John. "Masculinity in Politics and War in the Age of Nation-States and World Wars, 1850–1950." In *Masculinities in Politics and War: Gendering Modern History,* edited by Stefan Dudink, Karen Hagemann, and John Tosh, 23–40. Manchester: Manchester University Press, 2004.

Horne, John, and Alan Kramer. *German Atrocities, 1914: A History of Denial.* New Haven: Yale University Press, 2001.

Höroldt, Dietrich. "Mischehen und konfessionelle Kindererziehung im Bereich der rheinischen Landeskirche seit 1815." *Rheinische Vierteljahrsblätter* 39 (1975): 147–188.

Horstmann, Johannes, and Antonius Liedhegener, eds. *Konfession, Milieu, Moderne. Konzeptionelle Positionen und Kontroversen zur Geschichte von Katholizismus und Kirche im 19. und 20. Jahrhundert.* Schwerte: Katholische Akademie Schwerte, 2001.

Howard, Thomas Albert. *Protestant Theology and the Making of the Modern German University.* Oxford: Oxford University Press, 2006.

Hroch, Miroslav. *Das Europa der Nationen: Die moderne Nationsbildung im europäischen Vergleich.* Göttingen: Vandenhoeck and Ruprecht, 2005.

Huber, Augustin Kurt. *Kirche und deutsche Einheit im 19. Jahrhundert: Ein Beitrag zur österreichisch-deutschen Kirchengeschichte.* Königstein: Königsteiner Institut für Kirchen- und Geistesgeschichte der Sudetenländer, 1966.

Hübinger, Gangolf. "Geschichte als leitende Orientierungswissenschaft im 19. Jahrhundert." *Berichte zur Wissenschaftsgeschichte* 11 (1988): 149–158.

———. *Kulturprotestantismus und Politik: zum Verhältnis von Liberalismus und Protestantismus im wilhelminischen Deutschland.* Tübingen: J.C.B. Mohr, 1994.

———. "Confessionalism." In *Imperial Germany: A Historiographical Companion,* edited by Roger Chickering, 156–184. Westport, CT: Greenwood, 1996.

Hüser, Dietmar. "Selbstfindung durch Fremdwahrnehmung in Kriegs- und Nachkriegszeiten. Französische Nation und deutscher Nachbar seit 1870." In *Das Bild "des Anderen". Politische Wahrnehmung im 19. und 20. Jahrhundert,* edited by Birgit Aschmann and Michael Salewski, 55–79. Stuttgart: Steiner, 2000.

Hüther, Andreas. "A Transnational Nation-Building Process: Philologists and Universities in Nineteenth-Century Ireland and Germany." In *Ireland and Europe in the Nineteenth Century,* edited by Leon Litvack and Colin Graham, 101–111. Dublin: Four Courts, 2006.

Jarausch, Konrad. *Students, Society, and Politics in Imperial Germany: The Rise of Academic Illiberalism.* Princeton: Princeton University Press, 1982.

———. *Deutsche Studenten 1800–1970.* Frankfurt am Main: Suhrkamp, 1984.

Jarausch, Konrad, and Michael Geyer. *Shattered Past: Reconstructing German Histories*. Princeton: Princeton University Press, 2003.

Jaworski, Rudolf. "Zwischen Polenliebe und Polenschelte." In *Das Bild 'des Anderen': Politische Wahrnemung im 19. und 20. Jahrhundert*, edited by Birgit Aschmann and Michael Salewski, 80–89. Stuttgart: Steiner, 2000.

Jedin, Hubert. "Freiheit und Aufstieg des deutschen Katholizismus zwischen 1848 und 1870." In *Kirche des Glaubens, Kirche der Geschichte: Ausgewählte Aufsätze und Vorträge*, edited by Hubert Jedin, 469–484. Freiburg: Herder, 1966.

Jeismann, Michael. *Das Vaterland der Feinde: Studien zum nationalen Feindbegriff und Selbstverständnis in Deutschland und Frankreich, 1792–1918*. Stuttgart: Klett-Cotta, 1992.

Kaelble, Hartmut. "Die vergessene Gesellschaft im Westen?: Das Bild der Deutschen von der französischen Gesellschaft, 1871–1914." *Revue d'Allemagne* 21 (1989): 181–196.

Keinemann, Friedrich. *Das Kölner Erieignis, Sein Widerhall in der Rheinprovinz und in Westfalen, Teil I*. Münster: Aschendorf, 1974.

Kelley, Alfred. *The Descent of Darwin: The Popularization of Darwinism in Germany, 1860–1914*. Chapel Hill: University of North Carolina Press, 1981.

———. "The Franco-Prussian War and Unification in German History Schoolbooks." In *German Unifications and the Change of Literary Discourse*, edited by Walter Pape, 37–60. Berlin: Walter de Gruyter, 1993.

Kennedy, Katharine D. "A Nation's Readers: Cultural Integration and the Schoolbook Canon in Wilhelmine Germany." *Paedagogica Historica* 33:2 (1997): 459–480.

Kipper, Rainer. *Der Germanenmythos im deutschen Kaiserreich: Formen und Funktionen historischer Selbstthematisierung*. Göttingen: Vandenhoeck and Ruprecht, 2002.

Kirchner, Hubert. *Das Papsttum und der deutsche Katholizismus 1870–1958*. Leipzig: Evangelische Verlagsanstalt, 1992.

Kisky, Wilhelm. *Der Augustinus-Verein zur Pflege der katholischen Presse von 1878 bis 1928*. Düsseldorf: Verlag des Augustinus-Vereins, 1928.

Kißling, Johannes Baptist. *Geschichte des Kulturkampfes im Deutschen Reiche*. 3 vols. Freiburg: Herder: 1911–1916.

Kitchen, Martin. *A History of Modern Germany, 1800–2000*. Malden, MA: Blackwell, 2006.

Klöcker, Michael "Das katholische Bildungsdefizit in Deutschland: Eine historische Analyse." *Geschichte in Wissenschaft und Unterricht* 32 (1981).

————. "Katholizismus und Bildungsbürgertum: Hinweise zur Erforschung vernachlässigter Bereiche der deutschen Bildungsgeschichte im 19. Jahrhundert." In *Bildungsbürgertum im 19. Jahrhundert, Teil 2: Bildungsgüter und Bildungswissen,* edited by Reinhart Koselleck, 117–138. Stuttgart: Klett-Cotta, 1990.

Kohl, Wilhelm. *Kleine Westfälische Geschichte.* Düsseldorf: Patmos, 1994.

Köhle-Hezinger, Christel. *Evangelisch, Katholisch: Untersuchungen zu konfessionellem Vorurteil und Konflikt im 19. und 20. Jahrhundert vornehmlich am Beispiel Württembergs.* Tübingen: Tübinger Vereinigung für Volkskunde, 1976.

Köhler, Joachim. "Die katholische Kirche." In *Geschichte Schlesiens,* Band III, edited by Josef Joachem Menzel, 226–228. Stuttgart: Thorbecke, 1999.

Kohn, Hans. *Nationalism: Its Meaning and History.* Princeton: Van Nostrand, 1955.

Kontje, Todd. *Women, the Novel, and the German Nation, 1771–1871: Domestic Fiction in the Fatherland.* Cambridge: Cambridge University Press, 1998.

Körner, Hans-Michael. *Geschichte des Königreichs Bayern.* Beck: Munich, 2006.

Koselleck, Reinhart, ed. *Bildungsbürgertum im 19. Jahrhundert, Teil II: Bildungsgüter und Bildungswissen.* Stuttgart: Klett-Cotta, 1990.

Koshar, Rudy. *From Monuments to Traces: Artifacts of German Memory, 1870–1990.* Berkeley; University of California Press, 2000.

Koszyk, Kurt. *Deutsche Presse im 19. Jahrhundert.* Teil II. Berlin: Colloquium, 1966.

Kramer, Gustav. *Die Stellung des Präsidenten Ludwig von Gerlach zum politischen Katholizismus.* Breslau: Marcus, 1931.

Kruft, Hanno-Walter. *Geschichte der Architekturtheorie.* 5th ed. Munich: C.H. Beck, 2004.

Kuhlemann, Frank Michael. "Niedere Schulen." In *Handbuch der deutschen Bildungsgeschichte, Band IV: 1870–1918,* edited by Christa Berg, 179–227. Munich: C.H. Beck, 1991.

————. "Das Kaiserreich als Erzeihungsstaat." *Geschichte in Wissenschaft und Unterricht* 49 (1998): 728–745.

Kühne, Thomas. *Handbuch der Wahlen zum Preussischen Abgeordnetenhaus 1867–1918: Wahlergebnisse, Wahlbündnisse und Wahlkandidaten.* Düsseldorf: Droste, 1994.

Kurtz, Johann Heinrich. *Church History.* Vol. III. Translated by John Macpherson. New York: Funk and Wagnalls, 1890.

Lamberti, Marjorie. "State, Church, and the Politics of School Reform during the Kulturkampf." *Central European History* 19 (1986): 63–81.

————. *State, Society, and the Elementary School in Imperial Germany.* New York: Oxford University Press, 1989.

Lange, Josef. *Die Stellung der überregionalen katholischen deutschen Tagespresse zum Kulturkampf in Preußen (1871–1878).* Frankfurt a.M.: Peter Lang, 1974.

Langer, Michael. *Zwischen Vorurteil und Aggression: Zum Judenbild in der deutschsprachigen katholischen Volksbildung des 19. Jahrhunderts.* Freiburg: Herder, 1994.

Langewiesche, Dieter. "Vom Gebildeten zum Bildungsbürger? Umrisse eines katholischen Bildungsbürgertum im wilhelminischen Deutschland." In *Liberalismus und Sozialismus: Gesellschaftsbilder-Zukunftsvisionen-Bildungskonzeptionen,* edited by Friedrich Lenger, 177–205. Bonn: Dietz, 2003.

Langewiesche, Dieter, and Georg Schmidt, eds. *Föderative Nation: Deutschlandkonzepte von der Reformation bis zum Ersten Weltkrieg.* Münich: Oldenbourg, 2000.

Laqueur, Walter. *Russia and Germany: A Century of Conflict.* New Brunswick, NJ: Transaction Publishers, 1990.

Large, David Clay. *Berlin.* New York: Basic Books, 2000.

Laube, Stefan. "Konfessionelle Brüche in der nationalen Heldengalerie— Protestantische, katholische und jüdische Erinnerungsgemeinschaften im deutschen Kaiserreich (1871–1918)." In *Nation und Religion in der deutschen Geschichte,* edited by Heinz-Gerhard Haupt and Dieter Langewiesche, 293–332. Frankfurt and New York: Campus, 2001.

————. *Fest, Religion und Erinnerung: konfessionelles Gedächtnis in Bayern von 1804–1917.* Münich: Beck, 1999.

Leerssen, Joep. "As Others See, Among Others, Us: The Anglo-German Relationship in Context." In *As Others See Us: Anglo-German Perceptions,* edited by Harald Husemann, 69–79. Frankfurt a.M: Peter Lang, 1994.

Lenoir, Timothy. *Politik im Tempel der Wissenschaft: Forschung und Machtausübung im deutschen Kaiserreich.* Frankfurt: Campus, 1992.

Lepp, Claudia. *Protestantisch-liberaler Aufbruch in die Moderne: Der deutsche Protestantenverein in der Zeit der Reichsgründung und des Kulturkampfes.* Gütersloh: Chr. Kaiser, 1996.

————. "Protestanten Feiern Ihre Nation—Die Kulturprotestantischen Ursprünge des Sedantages." *Historisches Jahrbuch* 118 (1998): 201–222.

Lepper, Herbert. *Volk, Kirche und Vaterland. Wahlaufrufe, Aufrufe, Satzungen und Statuten des Zentrums 1870–1933: Eine Quellensammlung zur Geschichte insbesondere der Rheinischen und Westfälischen Zentrumspartei.* Düsseldorf: Droste, 1998.

Lepsius, M. Rainer. "Parteiensystem und Sozialstruktur: Zum Problem der Demokratisierung der deutschen Gesellschaft." In *Deutsche Parteien vor 1918*, edited by Gerhard A. Ritter, 56–80. Cologne, 1973.

Lidtke, Vernon. *The Alternative Culture: Socialist Labor in Imperial Germany.* New York: Oxford University Press, 1985.

Liedhegener, Antonius. *Christentum und Urbanisierung: Katholiken und Protestanten in Münster und Bochum 1830–1933.* Paderborn: Schöningh, 1997.

Lill, Rudolf. "Die deutschen Katholiken und die Juden in der Zeit von 1850 bis zur Machtübernahme Hitlers." In *Kirche und Synagoge: Handbuch zur Geschichte von Christen und Juden*, Vol. 2, edited by Karl Heinrich Rengstorf and Siegfried von Kortzfleisch, 370–420. Stuttgart: Klett, 1970.

———. "Die deutschen Katholiken und Bismarcks Reichsgründung." In *Reichsgründung 1870/1871: Tatsachen, Kontroversen, Interpretationen*, edited by Theodor Schieder and Ernst Deuerlein, 345–365. Stuttgart: Seewald, 1970.

———. "Der Kulturkampf in Preußen und im Deutschen Reich (bis 1878)." In *Handbuch der Kirchengeschichte*, Vol. 6, no. 2, edited by Hubert Jedin, 28–47. Freiburg: Herder, 1973.

———. "The *Kulturkampf* in Prussia and in the German Empire until 1878." In *The Church in the Industrial Age*, edited by Hubert Jedin, Roger Aubert, and John Dolan, translated by Margit Resch, 26–45. London: Crossroad, 1981.

———. "Grossdeutsch und Kleindeutsch im Spannungsfeld der Konfessionen." In *Probleme des Konfessionalismus in Deutschland seit 1800*, edited by Anton Rauscher, 29–47. Paderborn: Schöningh, 1984.

———. "Katholizismus und Nation bis zur Reichsgründung." In *Katholizismus, nationaler Gedanke und Europa seit 1800*, edited by Albrecht Langner, 51–64. Paderborn: Schöningh, 1985.

Lipp, Carola. "Bräute, Mütter, Gefährtinnen. Frauen und politische Öffentlichkeit in der Revolution 1848." In *Grenzgängerinnen: Revolutionäre Frauen im 18. und 19. Jahrhundert. Weibliche Wirklichkeit und männliche Phantasien*, edited Helga Grubitzsch, Hannelore Cyrus, and Elke Haarbusch, 71–92. Düsseldorf: Schwann, 1985.

Liulevicius, Vejas Gabriel. *War Land on the Eastern Front: Culture, National Identity, and German Occupation in World War I.* Cambridge: Cambridge University Press, 2000.

Löffler, Klemens. *Geschichte der katholischen Presse Deutschlands.* M. Gladbach: Volksvereins-Verlag, 1924.

Lorenz, Chris. "Representations of Identity: Ethnicity, Race, Class, Gender and Religion. An Introduction to Conceptual History." In *The Contested*

Nation: Ethnicity, Class, Religion and Gender in National Histories, edited by Stefan Berger and Chris Lorenz, 24–59. Basingstoke: Palgrave, 2008.

Loth, Wilfried. "Zwischen autoritärer und demokratischer Ordnung: Das Zentrum in der Krise des Wilhelminischen Reiches." In *Die Minderheit als Mitte: Die Deutsche Zentrumspartei in der Innenpolitik des Reiches, 1871–1933,* edited by Winfried Becker, 47–69. Paderborn: Schöningh, 1986.

———. "Soziale Bewegungen im Katholizismus des Kaiserreichs." *Geschichte und Gesellschaft* 17 (1991): 279–310.

———. "Integration und Erosion: Wandlungen des katholischen Milieus in Deutschland." In *Deutscher Katholizismus im Umbruch zur Moderne,* edited by Wilfried Loth, 266–281. Stuttgart: Kohlhammer, 1991.

Marchand, Suzanne. *Down from Olympus: Archaeology and Philhellenism in Germany.* Princeton: Princeton University Press, 1996.

———. *German Orientalism in the Age of Empire: Religion, Race, and Scholarship.* Washington D.C.: German Historical Institute; New York: Cambridge University Press, 2009.

Martin, Matthias. *Der katholische Weg ins Reich: der Weg des deutschen Katholizismus vom Kulturkampf hin zur staatstragenden Kraft.* Frankfurt a.M.: P. Lang, 1998.

May, Joseph. *Geschichte der Generalversammlungen der Katholiken Deutschlands (1848–1902).* Cologne: Bachem, 1903.

Mazura, Uwe. *Zentrumspartei und Judenfrage 1870/71–1933: Verfassungsstaat und Minderheitenschutz.* Mainz: Matthias-Grünewald, 1994.

McClelland, Charles E. "Structural Change and Social Reproduction in German Universities, 1870–1920." *History of Education* 15 (1986): 177–193.

Meinecke, Friederich. *The Age of German Liberation, 1795–1815.* Translated by Peter Paret and Helmut Fischer. Berkeley: University of California Press, 1977.

Meiwes, Relinde. "Religiosität und Arbeit als Lebensform für katholische Frauen: Kongregationen im 19. Jahrhundert." In *Frauen unter dem Patriarchat der Kirchen: Katholikinnen und Protestantinnen im 19. und 20. Jahrhundert,* edited by Irmtraud Götz von Olenhusen et al., 69–88. Stuttgart: Kohlhammer, 1995.

———. *'Arbeiterinnen des Herrn': Katholische Frauenkongregationen im 19. Jahrhundert.* Frankfurt: Campus, 2000.

Mergel, Thomas. "Mapping Milieus Regionally: On the Spatial Rootedness of Collective Identities in the Nineteenth Century." In *Saxony in German*

History: Culture, Society, and Politics, 1830–1933, edited by James Retallack, 77–95. Ann Arbor: University of Michigan Press, 2000.

————. *Zwischen Klasse und Konfession: katholisches Bürgertum im Rheinland, 1794–1914.* Göttingen: Vandenhoeck and Ruprecht, 1994.

————. "Grenzgänger: Das katholische Bürgertum im Rheinland zwischen bürgerlichem und katholischem Milieu 1870–1914." In *Religion im Kaiserreich: Milieus—Mentalitäten—Krisen,* edited by Olaf Blaschke and Frank Michel Kuhlemann, 166–192. Gütersloh: Chr. Kaiser, 1996.

Mohr, Hubert. *Katholische Orden und deutscher Imperialismus.* Berlin: Akademie Verlag, 1965.

Molik, Witold. "Assimilation der polnischen Intelligenz im preußischen Teilungsgebiet durch Bildung 1871–1914." *Archiv für Sozialgeschichte* 32 (1992): 81–93.

Mommsen, Wilhelm. "Die Zeitung als historische Quelle." Reprinted in *Das Institut für Zeitungsforschung in Dortmund: 1926: Eine Disziplin nimmt Gestalt an; Festschrift zum 80jährigen Jubiläum,* edited by Gabriele Toepser-Ziegert and Karen Peter, 56–64. Dortmund: Insitut für Zeitungsforschung, 2006.

Morsey, Rudolf. "Die deutschen Katholiken und der Nationalstaat zwichen Kulturkampf und Erstem Weltkrieg." *Historisches Jahrbuch* 90 (1970): 31–64.

————. "Georg Graf v. Hertling." In *Zeitgeschichte in Lebensbildern: Aus dem deutschen Katholizismus des 20. Jahrhunderts,* edited by Rudolf Morsey, 43–52. Mainz: Grünewald, 1973.

————. "Der Kulturkampf." In *Der soziale und politische Katholizismus: Entwicklungslinien in Deutschland 1803–1963,* Band I, edited by Anton Rauscher, 80–89. Munich: Günter Olzog Verlag, 1981.

————. "Ludwig Windthorst. Größe und Grenzen von Bismarcks Gegenspieler." In *Von Windthorst bis Adenauer: Ausgewählte Aufsätze zu Politik, Verwaltung und politischem Katholizismus im 19. und 20. Jahrhundert,* edited by Ulrich von Hehl et.al., 145–157. (Paderborn: Schöningh, 1997).

————. "Streiflichter zur Geschichte der deutschen Katholikentage 1848–1931." In *Von Windthorst bis Adenauer: Ausgewählte Aufsätze zu Politik, Verwaltung und politischem Katholizismus im 19. und 20. Jahrhundert,* edited by Ulrich von Hehl et. al., 187–200. Paderborn: Schöningh, 1997.

Mosse, George. *The Nationalization of the Masses: Political Symbolism and Mass Movements in Germany from the Napoleonic Wars through the Third Reich.* New York: Fertig, 1975.

————. *Nationalism and Sexuality: Middle-Class Morality and Sexual Norms in Modern Europe.* Madison: University of Wisconsin Press, 1985.

————. *The Image of Man: The Creation of Modern Masculinity.* New York: Oxford University Press, 1996.

Müller-Dreier, Armin. *Konfession in Politik, Gesellschaft und Kultur des Kaiserreichs: Der Evangelische Bund 1886–1914.* Gütersloh: Chr. Kaiser, 1998.

Nägelke, Hans-Dieter. "Gelehrte Gemeinschaft und wissenschaftlicher Großbetrieb: Hochschulbau als Spiegel von Wissenschaftsidee und –praxis im 19. und frühen 20. Jahrhundert." *Berichte zur Wissenschaftsgeschichte* 21 (1998): 103–114.

Naujoks, Eberhard. "Bismarck und die Organisation der Regierungspresse." *Historische Zeitschrift* 205 (1967): 46–80.

Nippel, Wilfried. "'Rationeller Fortschritt' auf dem 'antiquarischen Bauplatz'—Mommsen als Architekt des 'Römischen Staatsrechts'." In *Theodor Mommsen: Wissenschaft und Politik im 19. Jahrhundert,* edited by Alexander Demandt, Andreas Goltz, and Heinrich Schlange-Schöningen, 246–258. Berlin: Walter de Gruyter, 2005.

Nipperdey, Thomas. *Deutsche Geschichte 1800–1866: Bürgerwelt und starker Staat.* Munich: Beck, 1983.

————. *Religion im Umbruch.* Munich: Beck, 1988.

————. *Deutsche Geschichte, 1866–1918.* 2 Vols. Munich: Beck, 1990.

Nowottnick, Georg. *Geburt, Hochzeit, Tod in Sitte, Brauch und Volksdichtung.* Berlin: Wiedmannische Buchhandlung, 1935.

O'Donnell, Krista, Nancy Reagin, and Renate Bridenthal, eds. *The Heimat Abroad: The Boundaries of Germanness.* Ann Arbor: University of Michigan, 2005.

O'Malley, Martin. *Wilhelm Ketteler and the Birth of Modern Catholic Social Thought: A Catholic Manifesto in Revolutionary 1848.* Munich: Utz, 2008.

Olenhusen, Irmtraud Götz von. *Wunderbare Erscheinungen: Frauen und katholische Frömmigkeit im 19. und 20. Jahrhundert.* Paderborn: Schöningh, 1995.

Orlowski, Hubert. *"Polnische Wirtschaft": Zum deutschen Polendiskurs der Neuzeit.* Wiesbaden: Harrassowitz, 1996.

Paddock, Troy R. E. *Creating the Russian Peril: Education, the Public Sphere, and National Identity in Imperial Germany, 1890–1914.* Rochester, NY: Camden House, 2010.

Paletschek, Sylvia. *Frauen und Dissens: Frauen im Deutschkatholizismus und in den freien Gemeinden 1841–1852.* Göttingen: Vandenhoeck and Ruprecht, 1990.

———. "Religiöser Dissens um 1848: Das Zusammenspiel von Klasse, Geschlecht und anderen Differenzierungslinien." *Geschichte und Gesellschaft* 18(1992): 161–178.

Parent, Thomas. *"Passiver Widerstand" im preußischen Verfassungskonflikt: die Kölner Abgeordnetenfeste.* Cologne: DME-Verlag, 1982.

Parenti, Michael. *Inventing Reality: The Politics of News Media.* New York: St. Martin's, 1986.

Pastor, Ludwig von. *Johannes Janssen: Ein Lebensbild, vornehmlich nach den ungedruckten Briefen und Tagebüchern desselben.* Freiburg: Herder, 1892.

———. *August Reichensperger. Sein Leben und sein Wirken auf dem Gebiet der Politik, der Kunst, und der Wissenschaft.* Vol. II. Freiburg im Breisgau: Herder, 1899.

———. "Johannes Janssen." In *Allgemeine Deutsche Biographie*, Bd. 50, 733–741. Leipzig: Dunker and Humblot, 1905.

Pauley, Bruce F. *From Prejudice to Persecution: A History of Austrian Anti-Semitism.* Chapel Hill: University of North Carolina Press, 1992.

Paz, D. G. *Popular Anti-Catholicism in Mid-Victorian England.* Standford: Stanford University Press, 1992.

Peterson, Brent O. "The Fatherland's Kiss of Death: Gender and Germany in Nineteenth-Century Historical Fiction." In *Gender and Germanness: Cultural Productions of the Nation*, edited by Patricia Herminghouse and Magda Mueller, 82–97. Providence: Berghahn, 1997.

———. *History, Fiction, and Germany: Writing the Nineteenth-Century Nation.* Detroit: Wayne State University Press, 2005.

Pickus, Keith H. *Constructing Modern Identities: Jewish University Students in Germany 1815–1914.* Detroit: Wayne State University Press, 1999.

Pierson, Ruth Roach. "Nations: Gendered, Racialized, Crossed with Empire." In *Gendered Nations, Nationalism and Gender Order in the Long Nine-teenth Century*, edited by Ida Blom, Karen Hagemann, and Catherine Hall, 41–62. Oxford: Berg, 2000.

Pleitner, Berit. *Die 'vernünftige' Nation: zur Funktion von Stereotypen über Polen und Franzosen im deutschen nationalen Diskurs 1850 bis 1871.* Frankfurt a.M: Peter Lang, 2001.

Plessen, Marie-Louise von, ed. *Marianne und Germania 1789–1889: Frank-reich und Deutschland: Zwei Welten—Eine Revue: Eine Ausstellung der Berliner Festspiele GmbH im Rahmen der ›46. Berliner Festwochen 1996‹ als Beitrag zur Städtepartnerschaft Paris-Berlin im Martin-Gropius-Bau, Stresemannstraße 110 vom 15. September 1996 bis 5. Januar 1997.* Berlin: Argon, 1996.

Pohlsander, Hans A. *National Monuments and Nationalism in 19th Century Germany.* Bern: Lang, 2008.

Quataert, Jean H. *Staging Philanthropy: Patriotic Women and the National Imagination in Dynastic Germany, 1813–1916.* Ann Arbor, University of Michigan Press, 2001.

Raab, Heribert. "'Katholische Wissenschaft,'—Ein Postulat und seine Variationen in der Wissenschafts- und Bildungspolitik deutscher Katholiken während des 19. Jahrhunderts." In *Katholizismus, Bildung und Wissenschaft im 19. Jahrhundert,* edited by Anton Rauscher, 61–91. Paderborn: Schöningh, 1987.

Rahden, Till van. *Juden und andere Breslauer: die Beziehungen zwischen Juden, Protestanten und Katholiken in einer deutschen Grossstadt von 1860 bis 1925.* Göttingen: Vandenhoeck and Ruprecht, 2000.

Rassem, Mohammed, and Justin Stagl. "Zur Geschichte der Statistik und Staatsbeschreibung in der Neuzeit." *Zeitschrift für Politik* 24 (1977): 81–86.

Reagin, Nancy R. "Review: Recent Work on German National Identity: Regional? Imperial? Gendered? Imaginary?" *Central European History* 37 (2004): 286–288.

———. *Sweeping the Nation: Domesticity and National Identity in Germany, 1870–1945.* New York: Cambridge University Press, 2007.

Reeken, Dietmar von. *Kirchen im Umbruch zur Moderne: Milieubildungsprozesse im nordwestdeutschen Protestantismus, 1849–1914.* Chr. Kaiser: Gütersloh, 1999.

Reiber, Hans Joachim. *Die katholische deutsche Tagespresse unter dem Einfluß des Kulturkampfes.* Görlitz: Hoffmann and Reiber, 1930.

Ribbe, Wolfgang, and Jürgen Schmädeke. *Kleine Berlin-Geschichte.* 3rd ed. Berlin: Stapp, 1994.

Ricciotti, Giuseppe. *Julian the Apostate.* Translated by Joseph Costelloe. Milwaukee: Bruce, 1960.

Riesenberger, Dieter. "Katholische Militarismuskritik im Kaiserreich." In *Militarismus in Deutschland 1871 bis 1945: Zeitgenössiche Analysen und Kritik,* edited by Wolfram Wette, 97–114. Münster: Lit, 1999.

Ringer, Fritz. "Higher Education in Germany in the Nineteenth Century." *Journal of Contemporary History* 2 (1967): 123–138.

———. "Comparing Two Academic Cultures: the University in Germany and in France Around 1900." *History of Education* 16 (1987): 181–188.

———. "Bildung: The Social and Ideological Context of the German Historical Tradition." *History of European Ideas* 10 (1989): 193–202.

———. "A Sociography of German Academics, 1863–1938." *Central European History* 25 (1992): 251–280.

Ritter, Gerhard, and Merith Niehuss. *Wahlgeschichtliches Arbeitsbuch: Materialien zur Statistik des Kaiserreichs 1871–1918.* Munich: Beck, 1980.

Rohe, Karl. *Wahlen und Wählertraditionen in Deutschland: kulturelle Grundlagen deutscher Parteien und Parteiensysteme im 19. und 20. Jahrhundert.* Frankfurt am Main: Suhrkamp, 1992.

Roos, Lothar. "Wilhelm Emmanuel Frhr. von Ketteler." In *Zeitgeschichte in Lebensbildern: aus dem deutschen Katholizismus des 19. und 20. Jahrhunderts,* edited by Jürgen Aretz, Rudolf Morsey, and Anton Rauscher, 22–36. Mainz: Matthias-Grünewald, 1980.

Rösener, Werner. "Das katholische Bildungsdefizit im deutschen Kaiserreich— ein Erbe der Säkularisation vom 1803?" *Historisches Jahrbuch der Görres-Gesellschaft* 112 (1992): 104–127.

Ross, Ronald. *The Failure of Bismarck's Kulturkampf: Catholicism and State Power in Imperial Germany, 1871–1887.* Washington D.C.: Catholic University of America Press, 1998.

Rublack, Ulinka. "Wench and Maiden: Women, War and the Pictorial Function of the Feminine in German Cities in the Early Modern Period." *History Workshop Journal* 44 (1997): 1–21.

Ruff, Mark Edward. "Integrating Religion into the Historical Mainstream: Recent Literature on Religion in the Federal Republic of Germany." *Central European History* 42 (2009): 307–337.

Ryan, Mary. *Civic Wars: Democracy and Public Life in the American City during the Nineteenth Century.* Berkeley: University of California Press, 1997.

Saal, Friedrich Wilhelm. "Die katholische Kirche in Dortmund und die Industrialisierung im Ruhrgebiet." In *Seelsorge und Diakonie in Berlin,* edited by Kasper Elm and Hans-Dietrich Loock, 136–143. Berlin: Walter de Gruyter, 1990.

Schaefer, Richard. "Program for a New Catholic *Wissenschaft*: Devotional Activism and Catholic Modernity in the Nineteenth Century." *Modern Intellectual History* 4 (2007): 433–462.

Schama, Simon. *Landscape and Memory.* New York: Knopf, 1995.

Schambach, Karin. *Stadtbürgertum und Industrieller Umbruch: Dortmund, 1780–1870.* Munich: Oldenbourg, 1996.

Schaser, Angelika. "The Challenge of Gender: National Historiography, Nationalism, and National Identities." In *Gendering Modern Germany*

History: Rewriting Historiography, edited by Karen Hagemann and Jean H. Quataert, 39–62. Oxford: Berg, 2007.

Schauff, Johannes. *Das Wahlverhalten der deutschen Katholiken im Kaiserreich und in der Weimarer Republik: Untersuchungen aus dem Jahre 1928.* Edited by Rudolf Morsey. Mainz: Matthias-Grünewald, 1975.

Schellhase, Kenneth C. *Tacitus in Renaissance Political Thought.* Chicago: University of Chicago Press, 1976.

Schenk, Frithjof Benjamin. "Mental Maps. Die Konstruktion von geographischen Räumen in Europa seit der Aufklärung." *Geschichte und Gesellschaft* 28 (2002): 493–514.

Schieder, Wolfgang. "Kirche und Revolution. Sozialgeschichtliche Aspekte der Trierer Wallfahrt von 1844." *Archiv für Sozialgeschichte* 14 (1974): 419–454.

Schiele, Friedrich Michael. "Apostolikumstreit." In *Die Religion in Geschichte und Gegenwart,* 1st ed., Band I, edited by H. D. Betz, 601–605. Tübingen: Mohr Siebeck, 1909.

Schlange-Schöningen, Heinrich. "Konstantin der Große und der 'Kulturkampf': Bemerkungen zur Bewertung des ersten christlichen Kaisers in Theodor Mommsens Römischer Kaisergeschichte." *Gymnasium* 104 (1997): 385–397.

Schmidt-Volkmar, Erich. *Der Kulturkampf in Deutschland 1871–1890.* Göttingen: Musterschmidt, 1962.

Schmolke, Michael. *Die schlechte Presse. Katholiken und Publizistik zwischen "Katholik" und "Publik" 1821–1968.* Münster: Regensberg, 1971.

Schöllgen, Gregor. *Imperialismus und Gleichgewicht: Deutschland, England und die orientalische Frage 1871–1914.* Munich: Oldenbourg, 2000.

Schörs, Heinrich. "Hermesianische Pfarrer." *Annalen des Historischen Vereins für den Niederrhein* 103 (1919): 76–183.

Schwarz, Angela. *Der Schlüssel zur modernen Welt: Wissenschaftspopularisierung in Großbritanien und Deutschland im Übergang zur Moderne (ca. 1870–1914).* Stuttgart: Steiner, 1999.

Sheehan, James. *German Liberalism in the Nineteenth Century.* Chicago: University of Chicago Press, 1978.

Shibata, Masako. "Controlling National Identity and Reshaping the Role of Education." *History of Education* 33 (2004): 75–85.

Silverman, Dan P. "Political Catholicism and Social Democracy in Alsace-Lorraine, 1871–1914." *The Catholic Historical Review* 52 (1966): 39–65.

Smith, Helmut Walser. "Religion and Conflict: Protestants, Catholics, and Anti-Semitism in the State of Baden in the Era of Wilhelm II." *Central European History* 27 (1994): 283–314.

————. "The Learned and the Popular Discourse of Anti-Semitism in the Catholic Milieu of the Kaiserreich." *Central European History* 27 (1994): 315–328.

————. *German Nationalism and Religious Conflict: Culture, Ideology, Politics, 1870–1914.* Princeton: Princeton University Press, 1995.

————. *The Continuities of German History: Nation, Religion, and Race across the Long Nineteenth Century.* Cambridge: Cambridge University Press, 2008.

Smith, Helmut Walser, ed. *Protestants, Catholics, and Jews in Germany, 1800–1914.* Oxford: Berg, 2001.

Smith, Woodruff D. *Politics and the Sciences of Culture in Germany, 1814–1920.* New York: Oxford University Press, 1991.

Sontag, Raymond James. *Germany and England: Background of Conflict, 1848–1894.* New York: D. Appleton-Century, 1938.

Southern, Pat. *The Roman Empire from Severus to Constantine.* London: Routledge, 2001.

Spael, Wilhelm. *Görres-Gesellschaft, 1876–1941.* Paderborn: Schöningh, 1957.

Spencer, Elaine Glovka. *Police and the Social Order in German Cities: The Düsseldorf District, 1848–1914.* DeKalb: Northern Illinois Press, 1992.

Spencer, Philip, and Howard Wollman, eds. *Nationalism: A Critical Introduction.* London: SAGE, 2002.

Sperber, Jonathan. "Roman Catholic Religious Identity in Rhineland-Westphalia, 1800–70: Quantitative Examples and Some Political Implications." *Social History* 7 (1982): 305–318.

————. *Popular Catholicism in Nineteenth-Century Germany.* Princeton: Princeton University Press, 1984.

————. "Festivals of National Unity in the German Revolution of 1848–9." *Past and Present* 136 (1992): 114–148.

————. *The Kaiser's Voters: Electors and Elections in Imperial Germany.* Cambridge: Cambridge University Press, 1997.

Stambolis, Barbara. "Nationalisierung trotz Ultramontanisierung oder: 'Alles für Deutschland. Deutschland aber für Christus': Mentalitätsleitende Wertorientierung deutscher Katholiken im 19. und 20. Jahrhundert." *Historische Zeitschrift* 269 (1999): 57–97.

Stargardt, Nicholas. *The German Idea of Militarism: Radical and Socialist Critics, 1866–1914.* Cambridge: Cambridge University Press, 1994.

Stehlin, Stewart A. "Bismarck and the Secret Use of the Guelph Fund." *Historian* 33 (1970): 21–39.

Steinhoff, Anthony. "Christianity and the Creation of Germany." In *The Cambridge History of Christianity: World Christianities*, Vol. 8, edited by

Sheridan Gilley and Brian Stanley, 282–300. Cambridge: Cambridge University Press, 2006.

————. *The Gods of the City: Protestantism and Religious Culture in Strasbourg, 1870–1914.* Leiden: Brill, 2008.

Stoetzler, Marcel. *The State, the Nation and the Jews: Liberalism and the Antisemitism Dispute in Bismarck's Germany.* Lincoln: University of Nebraska Press, 2008.

Stökl, Günther. *Osteuropa und die Deutschen: Geschichte und Gegenwart einer spannungsreichen Nachbarschaft.* 3rd ed. Stuttgart: Hirzel, 1982.

Stroh, Wilfried. *Latein ist tot, es lebe Latein!: kleine Geschichte einer großen Sprache.* Berlin: List, 2007.

Struck, Bernhard. *Nicht West—Nicht Ost: Frankreich und Polen in der Wahrnehmung deutscher Reisender zwischen 1750 und 1850.* Göttingen: Wallstein, 2006.

Swartout, Lisa. "Culture Wars: Protestant, Catholic, and Jewish Students at German Universities, 1890–1914." In *Religion und Nation, Nation und Religion: Beiträge zu einer unbewältigten Geschichte,* edited by Michael Geyer and Hartmut Lehmann, 157–175. Göttingen: Wallstein, 2004.

Szöllösi-Janze, Margit. "Science and Social Space: Transformations in the Institutions of *Wissenschaft* from the Wilhelmine Empire to the Weimar Republic." *Minerva* 43 (2005): 339–360.

Tacke, Charlotte. *Denkmal im sozialen Raum: Nationale Symbole in Deutschland und Frankreich im 19. Jahrhundert.* Göttingen: Vandenhoeck and Ruprecht, 1995.

Tal, Uriel. *Christians and Jews in Germany: Religion, Politics, and Ideology in the Second Reich, 1870–1914.* Ithaca: Cornell University Press, 1975.

Thijs, Krijn. "The Metaphor of the Master: 'Narrative Hierarchy' in National Historical Cultures of Europe." In *The Contested Nation: Ethnicity, Class, Religion and Gender in National Histories,* edited by Stefan Berger and Chris Lorenz, 60–74. Basingstoke: Palgrave, 2008.

Timm, Hermann. "Bildungsreligion im deutschsprachigen Protestantismus— eine grundbegriffliche Perspektiverung." In *Bildungsbürgertum im 19. Jahrhundert, Teil II: Bildungsgüter und Bildungswissen,* edited by Reinhart Koselleck, 57–79. Stuttgart: Klett-Cotta, 1990.

Tipton, Frank B. *A History of Modern Germany since 1815.* Berkeley: University of California Press, 2003.

Tooze, J. Adam. *Statistics and the German State, 1900–1945: The Making of Modern Economic Knowledge.* Cambridge: Cambridge University Press, 2001.

Umbach, Maiken, ed. *German Federalism: Past, Present, Future.* Basingstoke: Palgrave, 2002.

Ungern-Sternberg, Wolfgang von. "Medien." In *Handbuch der deutschen Bildungsgeschichte,* Band III, edited by Karl-Ernst Jeismann and Peter Lundgreen, 382. Munich: C.H. Beck, 1987.

Verdery, Katherine. "Whither 'Nation' and 'Nationalism'?" *Daedalus* 122 (1993): 37–45.

Vick, Brian. *Defining Germany: The 1848 Frankfurt Parliamentarians and National Identity.* Cambridge, MA: Harvard University Press, 2002.

Vinzent, Markus. *Der Ursprung des Apostolikums im Urteil der kritischen Forschung.* Göttingen: Vandenhoeck and Ruprecht, 2006.

Vital, David. *A People Apart: The Jews in Europe, 1789–1939.* Oxford: Oxford University Press, 1999.

Vogel, Jakob. "Militärfeiern in Deutschland und Frankreich als Rituale der Nation (1871–1914)." In *Nation und Emotion. Deutschland und Frankreich im Vergleich. 19. und 20. Jahrhundert,* edited by Étienne François, Hannes Siegrist, and Jakob Vogel, 199–214. Göttingen: Vandenhoeck and Ruprecht, 1995.

———. "Zwischen protestantischen Herrscherideal und Mittelaltermystik. Wilhelm I. und die 'Mythomotorik' des Deutschen Kaiserreichs." In *"Gott mit uns": Nation, Religion und Gewalt im 19. und frühen 20. Jahrhundert,* edited by Gerd Krumeich and Hartmut Lehmann, 213–230. Göttingen: Vandenhoeck and Ruprecht, 2000.

Vögler, Max. "Similar Paths, Different 'Nations'?: Ultramontanism and the Old Catholic Movement in Upper Austria, 1870–71." In *Different Paths to the Nation: Regional and National Identities in Central Europe and Italy, 1830–70,* edited by Laurance Cole, 180–199. Basingstoke: Palgrave, 2007.

Warner, Marina. *Alone of All her Sex: The Myth and the Cult of the Virgin Mary.* New York: Knopf, 1976.

Weber, Christoph. "Der deutsche Katholizismus und die Herausforderung des protestantischen Bildungsanspruchs." In *Bildungsbürgertum im 19. Jahrhundert, Teil II: Bildungsgüter und Bildungswissen,* edited by Reinhart Koselleck, 139–167. Stuttgart: Klett-Cotta, 1990.

———. *"Eine starke, enggeschlossene Phalanx": Der politische Katholizismus und die erste deutsche Reichstagswahl 1871.* Essen: Klartext, 1992.

Weber, Thomas. *Our Friend "the Enemy": Elite Education in Britain and Germany before World War I.* Stanford: Stanford University Press, 2008.

Weichlein, Siegfried. *Nation und Region: Integrationsprozesse im Bismarck-reich.* Düsseldorf: Droste, 2004.

Weindling, Paul Julian. *Darwinism and Social Darwinism in Imperial Germany: The Contribution of the Cell Biologist Oscar Hertwig (1849–1922)*. Stuttgart: Fischer, 1991.

Wells, Colin. *The Roman Empire*. 2nd ed. Cambridge, MA: Harvard University Press, 1992.

Wende, Peter. "Models of Britain for Nineteenth-Century Germany." In *Britain as a Model of Modern Society? German Views*, edited by Arnd Bauerkämper and Christiane Eisenberg, 25–39. Augsburg: Wissner-Verlag, 2006.

Westergaard, Herald. *Contributions to the History of Statistics*. London: P.S. King & Son, Ltd., 1932.

Wette, Wolfram. *Militarismus in Deutschland: Geschichte einer kriegerischen Kultur*. Frankfurt a.M.: Fischer, 2008.

White, Dan S. "Regionalism and Particularism." In *Imperial Germany: A Historiographical Companion*, edited by Roger Chickering 131–155. Westport, CT: Greenwood, 1996.

Williamson, George S. *The Longing for Myth: Religion and Aesthetic Culture from Romanticism to Nietzsche*. Chicago: University of Chicago Press, 2004.

Windell, George C. *The Catholics and German Unity 1866/1871*. Minneapolis: University of Minnesota Press, 1954.

Wolf, Hubert. "Der Historiker ist kein Prophet. Zur theologischen (Selbst-) Marginalisierung der katholischen deutschen Kirchengeschichtsschreibung zwischen 1870 und 1960." In *Die katholisch-theologischen Disziplinen in Deutschland 1870–1962*, edited by Hubert Wolf with Claus Arnold, 71–93. Paderborn: Schöningh, 1999.

Wolff, Larry. *Inventing Eastern Europe: The Map of Civilization on the Mind of the Enlightenment*. Stanford: Stanford University Press, 1994.

Wolfframm, Peter Bruno Max. *Die deutsche Außenpolitik und die großen deutschen Tageszeitungen, 1871–1890*. Zeulenroda: B. Sporn, 1936.

Woolf, Stuart. "Statistics and the Modern State." *Comparative Studies in Society and History* 31 (1989): 588–604.

Wyrwa, Ulrich. "Heinrich von Treitschke. Geschichtsschreibung und öffentliche Meinung im Deutschland des 19. Jahrhunderts." In *Zeitschrift für Geschichtswissenschaft* 51 (2003): 781–792.

Yonke, Eric. "The Problems of the Middle Class in German Catholic History: The Nineteenth-Century Rhineland Revisited." *Catholic Historical Review* 88 (2002): 263–280.

Yuval-Davis, Nira. "Gender and Nation." In *Women, Ethnicity and Nationalism: The Politics of Transition*, edited by Rich Wilford and Robert L. Miller, 23–35. London: Routledge, 1998.

Zalar, Jeffrey T. " 'Knowledge is Power': The *Borromäusverein* and Catholic Reading Habits in Imperial Germany." *Catholic Historical Review* 86 (2000): 20–46.

———. "The Process of Confessional Inculturation: Catholic Reading in the 'Long Nineteenth Century," in *Protestants, Catholics and Jews, 1800–1914*, edited by Helmut Walser Smith, 121–152. Oxford: Berg, 2001.

———. "Knowledge and Nationalism in Imperial Germany: A Cultural History of the Association of Saint Charles Borromeo, 1980–1914." PhD diss., Georgetown University, 2002.

Zantop, Suzanne. *Colonial Fantasies: Conquest, Family, and Nation in Precolonial Germany, 1770–1870*. Durham, NC: Duke University Press, 1997.

Index

Harvard University Press is a member of Green Press Initiative
(greenpressinitiative.org), a nonprofit organization working to
help publishers and printers increase their use of recycled paper
and decrease their use of fiber derived from endangered forests.
This book was printed on recycled paper containing 30%
post-consumer waste and processed chlorine free.